MANLINESS  CIVILIZATION

WOMEN IN CULTURE AND SOCIETY

A series edited by Catharine R. Stimpson

MANLINESS

CIVILIZATION

**A CULTURAL HISTORY OF GENDER AND
RACE IN THE UNITED STATES, 1880–1917**

GAIL BEDERMAN

THE UNIVERSITY OF CHICAGO PRESS
CHICAGO AND LONDON

The University of Chicago Press, Chicago 60637
The University of Chicago Press, Ltd., London
© 1995 by The University of Chicago
All rights reserved. Published 1995
Paperback edition 1996
Printed in the United States of America
04 03 02 01 00   4 5

ISBN: 0-226-04139-5 (paperback)

Library of Congress Cataloging-in-Publication Data

Bederman, Gail.
    Manliness & civilization : a cultural history of gender and race in the
United States, 1880–1917 / Gail Bederman.
        p.   cm. — (Women in culture and society)
    Includes bibliographical references and index.
    1. Sex role—United States—History.   2. Masculinity (Psychology)—
United States—History.   3. United States—Race relations.   4. White
supremacy movements—United States—History.   5. United States—
Civilization.   I. Title.   II. Title: Manliness and civilization.   III. Series.
    HQ1075.5.U6B43   1995
    305.3'0973—dc20   94-26936
                                                                              CIP

To my parents

CONTENTS

ILLUSTRATIONS

FOREWORD

Every society is known by the fictions that it keeps. When, for example, I was an American girl child, I was told that God walked and talked to a man named Adam in the splendid groves of Eden. The issue is not whether a society tells fictions to itself and others, but which fictions it calls true, which false, which art, which entertainment.

Manliness and Civilization is a revelatory study of the genesis and growth of a profoundly influential fiction that many Americans began to accept as true in the period between the end of the Civil War and the entrance of the United States into World War I. The purpose of this story was to construct and legitimate a vision of the best possible man, the masculine ideal. Gail Bederman recognizes that manhood, like womanhood, is not an ahistorical given. Rather, each is the consequence of "historical, ideological" processes. This best man was white. He was also the apex of civilization, the greatest achievement of human evolution, progress, and history. Literally embodying the survival of the fittest, he deserved to rule the globe and its various species. Not everyone bought into this myth. African-Americans, for example, resisted it in every possible way. Despite this gainsay, the myth gained sway and affects American men and women still.

Brilliantly, freshly, with fine authority, Bederman examines four very different figures who helped to write and revise the fiction of male supremacy. The first is Ida B. Wells, the militant African-American journalist and crusader. Undertaking her lonely struggle against the lynching of African-American men, she defiantly asked how the civilized white race could permit such barbarism. The second is G. Stanley Hall, the scholar, psychologist, and educator. Like many others, Hall worried that the advanced races might prove to be too delicate, that civilization might drain people of potency and energy. The then-current medical discourse diagnosed and warned of neurasthenia, a disease of the highly evolved. Hall wanted to bring up men, not sissies. His strategy was to train schoolboys to experience the evolution of the white race and to capture the primitive within their psyches. Cleverly, Bederman shows how the figure of Tarzan, whom Edgar Rice Burroughs invented in 1912, extends Hall's project of permitting white men to be civilized and savage at once.

The third figure is Charlotte Perkins Gilman, the feminist. Seeking to link women and civilization, she limited her linkage to women and the "advanced" race. Doing so, she too purveyed the myth of white supremacy. Finally, Bederman crisply anatomizes Theodore Roosevelt, a prime advocate of and actor in an international drama of virile white manhood. Fearful of "race suicide," Roosevelt encouraged white men and women to reproduce themselves. Fearful of the racial other, he transformed Native Americans into demons, African-Americans into inferiors, and the Japanese into fearsome competitors.

The title *Manliness and Civilization* evokes *Madness and Civilization,* the English title of one of Michel Foucault's magisterial works of history. Bederman describes her methodological debt to Foucault. That is, she explores the discourse of a society, its characteristic set of ideas and social practices. Aware of how contradictory and contestatory these ideas and practices can be, Bederman abhors vacuous oversimplification and respects the complexities of history. For example, she carefully traces the intricate development of the figure of the brutal savage rapist, a figure that eventually became a popular image of well-deserved punishment for uppity feminists. Happily for her reader, she balances her respect for complexity with an ability to take the measure of the structuring constants of a historical period. One constant that she foregrounds is the fusion of racism and sexism in America. We have constructed race and gender together. Indeed, Bederman closes the book with these words: "Male dominance and white supremacy have a strong historical connection. Here, surely, is a lesson that we can all learn from history."

Recently, I, no longer a girl child, was listening to a male relative tell me about his involvement in the contemporary men's movement. He spoke with cheerful awe about going off into the woods with a group of male friends, camping out and beating drums, recovering the lost, wild boy within him. Because I am fond of this man, because I know him to be a decent fellow who would never hurt a fly, I heard him out indulgently. After reading *Manliness and Civilization,* I am less sanguine about the meaning of his pastoral pastime. Like all important history, *Manliness and Civilization* forces and encourages us to discover the fictions of both past and present, the connections between them, and the reasons why we must dethrone some fictions that have so far reigned supreme.

Catharine R. Stimpson

ACKNOWLEDGMENTS

Despite the long hours we spend toiling alone over our word processors, historical scholarship is at base a communal enterprise. It is therefore a pleasure to thank my colleagues, advisers, and friends for their help, suggestions, and criticisms.

My deepest debt is to Mari Jo Buhle, who has been the perfect adviser and mentor. She has generously read and reread numerous drafts of the manuscript, always providing excellent suggestions and right-on-target criticism. Joan Scott, too, has provided crucial insights at critical moments and urged me to take more interesting approaches than I had first imagined. Elizabeth Francis, David Leverenz, and William G. McLoughlin all provided detailed and valuable criticisms of the entire manuscript, which have been essential in revising. I am also grateful to Barbara Bair, Sherri Broder, Oscar Campomanes, Nancy Cott, Carolyn Dean, Laura Edwards, Ruth Feldstein, Kevin Gaines, Jacquelyn Dowd Hall, Dagmar Herzog, Michael Kimmel, Suzanne Kolm, Barbara Melosh, Louise Newman, James Patterson, Mary Louise Roberts, Lyde Sizer, and John L. Thomas for their insightful and useful suggestions. Without the help of these colleagues, I could not have written this book.

I am grateful, as well, for the help of many archivists and librarians. I especially need to thank Beth Coogan of Brown University's Rockefeller Library Interlibrary Loan, and Stuart Campbell and Dorothy Mosakowski of the Clark University Archives. Thanks, too, to the Clark University Archives for permission to quote from Hall's unpublished papers.

For friendship and support during the writing process, thanks to Kit Bederman, Morrie Chantz, Carla Hansen, Karen Luther, Tim Sprouls, Barbara Tholfsen, my colleagues in the University of Notre Dame History Department, and especially George Schietinger.

Finally, I need to thank my parents, Henriet Bederman and Alfred Bederman, for their love, enthusiasm, and above all, their intellectual engagement with my work. This book is dedicated to them.

1

Remaking Manhood through Race and "Civilization"

At 2:30 P.M. on July 4, 1910, in Reno, Nevada, as the band played "All Coons Look Alike to Me," Jack Johnson climbed into the ring to defend his title against Jim Jeffries. Johnson was the first African American world heavyweight boxing champion. Jeffries was a popular white former heavyweight champion who had retired undefeated six years before. Although it promised to be a fine match, more than mere pugilism was at stake. Indeed, the Johnson-Jeffries match was the event of the year. Twenty thousand men from across the nation had traveled to Reno to sit in the broiling desert sun and watch the prizefight. Five hundred journalists had been dispatched to Reno to cover it. Every day during the week before the fight, they had wired between 100,000 and 150,000 words of reportage about it to their home offices. Most had assured their white readership that Jeffries would win. On the day of the fight, American men deserted their families' holiday picnics. All across America, they gathered in ballparks, theaters, and auditoriums to hear the wire services' round-by-round reports of the contest. Over thirty thousand men stood outside the *New York Times* offices straining to hear the results; ten thousand men gathered outside the *Atlanta Constitution*. It was, quite simply, a national sensation.[1]

Ever since 1899, when Jeffries first won the heavyweight championship, he had refused to fight any Negro challengers. Jack Johnson first challenged him as early as 1903. Jeffries replied, "When there are no white men left to fight, I will quit the business. . . . I am determined not to take a chance of losing the championship to a negro."[2] Jeffries' adherence to the color line was not unique. Ever since 1882, when John L. Sullivan had won the title, no white heavyweight champion had fought a black challenger, even though black and white heavyweights had previously competed freely.[3] Sullivan had announced he would fight all contenders—except black ones. "I will not fight a negro. I never have and never shall."[4] It was in this context that Jack

1

Johnson began his career, and eventually defeated every fighter, black or white, who faced him.

For two years Jeffries refused to fight Johnson, but when Jeffries retired in 1905, the remaining field of white contenders was so poor that the public temporarily lost interest in prizefighting. Finally in 1908, the reigning white champion, Tommy Burns, agreed to fight Johnson. By accepting Johnson's challenge, Burns hoped to raise both interest and prize money. Johnson promptly and decisively thrashed Burns, however, and won the title. Faced with the unthinkable—a black man had been crowned the most powerful man in the world!—interest in pugilism rebounded. The white press clamored for Jeffries to return to the ring. "Jeff must emerge from his alfalfa farm and remove that smile from Johnson's face. Jeff, it's up to you," implored Jack London in the *New York Herald*.[5] In April 1909, the *Chicago Tribune* printed a drawing of a little blond girl begging the former champion: "Please, Mr. Jeffries, are you going to fight Mr. Johnson?"[6] Across America, white newspapers pleaded with Jeffries to vindicate Anglo-Saxon manhood and save civilization by vanquishing the upstart "Negro."

Eventually the aging, reluctant Jeffries agreed to fight, reportedly explaining, "I am going into this fight for the sole purpose of proving that a white man is better than a negro."[7] From its inception, then, the Johnson-Jeffries fight was framed as a contest to see which race had produced the most powerful, virile man. Jeffries was known as the "Hope of the White Race," while Johnson was dubbed the "Negroes' Deliverer."[8] With few exceptions, predictions of the fight's outcome focused on the relative manliness of the white and the black races. For example, *Current Literature* predicted Jeffries would win because "the black man . . . fights emotionally, whereas the white man can use his brain after twenty rounds."[9] White men were confident that Jeffries's intrinsic Anglo-Saxon manhood would allow him to prevail over the (allegedly) flightier, more emotional Negro.

Thus, when Johnson trounced Jeffries—and it was a bloody rout—the defenders of white male supremacy were very publicly hoist by their own petards. They had insisted upon framing the fight as a contest to demonstrate which race could produce the superior specimen of virile manhood. Johnson's victory was so lopsided that the answer was unwelcome but unmistakable. After the fight, the black *Chicago Defender* exulted that Johnson was "the first negro to be admitted the best man in the world."[10]

The ensuing violence showed what a bitter pill that was for many white American men to swallow. Race riots broke out in every Southern state, as well as in Illinois, Missouri, New York, Ohio, Pennsylvania, Colorado, and the District of Columbia. Occasionally, black men attacked white men who were belittling Johnson. In most of the incidents, however, rampaging white men attacked black men who were celebrating Johnson's victory.[11] In Manhattan, the *New York Herald* reported, "One negro was rescued by the police from white men who had a rope around his neck. . . . In Eighth Avenue, between Thirty-Seventh and Thirty-Ninth Streets, more than three thousand whites gathered, and all the negroes that appeared were kicked and beaten, some of them into insensibility. . . . Three thousand white men took possession of Eighth Avenue and held against police as they attacked every negro that came into sight."[12] Contemporary reports put the overall national toll at eighteen people dead, hundreds more injured.[13]

Even the United States Congress reacted to the implicit aspersions Johnson's victory cast on white manhood. Before the Johnson-Jeffries fight, Congress had refused even to consider a bill suppressing motion picture films of prizefights. The prospect of the filmic reenactment of the "Negroes' Deliverer" thrashing the "White Hope" in hundreds of movie theaters across the nation was too much for them, however. Within three weeks, a bill suppressing fight films had passed both houses and was soon signed into law.[14]

Soon after Johnson won the championship, an even more scandalous public controversy arose: the "Negroes' Deliverer" was making no secret of his taste for the company of white women. White men worried: Did Johnson's success with white women prove him a superior specimen of manhood? The spectacle of dozens of white women in pursuit of Johnson's favor pleased Johnson and infuriated many whites. These women were mostly prostitutes, but racial etiquette held all white women were too "pure" for liaisons with black men.[15] It seemed bad enough that Johnson's first wife was white, although antimiscegenist doomsayers felt smugly vindicated when she committed suicide in 1912.[16] But when authorities discovered Johnson was having an affair with an eighteen-year-old blond from Minnesota, Lucille Cameron, they charged him with violating the Mann Act—that is, with engaging in white slavery. The white American public, north and south, was outraged. In Johnson's hometown, Chicago, a man threw an inkwell at him when he made an appearance at his bank. Effigies of Johnson were hung from trolley and electric poles around the city. Wherever Johnson went he was greeted with cries of "Lynch him! Lynch the nigger!"[17] It didn't matter that Lucille Cameron insisted she was in love with Johnson and soon married him. It made no difference that she turned out to have been an established prostitute, not a seduced virgin. It didn't even matter that no violations of the Mann Act had occurred, and the original charges had to be dropped. By winning the heavyweight championship and by flaunting his success with white women, Johnson had crossed the line, and the white public demanded punishment.[18]

The national Bureau of Investigation was ordered to conduct a massive search to find something to pin on Johnson. After an expensive and exhaustive inquiry, it dredged up some old incidents in which Johnson had crossed state lines with a long time white mistress. Although the government usually invoked the Mann Act only to combat white slavery and commercial prostitution, officials made an exception for Johnson. He was convicted of crossing state lines with his mistress and of giving her money and presents. For most American men, these were perfectly legal activities. Johnson, however, was sentenced to a year in prison and a thousand-dollar fine. Hoping to get rid of him, government employees tacitly encouraged him to jump bail and leave the country, which he did. For the next seven years, all Johnson's efforts to make a bargain and turn himself in were rebuffed. Only in 1920 was Johnson allowed to return to the United States to serve his sentence, an impoverished and greatly humbled former champion.[19] The photograph of him losing his last championship bout to white fighter Jess Willard in Havana in 1915 was a standard feature in white bars and speakeasies for many years thereafter.[20]

By any standard, white Americans' response to Jack Johnson was excessive. Why should a mere prizefight result in riots and death? What was it about Jack Johnson that inspired the federal government to use the Bureau of Investigation to conduct a vendetta against him? That moved Congress to pass federal legislation to mitigate his impact? That impelled prominent leaders like former President Theodore Roosevelt to condemn him in print?[21] That caused so many respected Americans to describe Johnson's activities as "a blot on our 20th century American Civilization?"[22] That caused American men to celebrate his ultimate defeat in their saloons for decades?

The furor over Jack Johnson was excessive, yet it was not unique. During the decades around the turn of the century, Americans were obsessed with the connection between manhood and racial dominance. This obsession was expressed in a profusion of issues, from debates over lynching, to concern about the white man's imperialistic burden overseas, to discussions of child-rearing. The Jack Johnson controversy, then, was only one of a multitude of ways middle-class Americans found to explain male supremacy in terms of white racial dominance and, conversely, to explain white supremacy in terms of male power.

This book will investigate this turn-of-the-century connection between manhood and race. It will argue that, between 1890 and 1917, as white middle-class men actively worked to reinforce male power, their race became a factor which was crucial to their gender. In ways which have not been well understood, whiteness was both a palpable fact and a manly ideal for these men. During these years, a variety of social and cultural factors encouraged white middle-class men to develop new explanations of why they, as men, ought to wield power and authority. In this context, we can see that Johnson's championship, as well as his self-consciously flamboyant, sexual public persona, was an intolerable—and intentional—challenge to white Americans' widespread beliefs that male power stemmed from white supremacy. Jack Johnson's racial and sexual challenge so upset the ideology of middle-class manhood that both the white press and the United States government were willing to take extraordinary measures in order to completely and utterly annihilate him.

The Jack Johnson controversy, then, simply exemplifies one of many ways Progressive Era men used ideas about white supremacy to produce a racially based ideology of male power. Hazel Carby has called for "more feminist work that interrogates sexual ideologies for their racial specificity and acknowledges whiteness, not just blackness, as a racial categorization."[23] This study attempts precisely that task.

In order to understand why turn-of-the-century middle-class Americans were so interested in using race to remake manhood, we need to outline a larger historical and analytical context. Thus, the rest of this chapter will consider three points. First, it will consider a question which is not as self-evident as it appears: precisely what do we mean by "manhood," and how do we study its history? Second, it will outline what was happening to middle-class manhood at the turn of the century, and why the middle class believed manhood needed to be remade. Finally, it will introduce a central set of ideas that turn-of-the-century Americans frequently used to tie male power to racial dominance—the discourse of "civilization."

"Manhood": What Is It, and How Does It Work?

What do we mean by manhood? This question is not as simpleminded as it appears. Although most people can easily identify certain human beings as men, manhood has been defined quite differently in different times, places, and contexts.[24] Moreover, historians of American manhood have based their analyses on very disparate assumptions about the meaning of manhood, which has led to confusion and misunderstanding. (I am purposely using the term "manhood" instead of "masculinity" here because, as we will see, the noun "masculinity" was only beginning to be widely adopted by 1890 and had very specific connotations which have been largely forgotten today.)

Many historians have simply assumed that manhood is an unproblematic identity—an unchanging essence—inherent in all male-bodied humans. These historians see manhood as a normal aspect of human nature, transparent and self-evident, which simply needs to be expressed without inhibiting factors like "anxiety." Although they recognize that manhood might be expressed differently at different times, they nonetheless assume that its underlying meaning remains basically the same. Historians using this sort of theoretical approach have tended to write about what men have done, historically, to express their manhood. For example, they have written fine accounts of men's activities in fraternal organizations and in the Boy Scouts. Moreover, these historians, by raising such questions as whether the Progressives experienced a "masculinity crisis," were among the first to identify male gender issues as proper subjects of historical analysis—in itself, a major contribution. However, their approach has the drawback of *assuming* what it ought to *investigate*. What did "masculinity" mean to men in organizations like the Boy Scouts? Why was it so important to them? Why would its presumed loss be painful enough to cause a "crisis"? Does power or authority have anything to do with manhood? By ignoring these historically important questions, this approach leaves the impression that manhood is a transhistorical essence, substantially unchanging over time, rooted in biology, and therefore not amenable to historical analysis—or to human efforts to change gender relations.[25]

Other historians have seen manhood as a culturally defined collection of traits, attributes, or sex roles. For example, one historian renders the Victorian definition of manhood as a list of adjectives: "a man was self-reliant, strong, resolute, courageous, honest."[26] These historians often analyze how the traits or occupations which are seen as masculine change from period to period or class to class. For example, colonial American men were socialized to be strong patriarchal fathers, while nineteenth-century middle-class men were shunted off to a "separate sphere" to be competitive businessmen. By investigating how manhood changes over time, historians using this approach encourage readers to see gender relations as mutable and improvable. Yet this approach, too, has its limitations. Attempting to define manhood as a coherent set of prescriptive ideals, traits, or sex roles obscures the complexities and contradictions of any historical moment. For example, some historians argue that middle-class Progressive manhood was most characterized by chest-thumping virility, vigorous outdoor athleticism, and fears of feminization. Others disagree, and stress Progressive men's growing interest in erstwhile "feminine" occupations like parenthood and domesticity. Envisioning manhood as a unified set of traits gives us no way to consider the relations between these two coexisting but contradictory aspects of Progressive manhood, nor does it give us a way to understand how men themselves negotiated the contradictions.[27]

This study is based on the premise that gender—whether manhood or womanhood—is a *historical, ideological process*.[28] Through that process, individuals are positioned and position themselves as men or as women. Thus, I don't see manhood as either an intrinsic essence or a collection of traits, attributes, or sex roles. Manhood—or "masculinity," as it is commonly termed today—is a continual, dynamic process. Through that process, men claim certain kinds of authority, based upon their particular type of bodies. At any time in history, many contradictory ideas about manhood are available to explain what men are, how they ought to behave, and what sorts of powers and authorities they may claim, as men. Part of the way gender functions is to hide these contradictions and to camouflage the fact that gender is dynamic and always changing. Instead, gender is constructed as a fact of nature, and manhood is assumed to be an unchanging, transhistorical essence, consisting of fixed, naturally occurring traits. To study the history of manhood, I would argue, is to unmask this process and study the historical ways different ideologies about manhood develop, change, are combined, amended, contested—and gain the status of "truth."[29]

To define manhood as an ideological process is not to say that it deals only with intellectuals or ideas. It is, rather, to say that manhood or masculinity is the cultural process whereby concrete individuals are constituted as members of a preexisting social category—as men. The ideological process of gender—whether manhood or womanhood—works through a complex political technology, composed of a variety of institutions, ideas, and daily practices. Combined, these processes produce a set of truths about who an individual is and what he or she can do (based upon his or her body.) Individuals are positioned through that process of gender, whether they choose to be or not. Although some individuals may reject certain aspects of their positioning, rare indeed is the person who considers "itself" neither a man nor a woman. And with that positioning as "man" or "woman" inevitably comes a host of other social meanings, expectations, and identities. Individuals have no choice but to act upon these meanings—to accept or reject them, adopt or adapt them—in order to be able to live their lives in human society.

Another way to say this is to define manhood as the process which creates "men" by linking male genital anatomy to a male identity, and linking both anatomy and identity to particular arrangements of authority and power. Logically, this is an entirely arbitrary process. Anatomy, identity, and authority have no intrinsic relationship. Only the process of manhood—of the gender system—allows each to stand for the others.

We can see more concretely how this cultural process works by returning to our discussion of Jack Johnson and considering how Johnson's championship was construed by his culture's historically specific way of linking male anatomy, identity, and authority. Late Victorian culture had identified the powerful, large male body of the heavyweight prizefighter (and not the smaller bodies of the middleweight or welterweight) as the epitome of manhood. The heavyweight's male body was so equated with male identity and power that American whites rigidly prevented all men they deemed unable to wield political and social power from asserting any claim to the heavyweight championship. Logically, there was no reason to see a heavyweight fighter's claim to bodily strength as a claim to public power. Yet the metonymic process of turn-of-the-century manhood constructed bodily strength and social authority as identical. Thus, for twenty-seven years African American men, whom whites saw as less manly than themselves, were forbidden to assert any claim to this pugilistic manhood. When Johnson actually won the heavyweight title, white men clamored for Jeffries to ameliorate the situation and restore manhood to what they believed was its proper functioning.

Yet Johnson was not only positioned by these cultural constructs—he also actively used them to position himself. Embittered by years of vainly seeking a title bout, Johnson consciously played upon white Americans' fears of threatened manhood by laying public claim to all three of the metonymic facets of manhood–body, identity, and authority. During his public sparring matches, Johnson actually wrapped his penis in gauze to enhance its size. Clad only in his boxing shorts, he would stroll the ring, flaunting his genital endowments for all to admire, displaying his superior body to demonstrate his superior manhood.[30] In his private life, Johnson also took great pleasure in assuming a more conventional middle-class manly identity, sometimes taking on the persona of a successful self-made man. In 1912, he publicly claimed the right to move into an exclusive white suburb until the horrified residents took steps to prevent him.[31] He also dressed both his beautiful blond wives in jewels and furs and paraded them in front of the press. Johnson, who grew up in Texas, was well aware that throughout the South black men were regularly tortured and lynched for consorting with white women, and that even Northern whites feared that black men lusted irrepressibly after pure white womanhood. Therefore, he made certain the public could not view his wives as pathetic victims of Negro lust. Instead, he presented his wives as wealthy, respectable women whose husband was successful and manly enough to support them in comfort and luxury.

Johnson was equally insistent upon his masculine right to wield a man's power and authority. He treated minor brushes with the law—his many speeding tickets and automobile violations—contemptuously, as mere inconveniences which he was man enough to ignore.[32] In his autobiography,

Fig. 1. An elegantly dressed Jack Johnson strikes a manly pose for a photographer in 1911, the year after he won the world heavyweight championship. Courtesy of Photos and Prints Division, Schomburg Center for Research in Black Culture, The New York Public Library, Astor, Lenox, and Tilden Foundations.

he claims (falsely, according to his biographer) to have "mingled . . . with kings and queens; monarchs and rulers of nations have been my associates."[33] On a more sinister note, he physically beat and emotionally maltreated his wives and mistresses, implicitly claiming a man's right to dominate women.[34] In short he recognized that dominant white usage prevented him from being treated as the epitome of manhood, as a white heavyweight champion would be treated. Nevertheless he scornfully refused to accept this racial slight. Defiantly, Johnson positioned himself as a real man by laying ostentatious claim to a male body, male identity, and male power.

As Jack Johnson's example suggests, then, gender ideology, although coercive, does not preclude human agency. Numerous ideological strands of gender, class, and race positioned Johnson in a web which he could not entirely escape. He was inescapably a man, a black man, the son of a freed slave brought up in poverty, and so on. Yet although these discourses inescapably defined him, Johnson was able to take advantage of the contradictions within and between these ideologies in order to assert himself as a man and a pro-active historical agent. Recognizing that "Negroes" were considered less than men, he sometimes asserted his manliness in a race-neutral context, as a champion, a self-made man, and a world-famous hero. In other situations, he played upon his blackness, using his champion's body to present himself as an embodiment of highly sexed Negro masculinity. In all these ways, Johnson reinforced his claim to powerful manhood.

In other words, ideologies of gender are not totalizing. Like all ideologies, they are internally contradictory. Because of these internal contradictions, and because ideologies come into conflict with other ideologies, men and women are able to influence the ongoing ideological processes of gender, even though they cannot escape them. Men and women cannot invent completely new formations of gender, but they can adapt old ones. They can combine and recombine them, exploit the contradictions between them, and work to modify them. They can also alter their own position in relation to those ideologies, as Jack Johnson did. Thus, looking at manhood as an ongoing ideological process—instead of as an inherent essence, or a set of traits or sex roles—allows historians to study the ways people have been historical agents of change.[35]

Class, Gender, and the Impulse to Remake Manhood

Historians have long been aware that turn-of-the-century middle-class men seem to have been unusually interested in—even obsessed with—

manhood. They have spoken of a "virility impulse" among the Progressives, a cult of the "strenuous life," and, most frequently, a "masculinity crisis" among American men, pointing to the popularity of cowboy novels, the craze for hunting and fishing, and the profusion of "he-man" rhetoric.[36] Other historians have denied such a "masculinity crisis" existed, correctly noting that despite virile, chest-thumping rhetoric, most middle-class men did not flee to the Western frontier but remained devoted to hearth and home.[37]

Both positions have merit. Middle-class men were unusually obsessed with manhood at the turn of the century; yet I would hesitate to call this obsession a "crisis." For one thing, there is no evidence that most turn-of-the-century men ever lost confidence in the belief that people with male bodies naturally possessed both a man's identity and a man's right to wield power. They might not have been entirely certain *how* these three factors were related, but few seem to have lost confidence *that* they were related. Moreover, to imply that masculinity was in crisis suggests that manhood is a transhistorical category or fixed essence that has its good moments as well as its bad, rather than an ideological construct which is constantly being re-made. Gender, which we have defined as an ongoing ideological process, implies constant contradiction, change, and renegotiation. Thus, change in the gender system—even extensive change—doesn't necessarily imply a "crisis." In any event, by 1890 a number of social, economic, and cultural changes were converging to make the ongoing gender process especially active for the American middle class. These factors were influencing middle-class views of men's bodies, men's identities, and men's access to power.

Class issues underlay many of these changes. By the last decades of the nineteenth century, middle-class power and authority were being challenged in a variety of ways which middle-class men interpreted—plausibly —as a challenge to their manhood. Ever since the middle class had begun to define itself as a class in the early nineteenth century, ideals of gender and of "manliness" had been central to middle-class consciousness.[38] Between 1820 and 1860, as increasing numbers of men had begun to earn comfortable livings as entrepreneurs, professionals, and managers, the middle class had begun to differentiate itself from other classes by stressing its gentility and respectability.[39] Gender was central to this self-definition, as the middle class celebrated true women as pious, maternal guardians of virtue and domesticity.[40] True manhood was equally crucial to antebellum middle-class identity. Middle-class parents taught their sons to build a strong, manly "character" as they would build a muscle, through repetitive exercises of control over impulse.[41] The middle class saw this ability to control powerful masculine passions through strong character and a powerful will as a primary source of men's strength and authority over both women and the lower classes. By gaining the manly strength to control himself, a man gained the strength, as well as the duty, to protect and direct those weaker than himself: his wife, his children, or his employees.

The mingled honor, high-mindedness, and strength stemming from this powerful self-mastery were encapsulated in the term "manliness."[42] Throughout the nineteenth century, ideals of manliness remained central to middle-class male identity. In the context of the market economy's unpredictability, a manly character built on high-minded self-restraint was seen as the rock on which middle-class men could build their fortunes. Middle-class men were awarded (or denied) credit based on others' assessment of the manliness of their characters, and credit raters like Dun and Bradstreet reported on businessmen's honesty, probity, and family life.[43] Manly control over impulse also helped the middle class develop their distinctive family practices. Celebrations of manly self-restraint encouraged young men to postpone marriage until they could support a family in proper middle-class style, to work hard and live abstemiously so that they could amass the capital to go into business for themselves.[44] In short, by the end of the century, a discourse of manliness stressing self-mastery and restraint expressed and shaped middle-class identity.

By the 1890s, however, both "manliness" and middle-class identity seemed to falter, partly because economic changes had rendered earlier ideologies of middle-class manhood less plausible. Middle-class manliness had been created in the context of a small-scale, competitive capitalism which had all but disappeared by 1910. Between 1870 and 1910, the proportion of middle-class men who were self-employed dropped from 67 percent to 37 percent.[45] At the same time, the rapid expansion of low-level clerical work in stores and offices meant that young men beginning their careers as clerks were unlikely to gain promotion to responsible, well-paid management positions, as their fathers had.[46] Moreover, between 1873 and 1896, a recurring round of severe economic depressions resulted in tens of thousands of bankruptcies and drove home the reality that even a successful, self-denying small businessman might lose everything, unexpectedly and through no fault of his own. Under these conditions, the sons of the middle class faced the real possibility that traditional sources of male power and status would remain closed to them forever—that they would become failures instead of self-made men.

Under these changing conditions, manly self-denial grew increasingly unprofitable. No longer would the dream of manly independent entrepreneurship be achievable for most middle-class men. In this context, Victorian codes of manly self-restraint began to seem less relevant. Increasingly, middle-class men were attracted to new ideals—ideals at odds with older codes of manliness.

Concurrent with middle-class men's narrowing career opportunities came new opportunities for commercial leisure. The growth of a consumer culture encouraged many middle-class men, faced with lowered career expectations, to find identity in leisure instead of in work.[47] Yet codes of manliness dictated they must work hard and become economically independent. The consumer culture's ethos of pleasure and frivolity clashed with ideals of manly self-restraint, further undermining the potency of middle-class manliness.[48] Economically based changes in middle-class culture were thus eroding the sense of manliness which remained so essential to nineteenth-century men's identity.

At the same time middle-class ideals of manliness were eroding from within, middle-class men's social authority faced an onslaught from without—from working-class men, competing with them for control over the masculine arena of politics. During the nineteenth century, electoral politics had been viewed as part of the male sphere, as an exclusively male bailiwick. Indeed, as Paula Baker has shown, partisan politics were seen as a proving ground for male identity. Political campaigns were male rituals celebrating participants' identities both as party members and as men. At the same time, electoral politics dramatized and reinforced men's connection, as men, to the very real power of the government.[49] Men objected so strenuously to woman suffrage precisely because male power and male identity were both so central to nineteenth-century electoral politics. In this light, immigrant men's contestation for control of city governments can be seen, in a very real sense, as a contestation of manhood. As immigrants wrested political control from middle-class men in one city after another, a very real basis of urban middle-class men's manhood received both symbolic and material blows. Immigrant men's efforts to control urban politics were, in a very real sense, contests of manhood—contests which the immigrants frequently won.[50]

While immigrant working men were challenging middle-class men's manly power to govern the cities, other laboring men were challenging their manly power to control the nation. Beginning with the Great Uprising of 1877, the Gilded Age had seen an abundance of labor unrest. Between 1881 and 1905 there were nearly thirty-seven thousand strikes, often violent, involving seven million workers—an impressive number in a nation whose total work force in 1900 numbered only twenty-nine million.[51] To many, class war seemed imminent. The strength of socialist and anarchist movements reinforced these fears. Middle-class men worried that they were losing control of the country. The power of manhood, as the middle class understood it, encompassed the power to wield civic authority, to control strife and unrest, and to shape the future of the nation. Middle-class men's inability to fulfill these manly obligations and exercise this manly authority, in the face of challenges by working class and immigrant men, reinforced their focus on manhood.

Immigrant and working-class men were not the only ones challenging middle-class men's claims on public power and authority. Concurrently, the middle-class woman's movement was challenging past constructions of manhood by agitating for woman's advancement. "Advancement," as these New Women understood it, meant granting women access to activities which had previously been reserved for men. Small but increasing numbers of middle-class women were claiming the right to a college education, to become clergymen, social scientists, and physicians, and even to vote. Men reacted passionately by ridiculing these New Women, prophesying that they would make themselves ill and destroy national life, insisting that they were rebelling against nature. As one outraged male clergyman complained, feminists were opposing "the basic facts of womanhood itself. . . . We shall gain nothing in the end by displacing manhood by womanhood or the other way around."[52] Yet the New Woman did "displace manhood by womanhood," if only because her successes undermined the assumption that education, professional status, and political power required a male body. The woman's movement thus increased the pressure on middle-class men to reformulate manhood.[53]

These challenges from women, workers, and the changing economy not only affected men's sense of identity and authority, they even affected men's view of the male body. White middle-class men now learned that they were threatened by a newly discovered disease, "neurasthenia." According to doctors, neurasthenia was spreading throughout the middle class, due to the excessive brain work and nervous strain which professionals and businessmen endured as they struggled for success in an increasingly challenging economy.[54] This discovery of neurasthenia led many to fear that middle-class men as a sex had grown decadent. Working class and immigrant men, with their strikes and their "primitive" customs, seemed to possess a virility and vitality which decadent white middle-class men had lost.

Not coincidentally, while some doctors were focusing their attention on the neurasthenic male body, other physicians and medical investigators began to pay a great deal of attention to male homosexuals. After the 1880s, medical experts ceased to see homosexuality as a punishable act, and began to see it as an aberrant and deficient male identity, a case of the male body gone wrong through disease or congenital deformity.[55] Attention to the figure of the homosexual man—newly dubbed the "invert"—was one way to investigate, medicalize, and contain the wider social, cultural, and economic forces that threatened the potency of middle-class manhood.

Although some medical experts were discovering new identities and illnesses which threatened men's bodies, other middle-class men were finding new ways to celebrate men's bodies as healthy, muscular, and powerful.[56] Even the popular imagery of a perfect male body changed. In the 1860s, the middle class had seen the ideal male body as lean and wiry. By the 1890s, however, an ideal male body required physical bulk and well-defined muscles. A prime example would be Jim Jeffries' heavyweight prizefighter's body.[57] Middle-class men's new fascination with muscularity allowed strongmen Eugene Sandow and Bernarr McFadden to make fortunes promoting themselves and marketing bodybuilding magazines like *Physical Culture*.[58] By the 1890s, strenuous exercise and team sports had come to be seen as crucial to the development of powerful manhood. College football had become a national craze; and commentators like Theodore Roosevelt argued that football's ability to foster virility was worth even an occasional death on the playing field.[59]

Between 1880 and 1910, then, middle-class men were especially interested in manhood. Economic changes were undermining Victorian ideals of self-restrained manliness. Working class and immigrant men, as well as middle-class women, were challenging white middle-class men's beliefs that they were the ones who should control the nation's destiny. Medical authorities were warning of the fragility of men's bodies, and athletes like Jim Jeffries, boxing's "White Hope," were providing new models of muscular manhood to emulate. All this activity suggests that men were actively, even enthusiastically, engaging in the process of remaking manhood. Yet although older meanings of manhood were gradually losing their persuasiveness, masculinity was hardly in crisis. Middle-class men were clearly still convinced that manhood was powerful, that it was part of their identity, and that all beings with healthy male bodies had it. Indeed, the passions inspired by Jack Johnson's heavyweight championship and his interracial marriages demonstrate the vitality of the ongoing process of remaking manhood.

Multiple Strategies to Remake Manhood: Sex, Class, Race, and the Invention of "Masculinity"

Facing a variety of challenges to traditional ways of understanding male bodies, male identities, and male authority, middle-class men adopted a variety of strategies in order to remake manhood. Uncomfortable with the ways their history and culture were positioning them as men, they experimented with a host of cultural materials in order to synthesize a manhood more powerful, more to their liking. In the process, they began to formulate new ideologies of manhood—ideologies not of "manliness" but of "masculinity."

Many men tried to revitalize manhood by celebrating all things male. Millions joined fraternal orders like the Red Men, the Freemasons, and the Oddfellows.[60] Others concentrated on making boys into men through organizations like the Boy Scouts and YMCA.[61] Many, as we have already seen, glorified the athletic male body through muscular sports like prizefighting, college football, and bodybuilding.[62] Some wrote books about old-fashioned manliness, like Senator Albert Beveridge's popular, platitude-filled *The Young Man and the World*.[63]

Other men believed they could revitalize manhood by opposing excessive femininity. Some focused on strong-minded women as the problem, and complained about feminism, coeducation, divorce, and the suffragists.[64] Others worked to safeguard little boys' masculinity by recruiting more male teachers.[65] Still others warned that Victorian culture itself was "effeminate" and insisted that men must re-virilize their society. As Henry James had Basil Ransom put it in *The Bostonians* (1886),

> The whole generation is womanized; the masculine tone is passing out of the world; it's a feminine, nervous, hysterical, chattering canting age, an age of hollow phrases and false delicacy and exaggerated solicitudes and coddled sensibilities. . . . The masculine character, the ability to dare and endure, to know and yet not fear reality, to look the world in the face and take it for what it is . . . that is what I want to preserve, or rather . . . recover; and I must tell you that I don't in the least care what becomes of you ladies while I make the attempt![66]

Conversely, other men, perhaps feeling that women had appropriated too much of the male sphere, worked to take control of erstwhile "feminine" occupations away from women. For example, men began to take a greater interest in fatherhood and to claim an active role in raising their children.[67] At the same time, the mainline Protestant denominations tried strenuously to "masculinize" the churches through organized activities like the Men and Religion Forward Movement of 1911–12, which aimed to find "1,000,000 missing men" to virilize the churches.[68]

Class, too, provided materials to remake manhood. Just as some men were remaking middle-class manhood by appropriating activities which had been deemed feminine, others appropriated activities which had been deemed working-class. Throughout the nineteenth century, many working-class men had embraced a "rough" code of manhood formulated, in part, to resist the respectable, moralistic manliness of the middle class. This rough, working-class masculinity had celebrated institutions and values antitheti-cal to middle-class Victorian manliness—institutions like saloons, music halls and prizefights; values like physical prowess, pugnacity, and sexu-ality.[69] Since the 1820s, advocates of this rough working-class manhood had ridiculed middle-class manliness as weak and effeminate, while respectable middle-class men had derided this rough masculine ethos as coarse and backward. By the 1880s, however, as the power of Victorian manliness eroded, many middle-class men began to find this rough working-class mas-culinity powerfully attractive. In fashionable New York, for example, luxu-rious "lobster palaces" and Broadway restaurants provided daring middle-class men with a genteel analogue to the working man's saloon.[70] Boxing and prizefighting, too—long associated with the working class—became fas-cinating to middle- and upper-class men. Amateur sparring became popular and respectable enough for even YMCAs to offer instruction. By the time Jack Johnson became champion in 1908, many middle-class men had come to accept boxing champions like Jim Jeffries as embodiments of their own sense of manhood.[71]

As men worked to remake manhood, they adopted new words which could express their dynamic new understandings of the nature of male power. During the 1890s, they coined the new epithets "sissy," "pussy-foot," "cold feet" and "stuffed shirt" to denote behavior which had once appeared self-possessed and manly but now seemed overcivilized and effeminate.[72] Indeed, the very word "overcivilized" was coined during these years.[73] Most telling, however, was the increasing use of a relatively new noun to describe the essence of admirable manhood. This newly popular noun was "mas-culinity."

Although historians usually use the terms "manly" and "masculine" in-terchangeably, as if they were synonymous, the two words carried quite different connotations throughout the nineteenth century. Until about 1890, literate Victorians rarely referred to individual men as "masculine." Instead, admirable men were called "manly."[74] After 1890, however, the words "masculine" and "masculinity" began to be used far more frequently —precisely because they could convey the new attributes of powerful manhood which middle-class men were working to synthesize.

To understand the difference between "manliness" and "masculinity," we can consult *The Century Dictionary* (an American version of the *Oxford English Dictionary*) which, in 1890, outlined the differences between the two terms. "Manly," as there defined, had what we would now term a moral dimension: "Manly . . . is the word into which have been gathered the highest conceptions of what is noble in man or worthy of his manhood." "Manly" was defined as "possessing the proper characteristics of a man; independent in spirit or bearing; strong, brave, large-minded, etc." and was synonymous with "honorable, highminded." "Manliness" was "character or conduct worthy of a man."[75] In other words, "manliness" comprised all the worthy, moral attributes which the Victorian middle class admired in a man. Indeed, historians rightly use the term "manliness" to mean "Victorian ideals of manhood"—for example, sexual self-restraint, a powerful will, a strong character.[76] "Manliness," in short, was precisely the sort of middle-class Victorian cultural formulation which grew shaky in the late nineteenth century. Thereafter, when men wished to invoke a different sort of male power, they would increasingly use the words "masculine" and "masculinity."

Unlike "manly," which referred to the "highest conceptions" of manhood, the adjective "masculine" was used to refer to any characteristics, good or bad, that all men had. As *The Century Dictionary* put it, "Masculine . . . applies to men and their attributes." "Masculine" was defined as "having the distinguishing characteristics of the male sex among human beings, physical or mental . . . suitable for the male sex; adapted to or intended for the use of males."[77] During the early nineteenth century, "masculine" was most frequently employed to differentiate between things pertaining to men versus women—for example, "masculine clothing," "a masculine gait," or "masculine occupations." Thus "masculine," more frequently than "manly," was applied across class or race boundaries; for, by definition, *all* men were masculine.

"Masculine" thus existed as a relatively empty, fluid adjective—devoid of moral or emotional meaning—when the cultural changes of the 1890s undermined the power of "manliness." This very fluidity and emotional neutrality made the word "masculine" attractive to people casting about to synthesize new explanations and descriptions of male power.

As the adjective "masculine" began to take on these new sorts of connotations, people began to need a *noun* to mean "masculine things in the aggregate," a word they hadn't needed before "masculine" began to carry such powerful freight. It is probably not coincidental, then, that in the mid-nineteenth century, a new English noun was adopted from the French and very slowly made its way into popular usage—"masculinity."[78] While the noun "manliness" was in common usage throughout the nineteenth century, as late as 1890 Merriam and Webster's dictionary labeled the noun "masculinity" "rare." Earlier dictionaries frequently omit "masculinity" altogether.[79] The 1890 *Century Dictionary,* however, defined masculinity as "the quality or state of being masculine; masculine character or traits."

As middle-class men worked to add new shades of meaning and new powers to that masculine "quality or state," the words "masculine" and "masculinity" took on increasingly definite shades of meaning. By 1930, "masculinity" had developed into the mix of "masculine" ideals more familiar to twentieth-century Americans—ideals like aggressiveness, physical force, and male sexuality. Of course, these ideals had been associated with manhood from very early times. Yet with the rise of the middle class in the early nineteenth century, new "manly" ideals of manhood had partially eclipsed these traditional male values for most "respectable" Americans, although "rough" working-class male culture had continued to celebrate them.[80] It took several generations for the new formulations of "masculinity" to overtake Victorian "manliness" as the primary middle-class ideology of powerful manhood. Indeed, in 1917, when this study ends, middle-class Americans were equally likely to praise a man for his upright "manliness" as for his virile "masculinity." Yet in retrospect, the overarching direction of change—from "manliness" to "masculinity"—can clearly be seen.

Thus, in 1910, when Jack Johnson stepped into the ring to challenge Jim Jeffries for the championship, he was entering a larger arena as well—an arena in which white middle-class men were casting about for new ways to explain the sources and nature of male power and authority. Men were not only flocking to entertainments which had been associated with rough working-class men, like prizefighting; they were also joining male-only institutions like the Freemasons, working to masculinize the high schools by recruiting male teachers, ridiculing woman suffrage and coeducation, and even changing the very language associated with manhood with new words like "sissy" and "masculinity." Many other middle-class strategies of remaking manhood during these years could be discussed as well.[81] This study, however, will focus on only one type of strategy—the ways middle-class men and women worked to re-define manhood in terms of racial dominance, especially in terms of "civilization."

Constructing Male Dominance through Racial Dominance: An Ongoing Strategy

As the middle class worked to remake manhood, many turned from gender to a related category—one which, like gender, also linked bodies, identities, and power. That category was race.[82] In a variety of ways, Americans who were trying to reformulate gender explained their ideas about manhood by drawing connections between male power and white supremacy, as we have already seen with white men's hysterical response to Jack Johnson's heavyweight championship.

In itself, linking whiteness to male power was nothing new. White Americans had long associated powerful manhood with white supremacy. For example, during the first two-thirds of the nineteenth century, American citizenship rights had been construed as "manhood" rights which inhered to white males, only. Framers of state constitutions in sixteen northern and western states explicitly placed African American men in the same category as women, as "dependents."[83] Negro males, whether free or slave, were forbidden to exercise "manhood" rights—forbidden to vote, hold electoral office, serve on juries, or join the military. Similarly, white working men insisted that, as men, they had a claim to manly independence that women and Negro men lacked.[84] The conclusion was implicit but widely understood: Negro males, unlike white males, were less than men.

Conversely, African American men understood that their purported lack of manhood legitimized their social and political disfranchisement. They therefore protested that they were, indeed, men. Male slaves agitating for their freedom demanded their "manhood rights."[85] Frederick Douglass said that his first overt resistance to a whipping, as a sixteen-year-old slave, "revived within me a sense of my own manhood."[86] David Walker complained in 1828 that "all the inhabitants of the earth, (except, however, the sons of Africa) are called *men,* and of course are, and ought to be free. But we (colored people) and our children are *brutes!!* and of course are, and *ought to be* SLAVES. . . . Oh! my colored brethren, when shall we arise from this death-like apathy!—and be men!!"[87] During the Civil War, 180,000 black men enlisted in the Union Army, despite unequal and offensive treatment, because they understood that enlisting was their most potent tool to claim that they were men and should have the same rights and privileges as all American men.[88] These African Americans all understood that the only way to obtain civic power was through gender—by proving that they, too, were men.

Although linking manhood to whiteness was no novelty, by the 1880s middle-class white Americans were discovering an extraordinary variety of ways to link male power to race. Sometimes they linked manly power with

Fig. 2. A manly European explorer is implicitly contrasted with "inferior" African pygmies in this illustration from a 1908 issue of the *National Geographic*. Courtesy of Brooke Hammerle.

the racial supremacy of civilized white men. For example, popular anthropology magazines like the *National Geographic*, first published in 1889, achieved a large circulation by breathlessly depicting the heroic adventures of "civilized" white male explorers among "primitive" tribes in darkest Africa.[89] A photographic illustration from a 1908 article, "A Journey through the Eastern Portion of the Congo State," encapsulates this dynamic. A tall white explorer, dignified, blond, carefully clad in jacket, hat, boots, socks, and knickers, and carrying a state-of-the-art rifle, is flanked—and implicitly contrasted with—two black "pygmy trackers." Savage-looking, naked, and armed only with bow and arrows, the pygmies reach barely to his shoulders. In both stature and armament, they are implicitly less powerful, less manly than the white man.[90] Similarly, Anglo-Saxonist imperialists insisted that civilized white men had a racial genius for self-government which necessitated the conquest of more "primitive," darker races. Like civilized women (whose efforts to vote had been met by howls of outraged manhood), primitive men lacked the racial genius to exercise "manhood rights." "God has not been preparing the English-speaking and Teutonic peoples for a thousand years for nothing but vain and idle self-contemplation and self-admiration. No! He has . . . made us adepts in government that we may administer government among savage and senile peoples," insisted Senator Albert Beveridge in 1900, calling on the white men of the Senate to organize a government for the Filipinos.[91] In a variety of venues and contexts, white Americans contrasted civilized white men with savage dark-skinned men, depicting the former as paragons of *manly* superiority.

Yet in other contexts, middle-class white men adopted a contrasting strategy and linked powerful manhood to the "savagery" and "primitivism" of dark-skinned races, whose *masculinity* they claimed to share. According to historian E. Anthony Rotundo, by 1870 middle-class men's letters and diaries had become infused with a new sense of primal manhood very different from moral Victorian manliness. These late-nineteenth-century men—unlike their fathers' generation—believed that true manhood involved a primal virility which Rotundo has called the "masculine primitive." According to him, this masculine primitive stressed "the belief that all males—civilized or not—shared in the same primordial instincts for survival," and that "civilized men—more than women—were primitives in many important ways."[92] Middle-class men who saw themselves in terms of this masculine primitive ethos were drawn to a variety of "savage" activities. White men joined fraternal organizations like the Improved Order of Red Men in order to perform elaborate weekly rituals imitating their fantasies of American Indian adventures.[93] Interest in camping, hunting, and fishing—seen as virile survival skills of primitive man—flourished as never before. Middle-class men began to read heroic adventure stories: Jack London's novels, westerns like *The Virginian*, swashbucklers like *Graustark*.[94] Primitive heroics so permeated popular literature that one genteel critic complained, "Must a man have slain his lion and his bear to be anointed king, and is there no virtue in being a simple shepherd? Are we so barbarous?"[95]

"Civilization" and Its Malcontents: Linking Race to Middle-Class Manhood through the Discourse of Civilization

How could middle-class white men simultaneously construct powerful manhood in terms of both "civilized manliness" and "primitive masculinity?" Although these strategies may seem contradictory, they appeared coherent at the time because they both drew on the powerful discourse of civilization. "Civilization," as turn-of-the-century Americans understood it, simultaneously denoted attributes of race and gender. By invoking the discourse of civilization in a variety of contradictory ways, many Americans found a powerfully effective way to link male dominance to white supremacy.[96]

"Civilization" was protean in its applications. Different people used it to legitimize conservatism and change, male dominance and militant feminism, white racism and African American resistance. On the one hand, middle- and upper-class white men effectively mobilized "civilization" in order to maintain their class, gender, and racial authority, whether they invoked primitive masculinity or civilized manliness. Yet as effective as "civilization" was in its various ways of constructing male dominance, it was never totalizing. People opposed to white male dominance invoked civilization to legitimize quite different points of views. Feminists pointed to civilization to demonstrate the importance of woman's advancement. African Americans cited civilization to prove the necessity of racial egalitarianism.

Thus, the interesting thing about "civilization" is not what was meant by the term, but the multiple ways it was used to legitimize different sorts of claims to power. Therefore, rather than trying to reduce civilization to a set of specific formulations or points, I will be discussing it as a discourse that worked, albeit unevenly, to establish (or to challenge) white male hegemony. In other words, this study's focus will be the *process of articulation,* itself. Rather than trying to isolate commonalities about what people meant by "civilization"—and perhaps flattening out contradictions and complexities —I will be concentrating on the different, even contradictory, ways people invoked the discourse of civilization to construct what it meant to be a man.

A brief tangent on methodology is in order. Like many recent historians, I have been influenced by Michel Foucault and his ideas of discourse. By "discourse," I mean a set of ideas and practices which, taken together, organize both the way a society defines certain truths about itself and the way it deploys social power. This sort of methodology shifts intellectual history in three useful ways.[97]

First, unlike traditional intellectual history, this methodology does not differentiate between intellectual ideas and material practices, or between superstructure and base. Discourses include both intellectual constructs and material practices. Following Foucault, historians who use this methodology presume that intellectual knowledge and concrete power relations are mutually constitutive. On the one hand, the daily practices which enforce a society's power relations—its institutions, customs, political movements— determine what sort of knowledges will appear to be true. On the other hand, ideas widely accepted as true determine what sorts of power relations people believe are desirable, as well as what sorts of political aims and strategies they can imagine. This simultaneous focus on intellectual constructs and material practices allows historians to simultaneously analyze ideas and practices, agency and power.

Second, this methodology assumes that the ideas and practices comprising any discourse will be multiple, inconsistent, and contradictory. As we've already begun to see with "civilization," discourses can be complex. Their very contradictions frequently give them a tenacious power over people's thoughts and actions. Rather than attempting to catalogue a unified set of ideas, or to reconcile the inconsistencies, this methodology interrogates the very different ways discourses are articulated in different situations.

Finally, because it interrogates these inconsistencies, this methodology implies a particular emphasis on human agency and the possibility of intentional change. As we saw earlier with Jack Johnson, the inherent contradictions and inconsistencies within and between discourses allow people to bend them to their own purposes. Discourse theory does not leave open an infinite possibility for intentional change. Only certain types of truths, and therefore only certain possibilities for action, are imaginable under the terms of existing discourses. Yet because so many potential ambiguities and contradictions exist within any discourse many possibilities for dissent and resistance always remain.

Bearing these methodological assumptions in mind, let us return to our discussion of "civilization." By about 1890, the discourse of civilization had taken on a very specific set of meanings which revolved around three factors: race, gender, and millennial assumptions about human evolutionary progress. Feminist and antiracist versions of civilization might combine these three variables quite differently from hegemonic versions; yet race, gender, and millennialism—in some form—were central to all.

To understand the counterhegemonic versions, we first need to understand the dominant version of civilization, and the way it interwove race, gender, and millennialism. To begin with race: In the context of the late nineteenth century's popularized Darwinism, civilization was seen as an explicitly racial concept. It meant more than simply "the west" or "industrially advanced societies." Civilization denoted a precise stage in human racial evolution—the one following the more primitive stages of "savagery" and "barbarism." Human races were assumed to evolve from simple savagery, through violent barbarism, to advanced and valuable civilization. But only white races had, as yet, evolved to the civilized stage. In fact, people sometimes spoke of civilization as if it were itself a racial trait, inherited by all Anglo-Saxons and other "advanced" white races.[98]

Gender, too, was an essential component of civilization. Indeed, one could identify advanced civilizations by the degree of their sexual differentiation.[99] Savage (that is, nonwhite) men and women were believed to be almost identical, but men and women of the civilized races had evolved pronounced sexual differences. Civilized women were womanly—delicate, spiritual, dedicated to the home. And civilized white men were the most manly ever evolved—firm of character; self-controlled; protectors of women and children. In contrast, gender differences among savages seemed to be blurred. Savage women were aggressive, carried heavy burdens, and did all sorts of "masculine" hard labor. Savage men were emotional and lacked a man's ability to restrain their passions. Savage men were creatures of whim who raped women instead of protecting them. Savage men abandoned their children instead of providing for them. Savage men even dressed like women, in skirts and jewelry. In short, the pronounced sexual differences celebrated in the middle class's doctrine of separate spheres were assumed to be absent in savagery, but to be an intrinsic and necessary aspect of higher civilization.[100]

Finally, the discourse of civilization linked both male dominance and white supremacy to a Darwinist version of Protestant millennialism. A Christian millennialist interpretation of human progress had been rooted in

American culture for centuries. According to these doctrines, ever since Adam and Eve, human history had one cosmic purpose: the millennial fight against evil. Human history was itself the battleground, as Christian men and women, directed by the hidden hand of God, struggled against evil. Each small victory brought the world closer to the millennium—the day when evil would be vanquished, and Christ would rule over one thousand years of perfect peace and righteousness on earth.[101]

After Darwin's theories about evolution became widely accepted, however, many Protestants became confused about their place in this millennial scenario. As most educated Americans understood Darwin, the world evolved through survival of the fittest. Random conflict and violence had shaped the world's history, not the hand of God. Moreover, Darwin provided no cosmic telos to human evolution: one could hardly expect violent natural selection to culminate in a peaceful millennium.[102]

American Protestants who accepted Darwinism, but could not bear to jettison the belief that they were part of a cosmic plan to perfect the world, found in "civilization" a way to reconcile the seemingly contradictory implications of Darwinism and Protestant millennialism. Discourses of civilization gave millennialism a Darwinistic mechanism. Instead of God working in history to perfect the world, believers in civilization described evolution working in history to perfect the world. Instead of Christians battling infidels, they envisioned superior races outsurviving inferior races. Eventually, perfect human evolution would triumph. The most advanced, civilized races—that is, the white races—would be perfected. Part of this perfection would be the evolution of the most perfect manliness and womanliness the world had ever seen. And it was the duty of all civilized people to do what they could to bring about this perfect civilization, just as it had once been the duty of all Christians to take up the banner of the Lord. This millennial vision of perfected racial evolution and gender specialization was what people meant when they referred to "the advancement of civilization."[103]

"Civilization's" greatest cultural power, however, stemmed not from any of these elements individually but from the way the discourse interwove middle-class beliefs about race, gender, and millennialism. By harnessing male supremacy to white supremacy and celebrating both as essential to human perfection, hegemonic versions of civilization maintained the power of Victorian gender ideologies by presenting male power as natural and inevitable.

For one thing, hegemonic discourses of civilization conflated racial differentiation with the millennial drama of growing human perfection—that is, it conflated biological human evolutionary differences with moral and intellectual human progress. In 1897, a young Harvard-educated intellectual explained this connection. "The history of the world is the history . . . of races, and he who ignores or seeks to override the race idea in human history ignores and overrides the central thought of all history." The spirit and ideal of race, he continued, was "the vastest and most ingenious invention for human progress" which had ever been invented. As the world's greatest races had evolved, their spiritual and mental traits—which were based on, but transcended, their physical traits—had grown increasingly differentiated. These "race groups are striving, each in its own way, to develop for civilization its particular message, its particular ideal, which shall help to guide the world nearer and nearer that perfection of human life for which we all long, that 'one far-off Divine event.'" That "'one far-off Divine event'" was, of course, a reference to the millennium, the perfection of civilization. The author of these lines was the African American intellectual, W. E. B. Du Bois. The fact that even Du Bois, a militant advocate of racial justice, accepted this racial evolutionary view of civilization suggests both the possibilities for counterhegemonic versions of the discourse and the pervasiveness of these millennialist assumptions.[104]

Ideologies of "manliness," like ideologies of race, were imbued with "civilization's" millennial evolutionism. As we have seen, manliness was not something which was intrinsic to all men, as we today think of masculinity. Instead, manliness was a standard to live up to, an ideal of male perfectibility to be achieved. As *The Century Dictionary* put it, "manly" denoted "the highest conceptions of what is noble in man or worthy of his manhood."[105] Ideologies of manliness were thus similar to—and frequently linked with— ideologies of civilization. Just as manliness was the highest form of manhood, so civilization was the highest form of humanity. Manliness was the achievement of a perfect man, just as civilization was the achievement of a perfect race. (Masculinity, we should remember, was usually not associated with civilization, because it dealt with "attributes which all men had," including savages. Manliness, in contrast, dealt with moral achievements which only the most civilized men could attain.)

Scientific theories corroborated this belief that racial difference, civilization, and manliness all advanced together. Biologists believed that as human races slowly ascended the evolutionary ladder, men and women evolved increasingly differentiated lives and natures. The most advanced races were the ones who had evolved the most perfect manliness and womanliness. Civilized women were exempt from heavy labor and ensconced in the home.

Civilized men provided for their families and steadfastly protected their delicate women and children from the rigors of the workaday world. As Herbert Spencer put it, "up from the lowest savagery, civilization has, among other results, caused an increasing exemption of women from bread-winning labour, and . . . in the highest societies they have become most restricted to domestic duties and the rearing of children."[106] In short, as civilized races gradually evolved toward perfection, they naturally perfected and deepened the sexual specialization of the Victorian doctrine of spheres.

"Savage" (that is, nonwhite) races, on the other hand, had not yet evolved pronounced sexual differences—and, to some extent, this was precisely what made them savage. Savage men had never evolved the chivalrous instinct to protect their women and children but instead forced their women into exhausting drudgery—cultivating the fields, tending the fires, carrying heavy burdens. Overworked savage women had never evolved the refined delicacy of civilized women.[107] Racist humorists frequently drew on these beliefs by depicting African American men as weak and henpecked, dominated by their robust and overbearing wives. For example, in 1910 the *Literary Digest* reprinted a joke from the *Woman's Home Companion:*

> Mrs. Quackenboss—"Am yo' daughter happily mar'd, Sistah Sagg?"
> Mrs. Sagg—"She sho' is! Bless Goodness, she's done got a husband tat's skeered to death of her!"[108]

In these contexts, African Americans were depicted as unsexed primitives who had never evolved the perfect manhood or womanhood characteristic of more civilized races.

Although to twentieth-century sensibilities, "civilization" seems to confuse biology and culture, Victorian ideas of race were predicated on precisely that conflation. Historian of anthropology George Stocking has persuasively argued that Victorians understood "race" to mean a seamless mix of biology and culture. For example, when Charles Darwin met a group of Indians in Tierra del Fuego, their physical and cultural attributes seemed equally strange to him. Lacking any complex theory of culture (which would not be developed until the early twentieth century) he assumed both physical and social attributes were equally characteristic of biological race.

> What Darwin observed among the Fuegians was a kind of unhurried ethnographic gestalt, in which paint and grease and body structure blended into a single perception of physical type, percep-

tually unseparated from what he heard as discordant language and saw as outlandish behavior—a gestalt that he subsumed under the term "race." This was in fact quite consistent with the natural historian's treatment of other animal species, in which body type, cries or calls, and habitual behavior were all data to be used in distinguishing a variety or "race." Given the somewhat "Lamarckian" notion of adaptation which Darwin at that time still shared with so many of his contemporaries, this idea of "race," when applied to humans, inevitably had a mixed biocultural character.[109]

Lacking the conceptual framework to differentiate between physical morphology and cultural traits, educated Victorians subsumed both into a gestalt which they termed "race." Thus, white Americans' belief that primitive men were biologically incapable of achieving manliness was not a confusion between biology and culture, as some historians have argued, but a logical, if noxious, conclusion based upon their understandings of race.

Lamarckian biological theories about human heredity, too, supported "civilization's" assumption that racially primitive men lacked the biological capacity to be manly. Mendelian genetics had not yet been accepted, nor had the concept of genetic mutation. Until 1900, most biologists still assumed that the only way human races could evolve toward a higher civilization was for each generation to develop a bit more, and to pass these learned traits, genetically, on to their offspring. The educated public retained these beliefs decades longer than scientists. Thus, many middle-class whites felt scientifically justified in believing that no racially primitive man could possibly be as manly as a white man, no matter how hard he tried. Primitive races, lacking the biological capacity to develop racially advanced traits like manliness of character, would require many generations to slowly acquire manliness and pass these civilized capacities on to their offspring.

Civilization thus constructed manliness as simultaneously cultural and racial. White men were able to achieve perfect manliness because they had inherited that capacity from their racial forebears. Black men, in contrast, might struggle as hard as they could to be truly manly, without success. They were primitives who could never achieve true civilized manliness because their racial ancestors had never evolved that capacity.

By stressing the biological causation of race and gender, turn-of-the-century discourses of civilization tended to obscure the importance of another crucial category: class. Class issues had long been implicit in ideas of civilization, as historians have more frequently argued. Ever since at least the

eighteenth century, the refinement of more privileged classes had been associated with the highest civilization and contrasted with the coarse tastes of
the unwashed masses.[110] By the late nineteenth century, a variety of "civilized" arts and graces had become indelibly associated with the middle and
upper classes, ranging from the enjoyment of Shakespeare and fine paintings
to elaborate codes for polite management of bodily functions.[111]

Yet by insisting that these "civilized" tastes and customs were racial and
by downplaying the importance of mores and culture, the middle class was
able to obscure the continuing importance of class. In the light of civilization, the middle class could depict its own preferences and styles as biologically determined, superior racial traits. Evolution—and not financial
resources—gave the middle class the ability to enjoy and create great art,
classical music, and their elaborately furnished homes. Evolution—and not
middle-class cultural standards—had made white, middle-class women so
delicate and domestic. Evolution—and not economic self-interest—had
given white middle-class men the manly self-restraint which allowed them
to become self-made men. The large proportion of immigrants in the working class lent credence to these ideas: one could hardly expect the Slavic or
Mediterranean races to share the advanced, civilized tastes of Anglo-Saxons!
In the light of "civilization," these class-based differences could be coded
"racial."

Moreover, the evolutionary millennialism embedded in discourses of civilization provided more satisfying ways for middle-class men to contain
class-based challenges to their manly social authority. For example, middle-
class Americans had long believed that a man's hard work and talent would
inevitably be rewarded with riches and success. Yet by 1880 an increasingly
corporate economy, as well as recurring rounds of bankruptcy-spawning
depressions, meant fewer middle-class men could achieve manly power as
successful, independent entrepreneurs. In the light of "civilization," however, these economic setbacks could appear temporary and insignificant:
Middle-class whites' racial destiny was to approach civilized perfection, so
eventually they or their children would inherit the earth, anyway. Similarly,
recurring and seemingly unstoppable strikes by hostile working men might
seem to threaten middle-class men's control over the nation's future; yet discourses of civilization suggested these challenges were irrelevant. In the long
run, middle-class men's evolutionary destiny as members of highly civilized
northern European races would allow them to prevail over a predominantly
immigrant, and therefore racially inferior, working class. Thus, class-based
challenges to the power of middle-class manhood seemed to disappear be-

hind civilization's promise that the hard-working, meritorious, virile Anglo-Saxon man was inexorably moving toward racial dominance and the highest evolutionary advancement.

Race, Gender, and Civilization at the Columbian Exposition

To understand more concretely how "civilization" built hegemonic male power out of white supremacy and evolutionary millennialism—as well as how feminist and antiracist challenges to that power could be mounted—let us consider a familiar example: the 1893 World's Columbian Exposition in Chicago. In authorizing the exposition, Congress had called for it to be "an exhibition of the progress of civilization in the New World."[112] And, indeed, millennial assumptions were embedded in the exposition's rationale. As James Gilbert has pointed out, many of the civic leaders most active in organizing the Columbian Exposition were reared in the "burned over district" of New York, and the evangelical millennialism they had imbibed as youths underlay their visions of an exposition to demonstrate American civilization's astonishing progress toward human perfection.[113]

The millennial perfection embodied in the exposition was composed of equal parts of white supremacy and powerful manhood. As Robert Rydell has shown, organizers divided the World's Fair into two racially specific areas. The White City depicted the millennial advancement of white civilization, while the Midway Plaisance, in contrast, presented the undeveloped barbarism of uncivilized, dark races.[114] The civilized White City was intended to suggest a millennial future—what a city might look like as advanced white races worked toward a perfect civilization. Organizers employed the most eminent architects and city planners; and visitors commented upon the White City's breathtaking perfection.

In the White City, white racial perfection was repeatedly connected to powerful manhood. The White City's focal point was the majestic Court of Honor, a formal basin almost a half-mile long, surrounded by massive white beaux arts buildings. "Honorable," according to the 1890 *Century Dictionary,* was a synonym for "manly," and contemporaries would not have missed the Court's association with manhood.[115] The seven huge buildings framing the Court of Honor represented seven aspects of civilization's highest scientific, artistic, and technological achievements—Manufactures, Mines, Agriculture, Art, Administrations, Machinery, and Electricity. All were presented as the domain of civilized white *men.* These buildings housed thousands of

Fig. 3. The Court of Honor at the World's Columbian Exposition, 1893, epitomized the grandeur and advancement of manly white civilization. Courtesy of the Chicago Historical Society.

enormous engines, warships, trains, machines, and armaments—all self-consciously presented as artifacts built and employed by men, only. The White City also glorified the masculine world of commerce, exhibiting the most advanced products and manufacturing processes—"dynamos and rock drills, looms and wallpaper"—and housing these exhibits in magnificent white temples.[116] Thus, by celebrating civilization, the organizers celebrated the power of white manhood. Men alone, as they saw it, were the agents who lifted their race toward the millennial perfection God and evolution intended for them. As one poet put it, the White City was "A Vision of Strong Manhood and Perfection of Society."[117]

The men who organized the Columbian Exposition made certain that the White City's advanced civilization appeared overwhelmingly male. They firmly excluded women's products from most of the exhibits, even though a large group of upper-class white women had worked tirelessly—if fruitlessly—to gain women equal representation. In 1889, over one hundred prominent women including Susan B. Anthony and the wives of three Supreme

Court justices had petitioned Congress to name some women to the exposition's governing commission.[118] Congress refused. Instead, it established a "Board of Lady Managers." (Even the title was patronizing and ridiculous, many women complained.)[119] Congress gave them almost no authority, yet through persistent efforts the Lady Managers were able to make themselves an important part of the exposition. Led by Bertha Palmer, they organized and built one of the most well-attended exhibits in the White City, the Woman's Building.

Yet the Lady Managers believed the Woman's Building was merely one aspect of their greater task—to make sure that the White City did not depict civilization as intrinsically male. Earlier expositions, they complained, had hidden women's manifold contributions to civilization by confining women's exhibits to only one small building. Therefore, they originally planned the Woman's Building as a small historical museum, illustrating the progress women had made toward millennial perfection over the centuries. The main display of woman's place in civilization would be found, not in the Woman's Building, but in exhibits mounted by women throughout the White City. By exhibiting women's technological, intellectual, and artistic achievements next to men's, they would demonstrate that civilization was as womanly as it was manly. Thus, the Lady Managers made it their task to actively solicit women's exhibits, to forward them to the appropriate administrators, and to make certain women's applications received fair and equal treatment. They also planned to place placards throughout the White City informing fair-goers what proportion of each exhibit was produced by women's labor.[120]

Alas, the Lady Managers' plans met with complete resistance. Male exhibitors refused to let the Lady Managers' placards about women's labor anywhere near their displays.[121] Moreover, it soon became obvious that nearly all women applying for exhibit space in the White City were receiving rejections. In January, five months before the fair's opening, Palmer received official notification: "It is useless for the ladies to send in any more applications for ladies' work." Although Palmer ultimately got this policy reversed, by then the point was moot: almost no exhibit space was left.[122] Reluctantly the Lady Managers decided that devoting large areas of the Women's Building to women's commercial exhibits was better than excluding women's work from the White City altogether.[123]

As they had originally feared, using the Woman's Building as an exhibit hall marked all the rest of the White City—and, by extension, civilization itself—as male. At the Horticulture Building, for example, Lady Manager

Rebecca Felton complained, "everywhere the work has been credited to men. . . . The work of women in the farm exhibits is so intermingled and indissolubly joined to that of men, that we might as well seek to number and classify the pebbles on the shore, or the waves on beautiful Lake Michigan."[124] Despite their best efforts, the Woman's Building was perceived as a place apart. The message was inescapable: The White City's civilization was built by men, only. Exhibiting men's achievements required the entire White City, while women's achievements could fit into the smallest exhibition hall at the fair. (Only the Administration Building was smaller than the Woman's Building.)[125]

Worse, segregating women's exhibits in one small building suggested that women's contributions to civilization were completely different from men's. Visitors were impressed mostly by the Woman's Building's softness, compared to the masculine dynamos and technological marvels of the manly exhibits of the White City. For example, the *New York Times* suggested that while some men might say, "the Woman's Building and all of its varied exhibits simply serve to demonstrate the superiority of man," such sentiments were beside the point:

> The atmosphere of the entire building is not . . . woman's right to invade the domain of man, but the sublimely soft and soothing atmosphere of womanliness . . . the achievements of man [are] in iron, steel, wood, and the baser and cruder products . . . [while] in the Woman's Building one can note the distinct demarcation in the female successes in the more delicate and finer products of the loom, the needle, the brush, and more refined avenues of effort which culminate in the home, the hospital, the church, and in personal adornment.[126]

The Lady Managers had worked tirelessly to prove that women and men had contributed equally to the advancement of civilization. Yet, as the *Times* quote suggests, they failed. The lesson most people took from the Women's Building was that there was a "distinct demarcation" between men's contributions to civilization—machines, technology, commerce—and women's —needlework, beauty, domesticity.

Even the location of the Woman's Building underlined white women's marginality to civilization. Not only did the commissioners place the Woman's Building at the very edge of the civilized White City, far from the manly Court of Honor, they also situated it directly opposite the only exit to the *uncivilized* section of the fair, the Midway. On the border between civilized and savage (as befit women who, according to scientists, were biologically more primitive than men), the Woman's Building underlined the essential manliness of the white man's civilization.[127] Deflecting the counterhegemonic assertions of the Board of Lady Managers, the White City remained a monument to civilization's essential male supremacy.

The Columbian Exposition depicted white women as marginal to the White City; but at least white women got a building and an official board of Lady Managers. Men and women of color, on the other hand, were not marginal but absent from the White City. Although African American men and women objected vehemently to this policy, the white organizers—including the Board of Lady Managers—ignored them. In the Columbian Exposition's schema of hegemonic civilization, only whites were civilized. All other races were uncivilized and belonged not in the White City but on the Midway Plaisance.

As Robert Rydell has demonstrated, the Midway specialized in spectacles of barbarous races—"authentic" villages of Samoans, Egyptians, Dahomans, Turks, and other exotic peoples, populated by actual imported "natives."[128] Guidebooks advised visitors to visit the Midway only after visiting the White City, in order to fully appreciate the contrast between the civilized White City and the uncivilized native villages.[129] Where the White City spread out in all directions from the Court of Honor, emphasizing the complexity of manly civilization, the Midway's attractions were organized linearly down a broad avenue, providing a lesson in racial hierarchy. Visitors entering the Midway from the White City would first pass the civilized German and Irish villages, proceed past the barbarous Turkish, Arabic, and Chinese villages, and finish by viewing the savage American Indians and Dahomans. "What an opportunity was here afforded to the scientific mind to descend the spiral of evolution," enthused the *Chicago Tribune,* "tracing humanity in its highest phases down almost to its animalistic origins."[130]

Where the White City celebrated the white man's civilization as outstandingly manly, the Midway depicted savagery and barbarism as lacking manliness entirely. In the Persian, Algerian, Turkish, and Egyptian villages, for example, unmanly dark-skinned men cajoled customers to shed manly restraint and savor their countrywomen's sensuous dancing.[131] Male audiences ogling scantily clad belly dancers could have it both ways, simultaneously relishing the dancers' suggestiveness and basking in their own sense of civilized superiority to the swarthy men hawking tickets outside, unashamedly selling their countrywomen's charms.[132] Men who had just visited the White City would be especially conscious of their own racially superior manliness. Civilized womanliness, too, was absent on the Midway. Although few American women deigned to see the exotic belly dancers, they understood the message: White women's place in civilization might be marginal, but at least it was moral and safe. Under barbarism, however, women experienced not respect and equality but sexual danger and indecent exploitation.

Least manly of all the Midway's denizens, according to many commentators, were the savage Dahomans, who seemed to lack gender difference entirely. The *New York Times* described "The Dahomey gentleman, (or perhaps it is a Dahomey lady, for the distinction is not obvious,) who may be seen at almost any hour . . . clad mainly in a brief grass skirt and capering nimbly to the lascivious pleasings of an unseen tom-tom pounded within. . . . There are several dozen of them of assorted sexes, as one gradually makes out."[133] Asserting that he could only "gradually" make out the difference between the sexes, the columnist suggests that savages' sexual difference was so indistinct that the Dahomans might have a larger "assortment" of sexes than the usual two. Uncivilized, and thus unable to evince the self-restraint of true manliness, the Dahoman (who was clearly no "gentleman," despite the ironic appellation) publicly cavorts to the drums' "lascivious pleasings." He even wears "skirts."

In short, the Columbian Exposition demonstrated, in a variety of ways, that "nonwhite" and "uncivilized" denoted "unmanly" and, conversely, that whiteness and civilization denoted powerful manhood. Whether they looked like women or pandered their women's sexuality, the "savage" and "barbarous" men of the Midway served as reminders that, in comparison, white American men were far more manly. At the same time, by relishing the exotic native dancing girls, white American men could savor their own primitive masculinity. Either way, the Midway's deployment of civilization allowed white men to see their own manhood as especially powerful.

The exposition's logic of constructing manly white civilization in opposition to unmanly swarthy barbarism made it impossible for the white organizers to accept the existence of fully civilized men and women who were not of European ancestry. Therefore, white organizers rebuffed the many African American men and women who demanded representation on the White City's organizing bodies.[134] In 1890, for example, leaders of the National Convention of Colored Men and the Afro-American Press Association urged President Benjamin Harrison to appoint at least one African American to the exposition's organizing commission. Harrison refused, saying it "would savor too much of sentimentality, [and] be distasteful to the majority

Fig. 4. The civilized grandeur of the manly White City contrasted with the rough savagery of the Dahomey Village, on the Midway. Note the Dahomey man wearing short "skirts" in the tower atop the building, as well as the life-size pictures of stereotypical "savages" waving their arms at the bottom.

of commissioners themselves." "Sentimental," of course, was synonymous with "unmanly." No black commissioner was ever appointed.[135] The Lady Managers were equally exclusive. Despite their own repeated frustration in wringing concessions from the male commissioners, they firmly and repeatedly rebuffed black women—individuals and organizations—who demanded that one of the one hundred fifteen Lady Managers be African American.[136] Eventually, the Lady Managers allowed a small "Afro-American" exhibit to be installed in a distant corner of the Woman's Building but, like the male commissioners, the Lady Managers remained "simon-pure and lily white" themselves.[137] Aside from some porters and few underclerks, almost no African Americans had any official connection to the White City whatsoever.[138]

The Lady Managers did highlight the work of some "primitive" women in the Woman's Building, however. In conjunction with the Smithsonian Institution, they organized an exhibition entitled "Woman's Work in Savagery." This impressive collection of baskets, weavings, and other arts from African, Polynesian, and Native American women was intended to demonstrate that women had contributed productively to the advancement of civilization from the very dawn of time. As the "Preliminary Prospectus" put it, "The footsteps of women will be traced from prehistoric times to the present and their intimate connection shown with all that has tended to promote the development of the race." The contributions of these "primitive" women were acceptable to the Lady Managers, but only because they seemed historic: The African baskets, Samoan netting, and Navajo blankets were depicted, not as the products of living women of color, but as representations of the work of white women's own distant evolutionary foremothers. By proving that "women, among all the primitive peoples, were the originators of most of the industrial arts," organizers hoped to demonstrate that the talents of civilized women, like themselves, were important resources for civilization's further advancement.[139] Yet, ironically, constructing nonwhite women as representations of the distant past precluded their being accepted as fellow women in the present. Mrs. Palmer even tried to ban all contemporary Indian women's work from the exhibit, suggesting that Indian women's authentic artistic "instincts" were irrevocably "spoiled by contact with civilization."[140] The only acceptable primitive was the one who—anonymous, and preferably dead—could symbolize white women's racial past, in order to legitimize their contribution to the race's millennial future.

Although whites insisted tenaciously that civilization was built on white racial dominance, African Americans were equally tenacious in insisting that civilization was not necessarily white. This argument appeared in a widely circulated pamphlet, organized and partially written by Ida B. Wells and Frederick Douglass, that was explicitly designed to refute the fair's hegemonic, racist representations of civilization. It was addressed to the rest of the civilized world and was to be printed in English, French, German, and Spanish, so that all could read and learn why white Americans had excluded African Americans from the Columbian Exposition. Warning that "The absence of colored citizens from participating therein will be construed to their disadvantage by the representatives of the civilized world there assembled," they promised their pamphlet would set forth "the past and present condition of our people and their relation to American civilization."[141]

And it did. Entitled *The Reason Why the Colored American Is Not in the World's Columbian Exposition*, the pamphlet inverted the White City's depiction of "Negro Savagery" as the opposite of manly civilization. Instead, it suggested that both manhood and civilization were more characteristic of black Americans than of white. What better example of the advancement of American civilization then the phenomenal progress African Americans had made after only twenty-five years of freedom? Yet no such exhibit appeared in the White City. "Columbia has bidden the civilized world to join with her in celebrating the four hundredth anniversary of the discovery of America . . . but that which would best illustrate her moral grandeur has been ignored." For centuries, American blacks had "contributed a large share to American prosperity and civilization"; yet there was no hint of this at the fair.[142] Why, then, was the Colored American not in the World's Columbian Exposition?

The pamphlet's answer, left implicit to avoid excessive confrontation, was that the white American was not the manly civilized being he pretended to be. The white men who organized the exposition posed as exemplars of advanced civilization and superior manhood. Yet the truest American manhood and civilization were evinced, not by the white organizers, but by African Americans. By oppressing this true manhood, the Columbian Exposition demonstrated, not the advancement of white American civilization, but its barbarism, duplicity, and lack of manliness. Douglass lamented the unfortunate necessity of speaking plainly of wrongs and outrages which African Americans had endured "in flagrant contradiction to boasted American Republican liberty and civilization."[143] Far from embodying high civilization, white Americans still embraced "barbarism and race hate."[144] Nonetheless, the Negro was "manfully resisting" racist oppression, and "is now by industry, economy and education wisely raising himself to conditions of civilization and comparative well being."[145] Douglass concluded the chapter by insisting upon black manliness: "We are men and our aim is perfect manhood, to be men among men. Our situation demands faith in ourselves, faith in the power of truth, faith in work and faith in the influence of manly character."[146]

The balance of the pamphlet documented Douglass' assertion of black manhood. Since emancipation, African Americans had demonstrated manly character, making phenomenal strides in education, the professions, the accumulation of wealth, and literature. Nonetheless, white Americans had perversely attacked this youthful black manliness, through oppressive legislation, disfranchisement, the convict lease system, and the barbarism of lynch law. In closing, the pamphlet documented the exposition organizers' deliberate exclusion of blacks—except "as if to shame the Negro, the Dahomians are also here to exhibit the Negro as a repulsive savage."[147] In short, excluding the Colored American from the Columbian Exposition, far from glorifying white American civilization, demonstrated white American barbarism. Conversely, the truest exemplars of civilized American manhood were those excluded from the White City—African Americans.

Wells and Douglass had revised the hegemonic civilization discourse, which debarred African Americans from participating the World's Fair, and had turned it to their advantage. Headquartered in the White City's small Haitian Building, they distributed ten thousand copies of *The Reason Why* during the three months before the fair closed. (Debarred from representing his own nation, Douglass had been named Haiti's representative to the exposition.) Wells received responses from England, Germany, France, Russia, and India.[148]

In sum, the history of the World's Columbian Exposition exemplifies some of the many conflicting ways Americans deployed discourses of civilization to construct gender. Ostensibly, the exposition used civilization to assert white male hegemony. The White City, with its vision of future perfection and of the advanced racial power of manly commerce and technology, constructed civilization as an ideal of white male power. The Midway provided an implicit comparison between the White City's self-controlled civilized manliness and the inferior manhood of darkskinned primitive men who solicited customers for belly dancers or wore skirts and danced like women. Yet the Midway also allowed American men to play at being masculine barbarians themselves, savoring the visual pleasures of semiclad exotic dancers while simultaneously and inconsistently relishing their sense of superior, civilized, white manliness. By subsuming these ostensible contradictions within the larger experience of the World's Fair, these discourses of civilization provided powerful, persuasive representations and experiences of hegemonic white male power.

Yet the White City's powerful assertions of white male supremacy never succeeded in eliminating counterhegemonic assertions. The elite white women on the Board of Lady Managers tried to challenge the idea that civilization was especially male by placing women's work throughout the White City; although they failed in these efforts, their Women's Building nonetheless reminded fair-goers that white women did have a place in the White City. The Lady Managers' version of civilization rejected male supremacy, yet it shared the White City's racism. It fell to African Americans like Ida B. Wells and Frederick Douglass to develop a version of civilization that denied the implicit connections between advancement and skin color, and depicted non-whites as the truest exemplars of civilization.

All these versions of civilization linked assertions of millennial progress to issues of race and gender; thus, they were recognizably the same discourse. Yet different people, with different political agendas, defined and deployed "civilization" differently. It was this very mutability and flexibility, combined with the powerful linkage of race and gender, which made "civilization" such a powerful and ubiquitous discourse during these decades.

Conclusion

With this discussion of civilization in mind, let us take a final look at the Jack Johnson controversy, focusing on white journalists' reasons for expecting Jim Jeffries, the "Hope of the White Race," to prevail. Frequently, journalists predicted that Jeffries would beat Johnson because manly white civilization had long been evolving toward millennial perfection. *Collier's* magazine asserted that white men expected Jeffries to win because, unlike the primitive Negro, he was of a civilized race: "The white man has thirty centuries of traditions behind him—all the supreme efforts, the inventions and the conquests, and whether he knows it or not, Bunker Hill and Thermopylæ and Hastings and Agincourt."[149] The *San Francisco Examiner* agreed, predicting that the "spirit of Caesar in Jeff ought to whip the Barbarian."[150] Faced with rumors of a Johnson victory, the *Chicago Daily News* wailed, "What would Shakespeare think of this if he could know about it? . . . Could even Herbert Spencer extract comfort from so dread a situation?" Anglo-Saxon civilization itself might fall if Jeffries were beaten by the "gifted but non-Caucasian Mr. Johnson."[151] In these reports, a Johnson victory was depicted as an affront to the millennial advancement of civilization and the power of white manliness.

Yet in other reports, Jeffries was depicted, not as an exemplar of advanced civilization and high-minded manliness, but as a paragon of violent, primitive masculinity. In this context, Jeffries' eagerly awaited victory would show that white men's capacity for masculine violence was as powerful as black men's—that civilization had not undermined whites' primal masculinity. Journalists waxed lyrical about Jeffries' primal physical attributes, his "vast hairy body, those legs like trees, the long projecting jaw, deep-set scowling eyes, and wide thin, cruel mouth."[152] They printed pictures of him training for the fight by sawing through huge tree-trunks—which, in urban, twentieth-century America, had primitive connotations redolent of log cabins and the frontier.[153] Jack London, writing in the *New York Herald,* maintained that his own overwhelming desire to witness the match, like other white men's, was itself an Anglo-Saxon race trait. As he saw it, the love of boxing "belongs unequivocally to the English speaking race and . . . has taken centuries for the race to develop. . . . It is as deep as our consciousness and is woven into the fibres of our being. It grew as our very language grew. It is an instinctive passion of our race."[154] For these men, a Jeffries victory would prove that, despite being civilized, white men had lost none of the masculine power which had made their race dominant in the primeval past.

Because both approaches drew upon the discourse of civilization, few people saw any inconsistency. Under the logic of "civilization," Jeffries could be simultaneously a manly, civilized heir to Shakespeare and a masculine, modern-day savage lifted from the forests of ancient England. The crucial point was that Jeffries' racial inheritance made him the superior man; and his superlative manhood would prove the superiority of his race. Whether manly and civilized or masculine and savage, whites were confident that Jeffries would beat Jack Johnson.

Thus, many white men panicked when the black champion thrashed the white. By annihilating Jeffries so completely, Johnson implicitly challenged the ways hegemonic discourses of civilization built powerful manhood out of race. Johnson's victory suggested that the heirs of Shakespeare were not the manly, powerful beings they had thought—that "primitive" black men were more masculine and powerful than "civilized" white men. Many white men could not bear this challenge to their manhood. The men who rioted, the Congress that passed laws suppressing Johnson's fight films, the Bureau of Investigation authorities who bent the laws to jail him—all detested the way Johnson's victory shredded the ideologies of white male power embedded in "civilization."

In sum, when late nineteenth-century Americans began to synthesize new formulations of gender, hegemonic discourses of civilization explained concisely the precise relation between the male body, male identity, and male authority. White male bodies had evolved through centuries of Darwinistic survival of the fittest. They were the authors and agents of civilized advancement, the chosen people of evolution and the cutting edge of millennial progress. Who better to make decisions for the rest of humankind, whether female or men of the lower races? It was imperative to all civilization that white males assume the power to ensure the continued millennial advancement of white civilization.

The following chapters will consider a variety of ways American men and women utilized discourses of civilization in order to support or to resist this ideology of white male power. They will focus on four very different historical figures. Ida B. Wells, a journalist and antilynching activist, worked for racial justice in the United States. G. Stanley Hall, a scholar and college president, devoted his life to advancing the nascent science of psychology. Charlotte Perkins Gilman, a feminist theorist, was passionately committed to the cause of woman's advancement. Theodore Roosevelt, Republican politician and president of the Unites States, devoted himself to Progressive reform and imperialistic politics.

None of these figures knew one another, and their work and concerns were entirely unconnected. Yet they all labored to remake ideologies of manhood by revising and adapting discourses of civilization. I will not consider whether any of these four succeeded in transforming other Americans' beliefs about gender, but will instead consider the strategies they used in their efforts to remake manhood. These four figures show some of the different discursive positions it was possible to take in relation to race, manhood, and civilization. I am not suggesting that they are in any way representative, however. Since my methodology focuses specifically on the process of articulation, my main concern is to select a diverse group of people who left a large enough body of sources to reveal their cultural assumptions about race, manhood, and civilization. Other equally viable figures could have been chosen, however—for example, W. E. B. Du Bois, Jane Addams, or Jack London.

Chapter 2 will go into more depth about the relationship between manliness and civilization by focusing on the way Ida B. Wells worked to change Northern white men's views about lynching. Wells, a brilliant publicist, exploited the contradictions and inconsistencies in discourses of both manliness and civilization and succeeded in turning them against white Americans who tolerated lynch law. This chapter will also investigate the significance of "dangerous" black male sexuality (which we have already encountered in the Jack Johnson episode) in the context of "manly civilization."

The third chapter, on G. Stanley Hall, focuses less on manly civilization and more on the related topic of primitive masculinity. Hall believed strongly in the power and beneficence of manly civilization, but he worried that American middle-class men had lost the toughness and strength necessary to keep civilization evolving upward. Yet Hall, a psychologist and professor of pedagogy, believed he saw a way to "inoculate" boys against racial decadence, so that they could grow into virile, powerful civilized men. For Hall, the key to a powerful manly civilization lay in giving all males free access to the primitive. Parents and educators must encourage boys to relive the evolutionary progress of the race—to be savages and barbarians as boys, so that they would develop the strength to be both virile and civilized as men.

Charlotte Perkins Gilman, too, was passionately committed to the upward march of civilization; but her view of women's relation to civilization was very different from that of most of her contemporaries. Gilman worked to transform the ideology of civilization from one which linked civilization to manhood, to one which linked civilization to womanhood. In the process, she magnified the importance of race to civilization and minimized the importance of gender. To do this, she worked to exploit contradictions in the ideology of civilized manhood, much as Ida B. Wells had done. Gilman, however, writing two decades later than Wells, was unable to convince her political opponents that primitive masculine brutality was an unmitigated evil. Gilman's example, like Wells', reminds us that women, too, were engaged in the ongoing historical process of remaking manhood.

Theodore Roosevelt, more than any man of his generation, embodied virile manhood for the American public. Chapter 5 argues that one source of his vibrant virility was Roosevelt's talent for embodying two contradictory models of manhood simultaneously—civilized manliness and primitive masculinity. Combining manliness and masculinity, civilization and the primitive, Roosevelt modeled a new type of manhood for the American people, based firmly on the millennial evolutionary ideology of civilization. Through this new type of manhood, Roosevelt claimed not only a personal power for himself but also a collective imperialistic manhood for the white American race.

Taken collectively, these four figures suggest how flexible the discourse of civilization was, how useful for the project of remaking manhood. Each had a different political agenda, and each invoked a somewhat different version of civilization. At first glance, it might seem inappropriate to consider them as a group. Puzzled readers may wonder how an antilynching activist, a professor of pedagogy, a feminist theorist, and a president of the United States could possibly shed any light on each others' activities. Yet when taken together, it becomes clear that each is drawing on a recognizable and coherent set of assumptions about the historical relationship between race and manhood. Each accepts parts of this discourse, and each tries to change other parts. Strategies used by one person pop up, in slightly altered forms, in the writings of another. Together, they demonstrate the turn-of-the-century meanings of the term "civilization" and illuminate some of the complex ways that ideologies of race and of gender have constructed one another in American history.

2

"The White Man's Civilization on Trial": Ida B. Wells, Representations of Lynching, and Northern Middle-Class Manhood

"For, if civilization means anything, it means self-restraint; casting away self-restraint the white man becomes as savage as the negro."
RAY STANNARD BAKER, "WHAT IS A LYNCHING?"[1]

"It is the white man's civilization and the white man's government which are on trial."

IDA B. WELLS, *A RED RECORD*[2]

In March 1894, Ida B. Wells sailed to England in order to agitate against the rise of racial violence in the United States. She left a country where lynching was rarely mentioned in the white Northern press, and where she herself was unknown to most whites. Three months later, she returned to the United States a celebrity, vilified as a "slanderous and nasty-minded mulatress" by some papers but lauded by others.[3] Above all, she returned to a country where lynching was widely discussed as a stain on American civilization.

Wells' success in bringing lynching to the attention of the Northern middle class was due, in large part, to the ingenious ways she manipulated the discourse of civilization to play on their fears about declining male power. By playing on these anxieties about gender, Wells was able to raise the stakes among middle-class Northern whites, who had previously tolerated lynching as a colorful, if somewhat old-fashioned, Southern regional custom. (For example, the *New York Times* jovially editorialized in 1891, "the friends of order [in Alabama] have been in pursuit of a negro. . . . If they catch him they will lynch him, but this incident will not be likely to add to the prevailing excitement" of the more "serious" moonshining problem.)[4] Historians have long recognized Wells' success in debunking the myth of the black rapist, yet this was only part of her larger strategy.[5] She brilliantly and subversively manipulated dominant middle-class ideas about race, manhood, and civilization in order to force white Americans to address lynching. Wells, in short, convinced nervous white Northerners that they needed to take lynch law seriously because it imperiled both American civilization and American manhood.

Constructing White Manhood through Representations of Racial Violence

In order to understand the tactics Wells used in her antilynching campaign, we must first understand how the white press used discourses of civilization to tie powerful manhood to representations of lynching. Because most (though not all) lynchings took place in the South, few Northerners ever saw an actual lynching. Thus, for most of them, lynching was an imaginary scenario, constructed and fed by depictions in newspapers and literature. These representations of Southern lynching encouraged Northern white men to see themselves as manly and powerful and gave them a rich ground on which issues of gender, sexuality, and racial dominance could be attractively combined and recombined to depict the overwhelming power of their civilized white manliness.

Lynching, as whites understood it, was necessary because black men were uncivilized, unmanly rapists, unable to control their sexual desires. By the 1890s, most white Americans believed that African American men lusted uncontrollably after white women, and that lynchings occurred when white men were goaded beyond endurance by black men's savage, unmanly assaults on pure white womanhood. Yet this myth of the black rapist was relatively new. According to historian Joel Williamson, the idea that black men raped white women gained currency in the South only in the late 1880s.[6] Contemporaries recognized the newness of this charge. Whites often referred to rape as "the new Negro crime," while black spokesmen like Frederick Douglass complained that it strained credulity to imagine that black men had so suddenly become congenital rapists.[7] The actual number of rapes probably did not increase and might even have declined. Yet as the myth of the Negro rapist spread through the South, the incidence of Southern lynching soared. Black Southerners had always been in danger of white violence but, prior to 1889, most American lynchings occurred in the West, under frontier conditions, and mostly white men were lynched. After 1889, however, excited by rumors of "black beast rapists," Southern whites began to lynch African American men in record numbers. In 1892, the violence reached its apogee, with 161 African Americans murdered by white mobs. Ten years before, in 1882, only forty-nine black men had been lynched.[8] As lynchings grew in frequency, they also grew in brutality, commonly including burnings alive, castrations, dismemberments, and other deliberate and odious tortures.

Historians have tied the spread of Southern lynching to a variety of events, including Populism, economic depression, the uncertainty of a new market economy, and Southern politics.[9] Women's historians, however, are beginning to suggest that the spread of lynching might also have been connected to white Southerners' interest in bolstering male power and authority. According to LeeAnn Whites, Southern white women, betrayed by white men's inability to fulfill their manly responsibility to protect and provide for them after the losses of the Civil War, displaced their anger onto black men. By accepting the idea of the black male rapist, white women could express their dismay with white men's abdication of their manly responsibilities, while at the same time making common cause with white men over the issue of racial privilege.[10] Nell Irvin Painter has suggested that lynchings were "pornographic" rituals which maintained power relations, keeping black men powerless and exploitable for white men's economic needs.[11] Jacquelyn Dowd Hall argues that by constructing black men as natural rapists and by resolutely and bravely avenging the (alleged) rape of pure white womanhood, Southern white men were able to depict themselves as ideal men: "patriarchs, avengers, righteous protectors."[12]

Northerners, like Southerners, were drawn to lynching's forceful representations of white men's power.[13] When the notion that black men tended to rape white women arose in the late 1880s, it took hold as quickly in the North as it did in the South. In early 1892, for example, the *New York Times* asserted that the offense of rape was "especially, and with reason dreaded at the South, and one to which the African race is particularly prone."[14] Although white Northerners adopted this new myth of the black rapist as avidly as white Southerners, they were more ambivalent about lynching as an actual practice and rarely defended it, at least in print. Yet even when liberal Northern whites condemned lynching, they usually assumed that African American men tended to be rapists. An 1893 *New York Post* editorial denouncing lynching, for example, felt obliged to concede, "It would be unfair to say that Southern women do not run greater risks in this particular matter than Northern or European women."[15]

Whites' new belief in the "Negro rapist" drew heavily on Victorian ideologies about male sexuality. The middle class believed that men, unlike "naturally good" women, were beset by powerful gusts of sinful sexual desires.[16] This passionate masculine nature was considered simultaneously the source of men's greatest danger and of men's greatest power. Succumbing to overwhelming emotion or sexual passion would sap a man's force, rendering him weak and degenerate.[17] Therefore middle-class parents taught their sons to build a strong, manly "character" as they would build a muscle, through repetitive exercises of control over impulse.[18] The middle class saw this ability to control powerful masculine passions through strong character and a powerful will as a primary source of men's strength and authority. By gaining the manly strength to control himself, a man gained the authority, as well as the duty, to protect and direct those less manly than himself—whether his wife, his children, his employees, or his racial "inferiors."[19]

The more passionate a man's sexual desires, the more strength he manifested by keeping those desires under control. A powerful sexual passion was an intrinsic part of a loving marriage and demonstrated forceful virility and strong manliness. Indulging in masturbation, commercial sex, rape, or other illicit sexual activities, on the other hand, demonstrated not the strength of a man's desire but the weakness of his will. In other words, masculine sexual passion expressed within the context of a high-minded, civilized marriage denoted manliness; but expressed outside marriage, it connoted merely lust and weakness of character—unmanliness.[20] Of course, many men embraced less manly ideals of male sexuality, as the increasing numbers of middle-class men frequenting urban vice districts attest. Even so, they often remained confused and ambivalent about the meaning of their illicit sexual activity. Was it an inevitable outcropping of naturally explosive passionate masculinity? Or was it a sordid loss of self-controlled manliness and a sign of moral weakness?[21]

In short, Victorian ideas about male sexuality were complex. Male sexuality was both an intrinsic part of civilized manliness and its precise antithesis. This analysis supports Michel Foucault's observations that, rather than simply trying to repress sex, nineteenth-century Victorians were nearly obsessed with producing new ways of understanding sex as the key "truth" about men and women's natures. Physicians and scientists developed new types of knowledges about sex and claimed sexuality as a new field for their expertise. At the same time, new sorts of sexual transgressors—for example, the masturbating boy—became focuses of these new middle-class knowledges and technologies of sex.[22]

The explosion of interest in the "Negro rapist," I would argue, was another example of this burgeoning new attention to sexuality.[23] Like other Victorian sexualized figures, "the Negro rapist" produced a variety of new, and sometimes contradictory, knowledges about sexuality, manhood, and power. By focusing on this sexually dangerous image, white Northerners could investigate and construct a host of new formulations about the power of manhood.

On the one hand, representations of the Negro rapist demonstrated the continuing importance of civilized manliness. "Civilization" positioned African American men as the antithesis of both the white man and civilization itself. As such, black men embodied whatever was most unmanly and uncivilized, including a complete absence of sexual self-control. The horrors of the unfettered "Negro rapist" demonstrated to American society what could happen if civilized manliness lost its cultural power. Without manly self-restraint, civilized men would be no better than these vicious savages.

At the same time, however, because "the Negro rapist" represented the opposite of civilized manliness, he also represented primitive masculinity in its purest, most primal form. The male sex drive itself was widely considered a masculine trait—all men, regardless of race or moral status, had it.[24] By discussing the Negro rapist in such obsessive detail, white men were investigating new visions of what "masculinity" might be, unfettered by civilization. In the 1890s, these investigations were somewhat tentative, but by the 1910s, as we will see in chapter 4, these new visions of the primitive masculine rapist were increasing in social power.

Journalists invoked these ideas to describe lynching as a contest between manly civilization, represented by "the white man," and unmanly savagery, represented by "the Negro." According to them, "the Negro" was so unmanly, he was incapable of civilization.[25] As one article on lynching put it, "But a little way removed from savagery, [Negroes] are incapable of adopting the white man's moral code, of assimilating the white man's moral sentiments, of striving toward the white man's moral ideals. . . . They are, in brief, an uncivilized, semi-savage people, living in a civilization to which they are unequal, partaking to a limited degree of its benefits, performing in no degree its duties."[26]

If "the Negro" was constructed as unmanly and outside civilization, however, "the white man" actually meant "civilization." Although the trope "the white man" was not a new one, during the 1890s it took on added power from hegemonic discourses of civilization. In colloquial usage, the terms "civilization" and "the white man" were almost interchangeable. Columnists like the one above who invoked "the white man's moral code, . . . the white man's moral sentiments, . . . the white man's moral ideals" were invoking civilization's morals, civilization's sentiments, civilization's ideals. In other words, "the white man" was a metonym which simultaneously denoted a male of European ancestry and the advanced civilization of which he was a member.[27]

"The white man" represented "civilization" as a single human being defined equally by his whiteness and by his maleness. "The white man" was—in his very essence—*white*. The trope was meaningless unless it was juxtaposed to a reference to nonwhite races. For example, Kipling defined "The White Man's Burden" as the mission to civilize savage races, while the editors of the *Arena* entitled a symposium on several nonwhite ethnic groups, "The White Man's Problem."[28] Similarly, "the white man" was a *man*—not just any man, but a civilized man who embodied what was manly. Although the nonwhite counterparts to "the white man" were usually assumed to be male, they were almost never explicitly called "men"—they were "the Negro" or "the Indian." As one typical usage put it, "the Negro is especially prone to certain crimes of violence which are particularly obnoxious to the white man. . . . the Negro must, like the Indian, go down and out before the white man."[29] Whites rarely paired "the white man" with "the black man," even though that would have been the logical parallel construction. To refer to "the black man" would be to concede that black manliness paralleled white manliness—thus undercutting the ideological work of the phrase "the white man." By repeating these references to the manhood of "the white man," and omitting the parallel construction of "the red man" or "the black man," white usage reinforced the notion that only civilized white men were manly. "The white man," in short, linked white supremacy, male dominance, and evolutionary advancement in one powerful figure. He embodied the notion that nonwhite men were neither manly nor civilized. To speak of the white man was thus to link white males to the power and evolutionary advancement of civilization and to link black males to unmanliness and savagery.

Northern news reports of lynching, too, represented black men as savage and unmanly, and white men as the embodiment of civilization and manliness. Frequently (if improbably) they depicted white lynch mobs as paragons of disciplined, self-restrained manliness. For example, in 1893 the *Providence Journal* reported a Louisiana lynching: "Three Negroes were lynched in a quiet, determined manner by a mob of white men on Friday night. . . . The lynching was one of the coolest that has taken place in this section." The article contrasted the manly restraint of the white mob to the (alleged) criminal wildness of the unmanly black victims, one of whom, they repeatedly mentioned, was nicknamed "Chicken George."[30] Similarly, when the New York Times reported the Memphis lynching which started Ida B. Wells on her career as an antilynching activist, it contrasted the "quick and quiet" demeanor of the white men in the lynch mob with the unmanly emotion of the "shivering negroes" who were murdered.[31] In neither of these instances were the lynch victims accused of rape. Yet the widespread assumption that lynching punished rape colored Northern journalists' depictions of these lynchings, anyway. Events which otherwise might have been described as brutal gang murders took on the benign tones of a morality play, with the black lynch victims depicted as savage, unmanly cowards who deserved their fates, and the members of the white mob depicted as manly defenders of civilized values.

Although Northern news columns wrote admiringly of the lynch mobs' manliness, most Northern editorials condemned lynching as unmanly. Yet even these ostensibly antilynching editorials managed to depict the white man as far more manly and civilized than "the Negro." Typically, they would condemn white lynch mobs for being as despicably unmanly as primitive African or Indian savages. For example, in 1892, when an alleged rapist was burned alive in Arkansas, the New York Times editorialized, "Among the Pi-Utes or the dwellers in the neighborhood of Lake Tanganyika this would be regarded as a happy thought and a stroke of poetical justice, but civilized men and civilized women can regard it only with disgust."[32] In 1904 the Minneapolis Tribune condemned lynch mobs in similar terms: "A community capable of [lynching] has sunk lower in the human scale than Sixteenth century Iroquois or Nineteenth century Apaches."[33] Whites never noticed the bitter irony—that Apaches and Africans did not, in fact, burn accused rapists alive, while civilized white men did.[34] By linking unmanly, unrestrained lynching with nonwhite "savages," these editorialists reinforced the association of manliness with "the white man."

Often, Northern journalists included a third approach as well, demonstrating that although the Southern lynch mob was far manlier than the black lynch victim, the author himself was manlier than both. For example, a 1893 New York Times editorial took a jovially superior tone in ridiculing a Virginia lynch mob for botching the job. It invited readers to imagine the lynchers' "astonishment and disgust" when their victim turned up "in an unquestionably living state," and intimated these unmanly white yokels were not merely savages, but incompetents to boot! If the editorialist ever took up such primitive pursuits, he would presumably demonstrate his own manhood by killing "the Negro" more effectively.[35]

Combined, these ostensibly contradictory discourses about lynching reinforced the way the discourse of civilization linked powerful manliness to whiteness. On the one hand, the white lynchers' manly discipline and self-restraint contrasted with the uncontrolled, unmanly passions of the black "rapists." On the other hand, the white lynchers, too, were unmanly—but only because they acted like primitive African or Indian savages. Those Northern white journalists who opposed savage lynch law were manlier and more powerful than the Southern white lynchers, who were themselves more manly than the primitive black rapists. Either way, discussions of lynching identified manliness with whiteness and civilization, and denigrated men of "inferior" and uncivilized races as unmanly.

Ray Stannard Baker epitomized these ideas in his 1905 article, "What is a Lynching?" Baker was the one of the only Progressive white journalists ever to muckrake lynching. Thus, far from being extremely offensive, this was the best African Americans could expect from white Progressives.[36] Baker began by establishing that lynching was provoked only by the heinous crimes of unmanly "worthless negroes" who refused to work, abandoned their wives and children, committed crimes with no compunction, and above all, made "it unsafe for women to travel alone."[37] He concluded by insisting that the way to stop lynching was for "the white man" to embrace restrained, civilized manliness, eschew lynching and, thereby, to remain superior to "the negro."

> Nothing more surely tends to bring the white man down to the lowest level of the criminal negro than yielding to those blind instincts of savagery which find expression in the mob. The man who joins a mob, by his very acts, puts himself on a level with the negro criminal: both have given way to brute passion. For if civilization means anything, it means self-restraint; casting away self-restraint the white man becomes as savage as the negro.[38]

White manliness thus becomes the essential element of civilization. For the white man to remain the exemplary exponent of manliness, he must restrain his unmanly passions—otherwise he would become as unmanly and uncivilized as the negro. Thus, even in this most eloquent condemnation of lynching, Baker, like his contemporaries, used civilization to reinforce the idea that manly power was inextricably linked to whiteness.

[handwritten margin note: the most liberal white journalism]

By 1909, when Baker wrote, newer constructions of primitive "masculinity" were growing increasingly powerful, and notions of self-restrained manliness were on the defensive. In the early 1890s, however, when Ida B. Wells framed the terms of her antilynching campaign, Victorian manliness was only beginning to lose its persuasiveness. An inchoate sense of malaise linked to manly ideologies of male power permeated middle-class American culture. Ida B. Wells skillfully capitalized on this malaise by inverting the way the discourse of civilization linked manliness and racial dominance.

Ida B. Wells and the Memphis Lynching

Before March 1892, Wells had paid no particular attention to the growth of lynch law in the South. At age twenty-nine, Wells was already well known to literate African Americans as an experienced, militant activist and journalist who had long supported African Americans' claims to social and political equality. She had begun her antiracist activities in 1884 as a young schoolteacher when, having purchased a first-class railway ticket, she had refused to allow herself to be thrown out of the "ladies car," going so far as to bite the conductor's hand when he tried to grab her and pull her out of her seat. After being thrown off the train, Wells engaged a lawyer at her own expense to challenge Jim Crow accommodations in court—successfully—until the lower court ruling was overturned by Tennessee's Supreme Court in 1887.[39]

At roughly the same time, Wells had also begun her career as a journalist for the African American press. Although at first she wrote only for local newspapers, she soon began to be reprinted in black newspapers across the nation; and, in 1889, she was elected secretary of the National Afro-American Press Convention. Her columns, which she wrote under the pen name "Iola," dealt with a variety of both "race" and women's issues—from black nationalism to women's duty to uplift men.[40] By 1891, she had become the coeditor of Memphis' black weekly newspaper, the *Free Speech*, where she crusaded for a variety of issues including better black schools and black voting rights.[41]

Although Wells' early interests as an activist and journalist had little to do with lynching, on March 9, 1892, a tragic event changed both the focus of her activism and the course of her life. Three respected local businessmen, Thomas Moss, Calvin McDowell, and Will Stewart, were taken from the Memphis jail where they were awaiting trial, brutally tortured, and summarily murdered by a white mob. Moss and his wife were close friends of Wells.

From that moment on, Wells would devote much of her life to stamping out lynch law.

Wells, like the entire Memphis African American community, was devastated by the crime's brutality and by its utter cynicism. The lynchers' motivations seemed crassly economic. The three victims had committed the "crime" of opening a successful store, the People's Grocery, which competed with a nearby white-owned grocery. As the People's Grocery had grown increasingly prosperous, challenging the older store's monopoly, whites had threatened violence and tensions in the area rose. When gun-wielding white intruders burst threateningly into the grocery, the black owners had fired upon them in self-defense, only to discover that the intruders were deputy sheriffs in plain clothes, procured by their white competitor. Four days later at 3 a.m.—never having been tried—Moss and his partners were taken from their jail cells by a white mob and brutally shot to death. Moss was reported to have begged in vain for his life, for the sake of his wife, child, and unborn baby. McDowell, who had tried to grab his captors' gun, was found with his hand shot to bits and his eyes gouged out.

The viciousness of the murders was shocking enough; but the complacency of the white community was even worse. Memphis' white leaders refused to punish the lynchers, tacitly approving the murders. One morning newspaper had even postponed issuing its early edition until after the lynching so that it could regale its white readers with full details over breakfast. Nonetheless, white authorities piously declared the lynchers had been so secretive that they could find no clue as to their identities.

Moreover, the lynching seemed to serve no conceivable purpose, even given lynching's usual rationale. The standard white justification of lynching was that it punished heinous crimes like rape or murder, yet this lynching took place after the wounded whites were well out of danger. Clearly, the three men were lynched, not to avenge any terrible crime, but simply to discourage other black entrepreneurs from challenging white merchants' economic dominance. And, indeed soon after the lynching, white mobs plundered and destroyed the People's Grocery, thus restoring a monopoly to the older white-owned grocery.

The message was unmistakable. Even in one of the largest, most advanced cities in the South, white men could ignore any rights a black man claimed—could even murder black men with impunity—in order to retain absolute dominance. As Wells editorialized at the time, "The city of Memphis has demonstrated that neither character nor standing avails the Negro if he dares to protect himself against the white man or become his rival."[42]

Wells immediately set about trying to avenge her friends' murders, choosing tactics based on her previous experience. She had long lacked any faith that mere moral suasion could influence white Americans. Seven years earlier, in one of her earliest newspaper columns, she had dismissed as utterly useless the tactic of appealing "in honesty" to white Southerners' consciences, saying "they have been notably deaf to our calls of justice heretofore."[43] In 1887, when the Tennessee Supreme Court overturned her civil suit against Jim Crow accommodations, she had lost her faith in the legal system as well. She lamented this loss in her diary: "I have firmly believed all along that the law was on our side and would, when we appealed to it, give us justice. I feel shorn of that belief and utterly discouraged."[44] By 1892, she had become a confirmed follower of T. Thomas Fortune, echoing his calls for racial self-help and concerted pressure. As editor of the *Free Speech,* she had often praised communities who boldly banded together to boycott and otherwise use pressure to resist white oppression.[45] Yet Wells had also learned—again, through bitter experience—that economically vulnerable people often lacked the strength to resist white oppressors and risk losing the little they had.[46] In short, Wells' background had left her believing that only direct pressure would move "the white man."

Immediately after her friends' murders, then, Wells responded by devising a variety of economic pressure tactics designed to convince Memphis whites that lynch law's brutality also threatened their own well-being. From March through May, she helped lead a successful African American streetcar boycott which nearly bankrupted the company. She encouraged almost two thousand black Memphis residents to emigrate to Oklahoma, so that they could escape the lawlessness of Memphis—and so that whites could see how essential black workers and consumers were to Memphis' economy. (Wells herself traveled to Oklahoma and sent home detailed newspaper columns describing local conditions and encouraging emigration.) Direct economic pressure, she at first believed, was her most effective weapon against lynching.[47]

To build grassroots support for this movement, Wells wrote a series of blistering antilynching editorials in the *Free Speech.* Between March and May, she never raised the subject of rape. After all, the three murdered men had been accused of attempted murder, not rape. Then Wells wrote the famous editorial that got her thrown out of the South. As Wells had studied other lynchings, after the Memphis murders, she had grown increasingly dubious about the common wisdom linking lynching to rape. And in a short May 21 editorial, Wells briefly expressed her growing doubts. She reported that of eight men in four states lynched since the previous week's column, three were accused of murder and five of "the same old racket—the new alarm about raping white women. . . . Nobody in this section of the country believes the old thread bare lie that Negro men rape white women. If Southern white men are not careful, they will over-reach themselves and public sentiment will have a reaction; a conclusion will then be reached which will be very damaging to the moral reputation of their women."[48]

The virulence of white Memphis' reaction took Wells by surprise. Local editorials threatened the unknown author of those lines with castration and hanging. The Memphis *Evening Scimitar* urged citizens "to tie the wretch who utters these calumnies to a stake at the intersection of Main and Madison Sts., brand him in the forehead with a hot iron and perform upon him a surgical operation with a pair of tailor's shears."[49] Fortunately, Wells was out of town when her editorial appeared. Friends warned her that white men had learned she was the author and were watching her house, vowing to kill her on sight. Wells, unable to return home, was exiled to the North. For two years she lived in New York, although she spent much of 1893 organizing in Chicago; by 1894, she had settled in Chicago, where she would reside the rest of her life. Not until 1922 would she again dare to travel south of the Mason-Dixon line.[50]

Cut off from her Memphis constituency, Wells was forced to develop new tactics to pressure whites to stop lynching. Wells continued to urge African Americans to boycott, vote, and agitate against white oppressors.[51] Yet she believed these methods alone could not stop the national epidemic of lynching. Instead, as she later recalled, she focused her efforts on "the white press, since it was the medium through which I hoped to reach the white people of the country, who alone could mold public sentiment."[52] Yet because the white press, North and South, excluded most African American writers, she knew she could not rely solely on her own pen, as she had done in the past. To gain a hearing, Wells was forced to create forceful new arguments and tactics—and these tactics directly addressed "civilization's" interweavings of manly authority and white racial dominance.

Because the notion that black men were prone to rape white women was so new in 1892, many African Americans were unsure about how to respond to the charge. But Wells, always sensitive to cultural currents, understood intuitively that middle-class Americans were using "civilization" to remake Victorian ideologies of manhood. Wells herself—like many middle-class African Americans—was steeped in Victorian gender constructions. As a child, she recalled, "I had formed my ideals on the best of Dickens's stories,

Louisa May Alcott's, Mrs. A. D. T. Whitney's and Charlotte Brontë's books, and Oliver Optic's stories"—all exponents of the highest Victorian manliness and womanliness.[53] Many of Wells' earliest published articles were conventional hymns to pious, pure Victorian womanhood.[54] As a young woman, she had agonized about how to avoid appearing too forward in her very sedate courtship activities. Yet her own ambition occasionally led her to question the restrictions of womanliness. She once mused to her diary that although she enjoyed men's attentions, she had no desire to marry; and later wrote of her delight at finding a woman as ambitious as herself.[55]

Wells was equally conversant with ways nineteenth-century Americans used gender to uphold or resist white supremacy. As a very small child, she had overheard her father and grandmother discussing an incident from slavery days. Wells' grandmother had been used as a mistress by her white master, and the day after the master died, his jealous widow ordered her to be stripped and publicly beaten. The story made a deep impression on young Ida, who always felt it gave her great insight into the institution of slavery.[56] In her early articles, Wells, like many other black women, insisted that black women's chaste womanliness proved African Americans were as advanced and civilized as white Americans. For example, in an 1887 letter to a white Memphis newspaper, she complained, "Among the many things that have transpired to dishearten the Negroes in their effort to attain a level in the status of civilized races has been the wholesale contemptuous defamation of their women."[57] Similarly, she had written of black men's citizenship rights as their "manhood rights," complaining, for example, that "having destroyed the citizenship of the man, [whites] are now trying to destroy the manhood of the citizen. All their laws are shaped to this end—school laws, railroad car regulations, those governing labor liens on crops,—every device is adopted to make slaves of free men."[58] In short, Wells was quite familiar with Americans' interwoven constructions of gender and race.[59] She thus had all the background she needed to construct her own unique ways of resisting lynching by recasting whites' linkages of race and manliness.

Southern Horrors: Ida B. Wells Inverts the Civilization Discourse

In October 1892, soon after reaching New York, Wells published the pamphlet *Southern Horrors,* her first effort to reach a wide audience of white (as well as black) Americans. Its stated purpose was to document the charges she had made in her *Free Speech* editorial by debunking the idea that the black man was a rapist. But as Wells elaborated on her original charge, she began to develop the new, sophisticated arguments which would ultimately gain her a hearing. And in order to make those new arguments, she reworked the discourse of civilization.

In *Southern Horrors,* Wells refuted the lynching scenario by inversion. Where whites' scenario depicted black men as unmanly passion incarnate, Wells depicted black men as manliness personified. In Wells' framework, the African American men lynched for "rape," far from embodying unmanly, uncontrolled lust, were innocent victims, seduced into having consensual sex with carnal white women. As Wells put it, they were "poor blind Afro-American Sampsons who suffer themselves to be betrayed by white Delilahs."[60] Like the Biblical Samson, these black men had been manly towers of strength until they were ensnared and destroyed by the wiles of a wicked woman. The white Delilahs who falsely cried "rape" were the true embodiments of lust. To prove white women, and not black men, instigated these liaisons, Wells listed thirteen white women who willingly had sexual relationships with black men. Only upon discovery were these liaisons called rapes. Several of these white women were prostitutes, and Wells joked bitterly, "'The leading citizens' of Memphis are defending the 'honor' of *all* white women, *demi-monde* included."[61]

Where whites' lynching scenario depicted lynch mobs as disciplined, manly, and restrained, Wells depicted lynch mobs as vile, unmanly and cowardly, hiding their own rampant lusts with sanctimonious calls for chastity, and excusing their brutal murders by invoking the honor of harlots. Wells argued that Southern white men, including those who formed the lynch mobs, were enthusiastic supporters of rape and sexual abuse—as long as the victims were black. Far from suppressing lust, the white man gloried in it. His miscegenation laws, Wells wrote, "only operate against the legitimate union of the races; they leave the white man free to seduce all the colored girls he can," knowing he need neither marry nor support the victims of his unmanly lust.[62] Furthermore, Wells charged, Southern white men were "not so desirous of punishing rapists as they pretend." If they truly reviled rape, they would not so readily forgive the many white men who raped black women. Again, Wells names names and give dates, overwhelming the reader with cases of black women and little girls brutally raped by white men, with no objections from their white neighbors. Yet these sanctimonious white citizens of the South—rapists and accessories to rape—murdered black men who slept with willing white women, and piously proclaimed themselves defenders of chastity![63] Hypocrisy, licentiousness, and unrestrained passion —sexual lust and blood lust—characterized Southern white men, as Wells depicted them. Thus, in her account, the Southern lynch mob did not embody white manliness restraining black lust; it embodied white men's lust running amok, destroying true black manliness.

Finally, Wells attacked the idea that lynching showed the continuing power of manliness. On the contrary: Northern men could only regain their manliness by ending lynching. Her arguments echoed old antislavery arguments. Just as antislavery activists once warned that the slave power would spread north and contaminate free labor, so Wells warned that Southern men's unrestrained lust had spread north and corrupted Northern men's manliness. Northern white men had abrogated their manly duty to restrain vice. They had allowed white Southerners to rape, butcher, and burn black Americans alive, and this tolerance of vice had rotted their own manliness. Throughout America, Wells wrote, "Men who stand high in the esteem of the public for Christian character, for moral and physical courage, for devotion to the principles of equal and exact justice to all, and for great sagacity, stand as cowards who fear to open their mouths before this great outrage."[64]

More was at stake in these tactics than mere rhetoric. In refuting this discourse of civilization, Wells was trying to stop lynching by producing an alternative discourse of race and manhood. Hegemonic discourses of civilization positioned African American men as unmanly savages, incapable of controlling their passions through manly will. Northern whites, accepting the linkage of whiteness, civilization, and manliness, believed African American men were savage rapists. Therefore, they tolerated the brutal actions of Southern lynch mobs. Hazel Carby has shown that black women, including Wells, reconstructed the sexual ideologies of the nineteenth century to produce an alternative discourse of womanhood.[65] Similarly, Wells' antilynching propaganda constructed an alternative discourse of manhood. In *Southern Horrors,* Wells remade and redefined the ideology which whites deployed to marginalize black men and to construct white men as powerful and manly.

In 1892, however, most whites ignored Wells' pamphlet. A few scattered antilynching articles in white periodicals did borrow Wells' arguments. For example, in 1892 Albion Tourgée, the period's most forthright antiracist white, wrote in the Chicago *Daily Inter Ocean,* "Within a year half a score of colored men have been lynched for the crime of having white mistresses, while it does not seem to be thought necessary to hang or burn the white woman, nor is the white man who keeps a colored mistress in any danger of violence at the hands of his fellow citizens."[66] George C. Rowe, the sole black contributor to an 1894 symposium on lynching in the *Independent,* made a similar case.[67] But such articles were exceptional. Wells, like most African Americans, could only get her articles published in the black press, which few whites read. Despite the eloquence of *Southern Horrors,* Wells' objective of reaching white Northerners remained frustrated.

After publishing *Southern Horrors,* Wells began to discuss "civilization" more explicitly. When the white organizers of the World's Columbian Exposition refused to allow African Americans to participate in 1893, Wells decided to shame America "in front of the civilized world" for this exclusion and, with Frederick Douglass, wrote and distributed *The Reason Why the Colored American Is Not in the World's Columbian Exposition,* discussed in chapter 1. Although white Americans refused to listen to "primitive" black Americans, Wells reasoned, they might listen to "civilized" whites from Europe. Consequently, she hoped to translate the pamphlet into French, German, and Spanish; lacking the funding to do that, she included French and German translations of the introduction.[68] Yet although this pamphlet was well received, Wells' greatest success in turning the claims of "manly civilization" against white racism lay not in her World's Fair agitation but in her British campaigns against lynching of 1893 and 1894.

Wells' Two British Tours: 1893 and 1894

By 1893, after a year of writing and speaking in the North, Wells still had no access to the white American press. When offered the opportunity to tour England, she jumped at it, recognizing that although the white American press ignored her, they might not ignore the British.[69] Although her first tour, in 1893, got very little American press coverage, it laid the foundation for her 1894 tour, which got all the publicity she desired. When Wells returned to the states, she had become notorious; and white Americans had discovered that, due to their tolerance and practice of lynching, the rest of the world's Anglo-Saxons questioned whether white Americans were either manly or civilized.

Wells shaped both tours in terms of "civilization."[70] Her speeches, her writings, and even her demeanor framed her mission as an appeal from one civilized race to another for protection from violent white barbarians. As she told one British journalist, if Britain told America "the roasting of men alive on unproved charges and by a furious mob was a disgrace to the civilisation of the United States, then every criminal in America, white or black, would soon be assured of a trial under the proper form of law."[71] Wells spoke to British audiences, but her goal was to convince Americans that their tolerance of lynching rendered them unmanly savages in the eyes of the civilized world.

Wells knew that many white Americans felt a pleasurable sense of racial kinship with the English, whom they saw as fellow Anglo-Saxons, the most manly and civilized of all races. By forming an alliance with British reformers, Wells attacked this smug racial empathy. As she told an audience in Birmingham, England, "America cannot and will not ignore the voice of a nation that is her superior in civilisation. . . . I believe that the silent indifference with which [Great Britain] has received the intelligence that human beings are burned alive in a Christian (?) country, and by civilised (?) Anglo-Saxon communities, is born of ignorance of the true situation; and that if she really knew she would make the protest long and loud."[72] By enlisting "Anglo-Saxons" as her allies, Wells recruited precisely the spokesmen most able to disrupt the linkages between manliness and whiteness which kept white Americans tolerant of lynching.[73]

Throughout her tour, Wells hammered away at the myth of the black rapist. In the context of "civilization," though, her old arguments from *Southern Horrors* took on new weight. Since civilization, by definition, entailed pure womanliness and upright manliness, Wells could now show that white Americans' lasciviousness proved them uncivilized. Barbarous white men burned innocent black men alive for the "crime" of sleeping with willing white women, while they themselves brutally and boldly raped black women. The unchaste white women who took black lovers, then watched them burn, were also uncivilized; but, Wells claimed, unchastity was endemic to the white South: "Why should it be impossible to believe white women guilty of the same crime for which southern white men are notorious?"[74] Why should it be hard to imagine that depraved white men, whose crimes had peopled the South with mulattoes, begot depraved white daughters?

Most unmanly of all were the bloodthirsty lynch mobs. Wells argued passionately that by refusing to try accused African Americans in a court of law, and by engaging in the most horrific of tortures, lynch mobs and the Americans who tolerated them exposed themselves as unmanly barbarians.

> Make your laws as terrible as you like against that class of crime [rape]; devise what tortures you choose; go back to the most barba-

rous methods of the most barbarous ages; and then my case is just as strong. Prove your man guilty, first; hang him, shoot him, pour coal oil over him and roast him, if you have concluded that civilization demands this; but be sure the man has committed the crime first.[75]

No one but a brute, of course, could conclude that civilization demanded an accused criminal be burned alive, with or without benefit of trial.

Similarly, in describing an Alabama lynching, Wells ironically interwove references to race and gender, invoking "civilization" in order to condemn Americans as manifestly uncivilized. Bitterly she wrote, "the civilization which defends itself against the barbarisms of Lynch Law by stating that it lynches human beings only when they are guilty of awful attacks upon women and children" might have been expected to give these alleged *arsonists* a fair trial, especially since "one of the prisoners charged was a woman, and if the Nineteenth Century has shown any advancement upon any lines of human action, it is pre-eminently shown in its reverence, respect and protection of its womanhood." But, Wells argued, these uncivilized white men were entirely unmanly—anxious not to protect womanhood but to butcher it. The victims, Wells wrote, "were caged in their cells, helpless and defenseless; they were at the mercy of civilized white Americans, who, armed with shotguns, were there to maintain the majesty of American law." And these "brave and honorable white southerners . . . lined themselves up in the most effective manner and poured volley after volley into the bodies of their helpless, pleading victims, who in their bolted prison cells could do nothing but suffer and die."[76] Manliness and civilization, which stood for the rule of law, the defense of the weak, and the protection of womanhood, did not exist in the American South.

Conversely, Wells represented herself and her mission as modeling African Americans' civilized refinement, in marked contrast to white Americans' barbarism. Her newspaper reports from abroad, published in the white *Chicago Inter Ocean,* described the massive support she received from the most prominent, civilized British dignitaries. In column after column, Wells detailed dinners given in her honor by important members of Parliament, mass meetings called by eminent clergymen and reformers, and intimate gatherings organized by titled aristocrats. Indeed, Wells' dispatches sometimes read like gossip columns, full of references to the rich and famous, to delightful soirées and receptions in her honor. At first glance, this frivolity seems to jar with the seriousness of Wells' mission. Finally Wells had access to the white press, yet she never mentioned an actual lynching nor described the crime's barbarity. Yet by considering the columns in the context of "civilization," Wells' strategy becomes clear. Wells wanted to get British Anglo-Saxons to pressure American Anglo-Saxons. She wasn't trying to depict lynching's horrible cruelty, because she didn't believe white Americans would *care* that lynching was cruel, no matter how eloquent her denunciations. She knew white Americans wanted the British to admire the United States' advanced civilization, however. Thus, her columns stressed both the advancement of British civilization and English disgust for primitive American lynch law.

In all her columns, the most eminent and refined British celebrities express shock at American lynching's barbarity. Often she included stories of loutish white Americans whose incivility further convinced the British of American barbarism. For example, a "swell reception" was given for her at Princess Christian's Writer's Club, Wells wrote, and "The ubiquitous and (so far as I am concerned) almost invariably rude American was on evidence there. In a strident voice she pronounced my statements false. I found she had never been in the South and was a victim to her own imagination. I heard an Englishwoman remark after the encounter was over that she had seen a side of Mrs._____'s character which she never knew before."[77]

In contrast, Wells always carried herself with womanly dignity and restraint, and Britons clearly appreciated her as a true lady. Newspapers often remarked upon the quiet refinement of her speaking style and described her as "a woman of culture." (Indeed, Wells *was* a woman of culture. As her diary shows, she had devoted great effort in her early twenties to becoming as correct, accomplished, and refined—as womanly—as possible.) By presenting herself, her mission, and her race as embodying civilized values, Wells highlighted the barbarism of the white Americans who tolerated lynch law.[78]

Wells needed to model stainless womanliness, not only to embody African Americans' civilized status, but also because she understood that her message, as well as her race, made her vulnerable to imputations of unwomanliness. To speak publicly about topics related to sexuality—lynching and its connection to rape—was hardly a ladylike activity, especially for a young unmarried woman. Therefore, as often as possible Wells put her harshest accusations of lynching into the mouths of others. Rather than describe the brutalities of the lynch mobs herself, for example, she often quoted verbatim Southern newspapers' graphic and enthusiastic descriptions of human burnings and tortures. She also utilized statistics, culled from the white *Chicago Tribune,* to prove that fewer than one-third of all

Fig. 5. Ida B. Wells poses with the widow and orphans of Tom Moss, one of the three murdered Memphis grocers whose lynchings inspired Wells' campaign. Taken around the time Wells was traveling to England in 1893, the photo may have been a publicity piece meant to capture both the evils of lynch law—in the bereaved little family—and the womanly, protective part Wells was playing in agitating against it. Courtesy of the University of Chicago Library, Department of Special Collections, Ida B. Wells Papers.

lynch victims had even been accused of rape. In this way, Wells made lynching's apologists condemn themselves "out of their own mouths," while she modestly took the position of a womanly modern Deborah, forced to defend her people.

Wells understood, too, that her own behavior must be scrupulously correct because black women were frequently accused of being especially licentious and thus unwomanly and uncivilized.[79] Indeed, the *Memphis Daily*

Commerical attempted to discredit Wells' message by slandering her character, flooding England with newspapers accusing Wells of being a "negro adventuress" with an unsavory past. Yet Wells skillfully turned these slanders to her advantage by again using Americans' own words to prove their barbarism. She sent a response to newspapers throughout Great Britain, noting "so hardened is the Southern public mind (white) that it does not object to the coarsest language and most obscene vulgarity in its leading journals so long as it is directed against a negro." Moreover, she pointed out that because the *Daily Commercial* could not deny the barbarity of Southern lynching it had stooped to the ungentlemanly tactic of smearing her character. British papers were as shocked as Wells intended. It was neither manly nor civilized to slander a lady's character![80]

Nor was it *womanly* to denigrate a lady's character. Here Wells ran into problems herself when she correctly accused Frances Willard of refusing to oppose lynch law. Wells had found that British audiences, aghast at her stories of men burned and mutilated, repeatedly asked what Frances Willard, America's most famous reformer and beloved head of the Woman's Christian Temperance Union, was doing to stop lynching. And Wells was forced to answer—truthfully—not only that Willard was doing nothing but that she had publicly sympathized with white Southerners about the dangers of black rapists. In a published 1890 interview about the Southern race problem, Willard had expressed solidarity with the supposed sexual vulnerability of the "delightful" white women who had so warmly received her in her travels south: "The colored race multiplies like the locusts of Egypt. The grog-shop is its center of power. 'The safety of woman, of childhood, of the home, is menaced in a thousand localities at the moment, so that the men dare not go beyond the sight of their own roof-tree.'"[81] In 1893 Wells' audiences were so incredulous about Willard's statements that on her 1894 tour Wells was obliged to carry a copy of Willard's published interview to document her charges.[82]

Although Wells' charges about Willard's statements were unquestionably true, Willard's legions of well-placed British supporters were outraged and accused Wells of mean-spiritedly slandering Willard in order to gain publicity. The implication: Wells was no more womanly than the editor of the *Memphis Daily Commercial* was manly, for civilized people did not malign ladies in public. The whole mess degenerated into a nasty, yearlong public squabble which splintered Britain's reform community and detracted from Wells' otherwise successful mission to mobilize the British against American lynching.[83]

Why couldn't Willard and Wells ever resolve this antagonism? At first glance, the bitterness of their dispute appears puzzling, because the two shared so many essential assumptions. Both were active supporters of the movement for women's advancement. Both detested mob violence. Both enthusiastically endorsed the temperance movement. Indeed, in 1891, two years before the Memphis lynching, Wells had approvingly quoted Willard's statement that the grog-shop encouraged Negro men to menace white women, suggesting that, although too sweeping, Willard's statement had a kernel of truth about the dangers of alcohol.[84]

Yet despite these fundamental similarities, the two leaders could never resolve their dispute—in large part because of the opposite ways each deployed notions of womanly chastity. Frances Willard had built the W.C.T.U. on claims that women were inherently pure and needed a larger public influence to protect their womanly purity from corrupt men. Temperance was necessary because drunk men lost their manly self-restraint, and chaste womanhood bore the brunt of male lust.[85] Wells' arguments against lynching, on the other hand, pivoted around the assumption that it was possible —even common—for women to be so sexually licentious that they could victimize innocent men. According to Wells, large numbers of lascivious white women were seducing and betraying guiltless black men.

Although Willard supported Wells' antilynching campaign as a matter of general principle, she could hardly support Wells' vision of white women's widespread licentiousness. In an address at the next American W.C.T.U. convention, Willard objected that when Wells claimed that "white women [have] taken the initiative in nameless acts between the races, she has put an imputation upon half the white race in this country that is unjust, and, save in the rarest exceptional instances, wholly without foundation." Willard was willing to tie lynching-for-rape to *drink,* instead of to race, saying "An average colored man when sober is loyal to the purity of white women; but when under the influence of intoxicating liquors the tendency in all men is toward a loss of self-control." Willard even moved an antilynching resolution. Yet she was unable to abandon the myth of the Negro rapist and repeated her earlier assertion that Negroes' "nameless outrages perpetrated on white women and little girls were a cause of constant anxiety."[86] Willard could not publicly countenance the idea that white women and black men were having sex voluntarily, and therefore she repeatedly invoked the imagery of white womanhood sexually endangered by drunken black men. As far as she was concerned, simply condemning lynching was enough; the rest was immaterial—a mere matter of "rhetorical expressions," as she told Wells.[87]

Willard's continued allegations that lynching punished rape infuriated Wells.[88] Wells understood how powerful and dangerous the rape myth was, and insisted—correctly—that if Willard really understood and opposed lynching, she would publicly repudiate her suggestions that lynching was caused by rape, instead of airily describing her allegations as "rhetoric." Willard, however, could not publicly concede that white women were unchaste without undermining the basic ideological legitimation of her organization. The whole interlude left a bad taste, and Wells was forced to repeatedly justify and explain her side of the altercation.[89] Perhaps in reaction, Wells began to downplay her accusations of white women's unchastity and to emphasize even more white men's uncivilized lack of manliness.[90]

Results of Wells' British Agitation

Wells' powerful tactics convinced the British press and reformers that Americans' tolerance of lynching proved them uncivilized.[91] A *Westminster Gazette* writer said he could no longer "regard our American cousins as a civilized nation."[92] The *Christian World* thought American lynch law "would disgrace a nation of cannibals."[93] The *Birmingham Daily Gazette* editorialized, "The American citizen in the South is at heart more a barbarian than the negro whom he regards as a savage. . . . Lynch law is fiendishly resorted to as a sort of sport on every possible opportunity, and the negroes are butchered to make a Yankee holiday. . . . Either they mistrust their legal institutions or they murder in wantonness and for mere lust of blood."[94] Murdering in "wantonness," "lusting" for blood—Americans had degenerated past any claim to manliness or civilization.

Having convinced a large segment of the British public of American barbarism, Wells then called on the moral forces of Britain to put a stop to it. She convinced the gatherings she addressed to pass resolutions condemning lynching as uncivilized and warning the United States that its tolerance of lynch law was lowering it in the estimation of more civilized countries. She got the national conventions of major religious denominations—Baptist, Methodists, Quakers, Unitarians—to send resolutions to their counterparts in America condemning lynching as uncivilized and asking what they were doing to stop it. Individual churches and reform organizations followed suit, sending resolutions to American organizations, politicians, and publications, warning that the civilized world held all Americans, Northern or Southern, responsible for these "barbarisms."[95]

Wells ultimately convinced British reformers that they bore the responsibility of civilizing the United States. As Sir Edward Russell wrote in the *Liverpool Daily Post* (and as Wells quoted to her American readers), Americans were "horrifying the whole of the civilized world," and needed British uplift, for "when one reflects that [such things] still happen while we in this country are sending missions to the South Sea Islands and other places, they strike to our hearts much more forcibly, and we turn over in our minds whether it were not better to leave the heathen alone for a time and to send the gospel of common humanity across the Atlantic."[96] Moreover, the British were soon preparing to send such "missionaries." By the end of Wells' tour, prominent British reformers were organizing antilynching societies and planning to send representatives to the United States to investigate these atrocities first hand.[97] Such societies had been formed previously to protest Turkish and other exotic atrocities, but never to investigate fellow Anglo-Saxons.

All this British fervor finally got Wells her hearing in the white American press. Wells could be ignored; but the British were considered racial equals, qualified to pronounce upon civilized manliness. Thus, American men felt obligated to reply to British accusations.

Southerners typically insisted that lynching was a necessary evil because African Americans were savage rapists. According to the Atlanta *Constitution,* British agitation was futile, since "the negroes themselves are the only people who can suppress the evil, and the way for them to get rid of it is to cease committing" rape.[98] The *New Orleans Times-Democrat* opined that once Wells left Britain, she would no longer be believed, for Americans "know well that the Negro is not a model of virtue and the white man a cruel, bloodthirsty tyrant, as the Wells woman pretends."[99] A Southern educator complained, "stigmatizing [Southern men] as savages and barbarians" did no good—the real problem lay with the Negro, who was "still a semi-savage, far below the white man in the science and practice of civilization."[100]

Many Northern Democrats and Southerners complained that American lynch law was none of Britain's business.[101] In this they echoed British conservatives, like the *London Times* editorialist who accused Wells' British followers of having a "fanatical anxiety to impose our own canons of civilization upon people differently circumstanced." The *New York Times* approvingly reprinted this column, saying it reflected the sentiment of "a big majority of sensible Englishmen, who resent the meddlesome antics of a little and noisy minority."[102] Georgia's Governor Northen accused Wells of being funded by a syndicate of British and American capitalists who wanted to stop British immigration to the South.[103]

The last straw for those Americans upset about British "meddling" came in early September 1894, when the London Anti-Lynching Committee sent a small fact-finding delegation to tour the American South.[104] Fifteen governors made public statements condemning the British as "meddlers," including Governor Turney of Tennessee who huffed, "I think they had better purify their own morals before coming among a better people."[105] Governor Turney was embarrassed, however, when several days later six black men accused of arson were brutally lynched near Memphis. Jeered the Northern editors of the *Independent,* "It is very unfortunate . . . that just after Miss Wells's charges had been loudly pronounced false other such atrocious cases should have occurred, as if to justify all that she had said." Turney condemned these new murders and offered a reward of five thousand dollars for the lynchers' capture.[106]

Memphis' white civic leaders, too, found it expedient to take a public stand against this latest lynching. Although, two years before, they had destroyed Wells' presses and driven her north for protesting lynching, now they piously proclaimed their horror of lynch law. White merchants even demonstrated their civilized manliness by holding an indignation meeting where they raised one thousand dollars for the murdered men's widows and orphans.[107] Even the *Memphis Scimitar,* which two years earlier had demanded that Wells herself be castrated and lynched, had an apparent change of heart. "Every one of us is touched with blood-guiltiness in this matter, unless we prove ourselves ready to do our duty as civilized men and citizens who love their country and are jealous of its good name," it editorialized.[108] Thirteen white men were indicted, although never convicted, for the lynchings. According to historian David Tucker, the Memphis press never again condoned lynch law; and no new lynchings occurred in the area until 1917.[109]

Wells' campaign inspired many white Northerners to object more vocally to lynching, too. In Chicago, Brooklyn, and Santa Cruz, whites were reported to have formed antilynching societies, although these organizations seem to have been ephemeral.[110] While some Northern papers still defended lynching as necessary to deter rape, many others agreed with the *Cleveland Leader* that "Acts of barbarism have been committed in this country within the last twenty years by people claiming to be civilized which would scarcely have been credited to the cruelest and most bloodthirsty savages in Africa."[111]

In sum, Wells' British agitation had hit a nerve. White Americans, the cheers for the Columbian Exposition still ringing in their ears, were chagrined to discover prominent British reformers calling them unmanly barbarians. The United States, the glory of the civilized world, the epitome of evolutionary progress—accused of barbarism by fellow Angle-Saxons! The object of "missionaries"! Wells finally had the ear of the white American public. By enlisting the aid of British reformers, her campaign had forced indifferent American whites to address lynching. As Wells herself assessed it in the pamphlet she addressed to Americans upon her return ("Respectfully submitted to the Nineteenth Century civilization in 'the Land of the Free and the Home of the Brave,'" ran her ironic dedication), ever since her tour,

> governors of states, newspapers, senators and representatives and bishops of churches have all been compelled . . . to speak in one way or another in the defense of the charge against this barbarism in the United States. This has not been because there was any latent spirit of justice voluntarily asserting itself . . . but because the entire American people now feel, both North and South, that they are objects in the gaze of the civilized world and that for every lynching humanity asks that America render its account to civilization and itself.[112]

Wells could not force white Americans to *oppose* lynching but, in 1894, they could no longer *ignore* lynching.

How effective was Wells' agitation in the long run? Her campaign didn't stop lynching. Although lynching did decline after 1892, most historians credit factors other than Wells' efforts.[113] The British Anti-Lynching Committees, faced with white Americans' vehement complaints about the London Committee's visit, canceled further fact-finding tours and restricted their activities to letter-writing campaigns.[114] Southern lynchings continued, and Wells continued to agitate against them.

But even if Wells couldn't put an end to the violence, her success in putting American whites on the defensive did force some long-lasting, if subtle, shifts in whites' approaches to lynch law. White Americans had no stomach for being called unmanly and uncivilized by the British. After 1894, most Northern periodicals stopped treating lynching as a colorful Southern folkway. They dropped their jocular tones and piously condemned lynching as "barbarous." It became a truism that lynching hurt America in the eyes of the "civilized world." Nonetheless, journalists still implied one could do little to stop it.[115] At the same time, Wells' statistics forced the Northern press to acknowledge that most lynch victims had not been accused of rape. Nonetheless, the lynching-for-rape scenario retained its appeal as a dramatization of white male power, and the myth of the Negro rapist remained almost as strong as ever. Southern states began to pass antilynching laws, but these laws were almost never enforced.[116] While it is impossible to know whether these small changes actually deterred any prospective lynchers, in the context of the nation's overwhelming climate of racist violence, they must be seen as modest but definite victories.

Other Discourses, Other Implications: Lynching, "The Natural Man," and Primitive Masculinity

Despite Wells' efforts, whites continued to link lynching to manhood. The representations of racial manhood associated with lynching simply remained too powerful for white men to abandon—too useful for the project of reinventing manhood. Within five years, American whites had all but forgotten Wells' British campaign. Northern men refused to put an end to Southern lynching, even though Progressive fervor soon mobilized popular enthusiasm for other sorts of reform. White journalists like Ray Stannard Baker continued to associate lynching with rape and to describe "the white man" of the lynch mob as the epitome of manhood, in contrast to the unmanly "shivering Negro."

To understand the tenacity of lynching's hold on Northern white men's imaginations, we need to consider a different way of linking lynching to manhood—not in terms of "manliness," but in terms of "masculinity." In the short run, Wells' strategy of depicting lynching as uncivilized and unmanly was brilliantly effective, but in the long run it contained a fatal flaw. The ideologies of manliness upon which she had based so much of her British campaign were gradually losing persuasiveness, as we have seen. And as civilized manliness lost power, whites grew increasingly interested in a different figure that also combined racial supremacy with powerful manhood—not "the white man," who embodied civilized manliness, but "the natural man," who embodied primitive masculinity.

Although Wells and her followers had made a compelling case that lynching was entirely unmanly and uncivilized, contemporaries believed that the impulse to lynch might be an expression of the sort of powerful, primitive masculinity that swelled in the breast of "the natural man." For example, in 1891 the *Saturday Review* editorialized against mob violence but conceded that lynching had its attractions for the natural man: "We will not deny that the natural man is occasionally tempted to approve of the summary justice of Judge LYNCH. At least, after reading such a story as that reported last week from Kentucky, it is not unpleasing to learn that 'AMOS QUEEN stepped forward, and, raising his repeating rifle, blew out the brains of both the scoundrels.'" After indulging in this pleasurable fantasy about the savage joys of shooting two rapists, however, the editorialist recalls the exigencies of civilization: "One in this case rather envies AMOS QUEEN at that moment; but yet law, we have always understood, exists to control the impulses of the natural man." According to the editorialist, the law and civilization were invented because the natural man could not be allowed to rampage uncontrolled, however appealing the prospect.[117]

When turn-of-the-century Americans invoked the figure of "the natural man," as the above example suggests, they meant a man unfettered by civilization, exempt from manly self-restraint. In other words, "the natural man" was the opposite of the "the white man." Where "the white man" embodied civilized manliness, "the natural man" embodied primitive masculinity. Lacking civilized manly self-restraint, the natural man acted upon his "natural" impulses. And what kinds of "masculine" impulses were seen as "natural?" Precisely those characteristics which Victorian ideologies of manliness urged civilized men to restrain—especially selfish aggressiveness and sexual predation.

In the early twentieth century, journalists writing about lynching continued to assert that "masculine" impulses toward sex and violence, although savage and illicit, were "natural." In 1903, for example, B. O. Flower, editor of the *Arena,* argued that all men, even the most manly, had violent, brutal instincts. Civilized men, according to Flower, had evolved the capacity to suppress their unmanly passions, but when they joined lynch mobs, they allowed the savage within themselves free reign. As Flower saw it, within every man, "the savage is waiting to assert himself if only encouraged."[118] In 1904, Dean Richmond Babbitt explained lynching in similar terms. Babbitt argued that when white men formed a lynch mob, their "unconscious minds" took over. Lynch mobs were driven by men's "unconscious selves," which were inherent in all men, and rooted in "the primitive, the savage, the hereditary, the instinctive, the impulsive."[119] Both Flowers and Babbitt were liberals who attacked lynching. Yet, ironically, they served to reinscribe and promulgate the idea that lynching was natural, because the "natural man" carried within his breast a powerful primitive self—a "savage waiting to assert himself if only encouraged."

In 1903, the philosopher William James encapsulated these themes in an eloquent condemnation of lynching which was widely reprinted in the national press. James warned Americans that lynching suggested civilized men were increasingly willing to unleash the savage within them. Civilization had been designed to restrain men's innate capacity for murder and violence, but civilization's hold on modern men was tenuous, at best: "The average church-going Civilizee realizes, one may say, absolutely nothing of the deeper currents of human nature, or of the aboriginal capacity for murderous excitement which lies sleeping even in his own bosom. . . . But the water-tight compartment in which the carnivore within us is confined is artificial and not organic." An "aboriginal" tendency toward violence remained in the breast of even the most manly "Civilizee." If civilized Americans continued to tolerate lynching—that is, to allow civilization's repression of violence to weaken—civilization itself would crumble. As James saw it, civilization was far weaker than the primal violence of the natural man.[120]

James and his contemporaries saw a connection between lynching and the growing popularity of "masculine" activities like prizefighting. For example, James warned that "man hunt and negro burning" threatened to replace dogfights and prizefights as popular diversions. "The hoodlums in our cities are being turned by the newspapers into as knowing critics of the lynching game as they long have been of the prize-fight and football."[121] And, indeed, at the same time lynching was growing in the South, growing numbers of middle-class men were flocking to prizefights.[122] As we saw with Jack Johnson, middle-class men interpreted these violent struggles between men as a contest to prove superior masculinity.

Lynching, prizefighting, and the figure of the natural man reflected and reinforced the growing idea that an innate, uncivilized savagery lay simmering in the hearts of modern men. They suggest that by the 1890s, American men were increasingly attracted to the idea of a natural or primitive masculinity which was very different from civilized, self-restrained Victorian manliness. The natural man was violent and impulsive. He dominated others through physical force. He lacked any self-control or self-restraint. Above all else, he was untouched by civilization. He was the opposite of civilized—he was natural.

Redefining manhood in terms of the natural drew on a long tradition in Western thought. Ever since the Enlightenment, Westerners have invoked nature to explain whatever they found missing in their own cultures, societies, or civilizations. Yet as scholars have frequently pointed out, "nature" itself has no intrinsic meaning. At different times, nature has been defined as gentle and benevolent or as savage and violent; as an orderly model for people to emulate or as anarchic and chaotic. Recent scholars have argued that nature is itself a cultural construct, formulated in relation to existing cultural or political arrangements. Defining current arrangements as unnatural or natural allows people to formulate powerful criticisms or justifications of existing cultural conditions.[123] The figure of the violent, passionate "natural man" allowed turn-of-the-century Americans who were searching for alternative visions of manhood to imagine a manhood which was powerful but "uncivilized."

Thus, while some Americans were looking to the racially advanced superiority of "the white man" to uphold long-standing ideologies of upright, civilized "manliness," some Americans were interested in quite a different type of manhood. These Americans found a source of powerful manhood in a primal, untamed "masculinity," the opposite of "civilized manliness." This primal male power seemed to arise from the "natural man's" closeness to "nature." The "masculine" strength of the "natural man" was the sort of strength which *all* men had—civilized and savage. Here was a strength based not on manly self-control but on masculine "instinct." It was a violent strength— the strength of a "savage" or a "carnivore." This power, unlike that of high-minded "manliness," was weakened by civilization's restraining discipline. Just as "the white man" was the embodiment of "civilized manliness," "the natural man" was the embodiment of "primitive masculinity."

It is probably not coincidental, then, that as Ida B. Wells continued her campaign against lynching into the twentieth century, she gradually abandoned her tactic of calling racist white Americans unmanly or uncivilized. In the context of the increasing popularity of passionate, primitive masculinity, middle-class men were beginning to *like* thinking of themselves as a little bit "barbarous." Increasingly, Wells' twentieth-century antilynching writings were cast in the genre of the muckrakers, with Wells the investigative reporter and her antiracist arguments couched in the statistical language of social science.[124] By the time Wells wrote her autobiography in 1928, the whole strategy of rewriting "civilization" was so out-of-date that she didn't even bother to mention it when discussing the British campaigns.

Wells' sensitivity to whites' conflation of male power and white supremacy may have continued to shape her antiracist strategies, however. Between 1908 and 1917, she devoted much of her energy to organizing social services for African American *men*—a surprising tactic for a woman so steeped in the nineteenth-century woman's movement.[125] As Wells described it in her autobiography, she became aware that young men migrating from the South encountered a complete dearth of social services. Barred from settlement houses and YMCAs, they congregated in saloons and crime-infested neighborhoods and frequently got into trouble. Whites' interpretation of this situation added insult to injury: Instead of seeing high crime rates and unemployment as an indictment of exclusionary racist practices, whites found "proof" that the typical African American man was, like the "Negro rapist," a dangerous threat to "the white man." Perhaps by organizing her reading room, employment service, and men's lodging house, Wells was attempting, not only to fill these men's material needs, but also to address, once again, white America's assertion that black men's lack of manliness proved the inherent inferiority of the entire race.[126]

Conclusion

To appreciate how skillfully Wells conducted her antilynching campaign, one needs to understand, as Wells did, the subtle ways ideologies of race, manhood, and civilization were interwoven in the 1890s. In the face of social and cultural change, middle-class men had become fearful that their manhood was at risk. In order to strengthen faltering constructs of traditional manliness, they turned to race. By envisioning themselves as "the white man," whose superior manliness set them apart from more primitive dark-skinned races, middle-class men reassured themselves that manliness remained as strong as ever.

Wells inverted these linkages between manhood and white supremacy. Where white Northerners imagined lynching proved white men's superior manliness, Wells argued the reverse: lynching proved black men were far more manly than whites who tolerated lynching. Where white Americans constructed elaborate pageants like the Columbian Exposition to dramatize that white men were more manly and civilized than savage dark-skinned races, Wells mobilized the discourse of civilization to demonstrate the reverse: white Americans were despicably unmanly and uncivilized. American whites believed themselves civilized Anglo-Saxons, superior to primitive blacks, but Wells argued that the opposite was true: African Americans were highly civilized, whereas white Americans were brutal and barbarous. By mobilizing all these arguments, Wells convinced the British that American whites were unmanly barbarians who needed to be civilized, and convinced white American men that the civilized world would condemn them as unmanly barbarians until lynching was stopped.

By inverting "civilization" and challenging the links between white supremacy and manliness, Wells produced an antiracist discourse of manliness. Wells recognized that behind middle-class gender lay a fundamental assumption that all pure women and manly men were white. To attack that one point, as Wells and many of her contemporaries did, was to attack the entire edifice of middle-class identity and middle-class gender. Victorian ideologies of womanhood marginalized black women by depicting them as unwomanly harlots and contrasting them with white women, who were depicted as real women, high-minded and sexually pure. By resisting these ideas, and insisting on black women's pure womanliness, black women in effect produced an alternative discourse of womanhood, as Hazel Carby and Paula Giddings have shown.[127] In the same way, middle-class formulations of manliness marginalized black men by depicting them as unmanly rapists, whose uncontrolled sexuality contrasted with the restrained self-mastery and manliness of "the white man." By arguing that it was the white man, and not the black man, who was lustful and uncivilized, Wells produced a less damaging formulation of gender. By the early twentieth century, these tactics would be less powerful, having been eroded by the popularity of a more "primitive" masculinity. In 1894, however, Wells' rewriting of racist discourses of civilization had been very effective, indeed.

3

"Teaching Our Sons to Do What We Have Been Teaching the Savages to Avoid": G. Stanley Hall, Racial Recapitulation, and the Neurasthenic Paradox

G. Stanley Hall, unlike Jack Johnson and Ida B. Wells, lived nearly all his life out of the glare of public notoriety. A professor of pedagogy and psychology, he regularly contributed articles to genteel magazines and newspapers but almost never became the subject of public scrutiny himself. Yet, for a few weeks in 1899, this mild-mannered academic—the founder and president of Clark University—briefly and very uncomfortably became the focus of a local scandal in Chicago after he addressed a national kindergarten teacher's convention and told the teachers, on what he considered sound psychological evidence, that they should encourage the little boys in their care to act like savages.

Hall, like many of his contemporaries, feared overcivilization was endangering American manhood. As a nationally recognized expert on pedagogy, he believed it was his responsibility to make sure American boys received a virile education that avoided overcivilized effeminacy. He had thus welcomed the opportunity to address the leaders of the kindergarten movement, who he believed were hopelessly mired in feminine sentimentality. Hall was dumbfounded, however, when the Chicago newspapers, reporting his remarks, described him as a cruel and bloodthirsty advocate of "barbarism."

The headlines of the *Chicago Record* ran,

BOXING FOR BABIES.
DR. HALL'S UNIQUE DOCTRINES.
Recommends Tales of Bloodletting,
Painful Experiences, Sparring and
"Square" Dancing for the Cul-
tivation of the Young.[1]

The *Chicago Evening Post* made the point explicitly: Hall wanted to turn Americans' sons into savages. "The idea among the uncivilized peoples of the world to-day is that boys and men should fight. . . . To these people we send missionaries . . . and just as we are beginning to congratulate ourselves on reclaiming some men from barbarism Dr. Hall gets up and advises us to teach our sons to do what we have been endeavoring to teach the savages to avoid."[2]

Although these journalists sensationalized Hall's message, they reported it accurately. Hall *had* argued that boys should be seen as racially primitive savages. "The child is in the primitive age. The instinct of the savage survives in him. . . . The angry child doubles up its puny fists and strikes its mother. . . . That she is not killed or severely injured is not because of lack of will upon the part of the child, but of physical weakness. In his primitive, savage state, a man fought with his neighbor over a bone in a cave."[3] Like the advocates of "natural man," Hall believed that middle-class men could find an antidote to the effeminizing qualities of modern civilization in the "primitive." The *Evening Post* was correct: Hall did want to allow "our sons to do what we have been endeavoring to teach the savages to avoid." And although some scholars have tried to minimize Hall's insistence that small boys were—literally—savages, this belief was absolutely central to his theories of education and psychology.

G. Stanley Hall was as eager as any other man of his generation to remake manhood. Like many of his contemporaries, he never questioned the idea that manhood was and ought to be powerful, but he grew uncomfortable with Victorian ideologies of self-restrained manliness. Moreover, he shared the widespread belief that excessive civilization was threatening young American men with weakness and neurasthenic breakdown. Yet, as an educator, he believed he held the key to revitalizing American manhood. Men could be *made*. By adopting his methods, Hall believed, educators could raise boys to be strong and virile, immune from civilization's effeminizing tendencies. The key to building powerful virility in American men, as Hall saw it, was to encourage primitive savagery in American boys.

Why Did Hall Believe Manhood Needed to Be Remade? Manliness, Sexuality, and Self-restraint

G. Stanley Hall never really wanted little boys to actually *be* savages. As a respected college president and pillar of his community, he had every reason to uphold the manly power of "civilization." Indeed, that was precisely the point. Like many men of his generation, he was worried that civilization was becoming weak and that powerful manhood, as represented through Victorian ideologies of self-restrained manliness, was becoming impotent. Thus, he joined in the widespread cultural move to remake manhood. As an educator, Hall felt he could remake manhood by making men—literally. For what was education but the process of making boys into men? By encouraging educators to recognize the "savagery" in young boys, Hall believed he could find a way to allow boys to develop into adult men with the virility to withstand the effeminizing tendencies of advanced civilization. A brief consideration of Hall's own boyhood, and the way he himself learned about manhood, can help explain what Hall meant when he warned that civilized manliness was weak, and why he proposed to strengthen it with a healthy dose of boyhood primitivism.

As a young boy in New England, Hall (then called Stanley) was repeatedly taught that manliness was based on "character" and vigorous self-restraint. Born in 1844, Stanley was raised in a typical Yankee Protestant family in a small, not-too-prosperous, western Massachusetts farm community.[4] His parents—like most middle-class parents—strove diligently to help their son develop a strong and manly "character." Stanley learned he must control his instincts and deny himself momentary pleasures. Only a well-developed character—the strength born of total self-mastery—could make the boy strong enough to be a real man.[5]

Hall's parents described character as a muscle which needed to be strengthened and exercised through a program of moral calisthenics. By repeatedly holding fast to his good resolutions and eschewing any temptation to momentary pleasures, Stanley could exercise his will and build up a manly character. Conversely, however, if he habitually succumbed to temptation, he would grow up weak and unmanly. Hall's father, Granville, explained this dynamic to eight-year-old Stanley in an inspirational note: "Every good resolution you form, if it is carried into practice, will give you strength [to] practice greater virtues. But if you resolve, & fail, it will weaken your purpose and make you more irresolute till at last you cannot persevere in doing any thing that is good." If Stanley strove to exercise his will and build his character, his father promised, he would "rejoice at its good effect" when he became a man. But if Stanley let his will grow weak and flabby, he would turn into a shiftless and unmanly ne'er-do-well.[6]

Abigail Hall shared her husband's sentiments. As she warned Stanley at age fourteen, the smallest wrongdoing could fatally weaken his will and endanger his manliness. "We think you are placed in a situation where temptations meet you on every side. If you absolutely resist all enticements to wrong doing it will strengthen your moral principle and you will be a better man for it—but if you yield to the wrong in the smallest matter it will weaken your power of resistance in the future. I know you mean to make a good man, and to that end you must take care of the *Right* while a boy."[7] Stanley must practice resisting temptation while a boy so that he would develop into a good and powerful man.

One might think that few temptations would face a boy growing up in sleepy, rural Ashfield, Massachusetts. Yet, paradoxically, by positing manliness as the strenuous control of base masculine desires, Victorian parents like Granville and Abigail Hall constructed those base desires as a fundamental part of a boy's personality. The more a boy worked to repress his illicit desires, the more attention he focused on those desires and the more real they became. The more he struggled to remain obedient to his parents, the more he became aware of his desire to be disobedient. As he concentrated on repressing his pride, laziness, and gluttony, he could easily come to see himself as a proud, lazy glutton.

Chief among Stanley's illicit desires—too vile to discuss yet the most horrific of sins—was sex. Hall's recollections of his youth support the observations of Michel Foucault: sexual identity was *produced*, not repressed, by burgeoning Victorian discourses of sexual prohibition.[8] As a boy who longed to become manly by developing a powerful will, Stanley constructed his manhood in terms of a tortured sexuality which needed to be restrained but was potentially unrestrainable. Young Stanley learned to obsess on sex as the greatest possible obscenity. When the minister dwelt upon the "unpardonable sin" during sermons, Stanley assumed he was speaking of sex. His family called human genitals "the dirty place," and he understood this meant that genitals were unspeakably filthy—so vile a boy couldn't even speak their proper name. The dangers of sex pervaded his childhood. "The most degrading experience of my life," he recalled, was his yearly duty to drive the sows to mate with the boar. Everyone in town knew what he was taking those pigs to do, and Stanley was thoroughly humiliated. He also detested his task of holding screaming four-week-old piglets as they were castrated, one after the other. Hall was further traumatized by his schoolmates' sexual experimentation. Once he was mortified by an older girl who exposed herself to him. Worse, it "was common for the older boys to catch us younger ones, unless we were fleet enough to outrun them, and to strip and exhibit us to older boys and even girls."[9] How humiliating to have his "dirty place" exhibited before "even girls."

Yet the most dangerous results of these sexual episodes, according to Hall himself, lay not in his public humiliation but in the subversion of his manliness. All this exposure to sex gave Stanley lascivious thoughts, which undermined his self-control and imperiled his character and manhood. The more the boy tried to repress his sexual thoughts, the more interested in sex he became, and the more he saw himself as a vile, unmanly boy who harbored unclean desires.[10]

Unclean thoughts led to unclean habits. Soon Stanley was fatally addicted to masturbation. At first, he began to experiment with himself, "seeking assurance that function [was] normal," and this led to manipulation and then to masturbation. Upon discovering that his genitals were maturing, and he was on the road to becoming a man, his "new sense of virility" brought "a certain deep elation" and "a vaunting feeling of superiority." But boys like Stanley, schooled in the dangers of a flabby will, could not easily enjoy the pleasures of the flesh. Soon came "a sense of unworthiness, sin, pollution, and . . . convictions of foreboding disaster or penalty."[11] Stanley became obsessed with the thought that by his inability to repress his masturbatory passions, he was squandering all chance for manly power. Over and over again, Stanley made new resolutions, working to strengthen his will and abjure "self-abuse" forever. Always he failed, and waited for disaster to strike.

Even his father's scanty lectures on sexual purity only made him more aware of his own evil propensities. Once Granville warned Stanley away from sex by describing "a youth who abused himself and sinned with lewd women and as a result had a disease that ate his nose away until there were only two flat holes in his face for nostrils and who also became an idiot." Stanley, horrified, thus discovered new dangers. Not only could sex ruin his character and manhood; it could also cause imbecility and incurable, humiliating deformity. Instead of curbing Stanley's attention to sex, of course, this new knowledge gave Stanley new reasons to remain obsessed. "For a long time, if I had any physical excitation or nocturnal experience I was almost petrified lest I was losing my brains and carefully examined the bridge of my nose to see if it was getting the least bit flat," he recalled. Anxiously, Stanley began to inspect himself for physical signs of sexual degeneracy.[12]

Masturbation led to anxiety, but nocturnal emissions confirmed Stanley's worst forebodings. All he knew about ejaculation was that self-abuse and the loss of semen caused death and insanity. Now, all his parents' warnings about the dangers of a flaccid character seemed to be coming true in the most horrifying way possible. He had not kept his manly resolve to suppress his sinful desires. He had succumbed to the temptation of masturbation. His will had grown weak and useless. As a result, he had lost control entirely. Now, his body was masturbating *spontaneously,* even as he slept. Later in life Hall described these feelings:

> This causes fear, sometimes amounting to terror, lest control be lost and life now given over into the hands of blind and lethal powers against which conscious will and resolution are of no avail. Masturbation is felt to be controllable and the victim feels that he can stop at any time, but spontaneous emissions give a sense of being powerless in the hands of fate. . . . This frequently brings a dumb despair that saps all the joy of life, may make it intolerable and lead to suicide.[13]

He was powerless to control his masculine passions. His will was useless. Manliness would never be his. Disfigurement, madness, and death were his inevitable portion.

Sex was too vile to discuss with anyone, so Stanley had to face his disaster alone. He rigged up an apparatus to wake him if he got an erection, but this failed utterly. He secretly consulted a doctor in another town, who took his money, laughed at him, and gave him another stern lecture about insanity and unchastity. With great "anguish of soul," Hall concluded that he was "exceptionally corrupt . . . if I succeeded in making anything of myself it would be despite this private handicap. I should certainly never dare to marry and have children." By the time Hall discovered that wet dreams were normal, he was already in college.[14]

Hall's terrified battles with his masculine sexuality may have been extreme, but they were not unique. Throughout the nineteenth century, physicians and social purity experts churned out hundreds of widely circulated pamphlets offering lurid descriptions of the insanity and life-threatening diseases awaiting the masturbator.[15] Moreover, youths across America shared Hall's terror of nocturnal emissions. Medical experts warned them about the dangers of the life-threatening disease, "spermatorrhea," which consisted of the involuntary emission of semen. Legitimate doctors prescribed dozens of medicines and ingenious contrivances to suppress involuntary excitement and seminal leakage. Thousands of quacks built up flourishing mail-order businesses providing expensive nostrums to terrified youths unable to admit their condition to their family doctors.[16]

Why did male sexuality seem so dangerous? Why did young men fear that masturbation would make them insane, or that nocturnal seminal "leakage" could kill them? Protestant religious teaching, of course, had long depicted nonmarital sexuality as sinful, and Granville and Abigail Hall's teachings about manly self-control drew on this long-standing Christian tradition. Yet this terror of unrestrained male sexuality as potentially lethal drew less on religion than on Victorian medical science.

Victorian doctors believed that the human body contained a fixed and finite amount of "nerve energy." This nerve force was the energy which made life possible. Scientists had long been searching for a physical, mechanical explanation of the difference between inert matter and living things. By the early nineteenth century, they explained this difference in terms of the forces that animated the nervous system. In healthy bodies, this nerve force was evenly distributed throughout the organs. If any organ drew excessively on this limited quantity of nervous energy, however, the rest of the body would be starved of nervous force, and illness would result.[17]

According to medical experts, masturbation—or even too-frequent marital intercourse—threatened a man's health by wasting his limited stock of nerve force. Some experts believed this loss of nerve force stemmed from the loss of semen. Others held that the sex act itself exhausted the nervous force. Both sides agreed, however, that by giving in to sexual temptation, a man squandered his finite supply of nervous force and wrecked his health. As a frequently reprinted manual put it in 1857, masturbation "tends directly to weaken and destroy the force and energy of the physical system, and to impair the intellect, weaken the memory, and debase the mind; resulting often in early decrepitude, permanent nervous affections, amaurosis and blindness, fatuity and insanity."[18] Hundreds of books and pamphlets detailing these dangers were published and circulated during the nineteenth century.

When he matured, G. Stanley Hall, like an increasing number of his contemporaries, felt oppressed by this ideology of manly self-restraint, yet he had little else to put in its place. After he graduated from college he sneaked off for a year of study in Germany, where he developed a taste for beer, dancing, socializing on the Sabbath, and courting pretty girls—all in moderation.[19] Yet he could not entirely jettison his belief that manliness was based on iron self-mastery. It was entrenched in his identity, including his most intimate assumptions about the workings of his own body. It was the way he understood the sources of male power and authority, both of which he passionately desired. If he abandoned ideologies of "manliness," Hall would lack any coherent blueprint for becoming a powerful man. Despite his ambivalence, the young man remained enmeshed in his vision of manly power as the ability to restrain male sexuality, and of male sexuality as a dangerous drain on nervous energy.

Hall was not alone in his dissatisfaction with ideologies of manly self-restraint, as we have already seen. "Manliness" was thoroughly enmeshed in a moralistic Victorian culture which had already begun to lose its hold over the middle class by the last decades of the nineteenth century. Religious challenges from Darwinism and the new historical criticism of the Bible were undermining Victorianism's longstanding Protestant underpinnings. At the same time, the United States was beginning to develop a bureaucratic, corporate economy. As fewer men became able to achieve independent entrepreneurship, self-control and delayed gratification became a less profitable individual strategy. Instead, middle-class men began to find more pleasure in leisure and consumption, which further undermined the plausibility of manly self-restraint. Many men came to see Victorian culture, which stressed delayed gratification and sexual self-restraint, as "effeminate," and to yearn for some way to make it more "virile."[20] In short, Hall's dissatisfaction with ideologies of manly self-restraint was echoed by middle-class men across the nation.

Neurasthenia Defines the Paradox of the White Man's Body and "Civilization"

One of the many ways American men addressed the cultural weakness of manly restraint was to interpret it as a physical illness and attempt to treat it medically. "Neurasthenia" was in part an effort to construct the *cultural* weakness of self-restrained manliness as a *bodily* weakness, and to "cure" it. Civilized manly power was already seen as an attribute of the white male body. Thus, interpreting the cultural weakness of civilized manliness as a sickness of the white male body was not as outlandish as it might appear.[21]

Civilized manly power, under this formulation, stemmed from two combined factors: manhood and whiteness. To wield manly power, one must possess both a male body and the racial ability to restrain the masculine passions of that body. *All* healthy men, savage and civilized, were believed to have a strong and masculine sexual drive, because all men had male bodies and, thus, male desires. A man who lacked this sexual passion was like a woman—weak and undersexed, lacking the essential power of manhood. Yet the mere possession of powerful masculine sexuality was not enough to give one the vast power of civilized manliness, as we have seen in our discussions of Jack Johnson and the mythic Negro rapist. Primitive men, although they possessed powerful masculine passions, were believed to be unable to wield civilized manly power because they lacked the racial capacity for sexual self-restraint. Only civilized white men had evolved the advanced intellectual and moral capacity to master their masculine passions. As Hall's parents had told their son over and over, the only way that a civilized boy could build up a strong will and a manly character, and thus develop into a powerful man, was by struggling to restrain his sexual impulses.

As middle-class ideologies of manly self-restraint became less appealing, however, the power of civilized manliness began to appear problematic. Men like Hall who found the concept of iron self-mastery antiquated and unpersuasive began to face a number of questions about powerful manhood which they were unable to answer. If manly self-mastery was not the essence of white men's manly superiority to savages, what was? If manly strength and authority were not gained through manly self-restraint and a powerful will, where did they come from? Victorian middle-class ideologies of gender provided no answers to these questions.

Neurasthenia provided no answers, either, but it did provide a new way to frame the problem and an elaborate program to cure it. Although physicians today do not recognize neurasthenia as a disease, between 1870 and about 1915, physicians took it very seriously indeed.[22] By the early 1880s, neurasthenia had become a near epidemic, in large part because it so clearly expressed and explained this cultural problem.

Neurasthenia's cultural meaning was explained in the classic reference work on the subject, *American Nervousness* (1881), by George M. Beard.[23] Beard, the first man to discover the illness of neurasthenia, was widely considered the foremost American expert on the disease. He was also a very good friend of G. Stanley Hall. Hall, who was never one to offer praise lightly, characterized Beard as "a brilliant American physician who was prematurely cut off at the point of his highest promise." (Beard had died of pneumonia in 1883 at the age of forty-four.) Hall considered *American Nervousness* an important work and constructed his own mission to revitalize American manhood in very similar terms.[24]

Beard defined "neurasthenia" as "*nervelessness—a lack of nerve force.*"[25] Neurasthenia resulted when a highly evolved person seriously overtaxed his body's finite supply of nerve force—the same nerve force which masturbation squandered. Neurasthenia was thus not a mental illness. It was a neurological illness, a malfunction of bodily physics.[26] A neurasthenic, according to Beard, was like an undercharged electric battery. He lacked adequate power. When the demands on his nervous energy were greater than his "charge" he would grow ill. "Men, like batteries, need a reserve force, and men, like batteries, need to be measured by the amount of this reserve, and not by what they are compelled to expend in ordinary daily life."[27] A man, like a storage battery, had to live within his finite capacities—to avoid overdrawing his limited energies—or suffer severe and debilitating consequences. Beard lists two full pages of possible symptoms of neurasthenia, including headaches, dyspepsia, muscle spasms, and a variety of masculine sexual problems, including impotence, involuntary emissions, and spermatorrhea.[28]

It was not coincidental that neurasthenics and masturbators both suffered from the same sorts of sexual dysfunctions. Beard's explanations of neurasthenia paralleled Victorian explanations of masturbatory illness. Both diseases resulted from excessive expenditures of the body's limited supplies of nervous force. Just as masturbation would rob a body of its masculinity and male force by draining it of its nervous force, so neurasthenics who overtaxed their bodies would become weak and sickly, likewise drained of their nervous force.

Yet the moral implications of neurasthenia and masturbatory illness were very different. Masturbatory illness was the fault of the masturbator—of his moral weakness, his unmanly failure to master his masculine passions. Neurasthenia, however, was not necessarily the fault of the neurasthenic. It was, instead, the fault of the biological limitations and restraints of his highly evolved body. Thus, neurasthenia can be interpreted as a way to address the dangerously limited energies (and the questionable cultural power) of the white male body, without the stigma of masturbatory illness.

For neurasthenic illness was caused, not by unmanly self-abuse, but by manly modern civilization itself. As Beard put it, italicizing the key point, "The chief and primary cause of this development and very rapid increase of nervousness is *modern civilization*. . . . Civilization is the one constant factor without which there can be little or no nervousness, and under which in its modern form nervousness in its many varieties must arise inevitably."[29] In other words, neurasthenics were highly evolved white men who had overtaxed their vital energies by overstimulating themselves, not with sex, but with civilization.

Because it was caused by civilization, neurasthenia was thus a *racial* disease. It "scarcely exists among savages or barbarians, or semi-barbarians or partially civilized people."[30] Neurasthenics could be recognized by their European bodily traits, which contrasted utterly with the coarse features of the stereotypical "savage." Neurasthenics were distinguished by their "fine soft hair, delicate skin, nicely chiselled features." Neurasthenia was "frequently associated with superior intellect"—likewise widely considered a civilized racial trait.[31] In short, neurasthenia, like civilization and the most advanced manliness, affected only the most highly evolved white races.

Civilized men and women both developed neurasthenia, but because each sex had its own relation to civilization, the implications of neurasthenia varied by sex. Women became neurasthenics because civilization exposed them to more demanding mental activity, which drained their capacity to be healthy mothers.[32] Men, on the other hand, became neurasthenics because the increased pace and technological advancement of modern civilization placed greater demands on them as businessmen and professionals.

The men most in danger of developing neurasthenia were middle- and upper-class businessmen and professionals whose highly evolved bodies had been physically weakened by advances in civilization.[33] According to Beard, neurasthenia first developed after 1856, as American civilization was reaching its current eminence and as American men increasingly did work which stressed "labor of the brain over that of the muscles."[34] Because the body was a closed system with a limited amount of energy, by overdeveloping their intellects to meet the demands of civilization, men had enfeebled their bodies. The pace and technology of civilization drained men of their nervous force until they were as weak and useless as worn-out batteries. As steam power had quickened the rate and scale of production, and as the periodical press and telegraph informed the businessman of daily fluctuations in supply, cost, and marketing, the tempo of business life had increased, and the resulting increase in "brain work and worry" drained American businessmen of their nervous energy at a rate inconceivable even to their fathers.[35] Neurasthenia was thus implicitly a disease of the middle and upper classes. (The possibility of highly evolved Anglo-Saxons being laborers or factory workers instead of "brain workers" was simply not thinkable in this framework: again, "civilization's" foregrounding of race obscures the category of class.)

Civilization's repression of emotion caused neurasthenia, too, although to a lesser extent. Civilized men held their passions in check, but this manliness could be exhausting. "Constant inhibition, restraining normal feelings, keeping back, covering, holding in check atomic forces of the mind and body, is an exhausting process, and to this process all civilization is constantly subjected."[36] Here, too, the advancement of civilization led directly to neurasthenia by draining the force from white male bodies.

Indeed, civilization's demands on men's nerve force had left their bodies positively effeminate. According to Beard, neurasthenics had the organization of "women more than of men." They possessed "a muscular system comparatively small and feeble." Their dainty frames and feeble musculature lacked the masculine vigor and nervous reserves of even their most recent forefathers. "It is much less than a century ago, that a man who could not [drink] many bottles of wine was thought of as effeminate—but a fraction of a man." No more. With their dwindling reserves of nerve force, civilized men were becoming increasingly susceptible to the weakest stimulants until now, "like babes, we find no safe retreat, save in chocolate and milk and water."[37] Sex was as debilitating as alcohol for neurasthenics. For most men, sex in moderation was a tonic. Yet civilized neurasthenics could become ill if they attempted intercourse even once every three months. As Beard put it, "there is not force enough left in them to reproduce the species or go through the process of reproducing the species."[38] Lacking even the force "to reproduce the species," their manhood was clearly in jeopardy.

Neurasthenia thus expressed the *cultural* weakness of civilized, manly self-restraint in *medical* terms. According to Victorian doctrine, only civilized white men had the manly strength to restrain their powerful masculine passions. But what if civilized, manly self-restraint was not a source of power, but merely a symptom of nerve-exhaustion and effeminacy? What if civilized advancement led merely to delicacy and weakness? Then the male body becomes not a strong storage battery, highly charged with tightly leashed masculine sexuality, but a decadent wreck, an undercharged battery with a dangerous scarcity of nerve force. The "manly civilized man" takes on the sickly complexion of a masturbatory deviant who has lost his vital nervous energy and become weak and pathetic.

In short, neurasthenia posed a paradox. Only white male bodies had the capacity to be truly civilized. Yet, at the same time, civilization destroyed white male bodies. How could powerful, civilized manhood be saved? If civilized men were too delicate to tolerate civilization, who would lead the race to ever higher stages of evolution? Was civilization itself doomed to decay? Many educated men on both sides of the Atlantic feared this was the case, and intellectuals from Max Nordau to Madison Grant preached the dangers of racial degeneracy and the decline of civilization.[39] Humanity's future seemed bleak—unless a way could be found to reverse this evolutionary trend and to build a manhood powerful enough to withstand the emasculating tendencies of higher civilization. This was the task to which Hall devoted his energies.

G. Stanley Hall Solves the Paradox

George M. Beard and his fellow experts on neurasthenia had posed a paradox: only white manhood could create a higher civilization; yet higher civili-

Fig. 6. G. Stanley Hall, in the dignified, serious publicity photograph he typically included in his books. Courtesy Clark University Archives.

zation destroyed white manhood by draining men's bodies of their limited nervous force. G. Stanley Hall believed he could solve this paradox. The ambitious young boy from Ashfield had studied in Germany and earned a doctorate from Harvard. After much effort, he had become a prominent expert on psychology and pedagogy, finding some measure of manly power and authority in his personal professional advancement.[40] Yet the cultural contradictions embedded in civilized manly self-restraint remained a burning issue for Hall. Beginning in the 1880s, Hall began to look for new ways to raise middle-class boys with enough nervous force to withstand neurasthenia and modern civilization.

Hall was deeply affected by Beard's theories of neurasthenia and drew on them to frame an educational theory which would protect the manly power of civilized boys and, therefore, protect the future of civilization. Beard believed that excessive schooling drained boys' nervous energy and was one of the prime causes of neurasthenia in modern civilization.[41] Hall agreed and, beginning in the mid-1880s, peppered his pedagogical writings with warnings of the "real and grave danger"—the "national decay and calamity"—threatening American boys.[42] Like Beard, Hall believed neurasthenia was caused by civilization and warned of "a more and more predominant influence in the production of disease as civilization advances." He therefore warned against teachers who, by "overpressing" their students, "sow seeds of suffering and incapacity." For although education was essential to civilization, too much education led to neurasthenia. "The narrowness of mind and weakness of character, the paucity of information and slowness of intellect shown by so many originally bright boys after long years of expensive schooling, the long period of listlessness and perhaps depression, the 'loss of that keen interest in life which even healthy young animals should feel,' are the too common symptoms of that nervous exhaustion . . . which is distinctively school-bred."[43]

To avoid causing disease, educators must tread a tightrope: While a teacher must provide boys with the advanced knowledge they needed to be leaders of civilized society, excessive mental stimulation could lead to neurasthenia. In a speech given to a group of elite male students at Brown University in 1891, Hall vividly depicted the dilemma of modern young men trying to become manly and powerful while avoiding the dangers of neurasthenic collapse.[44] As Hall described it, an overpressed, neurasthenic student became as weak and ineffectual as a child. But unless a man underwent a strenuous education, he would remain stuck in mediocrity. Either danger would destroy manhood; either would leave a man powerless to lead civilized society. Education insured "individual success" and was the key to manly power and advancement, not only in civilized countries but even "in remote, and until lately, almost barbarous lands."[45] Yet while education was eradicating barbarism in foreign lands, Hall warned, it was also ruining schoolboys' health in civilized countries. American teachers were neglecting boys' bodies, allowing them "to atrophy, and chest, back, shoulders, hips, never to attain their fullest possible development."[46] Hall warned that this "mutilation" of civilized boys' bodies risked bringing a "sick and sterile epoch upon the world."[47] If civilized American men lost their health and became neurasthenics, how could they lead the fight for further evolutionary advancement? Overcivilized effeminacy and racial decadence loomed.

Hall was left with a paradox. Like so many educated men of his generation, Hall was face to face with the specter of racial degeneracy.[48] Civilization's advancement seemed to lead inevitably to its decay. The very educational methods which had previously caused civilization to advance now threatened modern man with degeneration and racial decline. As Hall lamented in 1894, "The modern school seems to be a force leading to physical degeneracy . . . and when we consider that children the civilized world over, and in countries barely civilized, all go to school, we see what a tremendous danger there is that the race will be imperfectly developed. How sad the thought that the race may, indeed almost must, degenerate in its efforts toward the realization of its loftiest ideals."[49]

Yet even as Hall penned these lines, he was well on the way to finding a solution. The neurasthenic paradox had posited a choice between two opposite and mutually exclusive alternatives. Men could either be civilized but neurasthenic weaklings, threatened by the limitations of their bodies, or they could be virile but less advanced primitives, banished from the millennial advancement of civilization. In other words, neurasthenia had posited a series of linked dualisms, structuring the relationship of white male bodies to civilization.

Barbarism	versus	Civilization
Masculinity	versus	Manliness
Primitive Race	versus	White Race
Bodily Strength	versus	Bodily Weakness
Ignorance	versus	Education
Excessive Masculine Passions	versus	Scarcity of Nerve Force
Virility	versus	Effeminacy

The second column was associated with neurasthenia; the first, with health. As long as these dualisms were seen as irreconcilable opposites, the paradox was unresolvable, and both manhood and civilization seemed on their way to certain decline.

Hall solved this paradox and suggested a new way to prevent neurasthenia by reconceptualizing the relationship between these linked dualisms. As Hall came to see it, these sets of pairs were related not dualistically but developmentally. They were not irreconcilable opposites, they were merely different stages of one developmental process. Through evolution, barbarism became civilization. Ignorance gave way to intellectual power. And thus, by extension, primitive masculinity could evolve into civilized manliness. The key here was to focus on the developmental process itself—on human evolution—and to replace neurasthenia's set of dualisms with a different set of pairs, which were all related developmentally:

Boys	evolve into	Adult Men
Barbarism	evolves into	Civilization
Masculinity	evolves into	Manliness
Primitive Race	evolves into	White Race
Ignorance	evolves into	Education
Primitive ancestors	evolve into	Contemporary Man
Savages	evolve into	Civilized Man

The first column was simply an earlier stage of the second. One turned into the other through the normal, developmental processes of growth and evolution.

By redefining the relationship between these related sets of pairs in terms of *developmentalism* instead of *dualism*, Hall found a way to get beyond the neurasthenic paradox. The neurasthenic paradox had rested on a linked set of dualistic opposites. Weakness, effeminacy, and civilization had been pitted against strength, male sexuality, and primitiveness. These dualisms were always constructed as opposites, continually at war with one another. Hall solved the paradox by reconciling these dualisms using recapitulation theory. He moved beyond these oppositions by redefining them all as related parts of one developmental process—evolution and human growth. While a man might be civilized as an adult, Hall insisted, as a *boy* he had been primitive. Boys, he insisted, had access to all the primitive strength lacking to civilized men. By elaborating on this insight, Hall developed an intricate, influential pedagogy based upon the premise that boys could avoid neurasthenic breakdown and become powerful civilized men by taking full advantage of their boyhood access to the primitive. Recapitulation theory, as a means to a primitive virility, became the centerpiece of Hall's pedagogy.

Hall's New Master Narrative: Recapitulation Theory

In the late nineteenth century, recapitulation theory was scientific orthodoxy among most American biologists. Medelian genetic theory was not known, even to most embryologists, until about 1900. Instead, scientists believed in Lamarck's theory that acquired traits could be inherited. Recapitulation theory provided scientists with a persuasive explanation of the mechanism by which an individual offspring could inherit its parents' learned traits. An individual would follow the developmental path its forebears took. Its ontogeny would recapitulate its phylogeny. As a child or young animal matured, it precisely repeated the evolutionary path its ancestors had taken, from the most distant protozoan upward. Thus, a human embryo could be seen to develop gills and would gradually ascend the evolutionary ladder. The newest advanced evolutionary traits, developed by the child's parents or grandparents, were simply added on at the very end of the child's growth period. Thus, human evolution could be consciously aided by making certain that each generation of boys was developed to its highest potential, so that this generation, in turn, could pass its racial improvement on to its sons.[50]

Advanced intelligence was the highest, final evolutionary development, and it came last, in adolescence. However, it could only come to members of advanced races whose forebears had ascended to the top of the evolutionary ladder, and thus added the most advanced stage to the end of their particular phylogenetic path. Scientists believed that until adolescence, Negro children were often as bright or brighter than white children. At adolescence, however, Negro children stopped developing, because their ancestors had never gone on to evolve a higher intelligence. Black adults were believed to be roughly as intelligent as Anglo-Saxon children, precisely because their intellectual development stopped in the evolutionary stage corresponding to white childhood. Hall was in the best scientific company, then, in believing that white children were the evolutionary equivalents of "primitive" savages.[51]

Although some historians have spoken of recapitulation theory as if it were metaphoric, the big distinction between recapitulation theory and previous notions of primitive immaturity is recapitulation theory's absolute literalness. Recapitulation theory held that children actually, physically relived the adult development of their primitive ancestors. From at least the sixteenth century, advocates of hierarchical rankings like the Great Chain of Being had written of "lesser races" as if they were children, but they rarely argued that nonwhites actually had children's morphological traits. Colonial New Englanders, for example, had believed that children had primitive, animalistic urges which needed to be tamed, just as wild animals or Indians needed to be tamed. According to recapitulation theory, however, children were not merely metaphoric savages; their somatic makeup made children physically recapitulate primitive evolutionary stages. You could no more train a child to perform tasks evolutionarily beyond him than you could train an adult savage. Both had the same biological capacity, because both were at the same evolutionary level. Following this logic, one must not only give up the idea of racial egalitarianism as unscientific—after all, lower races literally were children compared to whites—one must also recognize that children acted "savage," not because they were bad or willful, but because that was their nature at that stage of evolution.[52]

Although Hall was not the first to use recapitulation theory to link child study to the study of savages, his recapitulation-based theories were surely among the most ambitious. He believed that by applying Darwinism to the study of human development, he could do for psychology what Darwin had done for biology: he could bring psychology out of the rigid formal categories of the nineteenth century and make it more dynamic.[53]

It is impossible to overstate how literally Hall applied recapitulation theory to his theories of psychology and education. For him, the key to understanding child nature was to recognize that children grew up repeating the actual psychological experiences of their primitive adult ancestors. Child development, down to the most specific detail, could be explained by looking for correlations in the distant evolutionary past. For example, he suggested that modern children's tendency to pick scabs stemmed from their primitive ancestors' propensity to pick lice.[54] Civilized children laughed at human pain, even at death, because they were like men in primitive times, when one person's death meant more food for the rest.[55] Children feared animals with big teeth, big eyes, and rough fur because, only recently, their savage ancestors had been eaten by such creatures.[56] These examples could be multiplied almost indefinitely.[57] Hall even suggested that anthropologists should extrapolate from studies of civilized children to reconstruct the cultures of lost primitive races.[58] For example, he believed that the relative independence of modern children eight to twelve years old corresponded to a lost primitive "pigmoid" race, "when in a warm climate the young of our species once shifted for themselves independently of further parental aid."[59] Just as studying primitive savages could explain child development, so studying modern children could provide knowledge about lost stages and "missing links" in human evolutionary history.

Yet Hall's interest in recapitulation theory was more than scholarly. Hall believed his psychology was the basis of a practical pedagogy which would solve the neurasthenic paradox by building powerful manhood out of the primitive impulses of young boys. Hall described two ways that educators could build young boys into powerful men. First, by taking advantage of little boys' natural reliving of their ancestors' primitive evolutionary history, educators could "inoculate" them against the weakness of excessive civilization. Second, by taking advantage of the flood of inherited primitive traits which crowded in on young men at sexual puberty, educators could move them closer to being the "super-man." And, as valuable as this primal manhood would be for individual men, Hall believed more was at stake, here, than personal male power. By shoring up the collective masculine power of the civilized races, Hall believed he could not only save civilization from degenerating; he could help move civilization toward a millennial perfection.

Leading American Men toward a More Perfect Civilization:
The Savage Boy as "A Pillar of Smoke by Day, and Fire by Night"

Deeply ambivalent about manly self-restraint, Hall still believed in the manly power which stemmed from an iron will and a strong character. Yet in the light of the neurasthenic paradox, self-restraint seemed to stem less from an iron will than from a paucity of nervous force. Even the masculine passions their own grandfathers had safely enjoyed exhausted neurasthenic modern man. Men could no longer drink, love, or fight without suffering nervous exhaustion. Passion—sexual or otherwise—became the issue for Hall. It was both deeply desirable and dangerous. It made for manliness but could unman a neurasthenic. Hall began to look for ways to revitalize passionate and powerful manhood within advanced civilization.

Recapitulation theory allowed Hall to suggest ways to rear men with the strength to be both highly civilized and deeply passionate. The key was to take advantage of recapitulation and small boys' natural reliving of their ancestors' primitive emotionality. Children's "instincts and feelings . . . are reverberations from the remote ancestral past."[60] Civilized boys, unlike their fathers, still had access to the powerful emotions of their savage ancestors. By fully reliving their ancestors' vibrant passions, Hall suggested, little boys could incorporate a primitive's emotional strength into their adult personalities.[61]

Hall eloquently described this problem of overcivilized male passionlessness in 1903. In "our day and civilization," he lamented, "the hot life of feeling is remote and decadent. Culture represses, and intellect saps its root. The very word passion is becoming obsolete." What could civilized men, with their overdeveloped intellects and their weak and neurasthenic bodies, know of primitive passions, "of hate that makes men mad or bestial, of love that is not only uncalculating but is stronger than life, of fear that shakes the pulses and courage that faces death in its cruelest forms unflinchingly, of the wager of battle where men fight beasts or each other with teeth and knives and spitting revolvers, of torture, of joy that threatens sanity?" Lost was the passion which moved barbarians to fight "with teeth and knives and spitting revolvers." Men's hearts were "parched and bankrupt," and their "refined sensibilities" undermined their manhood.[62]

Yet just when the "hot life of feeling" seemed lost to civilized men forever, racial recapitulation restored it to them. Civilized men could rediscover their lost passions in the primitive emotions of their sons: "Happily for our craft, the child appears at the truly psychological moment, freighted as it is, body and soul, with reminiscences of what we were so fast losing. It is abandoned to joy, grief, passion, fear and rage. It is bashful, shows off, weeps, laughs, desires, is curious, eager, regrets and swells with passion, not knowing that these last two are especially outlawed by our guild." "Freighted body and soul" with "reminiscences" of the evolutionary past, children became men's safe island of primitive passion in civilization. "Despite our lessening fecundity, our over-schooling, city-fication and spoiling, the affectations we instill and the repressions we practice, they are still the light and hope of the world."[63]

Children's primitivism was "the light and hope" of the overcivilized world, not only because they were the next generation but because children's reliving of their evolutionary past provided an unfailing guide toward man's true evolutionary destiny. Here, Hall was drawing on the millennial subtext inherent in "civilization." To nineteenth-century Americans, "the advancement of civilization" always connoted a secularized version of Protestant millennialism: as the most civilized races advanced, they grew ever closer to human perfection on earth, ever closer to the highest evolutionary destiny.[64] Hall believed that racial recapitulation allowed psychologists to study the trajectory of this natural evolution toward human perfection, from the savage past toward the glorious future.

Child development thus had an oracular function, which Hall likened to the biblical image of God leading the children of Israel out of Egypt. Just as God had taken the form of a pillar of smoke by day and a pillar of fire by night for the Israelites journeying toward the promised land, so he had provided racial recapitulation as an infallible guide for man's evolutionary journey toward racial perfection. "Childhood and youth in their best impulses of development are not perverse but point more infallibly than anything else to the constant pole of human destiny. *Das ewige Kindliche* [the eternal child] is now taking its place beside, if not in some respects above, *Das ewige Weibliche* [the eternal feminine] as man's pillar of smoke by day and fire by night to lead him on."[65] Victorian society had revered the eternal feminine as the source of religion and morality. As Hall saw it, however, Victorian feminized religion had grown effeminate and empty.[66] The eternal child was a far surer source of a higher morality because he was rooted in the holy truths of evolution. The eternal child—eternal both in the divine truths he held and in the evolutionary trajectory he embodied—could become "man's pillar of cloud by day and fire by night" to lead him out of his overcivilized wilderness and into the promised land of racial advancement and powerful manhood.

Yet the most perfect civilization and the highest racial perfection could never be attained if civilized men remained weak and neurasthenic. Here Hall's interest in the savage little boy became a matter of practical pedagogy. By encouraging small boys to embrace their primitive passions instead of repressing them, educators could "inoculate" boys with the primitive strength they would need to avoid developing neurasthenia. As adults they could be safely civilized, refined, and cultured—but only if they had fully lived and outgrown a temporary case of savagery as small boys.

Hall described this reliving of primitive emotions as a sort of vaccination process.[67] In the same way that vaccination allowed people to resist smallpox by giving them a mild and controllable dose of the disease, reliving their ancestors' primitivism would allow boys to carry a weakened case of "savagery" in their systems and thus give them the primitive masculine strength to avoid neurasthenic breakdown and overcivilized effeminacy. Or, as Hall put it, the boy should have "been exposed to and already recovering from as many forms of ethical mumps and measles as, by having in mild form now he can be rendered immune to later when they become far more dangerous."[68] This bad childhood behavior denoted not moral weakness but moral development. A boy who misbehaves "is not depraved but only in a savage or half-animal stage." By allowing him to be true to his evolutionarily primitive nature, he would develop the antibodies necessary to render him "immune" to moral illnesses which could unman him later in life.

Hall specifically associated this childhood savagery with boys, not girls. Girls, he wrote, were more governed by adult motives, whereas "boys are nearer to primitive man."[69] Both boys and girls were buffeted by powerful feelings, but boys' emotions approached "savagery," whereas girls' emotions were characterized by "sentiment." This sexual difference in childhood emotion was even reflected in the difference between boys' and girls' preferred reading materials: "The boy who reads frontier stories till he is almost persuaded to be an 'Injun' is merely being vaccinated against savagery later in life." Girls, on the other hand, were more tame and tractable, so they read love stories.[70] Girls did not have this special link with savagery; nor did their feminine natures require such "inoculations." Only boys had the potential or need to be "vaccinated against savagery later in life" by reliving the moral savagery of their ancestors.

Of course, Hall didn't want little boys to actually *become* savages, any more than doctors wanted those they inoculated to die of smallpox. He merely wanted little boys to let their natural primitive tendencies express themselves fully so that, at the proper developmental stage, their savage tendencies could be replaced by the strongest, healthiest possible civilized traits. Eventually, at the proper recapitulatory moment (about age nine), boys would need to learn discipline.[71] Nor did Hall want small boys' savage tendencies to lead to dangerous violence. Boys simply needed to be encouraged to read bloody stories and engage in fisticuffs when necessary, in order to get the full benefit of racial recapitulation, and to avoid exacerbating civilization's excess of manly self-restraint.

To some extent, then, Hall's focus on boyhood savagery stemmed directly from his strategies of representation. In order to solve the neurasthenic paradox, he needed to represent the power of civilized manliness as developing naturally out of a pure, primal boyhood. Thus, for Hall, boyhood savagery was not a pedagogical end in itself. It was simply a means to allow young men to grow up masculine enough to avoid neurasthenia and other effeminizing tendencies of advanced civilization.

Yet although Hall intended to strengthen manly "civilization" by encouraging boyhood "savagery," at first some of his contemporaries found this distinction hard to understand. As we saw, when Hall opened a highly publicized 1899 education conference by calling on Chicago's kindergarten teachers to let small boys express their savage impulses, a minor scandal erupted. Addressing the teachers, Hall argued that educators should actively cultivate not only civilized emotions like love and virtue but also "primitive" emotions like anger, sin and pain.[72] Little boys who experienced only pleasure missed out on the healthful benefits of racial recapitulation, and lost the vital experience of repeating the savage experiences of the race. Lacking the ability to repeat evolution's advance, boys suffered evolutionary decay. Such boys were like the nautilus. Originally the nautilus had been a crab but, due to its excessively easy life, the species had degenerated into a helpless parasite. Now it had lost the use of its legs, eyes, skeleton, even its "reproductive apparatus."[73] In other words, the nautilus now had life so easy that it had—literally—lost its balls.

Civilized boys could avoid this horrifying emasculation by being exposed to judicious amounts of savagery. Hall condemned educators who never allowed boys "to fight, or to hear or read stories with bloodshed in them," who prevented them from learning "how it feels at the painful end of the rod," or from experiencing the "hard conditions of life, under which savage developed into civilized man." Hall, at base a partisan of civilization, conceded that pleasure was essential too. But, he argued, modern middle- and upper-class children got enough pleasure as it was. (Poor boys, he conceded parenthetically, needed more pleasure and less pain—again, "civilization's" larger emphasis on race allowed Hall to minimize the importance of class differences.)[74]

Underlying all these violent suggestions lay Hall's theories of racial recapitulation. Hall's speech is packed with images of little boys reliving the violent life of primitive man.

> The child is in the primitive age. The instinct of the savage survives in him, just as the physical peculiarities of the aquatic stage survive in his body and determine its conformations. . . . Boys are naturally robbers; they are bandits and fighters by nature. A scientific study has been made of boys' societies. . . . In every instance these societies have been predatory. All of the members thirsted for blood, and all of their plans were for thievery and murder. I recite these facts because they go to show, with many other facts, that a child repeats the history of his race.[75]

Boys must embrace primitive violence if they were to develop moral manliness. "Unless you want to make a selfish, knock-kneed weakling of him, teach him to double up his fist and strike back. . . . Physical courage is the foundation for moral courage later in life. One is to the child and the savage what the other is to the grown and cultured man."[76] Although Hall sometimes spoke of "the child," the context of his remarks makes it clear that he was really discussing only boys. He had no desire to see little girls engaged in fisticuffs. Boys, alone, must be little savages.

Hall objected strenuously to the sloppy effeminate sentimentality in current kindergartens: "All that rot they teach to children about the little raindrop fairies with their buckets washing down the windows must go." But he predicted that a virile reaction against effeminacy was setting in. "We shall go back to reading the old, bloody stories to children, and children will like to hear them because they are healthy little savages."[77] Once women stopped teaching boys about fairies and started teaching them about blood and guts, their innate savagery could blossom, and the little boys would grow up strong and manly enough to withstand the emasculating tendencies of civilization.[78]

Hall anticipated a cool reception from the organizers of the Kindergarten College, for he had frequently asserted that the kindergarten movement was degenerating into a sea of effeminate sentiment.[79] Yet although he was trying to be inflammatory, the lady teachers he wished to provoke listened politely, offering not a single dissenting opinion.[80] According to a local paper, "Dr. Hall, when he had concluded, confessed himself disappointed that he had not been more criticized, and he admitted having 'flaunted' some of his be-liefs, as it were, in the hope of meeting with opposition."[81]

The editors of Chicago's daily newspapers soon provided all the "opposi-tion" Hall could stand, however. In 1899, much of the middle class was still too enmeshed in Victorian culture to understand Hall's primitivist solution to the neurasthenic paradox.[82] The *Chicago Times Herald* called Hall a "preacher of pain and pessimism" and suggested that his message "sounds more like a disordered liver than psychology."[83] The *Chicago Evening Post* rejected Hall's insistence that civilization could be strengthened by a dose of savagery. "The whole training of early childhood is an attempt to turn the child from the savage instincts that are born in it, and to reverse the proce-dure would be to turn our faces again to the barbaric past."[84]

Moreover, some middle-class men—fearful of working-class men's chal-lenges to their authority—cared more about taming potentially disruptive working-class boys in the public schools than about combating overcivilized effeminacy. The Chicago Board of Education, charged with running orderly schools, objected to Hall's violent methods of promoting "virility in educa-tion." As Chairman Brenan explained, "We do not believe it will benefit the public school teachers to attend a convention where the speakers advocate teaching prize-fighting and bullying as an art. The boys will learn that fast enough without being taught." He therefore revoked the permission he had previously granted Chicago's teachers to dismiss classes early in order to at-tend the Kindergarten College.[85] To the Board, class war probably loomed as a more imminent danger than neurasthenia.

By the end of the conference, Hall had received all the opposition he could stomach and complained bitterly that he had been badly used by the press and the school board.[86] Hall was trying to rescue civilized manhood by infusing it with a dose of virile savagery. The press, however, accused Hall of attacking the civilized values he was trying to save. Small wonder Hall felt unjustly attacked and abused!

Yet not everyone misunderstood or attacked Hall. Several prominent men responded enthusiastically to Hall's message about boyhood primitivism. For example, Episcopal Bishop Samuel Fallows endorsed Hall's defense of boyish pugilism, claiming that without reenacting his violent "inherited pro-clivities," a boy could not grow into a strong man, ready for manly moral battle.[87] Most notably, Theodore Roosevelt wrote Hall a flattering letter agreeing that "the *barbarian virtues*" could keep civilized boys from becom-ing effeminate "milksops": "Over-sentimentality, over-softness, in fact washi-ness and mushiness are the great dangers of this age and of this people.

Unless we keep the *barbarian virtues,* gaining the civilized ones will be of little avail."[88] These men, like Hall, believed that overcivilized decadence could be held at bay, and overcivilized boys could be masculinized by embracing the primitive.

In glorifying the middle-class little boy as a savage, Hall was suggesting a solution to the neurasthenic paradox. By fully reliving their forebears' primitive passions, boys could grow up strong enough to survive the effeminizing tendencies of higher civilization. Boys must fight, bully, and dream of massive bloodshed. This juvenile savagery would "vaccinate" them with a controlled dose of the primitivism which would allow them to retain their virility as civilized adults. Combining the civilized power of higher races, with the masculine strength of primitive man, they would have the vitality to move humanity closer to millennial human perfection.

But reliving the savage emotions of boyhood was not the only strategy Hall found to remasculinize the civilized man. Adolescence, too, gave Hall a way to resolve the neurasthenic paradox by using recapitulation theory. And if the key for childhood was the figure of the savage little boy, the key for adolescence was the figure of the racially mutable adolescent boy.

Perfecting Manhood: Approaching the "Super-man" through the Racially Mutable Adolescent Boy

Adolescence was a very different stage of development than boyhood, as Hall saw it—a stage of far greater danger. Adolescent boys (those between the ages of fourteen and twenty–four) were especially vulnerable to civilization's two greatest energy-draining forces: neurasthenia and masturbation. On the one hand, the intellectual demands of high school and college were likely to drain an overstudious adolescent boy's nerve force and render him neurasthenic. On the other hand, with sexual puberty came the capacity for masturbation, which could lead to a host of physical and mental debilities. Moreover, neurasthenia and masturbation were both diseases of civilization: Both struck down highly evolved adolescent boys who overdrew their limited capital of nervous or sexual energies. Masturbation was "far more common among civilized than among savage races."[89] Neurasthenia was the quintessential disease of overcivilization. If the best of civilized adolescent boyhood was so vulnerable to neurasthenic weakness and masturbatory enervation, how could they develop the evolutionary vitality necessary to advance their race toward a perfect civilization?

Here, again, racial recapitulation allowed Hall to solve the neurasthenic paradox by representing his culture's dualistic formulations as merely different stages in an ongoing evolutionary process. Both masturbation and neurasthenia had gained their power by mobilizing a set of linked opposites to depict civilized men's nervous energies as endangered. Through that linked set of opposites, physicians like Beard had given men a choice: they could either be civilized, manly, and undervitalized or they could be primitive, masculine, and passionate. They couldn't be both. Hall rejected these dualistic formulations and represented them as different developmental stages of the same process. In his writings on childhood, Hall had represented the little boy as primitive, passionate, and masculine—and thus the larva of a civilized man strong enough to withstand the enervation of modern civilization. In his writings on adolescence, too, Hall dismantled the neurasthenic paradox by redefining neurasthenia's linked opposites as merely different developmental stages. Here, too, the key was to tie male power to racial power through the processes of evolution and racial recapitulation.

Hall began by assuming the central importance of sexual puberty to male adolescence. This focus on adolescent male sexuality was, of course, nothing new. Parents and educators, including Hall, had long warned that puberty was a uniquely dangerous time. Puberty predisposed young men to a precocious sexual expression which would exhaust their sexual "capital," leaving them too weak to develop into powerful men. Yet while Hall continued to believe that masturbation would lead to illness and neurasthenic collapse, in the 1890s he began to welcome the onset of male adolescent sexuality as a positive good instead of a danger.

On the one hand, Hall suggested, if channeled properly into nonsexual pursuits, a young man's nascent sexuality could give him renewed access to a powerful and manly vitality. When boys reached sexual awakening at puberty, according to Hall, they were suddenly flooded with sexual energy. This sexual energy was a valuable legacy: it was "capital" which, if carefully hoarded, would richly provide for a boy throughout his manhood. As Hall wrote in 1882 (drawing on a pervasive economic imagery comfortable to his class), "between the ages of twelve and sixteen . . . the young adolescent receives from nature a new capital of energy . . . and success in life depends upon the care and wisdom with which this energy is husbanded."[90] Hall had been raised and educated to assume that if this sexuality were carefully husbanded and a boy built a strong character by willfully suppressing his desires, he would develop into a manly and powerful man. If he squandered his sexual energy through masturbation or promiscuity, however, this expenditure of his "capital" would stunt the growth of true, virile manhood. His sexual growth would stop, and he would suffer premature degeneration.

By 1894, however, eager to solve the neurasthenic paradox by substituting developmentalism for dualism, Hall had begun to suggest that young men's new sexual energy could provide a healthful substitute for their scarce nervous energy. Educators need not concentrate on *repressing* adolescent boys' sexual energy; instead they could *channel* it into education. This would have the dual advantage, first, of keeping youths safe from sexual dissipation and, second, of giving them more energy to devote to higher education without becoming neurasthenic. "Every intellectual interest has some value as a palliative or alternative, or psycho-kinetic equivalent of inebriation or degraded love," Hall maintained.[91] By transforming young men's sexual passions into a source of scarce nervous energy, Hall was able both to mitigate the danger of neurasthenia and to reconstruct adolescent male sexuality in ways which did not stress self-restraint.

Hall did not believe the sexual maturity of puberty offered the same educational benefits to adolescent girls, however. He accepted Dr. Edward H. Clarke's widely held view that excessive education would divert necessary energies away from girls' developing reproductive systems, rendering them ill or even sterile.[92] Whereas boys protected their limited supply of sexual force by channeling it into their studies, girls would destroy their sexual force if they likewise channeled it into studies—they would permanently damage their reproductive capacities.[93] Thus, when Hall spoke of the regenerative opportunities of puberty, he was implicitly discussing only boys.

In embracing adolescent male sexuality as a positive good, Hall did more than merely suggest pubertal boys sublimate their new sexual energy. Hall described adolescent boys' sexual awakening as a spiritual awakening in the Protestant tradition of religious conversion, or "second birth." Among American Protestants, adolescence was the traditional age when young Christians experienced the spiritual "second birth" of religious conversion and became full-fledged church members.[94] Hall repeatedly insisted that puberty was a "physiological second birth," the moment of his physical development when the individual was born again as a full-fledged member of his race. Receiving the biological capacity to become a father constituted rebirth as a full member of the race, according to Hall, because now a youth could compete with other men to father the most superior offspring, and thus contribute to the ongoing evolutionary life of the race.

As Hall understood it, the "physiological second birth" of sexual maturity linked each individual boy to his race and the evolution of a perfect civiliza-

tion, just as the spiritual second birth of reborn Protestants had linked each
Christian to the true church and to the cosmic progress toward the millennium. Hall believed it was "no accidental synchronism of unrelated events
that the age of religion and that of sexual maturity coincide" for Protestants
as well as more primitive religions.[95] This was simply a religious reflection of
the high and holy truths embedded in the evolutionary process. At sexual
maturity, when a boy received the capacity for paternity, he ceased to exist
merely for himself, and began to exist as a potential contributor to the divine
process of racial evolution and the advancement of civilization. Adolescence
was thus a holy time, when sexuality and spirituality burst upon a young
man simultaneously, through the physiological second birth.[96]

Here, then, Hall had found a solution to the problem of manly self-
restraint, which had tormented him since his own adolescence. Sex was not
dirty; it was holy. It was God's means of creating healthier human specimens
and more advanced races.[97] In *Adolescence,* Hall waxed lyrical about the ecstatic, almost holy, pleasures of sex and orgasm, which he described as "the
sacred hour of heredity": "In the most unitary of all acts, which is the epitome and pleroma [abundance; plenitude] of life, we have the most intense of
all affirmations of the will to live, and realize that the only true God is love,
and the center of life is worship. . . . This sacrament [sex] is the annunciation
hour, with hosannas which the whole world reflects. . . . Now the race is
incarnated in the individual and remembers its lost paradise."[98] Hall believed
that for healthy, married adults, God was love, and love was Godly. Sex was
designed for procreation; procreation was the mechanism of evolution; and
evolution was God's way of progressing toward the millennium. "Nor is religion degraded by the recognition of this intimate relationship, save to those
who either think vilely about sex or who lack insight into its real psychic
nature and so fail to realize how indissoluble is the bond that God and nature
have wrought between religion and love."[99] All these delicious pleasures
were aspects of the holy evolutionary process.

Adolescent boys' new sexual maturity tied them in mystic and powerful
ways to the entire sweep of evolution, and gave them special racial gifts, gifts
which could regenerate a decadent civilization. On the one hand, puberty
linked a youth, via racial recapitulation, to his savage ancestors. On the other
hand, puberty linked a youth, as a potential father, to the race's evolutionary
future. By taking advantage of both factors, educators could bring American
boys ever closer to the "super-man that is to be."

Racial recapitulation was the key factor which could help educators evolve this super-man. With the onset of the physiological second birth at puberty, boys were suddenly flooded with ancestral tendencies and inheritances. As Hall put it, when a child reaches puberty, "very many of the remote ancestral strains of the blood appear. Blood from many different ancestral stocks is poured into the veins at once. We . . . each have some twenty million ancestors, if we reckon back to the time of William the Conqueror. These hereditary traits, then, are poured in, and appear at this time."[100] This onrush of atavistic ancestral traits fragmented an adolescent's personality and was the cause of adolescents' characteristic emotional turmoil.[101]

White American adolescents were at greater risk than Europeans because, the more ethnically diverse a child's ancestors, the more different primitive pasts he would relive and the more turbulent his adolescence would be. "The more mongrel the stock or the more numerous the strains of bloods of which it is composed, and the more unsettled the body of ethnic or national customs, traditions, and beliefs, the more critical does the whole adolescent period become."[102] (Note that Hall is talking about clashes not of environmentally based cultures, but of biological races—"numerous strains of blood" and "mongrel stocks.") Since each individual repeated the history of the race and since adolescence was a period when distant racial influences were particularly intense, it followed that any individual who was forced to repeat the histories of several races at once would be subjected to a severe multiplication of the normal stresses of adolescence. "Pure stocks with settled ways and ideals, which pass this ferment safely and quickly, are at one extreme, and a composite nation like our own, with new and diverse models of thought and life, and everything unsettled, is open to unparalleled dangers of arrested development."[103] White American youths' unstable racial inheritance (English, French, Dutch, German, and so on) threatened them with "arrested development."

Yet although American adolescents were in especial danger from their "mongrel" racial stock, Hall believed their very racial mix made it possible for them to achieve the most complete manhood ever evolved—to become, in fact, the "super-men" who could lead the nation to a millennial future: "In this country, with all its excitements and precocities, and especially with our mongrel blood . . . the seething is not only greater, but longer. But if there is increased danger of both stunting and collapse, there is also the possibility of later but higher and more complete unity in the 'cosmic, super-man' of the future."[104] White Americans' "mongrel blood" made their adolescence far more dangerous than that of more homogeneous races. Yet, precisely because of their racial liminality, American boys could develop into the cosmic super-man of the future.

Evolution's Lamarckian mechanism was what would make it possible for educators to help America's youths evolve toward super-men. If civilization's most gifted youths were properly educated to their full potential, they would pass their educational advancement on to their offspring genetically, thus raising the next generation to a higher evolutionary plane. As Hall informed the National Educational Association in 1894, "Evolution has taught the teacher that he or she is to be its chief agent in the march of progress. . . . In the vision of the super-man, if it is ever to be realized, it will be because the school, the college and university will succeed in bringing childhood to more complete maturity."[105]

The key in moving white American boys toward the super-man was to prolong their adolescence so that they could slowly and safely relive all the many competing primal pasts their multiple racial heritage was thrusting upon them. Educators must carefully allow boys to fully reexperience all the final stages from all their racially diverse ancestors, whether English, German, or Scandinavian. Racapitulation theory held that an organism's last developmental stages were the most advanced, because evolution's most recent beneficial adaptations were simply added on to the end of the growth process. By slowly and fully reliving this plethora of racially inherited stages, mongrel white adolescents could make the highest stages of *all* their racial ancestors fully their own. At the same time, they could move their racial inheritance to an even higher plane through their own advanced education. As fathers, they would pass this advancement on to their own children via Lamarckian inheritance, and this process could be repeated, ad infinitum. Thus, by slowly and carefully taking advantage of racial recapitulation, racially liminal adolescents could move the race ever closer to evolutionary perfection and the super-man.

But only *white* American mongrels could evolve into the super-man. The lower races simply did not have the white races' advanced final stages, so their adolescence was far shorter and there was no point prolonging it. "Colored children and those of low stock are often as bright as others, if not more so; but at from six to twelve they fall behind, and their educational period closes."[106] White "mongrel" adolescents, on the other hand, did inherit these advanced final stages. Indeed, those with an ethnically diverse heritage inherited several of them. The longer the adolescence, the more completely the child could relive, and thus make his own, his ancestors' evolutionary advancements. Scientists agreed that evolutionarily advanced species needed extended childhoods in order to fully assimilate all their ancestors' latest evolutionary advances: the longer a creature's immaturity, the more evolutionarily advanced the species. Because so many white American youths were of racially mixed European descent, Hall theorized, their adolescence could be almost infinitely extended, as they fully relived the most advanced stages of a profusion of highly evolved races. As Hall put it, even "if this period of adolescent immaturity is exceptionally prolonged and dangerous here, the possibilities of ultimate and complete manhood are correspondingly greater."[107] By taking advantage of their multiple racial heritage, and of adolescents' direct ties to all their primitive ancestors, American young men could bypass current threats to masculinity and develop the "ultimate and complete manhood" of the "cosmic super-man of the future."

When Hall prophesied the development of the "super-man" he did indeed mean *man*. Girls, unlike boys, could not develop into the super-man. Adolescent girls could develop their best potential; they could become excellent mothers and nurture the future race; they might even be flooded with racial memories when they hit puberty. Yet women's education could never bring about the super-man or advance the race.

Here, Hall based his theories on the biological axiom that females were generic, while males were variable.[108] According to contemporary science, only men had the evolutionary function of variability—of developing advantageous variations which they could pass on to their offspring. Sexual selection was driven by males' competing with one another in order to win females. Males needed to develop a multiplicity of attractive variations to please females. Thus men, being variable, were the only beings capable of becoming scientific geniuses and advancing civilization by passing this genius on to their children. Females, on the other hand, were generic. They were sexually passive and thus lacked the need to compete for their mates. Females therefore varied far less than males. This conservative, generic nature meant that women more rarely became idiots or degenerates, according to scientists; but they were also constitutionally unable to become geniuses. As respected British psychiatrist Harry Campbell put it in 1891, "Genius of the highest order is practically limited to the male sex."[109]

Hall's aim of prolonging adolescence in order to allow youths to take advantage of their ancestors' varied racial gifts was designed to encourage favorable variation, and thus referred only to males. When the most elite young men were given this opportunity to fully develop their potential, they would be able to pass their advancement on to their offspring (according to

Lamarckian theory), who would start from a higher evolutionary stage and be able to develop even further. They were thus, in a very real sense, advancing the race toward the super-man. Women, on the other hand, could not take advantage of this evolutionary mechanism of variability. Even if educators slowed girls' development, allowing them to relive their primitive evolutionary heritage, girls were biologically unable to develop inheritable genius. Moreover Hall believed that too much educational development could make a woman sterile, killing instead of improving her offspring.[110] The only being who could develop or pass on newly developed, evolutionarily advanced traits was the properly educated, slowly matured, racially liminal adolescent *boy*. Educating young women could not lead to the evolution of the superman.

The racially liminal adolescent boy—the larva of the super-man—embodied traits which had previously seemed impossibly dualistic and mutually contradictory. By reconciling these dualisms, Hall further resolved his neurasthenic paradox. For one thing, the "physiological second birth" combined sexuality with spirituality. Having just received his "capital" of sexual energy, the pubertal adolescent boy fairly glowed with virile sexual energy—no neurasthenic decadent, he! Yet as virile as he was, Hall's properly reared adolescent boy was perfectly pure, sublimating all his energy in his education. By constructing puberty as a physiological second birth, Hall allowed his adolescent boy to be both stainlessly virtuous and powerfully sexual. This let Hall abandon dualistic constructions of manly power which were based on unsatisfactory codes of self-restraint and repression.

Similarly, the racially mongrel adolescent boy combined the primitive and the civilized—qualities which had always seemed mutually exclusive. On the one hand, he was the future of civilization—part of the next wave of experts, businessmen, and scientists, and the father of future generations. On the other hand, despite his ties to advanced civilization, the adolescent boy was the heir of his primitive ancestors. Awash with the primal traits and memories of a profusion of distant racial ancestors, he had the strength to withstand the degenerative tendencies of modern civilization.

Hall was extremely serious about evolving the super-man. In article after article between 1894 and 1901, he invoked the vision of a perfectible man whom educators could develop by applying recapitulation theory to education. In 1896, Hall closed an article in the *Christian Register* by quoting Tertulian: "Stand forth, O soul of man, naked, genuine, real, just as thou dost come into the world from the hand of God, and having stood forth, grow to thy full perfection!"[111] In 1897, he insisted in a scholarly psychology article,

"Man is not the larva of an angel, but of a higher superman that is to be."[112] In 1899, he enthused to the New Jersey Association for the Study of Children and Youth, "You and I are 'poor critturs,' We are limited in action, knowledge and thought. . . . Let us say, All hail to the hereafter! The superman is yet to come."[113]

Hall repeatedly hinted at the earthshaking importance of his theories and at their revolutionary ability to contribute to human evolutionary advancement. He insisted that his evolutionary psychology had "begun a movement bigger than Darwinism,"[114] and predicted that in a few years the entire world would recognize its cosmic importance. In 1894, for example, he prophesied that within ten years his theories would have begun to completely regenerate the human race, leading to "a scientific reconstruction that aims at the top and is the salvation and ultimate development and end and aim of creation and of history."[115] Over the next ten years, Hall repeatedly claimed that by applying his theories to adolescent boys' education, he was finding a way to perfect the race, and to help turn white American boys into super-men.

Alas, Hall's grandiose ambitions of ushering in the evolutionary millennium—"the salvation and ultimate development and end and aim of creation and of history"—were thwarted. Ten years after Hall made his stirring prediction of future success, he had abandoned his plan to turn racially liminal adolescents into super-men. Between 1894 and 1904, Lamarckian theories of racial recapitulation had begun to be deeply discredited. August Weissman's theory that inheritance was determined by chromosomes, not by parental behavior, was on its way to becoming the standard scientific interpretation. With chromosomes as evolution's method of inheritance, scientists soon abandoned their belief that racial recapitulation was the way one generation's evolutionary advancement was passed on to the next.[116]

Thus, by 1904, when Hall published his magnum opus, the two volume, fourteen-hundred-page *Adolescence,* he was faced with a dilemma. It was his first major book and, at age sixty, he intended it to be the scholarly masterpiece which would cement his academic reputation.[117] He had been working on *Adolescence* since 1894 and was loathe to abandon ten years of work. Yet he knew his theory of the racially liminal adolescent would not be accepted by cutting-edge scholars because it was based almost entirely on the increasingly dubious theory of recapitulation. Therefore, although Hall expressed his continuing belief in the psychological applications of racial recapitulation, he took a cagey and defensive tone. "Realizing the limitations and qualifications of the recapitulation theory in the *biologic* field, I am now convinced that its *psychogenetic* applications have a method of their own," he insisted.[118] He even included a brief, half-hearted discussion of his theory's relevance to a Weismannist biological framework.[119]

After Lamarckianism was discredited, Hall, like many of his contemporaries, became discouraged about the possibility of engineering human racial improvement. If human evolution occurred, not through education passed down genetically to the next generation, but over long and dismal eons of genetic mutations, the development of superior individuals had no evolutionary utility at all. Educators could build better citizens or better people, but they lacked any power to engineer a better race. Thus, after 1903 Hall no longer argued publicly that educators could turn American boys into "super-men."[120]

Nonetheless, Hall remained committed to the millennial mission of furthering human evolutionary advancement. Although the demise of Lamarckianism doomed his theories of allowing racially liminal adolescents to evolve into super-men, Hall cast about for other methods of working toward racial perfection. By 1911 Hall, like many of his contemporaries, would find such a method in eugenics, arguing that severe "defectives" should be discouraged from reproducing and healthy people encouraged.[121] Yet in 1904 Hall remained skeptical of eugenics as a means of large-scale racial engineering, both for moral reasons (he believed in marriage for love, not breeding) and because he believed the scientific study of heredity was still too rudimentary.[122]

Adolescent Races

Between 1903 and 1911, Hall explored a different avenue toward human evolutionary perfection which he, as an educator, could further. He continued to devote most of his efforts to educating white adolescents; but rather than placing his millennial faith in their racial perfectibility, Hall began to find new hope in the evolutionary potential of primitive peoples, whom he saw as "adolescent races." As Hall himself put it in his introduction to *Adolescence,* man was "an organism in a very active stage of evolution. . . . Perhaps other racial stocks than ours will later advance the kingdom of man as far beyond our present standpoint as it now is above that of the lowest savage or even animals."[123] Primitive races themselves, who embodied savage traits more fully and completely than the racially recapitulating adolescent could ever do, temporarily became Hall's hope for human perfection in the distant future.

This was not Hall's only public cause during these years. Hall was working to safeguard and remake the power of manhood on a variety of different fronts. For example, at the same time that he was focusing on "adolescent races," he was also spending a great deal of effort on combating coeducation and the educational "sissification" of American boys. But through 1911 Hall's identity as a strong manly expert, bravely defending childish, weak primitives against the dangers of civilization, gave him a public platform to demonstrate his own manly power and authority as well as a way for him to work toward the "super-man that is to be."

This shift from racially mutable white adolescents to mutable nonwhite adolescent races as the millennial hope of the future was not as big a change as it might seem. Recapitulation theory held that as children's bodies developed, they actually repeated the evolutionary physical development of their forebears. American adolescents (on the brink of civilization) and primitive races (of all age groups) had long been, for Hall, precise equivalents. Substituting "races with adolescent characteristics" for "adolescents with racial characteristics" as candidates for bringing mankind toward the "super-man that is to be" was fully in keeping with Hall's overall theories. Thus, Hall came full circle in his use of race to vitalize—and virilize—effeminate civilization.

While most of *Adolescence* pulls together Hall's long-standing theories about white youths, the final chapter, entitled "Ethnic Psychology and Pedagogy, or Adolescent Races and Their Treatment," outlines Hall's vision of the evolutionary promise of primitive, nonwhite races.[124] Hall believed that "savages"—of all ages—were actually "adolescent races" who should be educated according to his larger principles of adolescent psychology. "Most savages in most respects are children, or, because of sexual maturity, more properly, adolescents of adult size. . . . Their faults and their virtues are those of childhood and youth. They need the same careful and painstaking study, lavish care, and adjustment to their nature and needs."[125] These adult primitives required the same educational care that young white adolescent boys did.

"Racial pedagogy" was simply Hall's program of adolescent white education applied to the education of adults of these "adolescent" races. As he described it, imperialists who forced primitive races to accommodate themselves to Western civilization were precisely analogous to teachers who overpressured civilized white adolescents. In both cases forcing the "adolescents" to become prematurely civilized left them weak and neurasthenic. "The inexorable laws of forcing, precocity, severity, and overwork, produce similarly disastrous results for both" children and savages.[126] Like overpressured children, these primitive adults were able to learn highly civilized skills. Yet because adolescent races had not evolved to a mature evolutionary stage, they lacked the moral and intellectual capacity to use these skills. "The whole history is summed up in 'a swift adoption of the externals of civilization going hand in hand with a steady physical decline, and a promising but suddenly arrested moral development.'"[127] Like a dissipated neurasthenic adolescent, overpressured adolescent races soon became sick and morally decadent.

Yet, like adolescent boys, adolescent races had the millennial capacity to evolve, someday, into super-men. Hall offered his readers a vision of the future greatness of some unknown, primitive adolescent race.

> In later ages other stocks now obscure, and perhaps other tongues now unstudied will occupy the center of the historic stage, appropriating the best we achieve, as we learn from Semites, Greeks, and Romans. If this be true, every vigorous race, however rude and undeveloped, is, like childhood, worthy of the maximum of reverence and care and study, and may become the chosen organ of a new dispensation of culture and civilization. Some of them now obscure may be the heirs of all we possess and wield the ever-increasing resources of the world for good or evil somewhat perhaps as we now influence their early plastic stages, for they are the world's children and adolescents.[128]

Hall reminded his civilized readers that their own age was not "the culminating period of history." The "best and greatest things have not happened yet." To nurture mankind's millennial future, civilized man must nurture the world's adolescent races. One day these primitive "stocks" could be the world's super-men.

It was thus crucial that civilized men protect the world's primitive races, just as enlightened educators protected adolescent boys. And, for a few years, Hall put his theories into practice by taking up the cause of anti-imperialism.[129] Having lost the possibility of building American adolescents into super-men, the only way Hall could continue his mission to perfect civilization was by safeguarding "adolescent races." In the process, however, Hall continued to reconstruct the power of middle-class white manhood.

Between 1903 and 1911, Hall actively set himself up as a professional expert on "racial pedagogy." This racial expertise allowed Hall to position himself as especially powerful and manly. By insisting that the world's non-white races were children who needed his enlightened protection, Hall constructed himself as a sort of racial pedagogue, a strong and manly civilized expert who must exercise paternal care over his weak charges. Savages, like children, were weak and vulnerable, and required the manly supervision of powerful civilized men like himself. As a racial pedagogue, Hall's manly strength and authority stood in stark contrast to the weakness and dependence of the "primitive" races he championed.

Hall's incarnation as racial pedagogue took a number of forms, both academic and political. He founded and coedited the *Journal of Race Development*. He established and taught a course entitled "Racial Pedagogy" at Clark University, where he was college president.[130] He organized a series of yearly conferences on the social problems of Asia, Africa, and the Near East.[131] He also set himself up as an authority on the education of African Americans and American Indians.[132]

Nor did Hall confine himself to the academic arena. His identity as manly racial pedagogue actually spurred him into temporarily becoming a leader in the anti-imperialist movement. Hall's somewhat short-lived (1905-8) public political activism was completely out of character—he usually confined his politicking to professional disagreements within the halls of academe. Most notable was Hall's public opposition to King Leopold's brutal regime in the Congo Free State. The Belgian king had annexed the Congo as his personal possession and had virtually enslaved the entire population. After 1905, horrifying reports of atrocities in the Congo were widely reported in the press. These reports galvanized the manly racial pedagogue. From early 1906 through late 1908, Hall served as president of the National Congo Reform Association. In this capacity, the scholarly academic took on the unfamiliar persona of the man of affairs, granting newspaper interviews, preparing position papers for the *Congressional Record,* and even traveling to Washington to meet with President Theodore Roosevelt.

Hall's speeches on behalf of the Congolese suggest that his desire to see "primitives" as unmanly children was at the heart of his anti-imperialism. A colonizer, he insisted, had a fatherly duty to treat its childish "wards" more as "its children, and less as its slaves."[133] Rather than being a manly protector of his African "children," Leopold was plundering the Congo and brutalizing its people. In numerous speeches, Hall luridly reported the evolutionary backsliding—Congolese men's indulgence in rape and cannibalism—

which had resulted from Leopold's abdication of manly paternalistic re-sposibility. Hall's descriptions of "photographs of cannibal feasts and of bodies of women being salted" for food simultaneously reinforced both contemporary myths of African men as unmanly primitives and Hall's own manly position as heroic protector of dependent and unmanly "adolescent races."[134]

Hall even suggested, in his persona as racial pedagogue, that the Congo situation provided a good opportunity for white men like himself to inculcate manliness in America's own "adolescent races"—in African American men. "What the black man here chiefly needs is self-respect: to be taught to be a manly negro . . . he needs a great cause such as interest in his brethren in the dark continent. . . . It is no argument against such a policy that the negro himself has not yet seen the full significance of this opportunity." Again, Hall holds himself up as a model of superior manhood, here in contradistinction to African American men, who (whether they recognized it or not) needed to learn about true manliness by emulating white men like himself.[135]

In constructing himself as the manly racial pedagogue, Hall was upholding a traditional view of manliness that encompassed the gentlemanly protection of the weak and dependent. Yet, ironically, in his advocacy of racial pedagogy, Hall was simultaneously reinforcing a contradictory view of manhood—one tied, not to self-restrained "manliness," but to newer formulations of passionate "masculinity." For, as Hall described it, the only reason racial pedagogy was needed was that evolution "naturally" spurred racially superior men to annihilate racially inferior men. In other words, Hall's identity as manly protector of inferior "adolescent races" depended on the idea that "masculinity" naturally predisposed men toward racial violence. We have previously encountered this view in journalists' discussions of the "natural man's" predilection for lynching. By insisting that men of superior races naturally desired to attack men of inferior races, Hall was reinforcing this new construction of "the natural man," with its passionate, primitive masculinity.

As Hall explained in *Adolescence,* from the moment of man's evolutionary origin, he had a passionate desire to eradicate all lower forms of life, whether animal or human. "Man early became the wanderer and destroyer par excellence. Less than any other animal, can man tolerate rivals in the struggle for existence."[136] As soon as man emerged as a species, he systematically set about destroying all his close evolutionary competitors.

This genocidal urge was a masculine impulse: Hall explicitly made men, and not women, the engines of this destructive evolutionary fury. He stressed the masculinity of "the hunting passion" that in prehistoric times drove man to exterminate numerous animals in his "long hot struggle . . . [to become] the lord of the animal creation." Like all "masculine" passions, this "hunting passion" was shared by all men; and civilized men, like their "savage" ancestors, still decorated their social clubs with their dismembered trophies. In contrast, the few animals who could coexist with man, then as now, were all domesticated by women. "Only the few score of animals which primitive woman domesticated for food or service can thrive beside him, and his clubrooms and dwellings are still decorated with the products of his head-hunting prowess."[137] Hall's figure of man the destroyer thus referred explicitly to men and to masculinity.

This instinctive masculine violence, a legacy of the Stone Age, was today leading civilized men to engage in imperialism, with its massive racial genocide. The contemporary masculine instinct for imperialistic racial extermination was

> the same instinct which in pre-historic times destroyed . . . the gigantic extinct mammals, and has forever scarred man's soul with fear, anger, and wanton cruelty. The same enmity against the lower races, which in our day has exterminated forever the Boethuks, the Tasmanians, and is reducing so many lower human ethnic stocks to make way for favored races, is but a relic of the rage which exterminated the missing links and made man for ages the passionate destroyer.[138]

Violence was the birthright of man the destroyer, the masculine exterminator who slaughtered animals and primitive men.

In this ostensible opposition between the benevolent racial pedagogue and man the bloodthirsty destroyer, Hall once again used race to rewrite problematic Victorian ideologies of manly self-restraint. The racial pedagogue was framed in terms of Victorian traditions of self-restrained manliness. Just as the boy Stanley had been taught to restrain his sexual passions—to allow his willful manliness to contain his masculine desires—so the adult Hall depicted the manly racial pedagogue restraining the violent masculine passions of man the destroyer.

Yet by making these masculine passions racial instead of sexual, their implications changed. As a boy Hall had learned that unbounded masculine passions—masturbatory desires or sexual dissipations—were a source of unmanly weakness. As a man, however, he depicted unbounded masculine passion—genocidal fury—as the evolutionary force which propelled the white races to their current position of racial supremacy. Like sexual passion, this racial passion was immoral. Yet it was precisely this masculine passion for racial violence that had allowed the white race to win the Darwinistic struggle for racial primacy, in the person of man the destroyer, enraged and cruel, who decimated all his racial competitors.

Thus, although self-restrained manliness and passionate masculinity remained at odds for Hall, they were also—paradoxically—linked. Civilized, manly man had achieved his self-restrained evolutionary eminence precisely because, in the past, he had shown his capacity for savage, passionate, violent masculinity. Ostensibly Hall was trying to discredit imperialistic racial violence. In spite of his good intentions, however, Hall nonetheless reinforced the increasingly prevalent idea that the capacity for "primitive" racial violence was an inherent part of masculinity.

After 1909, Hall began to concentrate his energies on Freudian psychology, and his interest in race gradually faded.[139] But although Hall concentrated less on the linkages between racial dominance and masculinity, many of his contemporaries retained their interest. The final word about Hall, race, and masculinity must be an extraordinary article in the *Boston Sunday American* of 1915, in which the newspaper's illustrator and editors directly translated Hall's use of racial primitivism into images of violent, aggressive masculinity.[140]

The text of the article, excerpted from a scholarly address Hall gave on anger, was a typical Hallian argument that primitive emotions (in this case, anger), when repressed and channeled, gave civilized people vitality enough to withstand the enervating effects of civilization. But the editor seems to have understood and approved Hall's subliminal message about the revitalization of overcivilized masculinity and presented it in a way his readers could understand more directly.

The newspaper fortified Hall's relatively tame article with headlines and illustrations which made primitive masculinity (though never directly referred to) the centerpiece. "How Rage, Anger and Hatred Help Us to Success. Why It is ANGER and NOT LOVE that 'Makes the World Go Round,' and Is the Secret of the Progress of Men and Nations," blared the headline. The gendered subtext would have been readily apparent to readers: where Victorians had counseled their sons to restrain their passions—to develop high-minded manliness—now experts believed "Rage, Anger, and Hatred" would lead "Men" to "Progress." Feminized Victorian morality was giving way to masculine aggression as the "Secret" which superior men needed to get ahead.

The three illustrations and their quoted captions drove the point home (see pp. 118–19 below).[141] Violent, aggressive emotion, as experienced by primitive men, was the source of power and masculinity. Two illustrations depicted angry, naked, black-skinned men in threatening postures. A hairy anthropoid, half man and half ape, shows his teeth and grasps a club as the caption announces "One Philosopher Argues That It was Anger that Made Primitive Man Lord of Creation by Inspiring Him to Fight." Above him, five glowering, war-painted black men crouch beside a howling man who clutches a spear in his clenched fists, as the caption explains, "Savages Work Themselves Into Frenzied Rage in Order to Fight Their Enemies." And, lest the reader miss the point that manly self-mastery and protection of the weak is not the sort of manhood that "anger" engenders, the illustrator depicts these "savages" working themselves into a frenzy over an enemy that has the rounded breasts and hips of a woman—no overcivilized manliness here!

The top illustration also depicts a naked man—but here, he is not black and angry but white and dying. Marat lays pitifully in his bath, having been murdered by the glaring virago, Charlotte Corday. Marat, like the savage naked men in the other illustrations, makes a fist. Yet Marat's fist impotently clutches not a club or spear but a bed sheet. We can read this illustration as a parable about the anemic weakness of civilized manliness and the need for the "Force-Creating Emotion" which would provide masculinity. Decimated by a too-strong woman—a feeling that in effeminate modern civilization, male power has evaporated—the old self-restrained manliness, like Marat, teeters on the brink of expiring. Yet male power can be rescued by something new—the primitive anger and raw quest for dominance echoed by bushmen in the neighboring illustration, who shake their fists over what appears to be the bound and helpless image of a naked woman. This racially based imagery, like Hall's figure of man the destroyer, was essential to the construction of new middle-class ideologies of violent, passionate "masculinity."

Conclusion

Hall had formed himself—and had been formed by—gender ideologies which constructed male power in terms of self-restraint. These ideologies of civilized manly power had represented the male body as animated by powerful but scarce nervous forces. The more control a man had over his own nervous forces, the more powerful he would be. It was the lack of this manly self-restraint which constructed nonwhite men, like Jack Johnson and the mythical Negro rapist, as weak and unmanly.

Yet Hall, like his contemporaries, was growing increasingly ambivalent

"One Philosopher Argues That It Was Anger That Made Primitive Man Lord of Creation by Inspiring Him to Fight."

"Savages Work Themselves Into Frenzied Rage in Order to Fight Their Enemies. This Is Well Illustrated by the Practise of the Australian Bushmen Who Throw Darts Into an Effigy of the Enemy Before Going in Pursuit of Him."

Figs. 7, 8, and 9. Hall's ideas illustrated in the *Boston Sunday American,* August 15, 1915. Clark University Archives. Photo by William Rice.

about these ideologies of manly self-restraint. For a variety of reasons—social, economic, and cultural—these ideologies were losing their persuasiveness by the 1880s and 1890s. Hall, like many of his contemporaries, began to work to synthesize new representations of the male body which could inform new ideologies of male power.

One of the most powerful representations of the male body, and of men's difficulties with manly restraint, was the disease of neurasthenia. In neurasthenia, physicians like George M. Beard had reconstructed middle-class men's discomfort with ideologies of civilized manly self-restraint as a physical illness. Neurasthenia resulted when white men, with highly evolved white bodies, overspent their scarce nervous forces on the enervating activities of civilization. In neurasthenia, the problematic nature of civilized manly self-restraint was laid out as a paradox. Only white men could lead

How Rage, Anger and Hatred Help

civilization to ever higher stages; yet civilization weakened white men's bodies and drained them of their scarce nerve force. How could white men retain their advanced civilized manliness, and still retain enough nervous energy to withstand the effeminizing tendencies of modern civilization?

Hall's project, as an educator, was to develop educational solutions to this neurasthenic paradox. Neurasthenia had been based on a series of dualistic opposites—most essentially, civilization versus savagery, and self-mastery versus passion. Hall worked to recast these dualisms into a monistic unified process of growth and evolution. Key to all his formulations were evolutionary theories of racial recapitulation, the process whereby children relived the primitive evolutionary stages of their ancestors. By constructing savagery, with its plentiful supplies of nervous force, as a characteristic of youth, Hall was able to argue that civilized men could develop powerful reserves of nervous forces by having a healthfully savage boyhood. Moreover, adolescent boys could develop the powerful manhood necessary to move the race toward the "super-man" by taking advantage of the racial variations of their primitive ancestors. Hall believed that by applying racial recapitulation to white boys' education, he could solve problems of overcivilized effeminacy and lead American civilization toward a millennial racial perfection.

By the early twentieth century, however, the abandonment of Lamarckian evolutionary theories, including racial recapitulation, had dashed Hall's hopes of developing white American boys into super-men. Hall temporarily salvaged his millennial hopes by changing his millennial agents. Adolescence remained the liminal time, but now Hall defined adolescence in terms of race stage instead of age stage. Instead of placing his hopes for a more virile civilization in the racial primitiveness of American youth, Hall began to look to more literal "primitives"—to nonwhite "adolescent" races. Hall was always one to take his metonymy literally. He had begun by arguing that white boys' access to the primitive could save civilization, but he ended by arguing that the hope of the future lay in primitive races untouched by the decadence and false development of modern civilization.

Yet even though Hall eventually stopped writing about the connections between race and manhood, others in his culture would remain interested in those connections. As the 1915 article in the *Boston Sunday American* suggests, white American men would continue to see nonwhite races, primitiveness, and violence as powerful ways to represent a virile masculinity, much desired by civilized man.

4

"Not to *Sex*—But to *Race!*" Charlotte Perkins Gilman,
Civilized Anglo-Saxon Womanhood, and the Return
of the Primitive Rapist

*"The dominant soul—the clear strong accurate brain, the perfect ser-
vice of a healthy body—these do not belong to sex—but to race!"*[1]

CHARLOTTE PERKINS GILMAN, 1891

Although "civilization" was usually invoked in order to assert and remake
white male supremacy, the discourse of civilization could also be used to
convey quite a different message. Just as Ida B. Wells inverted ideas about
civilization to combat American racism, so many white feminists recast ideas
about civilization to combat male dominance. Ideologies of civilization were
protean in their content and implications. "Civilization" always drew on ideologies of race and of gender, but people with very different political agendas
could deploy the discourse in a variety of ways.

"Civilization" was especially useful for making claims about "the woman
question." Antifeminists frequently used "civilization" to depict women as
less civilized than men, less able to contribute to the advancement of the
race. For example, as we have seen, the Columbian Exposition's male organizers located the Women's Building at the very edge of the civilized White
City, next to the Midway, at the border between civilization and savagery,
thereby constructing women's contributions to civilization as marginal. Yet
feminists were unwilling to concede civilization to their opponents and developed a variety of counterarguments. Some depicted primitive societies as
peaceful and prosperous matriarchies, ruled by women whose motherly altruism had led to centuries of orderly progress, cut short when men undermined civilized advancement by subjugating women. Others reinterpreted

evolutionary biology in order to prove that women were superior to men, not inferiors designed merely for reproduction. By reworking common assumptions about civilization, these women tried to undermine biologistic arguments that nature never intended woman to go to college, to have well-paid careers, or to vote.[2]

The most influential of these feminist exponents of civilization was Charlotte Perkins Gilman. From 1898 until the mid-1910s, Gilman was the most prominent feminist theorist in America.[3] She wrote prolifically—her bibliographer lists 2,168 published stories, poems, books, and articles—and made her living lecturing to women's groups throughout the United States.[4] The topics she addressed ranged from child care to architecture; from feminism to physiology; from fashion to international relations. In much of her work, Gilman used the discourse of civilization to create an effective and persuasive body of feminist theory. Her most successful book, *Women and Economics* (1898), which went through nine American printings by 1920, was an explicit attempt to revise antifeminist ideologies of civilization by making women central to civilization.[5] Reviewers hailed *Women and Economics* as "the book of the age" and the most brilliant and original contribution to the woman question since John Stuart Mill's essays on *The Subjection of Women*.[6] Florence Kelley called it "the first real, substantial contribution made by a woman to the science of economics"; Jane Addams simply called it a "Masterpiece."[7]

Gilman's contributions as a feminist foremother have been widely acknowledged, but historians have not recognized that her work was firmly based upon the raced and gendered discourse of civilization and, as such, was at its very base racist. One problematic result has been that scholars have seen Gilman's blatant racism as merely an unfortunate lacuna in an otherwise liberal philosophy.[8] Although they find her racism surprisingly inconsistent with her sexual egalitarianism, Gilman herself would have seen no inconsistency. Her feminism was inextricably rooted in the white supremacism of "civilization."

Because Gilman drew so deeply on the discourse of civilization, racial issues pervaded her feminism. Like G. Stanley Hall, Gilman always assumed that civilization's advancement occurred as individual races ascended the evolutionary ladder, and that the most advanced races—those closest to evolutionary perfection—were white. Gilman rarely made race the explicit focus of her analysis. Woman's advancement was her main interest, just as pedagogy was Hall's. Yet because Gilman's feminist arguments frequently revolved around women's relation to civilization, implicit assumptions about white racial supremacy were as central to her arguments as they were to Hall's.

When Gilman did turn her attention to explicitly racial issues, her white supremacism became apparent. For example, in a 1908 article in the *American Journal of Sociology*, Gilman suggested the government could solve "the Negro Problem" by forcing all African Americans who had not yet achieved "a certain grade of citizenship" to join compulsory, quasi-militaristic "armies" where they would be supervised, trained, and compelled to perform menial labor.[9] "Decent, self-supporting, progressive negroes" would not need to enlist in this army; but "the whole body of negroes who do not progress, who are not self-supporting, who are degenerating into an increasing percentage of social burdens or actual criminals should be taken hold of by the state."[10] Negroes who reached a certain level of advancement could "graduate" from this servitude; those who continued uncivilized had to remain in this army forever.

It might seem strange for a feminist who cared so passionately for political egalitarianism to advocate perpetual servitude for many African Americans; yet because Gilman's political philosophy was so enmeshed in the civilization discourse, she believed her proposal was profoundly egalitarian. Talented Negroes could advance to whatever degree of civilization they could muster, but those who were irredeemably savage would not cumber white Americans in their quest for a perfect civilization.

The mingled millennialism and racism inherent in the civilization discourse facilitated this strange mélange of racism and egalitarianism. On the one hand, "civilization" promised that humanity was infinitely perfectible. For many reformers, civilization's promise of human evolutionary perfectibility mandated the development of individual human potential. For Hall, civilization's advancement meant that boys could be turned into "supermen"; for Gilman, civilization's advancement meant that women must be freed from their subordinate position.

Yet, on the other hand, "civilization" as understood by most whites, including Gilman, remained irredeemably mired in white supremacism. By definition, civilized and savage races occupied different positions on the evolutionary ladder. Although liberals like Hall and Gilman insisted that all races had the *potential* to advance to higher levels, they likewise assumed that the savage races might take generations—even centuries—to catch up, even given the most careful, paternalistic attentions from benevolent Anglo-Saxons.[11]

Thus, the racism inherent in "civilization" became an essential part of

Gilman's feminist egalitarianism. Gilman used "civilization's" mingled ideologies of gender and race to argue that human advancement was a matter not of *gender* difference but of *racial* difference. Where the antifeminists had argued that women could contribute to civilization only as wives and mothers, Gilman argued that sex should not affect one's contribution to civilization—that race was the key factor. Gilman believed that white women and white men shared a racial bond that made them partners in advancing civilization. In a myriad of ways, Gilman worked to displace antifeminists' insistence on male supremacy in civilization by insisting on the centrality of white supremacy in civilization.

This chapter will investigate three ways in which issues of race and "civilization" pervaded Gilman's feminism. First, it will show how Gilman, as a child and young woman, learned to see the demands of her race as conflicting with the demands of her sex, and how she resolved this dilemma, after falling ill with neurasthenia. Second, it will show that in *Women and Economics,* Gilman revised male supremacist versions of "civilization" by invoking race to argue that women were essential to civilization's advancement. Third, in *The Man-Made World,* Gilman revised male supremacist versions of "civilization" by raising the racial specter of the savage rapist to argue that, compared to women, men were peripheral to civilization's advancement.

When Spheres Collide: Civilization, Womanhood, and Neurasthenia

Charlotte Perkins was born July 3, 1860. She grew up steeped in genteel Victorian values and Protestant evangelical culture. Her father, Frederick, was a member of the prominent Beecher family. Her mother, Mary, was a merchant's daughter who grew up with all the educational and cultural refinements of her class. Yet although both her parents had traditional Victorian upper-middle-class upbringings, Gilman herself grew up in near poverty. Her father was unable or unwilling to hold a job long enough to support his family, and by the time Charlotte was nine,[12] it was tacitly understood that he had deserted the family entirely. Gilman's mother, like most middle-class women, had neither the skills nor the opportunity to support herself. She and her two children were forced to take up the itinerant lifestyle of genteel "poor relations." Gilman spent her formative years—ages three to thirteen—moving between a succession of temporary homes in Rhode Island, Connecticut, and Massachusetts, living with a variety of often resentful relatives of her father.[13]

As young Charlotte grew up and learned what it meant to be a woman and a member of her class, certain aspects of the Victorian doctrine of spheres came to seem contradictory and incoherent. It was well known that God and nature had designed a sexual division of labor, and that men and women occupied separate spheres—woman's within the home, and man's in the workplace, outside. Civilization could only advance if both sexes remained within these spheres. Woman kept civilization high-minded and Christian by providing a domestic retreat for her husband and children. Man's contribution to civilization's advancement was more direct: man raised civilization toward increasing material and intellectual perfection by developing commerce, technology, and the sciences to ever higher levels. The greater the degree of sexual differentiation—the more domestic the woman, and the more specialized the man—the more advanced the civilization was believed to be.

In Charlotte's family, however, something had gone terribly wrong with the Victorian arrangement of spheres. Although Mary Perkins was perfectly willing—even eager—to make a domestic retreat for Frederick, she could not. When her husband abdicated the duties of his sphere, Mary lost the financial means to do justice by *her* sphere and was left homeless. Gilman described her mother's frustration over her involuntary exile from domesticity: "Mother's life was one of the most painfully thwarted I have ever known. . . . The most passionately domestic of home-worshipping housewives, she was forced to move nineteen times in eighteen years, fourteen of them from one city to another." Debt was Mary's greatest problem. It was so improper for married middle-class women to work that no jobs were available to them—at least, none with living wages. Deserted wives like Mary were cultural anomalies, relegated to the margins of society, where few noticed or provided for them. For ten years Mary moved from one house to another, living wherever Frederick "installed her" but always "fleeing again on account of debt," leaving town one step ahead of her creditors.[14] Watching her mother, Charlotte learned early and bitterly that woman's duty to civilization could easily founder on the rocks of feminine economic dependency.

Although Gilman could have interpreted her homeless childhood as a divine trial intended to build her character or as proof of her father's moral weakness, she interpreted it, instead, as a demonstration of the unjust limitations of "woman's sphere." In this, she was influenced by the growing woman's movement which, by the 1870s, had become extremely critical of just this sort of feminine economic dependency. Charlotte was probably exposed to these ideas when she boarded in the homes of her suffragist aunts Isabella Beecher Hooker and Harriet Beecher Stowe.[15]

Young Charlotte had no intention of sharing her mother's fate, and finding herself trapped and dependent in woman's sphere. Instead, she longed for artistic fame and intellectual success outside the home—achievements which she, like her culture, identified with man's sphere. As a young girl, she had envied her brother Thomas' access to the larger world and to her distant father's attention. Brighter than her brother, she had wooed her absent father by writing him to ask for books and magazines and by trying to dazzle him with her intellectual precocity.[16] Nonetheless, no one in her family saw fit to raise money for her education: she spent only four years in seven different schools before she turned fifteen.[17] Later, dull Thomas was sent to MIT while Charlotte had to beg to attend the Rhode Island School of Design.

Lacking much formal schooling to prepare her for important, remunerative work outside the home, she decided she must educate herself. In 1877, at the age of seventeen, she wrote her father, who was then working as assistant director of the Boston Public Library, informing him that she "wished to help humanity" and, in order to know where to begin, needed a reading list in history. In reply, Frederick sent her a list of nine books—not, as one might expect, about the history of modern social problems, or even about the history of modern nations. Instead, Frederick recommended scholarly tomes on ancient history and primitive anthropology.[18]

It was this reading list—the "beginning of my real education," according to Gilman—which taught her to identify the tantalizingly distant male sphere of intellectual achievement with the millennial mission to perfect the white races.[19] It also exposed her to the latest scholarly knowledge about the raced and gendered meaning of civilization. Frederick's list provided Charlotte with four of the central founding documents of a new type of Darwinist anthropology: Edward B. Tylor's *Researches into the Early History of Mankind and the Development of Civilization* (1865) and *Primitive Culture* (1871); and John Lubbock's *Pre-historic Times, as Illustrated by Ancient Remains, and the Manners and Customs of Modern Savages* (1869) and *The Origin of Civilization and the Primitive Condition of Man* (1870). These anthropologies extrapolate from the customs of "modern savages" to explain how the men of the white races had gradually evolved their advanced civilizations. In other words, these books—like G. Stanley Hall's pedagogy—stripped dark-skinned races of their status as people living in the nineteenth century and instead constructed them as ancient history texts—primitive survivals whose only importance to civilization was their capacity to provide information about the lost, primitive past of more "advanced" white races.[20] (Indeed, Hall, who cited both Tylor and Lubbock in *Adolescence,* drew on precisely this sort of anthropology when he looked to the customs of "savage races" in order to understand the impulses of "primitive" little boys.)[21] Frederick also sent Charlotte several issues of *Popular Science Monthly* to provide her with a grounding in evolutionary theory.[22] In short, Frederick's reading list depicted "the white man" as the cutting edge of civilization's advancement and the "primitive" races as evolutionary losers. All human history was a cosmic process of racial evolution, which was now thrusting the white races ever higher, toward a perfected civilization.

Inspired by her father's reading list, Charlotte soon moved to develop what she called her "religion"—a creed of the millennial importance of advancing the white races toward the highest possible civilization. Charlotte believed her studies of primitive history and anthropology gave her objective, scientific facts which she could use to answer her religious questions. It was the connectedness of her readings which impressed her, the way these seemingly unrelated books seemed to tie all human knowledge together in a "due order and sequence" which answered a variety of religious questions. As she put it, "they showed our origin, our lines of development, the hope and method of future progress."[23] Yet although she believed she saw a pattern in the *facts,* she really saw a pattern provided by the *discourse.* These texts, all shaped by the wider discourse of civilization, provided her with a ready-made philosophy of the millennial significance of racial evolution, which she discerned and adopted as her religion.

In taking evolution as the basis of her religion, Gilman was not unique. By the mid-1880s, a number of American Protestants were adopting evolution as a religious doctrine, including Gilman's great uncle, Henry Ward Beecher.[24] G. Stanley Hall, as we have already seen, also believed evolution had a profound religious significance, as it moved the race ever closer to millennial perfection.

Gilman's evolutionary religion differed from Beecher's and Hall's, however, in that it gave her a religious mandate to expand woman's sphere. By adopting this quest for a higher human evolution as her religion, Gilman was following in the footsteps of many Protestant women before her (including her great aunt Catharine Beecher) who had invoked religion to explain why it was necessary for women to do God's work outside the home.[25] For centuries, Protestant theologians had agreed there was no sex in Christ: both men and women were spiritual equals. Therefore, when Gilman substituted evolution for the older Christian doctrine, it was no great jump for her to assume that just as Christian men and women had once shared the duty of advancing Christendom toward the millennium, so evolutionist men and women shared the duty to advance their race toward human evolutionary perfection.

Gilman describes her discovery of this evolutionary religion in her autobiography. After completing her studies, she writes, she asked herself what God was, and answered that God was the force which moved evolution always higher.[26] She then asked, "What does God want . . . of us?" and answered, "I figured it out that the business of mankind was to carry out the evolution of the human race, according to the laws of nature, adding the conscious direction, the telic force, proper to our kind—we are the only creatures that can assist evolution."[27] According to Gilman, this evolutionary religion would remain "the essential part of my life."[28] She would continue to see her mission as a reformer in terms of "carry[ing] out the evolution of the human race, according to the laws of nature." And those laws of nature, as she had learned them from her father's reading list, included the special evolutionary fitness of the white races to advance toward the highest possible civilization.

Gilman's studies in evolution gave her a way to understand her ambitions in terms of race instead of sex. Important work in the male sphere wasn't simply masculine; it was racial. Productive work, outside the home, was part of the cosmic, divinely ordained process of keeping the white race moving ever onward, toward a perfect civilization. As a woman, she had a mission to provide a civilized home for her family; yet as an Anglo-Saxon, she had a mission to "carry out the evolution of the human race." The claims of racial evolution and of womanhood were thus set in opposition, according to young Gilman's understanding of the spiritual implications of civilization.

By the time Gilman reached twenty-one, her choices seemed clear. Either she could follow the claims of sex—marriage, motherhood, domesticity and dependency—or the claims of race—intellectual labor to advance the race toward millennial perfection. Choosing race meant choosing the male sphere, and thus abjuring the joys of love, sex, matrimony, and motherhood forever.[29] As she wrote when she was twenty-one,

> I am really glad not to marry. For the mother side of me is strong enough to make an interminable war between plain duties and in-

expressible instincts . . . . Whereas if I let that business alone, and
go on in my own way; what I gain in individual strength and development of personal power of character, *myself as a self,* you know,
not merely as a woman, or that useful animal a wife and mother, will
I think make up, and more than make up in usefulness and effect,
for the other happiness that part of me would so enjoy.[30]

Gilman was deeply ambivalent. She was emotionally attracted to love and
matrimony, but high-minded spinsterhood seemed the noblest option.
Gilman vowed to choose race over sex and prepared to meet her future as an
unmarried reformer.

Instead, she met her first husband. When Gilman was twenty-two, the
promising and handsome young artist Charles Walter Stetson asked for her
hand in marriage. Gilman was thrown into a quandary. She must either reject
the attractive Stetson, together with the deep joys of motherhood which
both the woman's movement and the civilization discourse told her was
woman's noblest portion; or she must betray her deep-felt calling to improve
the race, which she believed was the noblest possible occupation, albeit a
masculine one. Racial duty—her mission to advance civilization—warred
with her womanly duty and her own emotional desires. At first she refused
Stetson, citing the conflict between woman's sphere and racial advancement:
"If I were bound to a few [i.e., a husband and children] I should grow so fond
of them, and so busied with them that I should have no room for the thousand and one helpful works which the world needs."[31] Yet she wavered. "On
the one hand, I knew it was normal and right" for a woman to marry; "On the
other, I felt strongly that for me it was not right, that the nature of the life
before me [informed by her clarion calling to uplift the race] forbade it."[32]
For sixteen months, Stetson courted her until finally she agreed to marry
him. Still she had misgivings. She lamented to her diary, "Perhaps it was not
meant for me to work as I intended. Perhaps I am not to be of use to others. I
am weak. I anticipate a future of failure and suffering."[33] Charlotte and Walter were wed on May 2, 1884. Within two months, Gilman had fallen into an
agonizing state of paralysis and despair.[34]

For the next four years Gilman brooded on her faults. Having chosen the
claims of womanhood over race, she had failed as a woman. With everything
a woman could want—everything her mother had been denied—"a charming home; a loving and devoted husband; an exquisite baby, . . . a wholly
satisfactory servant"—still she "lay all day on the lounge and cried."[35] Unnatural! Worse, she had willfully and wickedly betrayed the cause of higher

civilization. "You did it yourself! You did it yourself!" she remembered thinking. "You were called to serve humanity, and you cannot serve yourself. No good as a wife, no good as mother, no good at anything. And you did it yourself!"[36] In desperation, she decided she must have a brain disease, uncharacteristically accepted a gift of a hundred dollars from a friend of her mother, and signed herself into the clinic of renowned neurologist Dr. S. Weir Mitchell, who diagnosed her as a victim of neurasthenia.[37]

Gilman herself already interpreted her own illness as the result of a conflict between her duty as a woman and her duty to her race, between woman's sphere and higher civilization. Neurasthenia was, thus, an appropriate diagnosis for her malaise. For, as we have already seen in our discussion of G. Stanley Hall and the neurasthenic paradox, neurasthenia was above all else a disease of higher civilization, which struck only men and women of the most advanced races, whose delicate, highly evolved nervous systems could not stand the demands of civilized life. Even Gilman herself ultimately agreed that the precipitating cause of her illness had been her society's insistence that the demands of womanhood must conflict with the demands of race.

Both sexes suffered from neurasthenia, yet the implications of neurasthenia differed for men and women, according to medical experts. Whereas men became neurasthenics because the mental labors of advanced civilization drained them of the nervous energy necessary to build a strong, masculine body, women became neurasthenics when they tried to combine their normal function—motherhood—with the masculine, enervating intellectual demands of modern civilization. Neurasthenic women lacked the nervous force to fully participate in modern civilization because their reproductive systems, unlike men's, were a constant drain on their nerve force. In fact, the most frequently cited single cause of female neurasthenia was reproductive disturbance.[38] This made the intellectual rigors of civilization especially dangerous for women. Indeed, George M. Beard repeatedly listed "the mental activity of women" as one of the five most dangerous developments of modern civilization.[39] Hall agreed and suggested that adolescent girls should take school holidays during their menses.[40]

Civilized intellectual activity and motherhood were thus medically incompatible for nervous women, according to the experts. Therefore, physicians' goals in curing neurasthenia were different for women than for men. While men must have their nervous forces recharged so they could return to the demanding intellectual pursuits of civilization, nervous women were advised to recognize their biological limitations and devote themselves exclusively to domesticity and the home. In other words, the neurasthenic man

must be returned to the civilized functions of the *race,* while the neurasthenic woman must recognize her biological limitations as a member of "the
sex" and return to woman's sphere.

These, then were the assumptions upon which Dr. Mitchell proposed to
treat the desperate Charlotte.[41] His first step was to disabuse her of her own
opinions about what ailed her—after all, that sort of intellectual activity was
what had made her ill, in the first place. Upon her arrival, Gilman had presented Mitchell with a long letter detailing the origins of her illness, which
the good doctor dismissed contemptuously as itself a neurasthenic symptom. "I've had two women of your blood here already," he told her
scornfully.[42] In order to recharge her nervous forces, he put her to bed and
gave her the most common treatment for neurasthenia, the "rest cure." This
consisted of complete bed rest; huge amounts of food, especially milk, hand-
fed by the nurse; soothing massages; passive dependence on doctor and
nurse; and complete isolation from one's old occupations and friends.[43]
Gilman found this regimen of infantilization and bodily pampering "agree-
able treatment," and responded so well that, after a month, Mitchell pronounced her cured and sent her home with strict advice on how to prevent a
neurasthenic relapse.

"Live as domestic a life as possible. Have your child with you all the time,"
Mitchell advised. "Lie down an hour after each meal. Have but two hours
intellectual life a day. And never touch pen, brush or pencil as long as you
live."[44] From now on, Gilman must remain in woman's sphere and forever
abjure her duty to her race. By devoting her scanty nervous energy to domestic duties and rationing her contact with intellectually stressful civilization,
she would be able to live a healthy, normal life. Diligently, Gilman tried to
follow this advice—with disastrous results. As she put it, she "came so near
the borderline of utter mental ruin I could see over."[45]

The most eminent medical expert had treated her, exiled her from civilization, and relegated her—as a mother, but like a child—to the home and
nursery. In despair and in rebellion, she regressed to early childhood, playing with toys and crawling on the floor. "I made a rag baby, hung it on a
doorknob and played with it. I would crawl into remote closets and under
beds—to hide from the grinding pressure of that profound distress."[46]

Yet perhaps we should see this behavior as a regression not to childhood
but to savagery. According to recapitulation theory, with which Gilman was
surely familiar, children were at the same evolutionary stage as savages.[47]
Gilman was forbidden to be civilized, forbidden to exercise the very functions which led to racial advance, the very gifts which had led her to believe
she had a mission to advance civilization. Very well then—if she couldn't be

civilized, she would be a savage.[48] Sixteen years later, Gilman elaborated on this line of logic in her book *The Home*, which argued that, as currently organized, the modern American home was an atavistic remnant of savagery. Although the civilized world was a place of specialization and intellectual challenge, civilized white women were forced to live at home, doing unspecialized drudgery in primitive conditions—in short, living the life of a savage "squaw."[49] Elsewhere, Gilman would make this argument more explicit: American women became neurasthenic because, as highly evolved, civilized human beings, they suffered from living an atavistic and primitive life in the home.[50] Gilman believed this because she had lived it: in 1887 she had found her total immersion in woman's sphere and domesticity unbearable and so uncivilized that it literally drove her to savagery.

Medical science had offered Gilman a choice—the female version of the neurasthenic paradox. She could be either a healthy but primitive woman, happy in woman's sphere and exiled from civilization, or a neurasthenic intellectual, weak and useless to civilization. Gilman, through her illness, reformulated her options: She could either be a crazy savage, cowering on the floor in woman's sphere, or she could rejoin civilization and, neurasthenic as she was, take up once again the mantle of her millennial mission to advance her race. It wasn't an easy decision but, in the end, only one choice was possible. Gilman left her husband and started a new life, working to uplift civilization as a writer and reformer. It had become clear that she simply couldn't survive in woman's sphere, exiled from civilization.

Nonetheless, her choice to rejoin civilization and abjure woman's sphere came at a price. From then on, Gilman considered herself a debilitated neurasthenic. Even forty years later, in 1927, Gilman insisted that "the effects of nerve bankruptcy remain to ths day."[51] She reported that she had suffered "lasting mental injury" from her neurasthenic breakdown; that she had lost the mental abilities she had enjoyed as a young woman; that ever since her first marriage she couldn't read, couldn't concentrate, couldn't work. Yet, as she complained bitterly, no one took her complaints of lasting damage seriously: "The humiliating loss of a large part of [my] brain power, of more than half of [my] working life, accompanied with deep misery and anguish of mind—this when complained of is met with amiable laughter and flat disbelief."[52] Well might her friends be incredulous—for Gilman's output after her divorce was prodigious! Between 1888, when she left her husband, and her death in 1935, Gilman wrote and published 8 novels, 171 short stories, 473 poems, and 1,472 nonfiction pieces (nine of them booklength).[53]

How could a woman so productive believe she was a neurasthenic in-

Fig. 10. This publicity photograph represents the civilized womanliness Charlotte Perkins Gilman worked so hard to construct for herself and her work. Gilman sits reading in a rocker. The atmosphere is homelike, with a Victorian lamp and furnishings. Yet this womanly domesticity is mingled with the "human" achievements of advanced civilization—the framed artwork on the table, and especially the shelves of thick, leatherbound books. Courtesy the Schlesinger Library, Radcliffe College.

valid? Perhaps her own solution to her personal neurasthenic paradox left her no other choice. She had gone into her marriage believing she must choose between woman's sphere and racial advance. She had wrestled with that choice until it nearly destroyed her. Only when faced with the complete destruction of her sanity could she give herself permission to desert woman's sphere and rejoin civilization and the race. Yet she never completely rejected the terms of the neurasthenic paradox, which posited womanly health as the opposite of intellectual achievement, womanly fulfillment as the opposite of racial contribution. In leaving her first husband, Gilman made her choice;

but she could not completely reject the terms of that choice even years later, after a happy and fulfilling second marriage, and a productive career. And forever after, she would live with what she felt were the consequences of that debilitating choice—permanent damage to her nervous energies.

Yet even though she could not escape the dualities of the neurasthenic paradox herself, she was determined to dismantle them for other women. Gilman would devote the rest of her life to insisting that women like herself—white women—were members of their race, as well as members of their sex. No white woman ought to have to make the choices she had been forced to make between her sex and her race. As racially advanced Anglo-Saxons, civilized advancement was women's concern and heritage as much as it was men's. As she told the Los Angeles Woman's Club in an eloquent lecture given only two years after she had left her husband and rejoined civilization:

> Some of you will say again that it is part of the male function in the human race to provide for the family, including under this head all the varied activities of our race, and the female function merely to serve the family . . . —in other words that the whole created human world, church and palace, book and picture, drama and oration, tool and weapon—can be produced only by the male sex, and that the female sex have no power beyond their functional ones! . . . But it is a lie! . . . Race function does not interfere with sex function. . . . The dominant soul—the clear strong accurate brain, the perfect service of a healthy body—these do not belong to *sex*—but to *race!*[54]

It was not true that all of civilization—"church and palace, book and picture, drama and oration, tool and weapon"—was part of man's sphere, and that the home was woman's only portion. "Race function" and "sex function" were as compatible for women as they were for men. The "dominant soul" of the highest brain and the healthiest body—of the most racially advanced, civilized members of the human family—"do not belong to *sex*—but to *race!*" This passionate tenet would remain the cornerstone of Gilman's feminism.

Making White Women Central to Civilization's Advancement: *Women and Economics*

In 1898, ten years after Gilman rejoined civilization, she published *Women and Economics,* her eloquent argument that women like herself—white women—were fully civilized beings, whose efforts were essential for the race to advance to the evolutionary millennium. It influenced countless American women, went through eight American printings by 1915 and was also published in translation in Japan, Hungary, Holland, Denmark, Italy, Germany, and Russia.[55] As the *New York City Review of Literature* put it thirty-five years after its publication, *Women and Economics* "has been considered by feminists of the whole world as the outstanding book on Feminism."[56]

Women and Economics: A Study of the Economic Relation between Men and Women as a Factor in Social Evolution was one of Gilman's fullest explications of her racially based feminism. Its whole point was to create an alternative ideology of civilization in which white women could take their rightful place beside white men as full participants in the past and future of civilization. In it, Gilman passionately refuted the ideas about women and civilization which she had found most oppressive: that extreme sexual difference was a hallmark of advanced civilization; that civilized women must devote themselves primarily to domesticity; that women's economic dependency was essential to civilization. As Gilman saw it, all these noxious ideas that had once forced her to choose between her womanhood and her race overstated the influence of sex. Civilization's advancement, she argued, should be seen primarily in terms of race, not sex. The choice she had once been offered—between her race and her sex—was a false choice, because as a member of her highly civilized race, she had an indisputable duty to work for evolutionary advancement and the perfection of civilization, whether she was a man or a woman.

In writing *Women and Economics,* Gilman drew on the white supremacist knowledges of civilization which she had originally learned from her father's reading program in evolutionary anthropology, and which she had adopted as her millennial religion. She assumed that human history had a cosmic telos, an evolutionary mechanism, and a racial basis: it was a story of advanced white races evolving ever higher, striving toward a perfect civilization. Gilman herself rarely specified which race she meant when she invoked the need to allow "the race" to evolve upward. She didn't need to. As we have seen with the Columbian Exposition, Ida B. Wells' antilynching campaign, and G. Stanley Hall, most educated whites assumed that only the white races had the capacity to advance to the highest future stages of civilization. Gilman's knowledge of the discourse of civilization made her understand that to specify "white" would be redundant.

Gilman began *Women and Economics* by discussing the evolutionary implications of women's economic dependence. Like G. Stanley Hall and most of her contemporaries, Gilman was a Lamarckian: she believed that children inherited their parents' acquired traits. The first chapter of *Women and Economics* argues that whatever creatures learned to do in order to obtain food was passed on genetically to their offspring and was the largest factor in the evolution of their species. For example, over the generations horses had evolved to be increasingly gentle creatures as they learned to depend on grazing for their livelihood, whereas tigers had become increasingly violent as they had learned ever more efficient ways to catch and dismember their prey.[57]

Women's economic dependence on men had made human beings evolve a most peculiar character. As Gilman put it, "We are the only animal species in which the female depends on the male for food, the only animal species in which the sex-relation is also an economic relation."[58] Gilman devoted her book to demonstrating how this "sexuo-economic" relation had distorted healthy human evolution and damaged civilization by making women develop sex traits at the expense of their race traits.

Gilman's condemnation of this sexuo-economic relation was the cornerstone of her feminist version of civilization. According to the masculinist civilization discourse, which Gilman was trying to rewrite, women's economic dependency on breadwinning husbands was indispensable to human evolution—an intrinsic part of civilized races' sexual difference. In *Women and Economics,* however, Gilman argued that women's economic dependence was entirely unnatural. Man's favor had become woman's bread-and-butter, and evolution had molded the human race accordingly. Woman had over-evolved those traits which men found sexually attractive. She had lost those robust qualities which normally led to *racial* advance, like physical size and strength, and had become specialized to man's *sexual* tastes. She was now delicate, soft, and feeble, unable to walk, run, or climb, or to perform any of the normal functions of the race. As Gilman put it, "our civilized 'feminine delicacy' . . . appears somewhat less delicate when recognized as an expression of sexuality in excess."[59] Excessive sexuality, and not advanced civilization, was the evolutionary result of women's economic dependence, according to Gilman.

In lower species, whose sole purpose was reproduction, this oversexed condition would not be a problem. Their females could afford to become "mere egg sac[s]," specialized entirely for sexual functions. But evolution intended human beings to develop a perfect civilization. As Gilman put it, "The duty of human life is progress, development . . . we are here, not merely to live, but to grow—not to be content with lean savagery or fat barbarism or sordid semi-civilization, but to toil on through the centuries, and build up the ever-nobler forms of life toward which social evolution tends."[60] Humanity in general, and the advanced white races in particular, had a sacred task to evolve the highest possible civilization.

Gilman insisted that despite conventional wisdom, civilized races' elaborate and excessive sexual differences were not intrinsic to civilization's advancement. On the contrary, throughout human history, these excessive sexual differences had always led to civilization's destruction. As she put it, "The inevitable trend of human life is toward higher civilization, but while that civilization is confined to one sex, it inevitably exaggerates sex-distinction, until the increasing evil of this condition is stronger than all the good of the civilization attained, and the nation falls." This danger was not merely national, but racial: "The path of history is strewn with fossils and faint relics of extinct races, — races which died of what the sociologist would call internal diseases rather than natural causes." And she quoted Byron's assertion that there is only one tale to History: "First Freedom, and then Glory; when that fails, Wealth, Vice, Corruption—barbarism at last."[61]

Now, as we have seen in our discussion of Hall, Gilman was not alone in warning of the dangers of overcivilized racial decadence and the potential decline of civilization. Part of the larger discourse of civilization—the necessary corollary of its millennial aspect—was the sense that if a race did not continue progressing upward toward a perfect civilization, it would inevitably backslide and fall into racial decay. The need for races to struggle to achieve a millennial future necessarily implied a potential for failure. In the Christian version of this millennial struggle, God's opponent was sin or the devil. In Darwinized versions, including both Hall's and Gilman's, the evil that threatened evolution was stunted growth or racial decadence. Ancient Greece and Rome were frequently held up as cautionary examples.

Although warnings of racial decline and overcivilized decadence were a ubiquitous part of her culture, Gilman's explanations of this peril facing civilization were unique, intended to counter the antifeminist implications of the larger discourse. Masculinist commentators insisted that to avoid the decline of civilization, sexual differences must be upheld and even increased, lest the two sexes become more alike and thus more like uncivilized savages. As Hall wrote in *Adolescence,* quoting biologist Alpheus Hyatt:

> In the early history of mankind the women and men led lives more nearly alike and were consequently more alike physically and mentally than they have become subsequently in the lives of highly civilized peoples. This divergence of sex is a marked characteristic of

progression among highly civilized races. Coeducation of the sexes, occupations of a certain kind, and woman's suffrage may have a tendency to approximate the ideals, the lives, and the habits of women to those of men in these same highly civilized races. Such approximation in the future . . . would not belong to the progressive evolution of mankind.[62]

These approximations between women and men, Hall continued in his own words, "would tend to virify women and feminize men, and would be retrogressive." This sort of "degenerative influence" must be avoided at all costs, because "one necessity of [continuous or certain progress] is that the sexes be not approximated, for this would inaugurate retrogressive evolution." Only the continuation and increase of sexual difference would allow civilization to move forward. If sexual difference decreased, evolution would move backward toward savagery, according to authorities like Hall and Hyatt.[63]

Gilman, on the other hand, argued the opposite: extreme sexual difference was not the proof of civilized advancement but the cause of overcivilized decadence and racial decay. "We, as a race, manifest an excessive sex-attraction, followed by its excessive indulgence, and the inevitable evil consequence. . . . What is the cause of this excessive sex-attraction in the human species? The immediately acting cause of sex-attraction is sex-distinction. The more widely the sexes are differentiated, the more forcibly they are attracted to each other."[64] Thus, for Gilman, extreme sex distinctions were dangerous devolutionary forces because they led to excessive sexuality in civilized men and women. In American civilization, this excessive sexuality manifested itself both within marriage (too much emphasis on sex) and outside marriage (in the seemingly ineradicable "social evil" of prostitution).[65] Thus, the sexuo-economic relation had deformed civilized men and women into a race of prostitute-like women, economically dependent on sexual allure, and of prostitute-patronizing men, who felt it was natural to support sexually attractive women.

Although Gilman was unique in seeing sexual difference as a cause of racial decadence, her view that excessive sexuality menaced civilization with racial decay was far more typical. Hall, for example, drew on these ideas when he constructed the figure of the masturbating, overstimulated youth as a metonym—cause and embodiment—of overcivilized decadence. For Gilman, the metonymic embodiment of civilization's impending decadence was the figure of the oversexed civilized woman—fat, weak, and ignorant—perverted from healthful evolutionary development and specialized, like a courtesan, for man's sexual pleasure. For both Hall and Gilman, however, excessive sex signified endangered civilization and racial extinction.

According to Gilman, advanced civilizations' seemingly inevitable slide to decadence could be explained by a general scientific law—a law which codified the relationship between race and sex. Race development and sex development, she argued, were inversely related. The more energy a race devoted to "sex activity," the less energy it had to devote to "race activity."[66] Most animals could devote only a limited amount of energy to sex activity because self-preservation dictated they devote most of their energy to race activity. For example, if the peacock's tail, with which he attracted a mate, got too large and gaudy, he would lose the capacity to move about and he would starve to death.[67] But civilized women, dependent on sex for their bread, could become infinitely oversexed without starving.

Only *civilized* women could become so dangerously oversexed; thus, only civilized races were imperiled by this sexually caused racial decay. Savage and barbarous women, too, were economically dependent on men; yet savage races avoided racial decadence because they were too poor and primitive for their women to withdraw completely from productive labor. Savage women still had to work outside the home, producing goods to allow their race to survive, and this "race activity" kept their "sex activity" within tolerable bounds.

Highly civilized races, on the other hand, could produce enough to survive and still devote all their women, full time, to "sex activity." Over the generations, civilized races would become increasingly sexualized and therefore increasingly unfit for "race activity." Their women would grow increasingly feeble and oversexed; and their sons and daughters would inherit this oversexed feebleness via Lamarckian evolution. Inevitably, the entire race would grow so weak and oversexed that, unable to maintain the forward drive of race activity and civilization, they would decline and fall, just as ancient Greece and Rome had. This would be the fate of the United States and the white American race if the sexuo-economic relation were not abandoned.[68]

Here, then, was another way Gilman revised antifeminist elements of the discourse of civilization. The masculinist proponents of civilization depicted sexual difference and racial difference as *directly* related. That is, as civilized races advanced, they grew ever more unlike their racial inferiors, and at the same time their women grew ever more unlike their men. Gilman, on the other hand, depicted sexual difference and racial difference as *inversely* related: As civilized races advanced, they grew ever more unlike their racial inferiors; but if sexual difference also increased, their racial superiority was likely to decrease, and they would degenerate back to the level of primitives. It was thus essential to civilized advancement that sexual differences not be exaggerated—otherwise racial devolution and the demise of civilization would result.

Here Gilman's millennialist evolutionary "religion" began to sound very much like the Protestant religion of her youth and her Beecher background. Like an Old Testament prophet—or one of her clergymen uncles—Gilman phrased her message as a warning that unless her people changed their ways, the fruits of their past sins would overwhelm them, and God/evolution would utterly destroy them. Civilization threatened to crumble at the very moment when humanity's perfection became conceivable. Holy evolution had brought the white races to a point where they had the potential to develop a civilization higher than any that had gone before. Yet despite this advancement, the white races' oversexed feebleness, born of their women's economic dependence on their men, threatened to destroy them and their civilization utterly.

To explain the higher evolutionary meaning of the sexuo-economic relation, Gilman drew on another story of thwarted divine intentions—the biblical story of Man's Fall in the Garden of Eden. These biblical echoes were probably unstudied, but they were powerful nonetheless, and structured her argument as a cosmic imperative. Just as God had originally intended Adam and Eve to live in happy perfection in the Garden, so Evolution had intended men and women to evolve happily and healthfully toward a perfect civilization. Yet evil had tempted man, and the Fall had occurred, as sin (the sexuo-economic relationship) had come into the world. *Women and Economics* contains two versions of this Fall—one prose version, contained in the text, and one version in verse, "Proem," which serves as a prologue.[69] Because the story they tell is substantially the same, the following discussion draws on both versions.

In the beginning, according to Gilman, "primitive man and his female were animals, like other animals," and, as with animals, the sexes were equal.[70]

> In dark and early ages, through the primal forests faring
> Ere the soul came shining into prehistoric night
> Twofold man was equal; they were comrades dear and daring,
> Living wild and free together in unreasoning delight.[71]

Originally, men and women were merely dual aspects of "twofold man" and their world was a paradise of "unreasoning delight." Primal woman was as "strong, fierce, . . . nimble and ferocious" as primal man and, like primal man, she fed herself on what she found in the forests. Both sexes lived happily and equally together, supporting themselves, and not relying on the other for their economic needs.

Then came the Fall. Primal innocence was shattered when primitive man discovered evil, in the form of excessive sensuality and rape. Man

> found the Tree of Knowledge, that awful tree and holy
> [And] he knew he felt, and knew he knew.

Gilman's Eve figure (male, unlike Genesis's) eats of the Tree of Knowledge and learns how to sin. He learns to eat for pleasure, drink for drunkenness, and imprison woman as his sexual possession:

> Then said he to Pain, "I am wise now, and I know you!
> No more will I suffer while power and wisdom last!"
> Then said he to Pleasure, "I am strong, and I will show you
> That the will of man can seize you,—aye, and hold you fast!
>
> Food he ate for pleasure, and wine he drank for gladness.
> And woman? Ah, the woman! the crown of all delight!
> His now,—he knew it! He was strong to madness
> In that early dawning after prehistoric night.

Primal man, who now knows evil, subjugates primal woman, keeping her too weak to flee him, and fans the "flame of passion" with unnatural arts and forces.

> Close, close he bound her, that she should leave him never;
> Weak still he kept her, lest she be strong to flee;
> And the fainting flame of passion he kept alive forever
> With all the arts and forces of earth and sky and sea.[72]

In future years, when Gilman lectured on the origins of woman's oppression, she continued to call this original discovery that man could violently compel woman to do his will—i.e. the birth of the primitive rapist—"the fall of man."[73]

Thus, the Fall from Evolution's original grace came when innocent primal man transformed himself from woman's equal into the first primitive rapist.

In her prose version, Gilman describes this development of the original savage rapist more explicitly than in the "Proem": "There seems to have come a time when it occurred to this amiable savage that it was cheaper and easier to fight a little female, and have it done with, than to fight a big male every time. So he instituted the custom of enslaving the female; and she, losing freedom, could no longer get her own food nor that of her young."[74] Man became intelligent enough to figure out how to circumvent the normal evolutionary process of sexual selection. He realized he didn't need to fight a big strong man every time he wanted sex—he could simply assault a small woman once, and then keep her weak and imprisoned. This was why men preferred small women to healthy large ones.

In other words, the origin of woman's subjection and the sexuo-economic relationship was the development of the primitive rapist—a figure we have met before. Like Northern white men, who demonstrated their own civilized manliness by contrasting it with the unrestrained lust of the mythic Negro rapist, Gilman was demonstrating women's capacity for higher civilization by contrasting virtuous primal woman with the unrestrained lust of primal man. Gilman intuitively understood the cultural power of the "primitive rapist," and, like most whites in her culture, she associated the "primitive rapist" with "the Negro." As she wrote in another context, Southern white "women suffer most frequently from masculine attack . . . by men of a lower grade of civilization to which no idea of chivalry has yet penetrated." Consciously or not, Gilman was drawing on the ubiquitous cultural images of manhood and Southern lynching against which Wells had fought so hard on her British tour, four years earlier.[75]

Gilman was not alone in seeing primal man as a rapist who destroyed a peaceful prehistoric period of sexual equality; the idea was already a commonplace among feminists who invoked a lost matriarchy. Yet by invoking the figure of the primitive savage rapist as the original enemy of sexual equality, feminists like Gilman were marshaling a powerful racist symbol for the cause of white women's advancement. The primitive rapist was already a figure of great cultural power in turn-of-the-century white America. Moreover, by making all men, including civilized white men, the evolutionary descendants of the original primal rapist—a figure indelibly coded Negro and therefore unmanly—Gilman was subtly arguing that men had no essential claim on civilization.

When man discovered rape, according to Gilman, he brought evil into the world, an evil which was now threatening the millennial future of all civilization. Evil, in Gilman's evolutionary religion, was whatever thwarted higher evolutionary development, and the evil which the primal rapist had unleashed in the Garden had perverted all subsequent human evolution.[76] Because of her sexuo-economic dependence, first enforced by the primitive rapist, woman had evolved into a weak, parasitic creature. She was permanently dependent on her powers of sexual attraction and therefore lower than a prostitute, whose debasement was at least temporary. She was cut off from the forces of natural selection and sheltered from the race activity which would normally have made her evolve characteristics such as strength, skill, endurance, and courage.[77] Indeed, if it were not for the racially advanced traits civilized women inherited from their fathers (who, unlike their mothers, regularly engaged in race activity and so developed racially advanced traits to pass on to their offspring), women would be the most primitive of beings.[78]

Man-the-rapist's perversion of evolution's true intentions had by now left the race so oversexed that the ultimate evolutionary catastrophe loomed: "All morbid conditions tend to extinction. One check has always existed to our inordinate sex-development—nature's ready relief, death. Carried to its furthest excess, . . . the nation itself has perished, like Sodom and Gomorrah."[79] This was the precarious condition in which civilized American men and women found themselves at that moment. The evil unleashed in the Garden had now grown to such an extent that it threatened to undermine the divine workings of evolution entirely, leaving evolution's most favored race on the brink of devolution and eternal night.

Yet evolution, like the Lord of Hosts, would never fail its chosen people. Nature would not have allowed a condition like the sexuo-economic relation to develop unless it had a higher purpose, an important part to play in the millennial drama of civilization's advancement. Although the sexuo-economic relation currently threatened civilization with decadence and dissolution (just as the devil had threatened Christendom with eternal damnation), the Fall from the sexually equal Garden had a higher meaning which would ultimately allow the development of a perfect civilization (just as the original Fall allowed God an ultimate triumph over evil, in a millennial future).

The sexuo-economic relation, Gilman now revealed, was only a temporary condition, designed by nature in order to make civilization possible. According to Gilman, civilization in its essence was social. The highest civilization was the one in which humans had developed the most specialized and efficient ways to serve one another: "To serve each other more and more widely; to live only by such service; to develop special functions, so that we depend for our living on society's return for services that can be of no direct use to ourselves—this is civilization, our human glory and race-distinction."[80] Yet this social feeling, which was the basis of civilization itself, was essentially feminine. (Gilman, as we will see later, believed in certain sex-based characteristics, which were aspects of biological motherhood or fatherhood.) Among animals, only females show any rudiments of social feeling, because only females were mothers. Female animals nursed their young, while male animals gratified only their own individual needs. Among the earliest primal humans, this animal dynamic continued: only females were social or altruistic. Primal woman developed social maternalism to new heights, developing primitive agriculture to feed her children, primitive architecture to house them, primitive industry to clothe them. Primal man, however, remained as individualistic as male animals, caring about nothing except himself. Had man remained this individualistic, civilization could never have evolved.

The sexuo-economic relation was evolution's way of forcing man to be social—and, ultimately, civilized—by harnessing his sexual passion to the cause of evolutionary advancement. It was only after man developed into the primitive rapist and imprisoned woman to serve as his concubine that he was forced, for the first time, to provide for beings other than himself. Captive, weakened females lost the ability to feed themselves and their children, and man was forced to support them himself.

> The subjection of woman has involved to an enormous degree the maternalizing of man. Under its bonds he has been forced into new functions, impossible to male energy alone. He has had to learn to love and care for some one besides himself. He has had to learn to work, to serve, to be human. Through the sex-passion, mightily overgrown, the human race has been led and driven up the long steep path of progress . . . until at last a degree of evolution is reached in which the extension of human service and human love makes possible a better way.[81]

Driven by his "mightily overgrown sex passion," the human male had gradually been driven up "the long steep path of progress." He had gradually been feminized and had become social, altruistic—civilized. Only this gradual feminization of man had made higher civilization possible.

According to Gilman, then, civilization is intrinsically feminine. Had men not been feminized, they could never have become either human or civilized. In other words, Gilman was inverting the more common idea, which had so paralyzed her during her marriage, that civilization was intrinsically masculine, and woman's place in it merely reproductive. Gilman encouraged modern woman to be proud of the crucial and unrecognized role she had played in the evolution of civilization. "With a full knowledge of the initial superiority of her sex and the sociological necessity for its temporary subversion, she should feel only a deep and tender pride in the long patient ages during which she has waited and suffered, that man might slowly rise to *full racial equality with her.*"[82] Woman was not, in other words, merely ancillary to civilization's advancement, as so many assumed. She was the central factor which had allowed the race to rise. "Women can well afford their period of subjection for the sake of a conquered world, a civilized man."[83] Man would have remained a pathetic animal had woman not suffered and sacrificed to raise him to her racial level, and to civilize him.

Now, however, the men of the most advanced races had finally become truly civilized. The women of those advanced races, therefore, could abandon their excessive sex distinctions. And it was imperative that they do so! It was a question of racial survival. We have seen that the sexuo-economic relation held in it the seeds of racial destruction. This had happened before; highly civilized races had always become oversexed and degenerated, while new, fresher races had risen to take their place. But white Americans today had the scientific and historic knowledge to understand the dangers and to develop a newer, better form of sex relation. As Gilman put it, they could "grasp the fruits of all previous civilizations, and grow on to the beautiful results of higher ones."[84] White, native-born Americans could choose either women's sexual dependence, leading to racial decline and barbarism, or women's sexual equality, leading to racial advance and the highest civilization ever evolved.

Sexual equality was, thus, a racial necessity. The white American woman must now abandon her primitive domestic labors in order to take her place as a civilized member of the Anglo-Saxon race. As Gilman put it, "the long-subverted human female" was now ready to emerge "to full racial equality."[85] And Gilman did, indeed, mean full *racial* equality, with all the trappings of white racial supremacy. It was because white Anglo-Saxon men had reached a civilized status that white Anglo-Saxon women could now claim the right to be treated as equal members of a civilized race.

Gilman didn't need to specify "white races" in *Women and Economics.* White readers, familiar with the discourse of civilization, could confidently and correctly assume that when Gilman mentioned "civilization," "women," or "racial advancement," she meant white civilization, white women, and white racial advancement, even if she rarely used the word "white." If we look for her to say this explicitly in *Women and Economics* we find only hints and implications. For example, when Gilman described women's current push toward equality, she wrote that "women in the most advanced races are standing free." In other words, not all women were evolutionarily prepared to throw off the sexuo-economic relation—only women in the most advanced races.[86] Similarly, Gilman suggested that women's push for "full racial equality" was stronger in the United States than in any other country partly because American women were mostly Anglo-Saxon.[87]

When asked directly, however, Gilman unhesitatingly made her white supremacist assumptions explicit. In 1904, while lecturing on "Woman as a Factor in Civilization," Gilman was asked whether her analysis applied equally to Negroes and whites. No, it did not, Gilman replied. She explained that the evolutionary purpose of the sexuo-economic relation was to raise man to woman's level, thus making civilization possible. The Negro race, unlike the white, had not yet become completely civilized. Therefore, until the Negro man no longer needed to be forced to work to support his family,· "it was best for the negro woman to remain at home and for the man to support her for yet awhile."[88] (Four years later, Gilman would expand on this point in the *American Journal of Sociology,* arguing that until they were civilized, most American Negroes should be conscripted into forced-labor armies.[89]) The Negro man still needed the spur of sex to teach him the virtues of hard work and altruism—to civilize him. Until the Negro man was civilized, Gilman saw no point in demanding equality or economic independence for the Negro woman. Anglo-Saxon whites, on the other hand, were already highly civilized. It was therefore time for Anglo-Saxon woman to become economically independent of Anglo-Saxon man and to begin engaging in "race activity."

The best known sections of *Women and Economics*—Gilman's suggestions that housework, food preparation, and child care be performed by paid professionals—were simply practical proposals to extricate Anglo-Saxon women from the primitive, unspecialized home, and allow them to rejoin civilization. Anglo-Saxon women had been exiled from true civilization and kept artificially primitive in comparison to Anglo-Saxon men. They were confined to the home, which was organized along primitive and inefficient lines—forced to do the work of a "savage squaw." Gilman therefore devotes several chapters to practical suggestions about how to reorganize housework in ways which would not only civilize home life but also free Anglo-Saxon women to engage in Anglo-Saxon race activity. In short, permitting civilized woman to abandon her sexuo-economic dependence would not merely give her *sex equality*—that is, parity with man—it would also give her *full racial equality*. It would allow her to claim her birthright as an evolutionarily advanced Anglo-Saxon.

At the end of the book, Gilman encapsulates her argument with a graphically racial metaphor of miscegenation. By artificially keeping Anglo-Saxon women in a painfully primitive condition and refusing to allow them to claim their civilized racial heritage, their society was committing the "innate perversion" of "moral miscegenation."[90] This perverted racial mixing had led the race to all kinds of social turmoil and needed to be stopped.

> Marry a civilized man to a primitive savage, and their child will naturally have a dual nature. Marry an Anglo-Saxon to an African or Oriental, and their child has a dual nature. Marry any man of a highly developed nation, full of the specialized activities of his race . . . to the carefully preserved, rudimentary female creature he has so religiously maintained by his side, and you have as a result what we all know so well . . . the innate perversion of character resultant from the moral miscegenation of two so diverse souls. . . . We have been injured in body and in mind by the two dissimilar traits inherited from our widely separated parents.[91]

Of course, white America's fears of miscegenation in 1898 stemmed less from intermarriage and more from its terror of the "savage Negro rapist"— the modern version of Gilman's primal sexual terrorist. By stirring up white terrors of the primal rapist and of a racially impure civilization—those same terrors which Ida B. Wells was trying to eradicate—Gilman was marshaling the most powerful available racist images to argue against keeping white women marginal to civilization.

White America, in Gilman's eyes, remained stunted in its growth and thwarted in its evolutionary development because it had committed a crime against nature, the crime of miscegenation. The white American race was as conflicted as the literary "tragic mulatto"—unable to rise to its civilized destiny; kept down by its primitive heritage. Yet, unlike the tragic mulatto, the white American race could remake itself as racially pure. Anglo-Saxon women no longer needed to remain racial primitives. When race development replaced sex development, white women would become civilized, and moral miscegenation would be replaced with a eugenic marriage between racial equals.

In sum, *Women and Economics* was Gilman's solution to the neurasthenic

Fig. 11. Cartoon from the *London Morning Leader,* March 2, 1905, illustrating Gilman's views (presented in a lecture during one of her many tours) that by forcing women to remain in the home, society made women "savages" compared to active, "civilized" men. Courtesy the Schlesinger Library, Radcliffe College.

agonies she had suffered as a young woman, when she had been forced to choose between her race and her sex. When Dr. Mitchell had tried to confine her to the nursery and to exile her from civilization, Gilman had nearly lost her sanity. *Women and Economics* proved that she had suffered needlessly. Her physician and her society had posed a false dualism: there was no need for her to choose between her womanhood and her race. Women like herself were central to civilization—to its original development, to its past history, and above all, to its future advancement. As Anglo-Saxons, they had every right and every duty to contribute their all to civilization's future by taking part in what had erroneously been called "the male sphere." This was their racial duty, a duty they dared not shirk. For if white women remained domestic "squaws," in a state of savagery, civilization itself was doomed. It was their duty, both as members of their sex and as members of their race, to take up the struggle to advance civilization.

Gilman's basic assumptions about civilization were quite similar to Hall's. Both Gilman and Hall wanted to help the most advanced white races evolve toward a millennial future, using the mechanisms of Lamarckian evolution. Both framed their mission as a struggle to prevent overcivilized decadence. Both argued that perverted gender and excessive sex threatened their society with overcivilized decadence. Both looked to quasi-anthropological studies of "primitive" man to understand the meaning of modern civilization.

When it came to their views about civilization and manhood, however, Hall and Gilman drew completely opposite conclusions. Hall invoked "civilization" in order to strengthen masculinity. He believed civilization had weakened men and saw civilization's opposite, the primitive, as a source of powerful manhood. Gilman, however, had no interest in finding a source of powerful manhood—she believed manhood was far too powerful, as it was! Instead, she found in "civilization" a way to strengthen womanhood. According to her, men had unjustly appropriated civilization for themselves, leaving women only those marginal spheres of activity associated with sex and reproduction. Therefore, in *Women and Economics,* she depicted the primitive past as a time of sexual equality, when primitive woman possessed a vibrant power which, if restored, could counter civilization's repeated tendency to decadence and collapse. Both Hall and Gilman looked to the primitive for a lost primal strength, in other words; but Hall found a lost, powerful manhood, while Gilman found a lost, powerful womanhood.

Yet although Gilman and Hall disagreed completely about the relation of civilization to modern manhood, their characterizations of primitve masculinity were quite similar. The unfettered violence and passion that Hall hoped to find in primitive man were echoed in Gilman's figure of the primal savage rapist. Indeed, as we saw with Ida B. Wells and Jack Johnson, many whites shared Hall's and Gilman's view that primitive masculinity implied unfettered sexual violence. Even scholarly anthropologists assumed that primal man was a rapist and that promiscuity and sexual violence were characteristic of savage races. For example, anthropologist John McLennan asserted "savages" were promiscuous or even rapists: when an aboriginal Australian wanted a woman, according to McLennan, "he forces her to accompany him by blows, ending by knocking her down and carrying her off."[92] Hall had found something powerful and exciting in this unfettered primal passion. Gilman, on the other hand, found it entirely reprehensible. Like Ida B. Wells lecturing in England, she assumed that unbounded masculine passion was unmanly, uncivilized, and therefore despicable. Yet, as she would soon discover, many American men were becoming as intrigued as Hall by this passionate, primal masculinity.

The Man-Made World and Primal Masculinity: "Desire, Combat, and Self-Expression"

Gilman didn't stop at making women central to civilization. Not long after *Women and Economics* was published, Gilman began to argue that, compared to women, men were peripheral to civilized advancement. For years, men had considered women to be merely "the sex," devoted by evolution to reproduction, and had assumed that only men could advance the race. Yet Gilman insisted the opposite was true: it was men who were "the sex," while women were the ones with the greatest capacity to advance the race. Indeed, by exiling women from civilization, and keeping racial advancement to themselves, men—"the sex"—had distorted civilization by permeating it with male sex traits.

Gilman made these arguments in a number of different, sometimes contradictory, ways. Sometimes she invoked biology, drawing especially on sociologist Lester Ward's "gynaecocentric theory." Ward had argued that the true meaning of sexual difference could be found by looking at sex's origins among insects and other invertebrates. When these sexually undifferentiated creatures first evolved into male and female, males were puny, inferior creatures designed merely to fertilize the female, whereas females carried all the species' superior and characteristic traits. Indeed, Ward argued, the presexual creatures who reproduced parthenogenetically ought themselves be seen as female.[93] Thus, females were the original organisms who had advanced evolution, while males' original evolutionary purpose was solely reproductive.

Gilman seized upon Ward's theory to refute the widespread assumption that biology dictated females' function to be merely maternal. Indeed, the opposite was true! As she gleefully pointed out (returning again to the Garden of Eden), Ward's evolutionary origin theory completely reversed Genesis, with all its antifeminist implications. Woman was not created out of Adam's rib as a mere afterthought and helpmeet for man. On the contrary, evolution had created her first and had created males merely for purposes of procreation.

Our ideas are all based on the primal concept expressed in the Adam and Eve story—that he was made first, and that she was made to assist him. On this assumption rests all our social structure as it concerns the sexes. Reverse this idea once and for all; see that woman is in reality the race-type, and the man the sex-type, and all our dark and tangled problems of unhappiness, sin and disease, as between men and women, are cleared at once.[94]

Once society realized that common wisdom had it backwards—that it was *man* who was the "sex type," and *woman* who was the "race-type"—modern social problems could be cleared up and civilization could be perfected.

Yet although sometimes Gilman insisted that woman was the race-type and man merely a creature of sex, at other times she insisted that men and women were equally creatures of sex and that both had an equal capacity for meaningful contribution to civilization. Gilman explained this by redefining the concept of separate spheres. It wasn't true that woman's sphere was the home and man's sphere the world, as she had been taught as a child. Instead, she insisted that there were three distinct spheres which needed to be differentiated. "As a matter of fact, there is a 'woman's sphere,' sharply defined and quite different from his; there is also a 'man's sphere,' as sharply defined and even more limited; but there remains a common sphere—that of humanity, which belongs to both alike."[95] Gilman called for a new system of classification which would differentiate between these spheres and labeled them, "masculine, feminine, and human."

Gilman explained the differences between the masculine, feminine, and human spheres by invoking the difference between lower and higher evolution. "That is masculine which belongs to the male sex, as such; to any and all males, *without regard to species* . . . That is feminine which belongs to the female sex, as such *without regard to species.*"[96] By definition, then, masculine and feminine traits were traits which people shared with animals—traits which remained unchanged as species ascended the evolutionary ladder. These traits were intrinsically sexual: they referred to reproduction, which worked alike in all species. Thus, for Gilman, masculinity and femininity were simultaneously sexual and animalistic.

Another way to say this is that Gilman (like so many others in her culture) saw "masculinity" as a primal trait, expressed as perfectly in animals or savagery as in civilization. "The male savage," Gilman wrote in another context, "is 'masculine' enough surely; but he is little else."[97] Femininity, too, was as perfectly expressed in animals or in savagery as in civilization. As she argued in *Women and Economics,* excluding civilized women from race activity forced them to develop the primal femininity of savage "squaws," without the advanced human attributes of civilization.

Unlike "masculine" and "feminine," which referred to all species, however, "human" referred to only one species—the one which had the capacity to become civilized. Indeed, the higher a species or race advanced toward a perfect civilization, the more human it was. As Gilman defined it, "That is human which belongs to the human species, as such, *without regard to sex.* Through all organic life we find the distinction between species steadily increasing as we rise, till in our own we find such marked differences as have enabled us to become long since the dominant race on earth. It is in this race distinction that every thought of humanity inheres."[98] Race distinctions, such as higher intelligence, were the hallmarks which distinguished true humanity. "That degree of brain development which gives us the human mind is a clear distinction of race. The savage who can count a hundred is more human than the savage who can count ten."[99] Once again, Gilman insisted that as human evolution advanced it was the distinctions between races which counted, not the distinctions between the sexes.

In short, sometimes Gilman minimized the importance of sex difference (pointing instead to the centrality of race difference), while at other times she made sex difference central to her analysis (arguing that femininity expressed the race-type, while masculinity merely expressed sexuality). The contradictory implications of these positions never bothered Gilman, even when she used both models simultaneously, as she frequently did. In fact, as Gilman used them, these ostensible contradictions buttressed one another. The world's supposedly ineradicable problems, until now excused as "human nature," were in fact simply excess masculinity. Conversely, the normal racial work of the world, commonly seen as masculine, was really human: "The task here undertaken is . . . to show that what we have all this time called 'human nature' and deprecated was really male nature, and good enough in its place; [and] that what we have called 'masculine' and admired as such, was in large part human, and should be applied to both sexes."[100] Once woman was recognized as human and not merely feminine, she would be able to address the true cause of civilization's problems: excessive masculinity. This was the argument of *The Man-Made World.*

The Man-Made World; or Our Androcentric Culture (1911; published serially 1909–10) demonstrated how woman could perfect civilization by ridding it of excessive masculinity. Gilman defined masculinity as consisting of three basic traits: "In these studies we must keep clearly in mind the basic masculine characteristics: desire, combat, and self-expression."[101] Gilman's characterization of masculinity looked much like the figure of the original primitive rapist. Desire, combat, and self-expression—lust, violence, and egotism—defined the crime of the primal rapist. Thus, *The Man-Made World* elaborated on the argument, already presented in *Women and Economics,* that the development of the primitive rapist was the original source of evil in the world. Rooting her analysis in the biology of sex differences, Gilman demonstrated precisely how modern civilization had been warped and damaged by the primal rapist's excessive masculinity, which lived on in modern, civilized man.

Gilman's definition of "excess masculinity" as "desire, combat, and self-expression" was drawn from a number of respected scientific sources. One was Patrick Geddes and J. Arthur Thompson's influential 1889 treatise, *The Evolution of Sex.*[102] Geddes and Thompson, prominent British biologists, argued that the basic differences between males and females of all species stemmed from essential differences in their cell metabolism. Females were characterized by the "anabolic" tendency to store up or conserve energy, which made them loving, intuitive, patient, altruistic, and maternal. Males, on the other hand, were characterized by the "katabolic" tendency to dissipate or expend energy, which made them passionate, forceful, strong, and aggressive.

The Evolution of Sex thus gave biological authority to Victorian middle-class assumptions about sexual difference, both feminist and antifeminist. Geddes and Thompson themselves were antifeminists: "What was decided among the prehistoric Protozoa cannot be annulled by Act of Parliament," they archly told woman suffragists.[103] Yet Gilman, like many other feminists of her generation, found in *The Evolution of Sex* a far more positive view of female biology than that held by antifeminist authorities like S. Weir Mitchell. Where Mitchell and his colleagues believed women's energy-hungry reproductive systems threatened to drain their bodies of the nervous force necessary to advance civilization, Geddes and Thompson depicted women as biologically different from men, but equally valuable; and feminists embraced the idea that women's anabolic energy gave them valuable, civilized attributes like altruism which katabolic men lacked.[104] Conversely, Gilman drew from Geddes and Thompson a much more pejorative view of masculinity than they ever intended. "Desire, combat and self-expression [were] all legitimate and right in proper use," she argued. But when allowed to run rampant (as in the masculine figure of the primal rapist) they were "mischievous," "excessive," "out of place," and a danger to human advancement.[105]

In defining desire, combat, and self-expression as the three essential masculine characteristics, Gilman was also drawing on Darwin's theories of sexual selection. Darwin had identified two biological mechanisms of sexual selection: male battle and female choice. Some male animals fought each other to win the female's favor (male battle); other males developed gorgeous plumage or impressive antlers in order to attract females (female choice).[106] Desire was a masculine trait, in this scenario, because it was always the male who initiated sexual pursuit and mating. (Here Victorian scientists were projecting Victorian notions of feminine sexual passivity onto animals.) Combat was a masculine trait because males fought one another in order to attract the female. Self-expression was a masculine trait because male animals developed elaborate bodily sex decoration (like wattles or manes) or engaged in elaborate courting dances and other ostentatious behavior in order to convince females to choose them for a mate.

As Gilman saw it, desire, self-expression, and combat were excellent characteristics—but only for sexual selection. When male sexuality was allowed to run rampant, coloring nonreproductive aspects of life, something was definitely wrong. When men wanted more sex than was necessary for reproductive purposes, for example, or when they engaged in mating behavior in nonsexual, "human" spheres of life, all civilization suffered. Modern civilization now found itself in precisely this desperate condition. Male sexuality had run amok and was now out of control, perverting all civilization. Men had claimed all civilization as theirs and had refused to allow women to participate in the so-called male sphere, which was actually the human sphere.[107] By excluding women's anabolic energy, men had warped nearly every aspect of civilized life. Excluding femininity was especially harmful because the female, unlike the male, was the race-type, and therefore closer to the true essence of humanity than the katabolic male. Only by restoring woman to her true position in the human sphere could civilization's excess masculinity be counteracted and the race be returned to normal.[108]

The Man-Made World documented a myriad of ways these excessive masculine sex-traits had perverted civilized institutions. For example, man's excessive tendency toward self-expression had perverted the arts, so that now the focus was on the artist himself, rather than on the artwork's beauty. The "ultra-masculine artist . . . uses the medium of art as ingenuously as the partridge-cock uses his wings in drumming on the log, or the bull moose stamps and bellows; not narrowly as a mate call, but as a form of expression of his personal sensations."[109] Similarly, man's love of combat had led historians to study wars and conquest, instead of the more important topic of social history, "our racial life."[110] Masculinity's perverse hold on ethics—and the excessive influence of the masculine passions of sex and combat—could be gauged by the popular proverb, "All's fair in love and war."[111] Even religion had been distorted by man's tendency toward desire, combat, and self-expression.[112] "What has the male mind made of Christianity? Desire—to save one's own soul. Combat—with the Devil. Self-Expression—the whole gorgeous outpouring of pageant and display."[113]

Economics, too, had been distorted by man's "basic spirit of desire and of combat": "Long ages wherein hunting [for game] and fighting [over women] were the only manly occupations have left their heavy impress. The predacious instinct and the combative instinct weigh down and disfigure our economic development."[114] As we saw in *Women and Economics,* the impulse to labor was feminine, stemming from mothers' need to provide for their children. Men could only be convinced to labor by depicting productive work as a struggle for dominance, a sort of prizefight: "to the male mind, the antagonist is essential to progress, to all achievement. . . . If you have not the incentive of [sexual] reward, or the incentive of combat, why work?" The debilitating result of this excessive masculinity in economics was cutthroat capitalist competition and class war.

What had caused the development of all this morbid masculinity? In *The Man-Made World,* Gilman blamed the same figure that she had in *Women and Economics*—the original primal rapist. The "great fundamental error" of the man-made world had been to make man, instead of woman, the sexual selector. This fundamental error originated when man assumed the illicit authority "to be the possessor of women, their owner and master, able at will to give, buy and sell, or do with as he pleases."[115] Woman lost her intrinsic feminine ability to say yes or no to sex; and man developed his excessive sexuality. Making man the sexual selector was unnatural, however, because sexual selection was based on male competition and female choice. Femininity entailed the capacity to choose the fittest mate, but masculinity entailed no such skills. Females naturally selected males who possessed the greatest genetic qualifications for paternity. Males, on the other hand, saw sex in terms of competition, so they tended to breed indiscriminately. They chose females out of mere sex attraction, regardless of the effect on their offspring. They liked women fat, weak, and tiny—traits antithetical to racial advancement. Males' usurpation of feminine choice had thus caused the race to become physically degenerate.[116]

These evolutionary drawbacks of man-as-selector were epitomized in the figure of the primal rapist. When man took on the essentially feminine function of sexual selection, he allowed his sexual desire to run rampant, and this excessive masculinity had led to racial devolution.

> If there is a race between males for a mate—the swiftest gets her first; but if one male is chasing a number of females he gets the slowest one first. The one method improves our speed; the other does not. If males struggle and fight with one another for a mate, the strongest secures her; if the male struggles and fights with the female (a peculiar and unnatural horror, known only among human beings) he most readily secures the weakest. The one method improves our strength—the other does not.[117]

Gilman could envision only two possibilities. Either men obeyed the natural imperatives of sexual selection by fighting other men to win a woman's favor; or men fought women and raped them. One was natural; the other was original sin. (Believing desire to be an exclusively masculine sex characteristic, Gilman could not conceive of a scenario in which females competed sexually for males. She considered Freudianism perverted.) Woman must return to the natural position of sexual selector so that eugenic matings could become the rule, instead of the exception.[118] Man as sexual selector—as rapist— must be abolished.

Whereas Gilman had once been forced to choose between her race and her sex, *The Man-Made World* argued that *men* must now choose between their race and their sex. Masculinity, as it had evolved, was completely antithetical to racial advancement and higher civilization. As Gilman defined it, masculinity was not even human: civilized masculinity was the same as animal masculinity. Lust, egotism, and violence were its primary components. Among animals, lust, egotism, and violence were kept under control by female sexual selection, but among humans, overly sexual, quasi-rapist men had subjugated the female and allowed male sexuality to run amok. Male sexuality must be curbed to save the race from decadence and restore the true path of upward civilization.[119] Just as in *Women and Economics,* the original primal rapist, with his violence, egotism, and overwhelming sexual desire, remained the origin of absolute evil and racial decadence. The higher development of civilization depended on cleansing the world of the influence of the primitive male rapist.

Thus Gilman in 1909, like Ida B. Wells in 1894, mobilized a figure of unrestrained male passion to signify the absolute opposite of higher civilization. Like Wells she assumed that the unfettered lust and violence of this unmanly figure would be anathema to her middle-class audience. Yet middle-class culture had changed in the fifteen years since Wells had returned triumphant from England, as Gilman would soon discover. So crucial to Gilman's analysis was this oppositional relationship between civilization and its nemesis, the primal savage rapist, that she was uncharacteristically flustered when antifeminist men began to champion the primal rapist as an expression of primitive virility and masculine dominance.

Gilman Confronts "the Brute in Man"

By about 1912, a new and "savage" note began to sound more frequently in popular expressions of middle-class manhood. Increasingly, male power and authority were being described as wild, primitive, and not all endangered by overcivilized decadence. Theodore Roosevelt had returned in triumph from his African safari; Edgar Rice Burroughs' *Tarzan of the Apes* had been published; and Charlotte Perkins Gilman was forced to come to terms with a popular image of primitive masculinity which, like hers, was based on combat, egotism, and desire, but which, unlike hers, was seen not as a reproach to, but as a legitimate source of, male dominance.

The middle-class interest in masculine primitivism was, of course, hardly new in 1914. We have already seen it in Hall's interest in boyhood primitivism and in the figure of the "natural man" so pervasive in journalists' accounts of lynching. Gilman herself had criticized it twenty years earlier. In 1894, she had attacked two popular symbols of primal masculinity by linking them to racial primitivism. Prizefighting, she wrote, showed the decay of civilization, and she quoted a press report condemning a New Orleans prizefight as "a scene of savagery which would not have been out of place in the heart of Africa."[120] She also objected to descriptions of bodybuilder Eugene Sandow as "the perfect man." Perfect manhood, in her opinion, implied development of the higher racial faculties which made man civilized. "It is good to see a man strong, healthy, well-developed—all men should be that at least; but to make beauty, much more perfection, requires more than this. The Dahomeyan is strong, healthy and well-developed; so is the Esquimaux; so is the Apache; so is many a proud athlete of the ring and track. But beauty is more, far more."[121] It wasn't physical culture that bothered Gilman: she was a great advocate of physical fitness for both men and women. Rather the celebration of manhood as primitive violence and mere physicality seemed to her racially atavistic and hostile to the primacy of civilization. In a rare use of the word, she even described prizefighting as lacking "manliness"—manliness, as we have seen, being commonly associated with "civilization."

Between 1894 and 1912, Gilman usually addressed the growing interest in primitive masculinity indirectly, if at all. Either she told origin stories depicting primitive man in the most unflattering light, as she did in *Women and Economics;* or she constructed primitive masculinity as the opposite of civilized advancement, as she did in *The Man-Made World.* Yet even as she wrote, a growing subcurrent in middle-class culture was constructing the capacity for selfish aggressiveness and sexual predation as an essential characteristic of the natural man. Many men who feared that excessive civilization was threatening American manhood continued to look to this "natural" masculinity for an antidote to effeminacy.

In a 1904 editorial in the *Woman's Journal,* Gilman attacked this figure of the natural man by likening him to the figure of the black male rapist. As we have seen in the Wells chapter, apologists for lynch mobs frequently asserted that the mobs were simply made up of "natural men" whose innate chivalry was so outraged by [alleged] black rapists that they were forced to lynch them. In this editorial, Gilman expressed only lukewarm opposition to lynching, but she vigorously attacked this idea of the innate chivalry of natural man. She insisted that it was not "natural" for men to protect women from rape, because it was entirely unnatural for women to lack the power to protect themselves, in the first place! Woman only began to need man's protection after the primal rapist had unnaturally subjugated her. By linking the "chivalrous" Southerner of the lynch mob—with his insistence on feminine dependence—to the original primal rapist, Gilman was implicitly likening the chivalrous white man to the unmanly "Negro rapist." In 1904, Gilman confidently assumed that this argument would be effective: no civilized white man would want to emulate the "Negro rapist," with his inferior and uncivilized lack of manhood.[122]

Gilman's confidence in the primacy of civilized manliness was misplaced, however. After 1912, she was forced to confront a more virulent figure of the natural man when antifeminist men began to glorify the primal savage rapist as a final answer to the woman suffragists. In 1911 militant English suffragists, led by Christabel Pankhurst, had declared a "Woman's War" on the male establishment, which culminated in 1912–14 with a systematic campaign of arson, vandalism, and destruction of private property. Horrified, the self-styled "civilized world" watched respectable upper- and middle-class Englishwomen smashing plateglass windows, fighting policemen, and going to jail. Antisuffragist men, distraught at the ostensibly oxymoronic prospect of violent femininity, began to look to the ubiquitous "natural man" to claim for themselves an even more violent masculinity which could overpower these "unnatural" women—a masculinity rooted in the primitive.

Two of the most vocal spokesmen for this position, both eminent scientists, were Sir Almroth Wright and Dr. William T. Sedgwick. Gilman detested them both and repeatedly invoked them as examples of the worst sort of antifeminism. Wright, a respected British bacteriologist who was offended by the suffragettes' destruction of property, penned an especially nasty attack on them in March 1912 which was published as a three-column letter to the *London Times*. Wright's column caused such an uproar in Britain that the National League for Opposing Women's Suffrage reprinted it as a pamphlet; Wright later expanded it into a full-length book, *The Unexpurgated Case against Women's Suffrage*. Accounts of the controversy and substantial excerpts from both letter and book were widely reported in the American press.[123]

Wright's most controversial assertions concerned men's right to use violence against women. Although chivalrous treatment of women was "of all the civilising agencies at work in the world . . . the most important," Wright opined, the feminists were mistaken if they assumed that respectful treatment was due women merely by virtue of their sex. Chivalry was a *contract* between men and women, and as such, could be broken. "When a man makes this compact with a woman, 'I will do you reverence, and protect you, and yield you service; and you, for your part, will hold fast to an ideal of gentleness, of personal refinement, of modesty, of joyous maternity, and [of] who shall say what other graces and virtues that endear woman to man,' that is *chivalry*."[124] If either sex broke this compact, all bets were off. When woman became violent, unrefined, ungrateful, or "when she places a quite extravagantly high estimate upon her intellectual powers," the contract was broken. Woman must then bear the brunt of unfettered masculine violence. "One always wonders if the suffragist appreciates all that woman stands to lose and all that she imperils by resort to physical force. One ought not to have to tell her that, if she had to fight for her position, her status would be that which is assigned to her among the Kaffirs—not that which civilised man concedes to her."[125] While it was a centuries-old truism that civilized women were sheltered from the hard labor which savage women had to perform, Wright's reference to "Kaffirs"—black South Africans—was surely a veiled reference to the figure of the black male rapist. If white women convinced white men to abandon chivalry, white men would be free to assault women just as the "Kaffirs" did.

Gilman was taken aback when Wright and his supporters claimed this affinity with the violent primal rapist. Gilman, too, believed that masculinity consisted of desire, egotism, and violence, but she never expected civilized men like Wright to agree with her so unashamedly. Soon after the publication of Wright's *Unexpurgated Case,* Gilman warned her readers of a "note of . . . frankly sinister import" among the antisuffragists. Inexplicably, antisuffragists were making arguments which seemed more comfortable in the mouths of the angriest feminists. "We are told that 'the brute in man' lies very near the surface and that women should have a care lest they tempt it too far and bring it forth in all its blind fury. If the suffragists themselves said this it would quite possibly be considered malicious and unfair, but it is said by the cautious editorial gentlemen who deprecate these violent maneuvers of belligerent Englishwomen." Gilman tried to turn the "brute in man" argument back against the antisuffragists by accusing them of proving the feminists' point: men's brutal treatment of the imprisoned suffragettes provided yet another "addition to that long black list of grievances which are at last rousing some women to acts of violence."[126] Yet if antisuffragists didn't *mind* being called brutes—if masculine brutality became an argument against woman suffrage instead of for it—Gilman needed to rethink her position.

Soon after the *Unexpurated Case* appeared as a book, Wright's veiled rape threat was repeated by the eminent American epidemiologist, Dr. William T. Sedgwick.[127] Sedgwick felt free to make his rape threat more explicit, possibly because in the United States, the popular discussion of the mythic black male rapist and the virtues of Southern lynching had already made the primal rapist a quasi-acceptable image of "natural man."

Speaking as a scientific expert—he was the head of Massachusetts Institute of Technology's department of biology and public health—Sedgwick rooted his argument in biology and, in a full-page *New York Times* interview, managed to employ all the antifeminist arguments Gilman most detested. Feminism was unscientific "biological bosh." Reproductive physiology fitted women to be only wives and mothers. Extreme sexual difference was the hallmark of advanced evolution.

> In the evolutionary process that nature has been carrying on through untold thousands of years, the development has on the whole been toward a greater differentiation of two sexes. On some of the lowest rungs of life's ladder are amoeba and other microbes that reproduce by parthogenesis—i.e. by birth without the cooperation of male and female elements. [Gilman and Lester Ward

had celebrated these as the original females, giving birth with no need for male help.] On the top rung is mankind in which the differentiation of sex and the reaction of sex upon both mind and body become strikingly complete.[128]

Here was precisely the antifeminist biology Gilman had worked so hard to refute with her own biological theories and origin stories.

Pivotal for Sedgwick, as it had been for Gilman, was the figure of the original primitive rapist. Sedgwick's story of human origins, like Gilman's account of the fall of man, begins at the prehistoric moment when primitive man first discovered he could rape women. Gilman saw this as the original sin, warping human development from then on, but Sedgwick saw this primal rape as merely a compelling example of natural man's inherent power, savagery, and sexual aggression. As man evolved and became civilized, his innate savagery was tamed by pure romantic love, and he developed chivalry toward women. But this civilized chivalry, according to Sedgwick, was all that protected modern woman from the naked masculine aggression of the original primal rapist. "Let the so-called 'advanced' but really retrogressive women carry on their crusade for a generation or two more," Sedgwick warned. Let men and women meet as economic competitors. Let marriage die and free love run rampant. Let women get involved in the fierce struggle of political life.

> Then will women indeed find that the knightliness and chivalry of gentlemen have vanished, and in their stead will arise a rough male power that will place women where it chooses. With all sense of chivalry, of tenderness, of veneration gone, and nothing but fleshly desire left, the status to which that masculine strength may relegate woman will be a subjection in fact, and not merely in theory. There is no dodging this hard, cold fact: man possesses always the brute strength; strip him of his chivalry, his tenderness and his respect for womanhood, and you leave naked, unfettered, and unashamed his more brutal appetites toward woman.[129]

If women continued to claim their own power, a "rough male power," rooted in primal masculinity, would rise up and effortlessly "place women where it chooses." Naked and unashamed, Sedgwick's primitive masculine rapist emerged from the distant moment of human origins to threaten modern feminists with the fate of their distant foremothers: a "subjection in fact" to man's most "brutal appetites."

As it always did in appeals to pure but corrupted origins, racial decadence loomed. "Any such state of affairs would mean a reversal of the whole social evolutionary process. As to what the ultimate outcome will be no one need be in doubt. The world is not long going to retrograde, but a single nation, a race, a civilization can." Racial decadence and the devolution of civilization threatened—for Sedgwick, as it had for Gilman. Here indeed was a threat to human evolutionary progress! Strip civilized man of his chivalry—his Christian, civilized manliness—and he would revert to the violent sexual brutality of his most distant forebear, to the masculine primitive. Manliness was merely a veneer over the natural man's essential violent masculinity, just as civilization was merely a veneer over his essential savagery. Sedgwick's return to the moment of human origins (and thus, to the essential truth about man) was not a return to Eden (as Gilman's was), but a menacing return to Chaos.

True to its classic form, however, Sedgwick's jeremiad held out a hope of salvation. If the race returned to the original intentions of evolution and biology, redemption and civilized advancement were certain. To escape racial decadence and the decline of American civilization, men must assert their dominance and force women to devote themselves to domesticity. "Long before any such sorry state of affairs becomes an actuality, man, seeing the things he most cherishes in danger of destruction, will firmly shut down on the Feminist activities, and putting the women back in their homes say: That is where you belong. Now stay there." Sedgwick's ultimate solution is thus Gilman's original problem: men imprisoning women in the home, exiling them from higher civilization.

Here in a nutshell was every argument Gilman most detested, yet they rested on her own views of masculinity. Sedgwick insisted that women's reproductive physiology precluded their participating in the wider civilization; that civilized advancement rested on the widest possible exaggeration of sexual differences; that woman belonged only in the home. At the same time, however, Sedgwick's premises about masculinity were disturbingly like Gilman's. Both agreed masculinity was composed of desire, egotism, and combat. Yet Gilman assumed men would be ashamed of that fact, while Sedgwick clearly relished modern man's kinship to the primal rapist. "There is a lot of the primitive in all of us, both men and women," he insisted; women enjoyed "being mastered," and men enjoyed "mastering" them.

Sedgwick's opinions touched off an extensive reaction in the United States, just as Wright's had in England. The *New York Times* praised Sedgwick for openly saying "things which have not been said before so plainly."[130] Feminists were less complimentary. Ida M. Metcalf wrote a letter to the editor asking whether, in the combative "charming . . . future civilization" Sedgwick envisioned, "all men unable to hold their own against a prize-fighter will be forcibly subdued and held in subjection?" This was a low blow. In 1914, when Metcalf wrote, the most famous American prizefighter was the exiled but still undefeated Jack Johnson, and white men remained uncomfortably aware that prizefighting was an unstable way to assert white male dominance. "Apparently the dictum of science, as expressed by this prophet, is that we are evolving backward toward the ancestor we share with the gorilla," she continued.[131] Several professors of medicine and physiology called Sedgwick's opinions bad science: men and women were not as different as he suggested.[132]

Gilman devoted two articles to condemning Sedgwick's ideas. The first, a March 1914 article entitled "The Biological Anti-Feminist," failed to disarm Sedgwick's threat to unleash the primal rapist. It began by stressing the distinction between race and sex, in order to refute the primacy Sedgwick placed on sexual difference.[133] In the past, men had invoked the "convenient Hebrew legend" of Adam and Eve in order to avoid seeing the truth about woman, but today "they have learned that the rib-and-apple story can scarce be quoted as an account of real facts in human origin and conduct," so they invent other origin tales.[134] Instead of spurious religion, they now turned to spurious science for an explanation of origins—to the ridiculous story that sexual difference increased as evolution advanced. This was untrue. A biologist like Sedgwick ought to know that it was "the increase in race characteristics which accompanies the development of the higher orders," and not the increase in sex characteristics. Once again, Gilman had returned to the point she had made in *Women and Economics*: civilized women should be seen in terms of their race, not their sex.

Gilman moved on to address Sedgwick's claim that chivalry protected (in Sedgwick's terms) "all women—womenkind." Balderdash. It didn't protect nonwhite women, whose menfolk were barbarians or savages: "We will leave out savages—they have not evolved. We will leave out all Asia—it is not perhaps claimed for the Orient." Moreover, Gilman pointed out, chivalry didn't protect civilized white women, either, despite the fact that chivalry was, allegedly, an attribute of civilization. Gentlemen seduced women poorer and weaker than themselves; employers paid their factory girls starvation wages; men accosted women in the street. "'Deeply ingrained in man's nature' indeed is this sweet tenderness," she jeered. Above all, chivalry must be a very poor thing if the moment woman varied from the demanded type, chivalrous man threatened wholesale rape. And Gilman quoted Sedgwick's bald assertion: "man possesses always the brute strength; strip him of his chivalry . . . and you leave naked, unfettered, and unashamed, his more brutal appetites."[135]

Here was the main point—Sedgwick's threat to unleash the primal rapist, naked, unfettered, and unashamed, upon the feminists. Men like Sedgwick insisted this "Brute" was "natural man," an essential, animalistic, masculine primitive who lurked within all men. Gilman, however, insisted the "Brute" was *unnatural*—characteristic only of the excessive masculinity which the sexuo-economic relation had bred into human beings. Male animals were instinctively respectful of their females' "superior value . . . to the race" as mothers. "No other male animal uses the strength and pugnacity developed by sex-combat between males for the unnatural dominance of the female which distinguishes our species." This was a "morbid phase" in *human* development, alone. As evolution advanced, it would pass, along with all the other distortions of oversexed masculinity.

Yet Gilman closed her article on an uneasy note. If civilized men cheerfully threatened to unleash their savage "Brute"—if men could no longer be shamed out of acting like the primal rapist—what should women do? Must they remain at men's mercy, and was woman's advancement doomed? Gilman had no viable solutions. Halfheartedly, she suggested women should carry daggers and pistols to defend themselves.[136] Literal sex war was not a solution she cherished, however; she had long argued combat was a masculine, not a feminine, sex characteristic. Gilman thus winds up as she began—unsure how to refute men who, like Sedgwick and Wright, were proud to claim man was intrinsically violent, in order to discredit feminism. Her old arguments against overly powerful, sexually rapacious masculinity were useless against "the Brute in Man."

About a year later, perhaps realizing the futility of her previous strategy, Gilman took an entirely different approach, and tried to defang the Brute with humor. In a popular magazine article, "What the 'Threat of Man' Really Means," she completely and improbably reversed her long-standing characterization of masculinity, and denied that civilized man bore any resemblance at all to the savage rapist.[137] Man's threat to unleash upon the world the "Brute in Man" was not a serious threat, as she had once argued; it was merely "funny." Here was modern man, portraying himself as an animal, with brutal passions poised to strike down menacing feminists. "Where is the joke, you ask? The joke is at home with you—at the table, peacefully eating, with propriety and ease; in the parlor, sitting under the evening lamp, reading paper, magazine or book, perhaps reading aloud to you and the children. . . . It grew up at your knee and you put on its little first trousers, and taught it how to button and unbutton them." Man a primitive rapist? Heavens, no! He was civilized, sitting in the parlor! Man a threat? Ridiculous! He was just a helpless little boy. Gilman could not have produced an image of man more benign—or more unlike all her previous images. Man was not a primal rapist, a figure of menacing sexuality. He lacked even the mastery to unbutton his own pants.

Gilman could not entirely jettison all her old arguments about masculinity. She conceded that men had sex characteristics that might, at first glance, appear alarming. Men were, to be sure, "more pugnacious than females, and more active . . . in their desires"; their fathers had left them a legacy of sexual excess which made it difficult for them to control their lusts. Yet now Gilman made light of this, suggesting that men could be taught to keep their primitive sexual impulses under control. "Even a Brute may be tamed and made useful, as the dog, for instance."

Yet there remained the niggling fear: What if man, unlike the dog, refused to be "tamed and made useful?" So Gilman reduced the threat to absurdity by taking it literally. "Now let us look at our joke from another standpoint. Suppose men really were as awful as they like to think." Suppose man really was a brute. "Man, run away with by his unbridled Brute, is supposed to fall upon [woman] promiscuous-like—a sort of Rape of the Sabines—in continuous performance." Precisely who would men rape? Most men are married—would they rape their own wives? Would they rape each other's wives? Would the other Brutish husbands stand idly by? Would they all desert their wives? Or would the Brutes all be bachelors, and their victims unmarried damsels? Would these damsels' brothers and fathers stand for it? Again, Gilman reduced the snarling Brute in Man to a small boy struggling to unbutton his pants: his grandiose plans were all very well, but the dear just wasn't being *practical*.

Then Gilman made a threat of her own, putting the Brute in his place like a benevolent mother outmonstering her rampaging son at bedtime. "Listen, listen carefully, O Threatening Male! There is a Brute in women, too! Not so big a one perhaps, but still strong, not so fierce a one perhaps, but fierce enough. Do those who make this silly threat, this humorous, absurd, impossible threat, imagine that the women of to-day would submit to the Brute in Man like those same Sabines?" Civilized women were not weak or frightened—they would calmly refuse to put up with any such Brutish behavior.

So all was well, and the article ended reassuringly. "The Brute in man is not so ferocious as he thinks. It is there, and at times rebellious, but the Human in man is as much stronger than the Brute in man as a horse is stronger than his ancestral eohippus." Man had become civilized, as the tiny eohippus had become a horse. The primal rapist—the Brute in Man—was no danger to civilized woman.

Yet although Gilman dismissed Sedgwick and Wright's argument by ridiculing it, there are signs she remained disturbed at the direction new formulations of manhood were taking. For example, her suggestion that husbands and brothers would protect women from rape stood in stark contrast to her customary insistence that women needed no help from chivalrous men to protect themselves. Similarly, her depiction of man as a civilized dear contrasted with her usual definition of masculinity as combat, egotism, and desire.

Most tellingly, she made a major character in her 1915 novel *Herland*, Terry, represent the new type of man who celebrated his masculine "Brute."[138] The misogynistic Terry is lustful, egotistical, and combative.[139] More important, he remains an untamable threat. *Herland*'s turning point comes when Terry attempts to rape the woman he loves, who has refused to allow him to "master" her. For this sin, Terry (like the primal rapist of *Women and Economics'* "Proem") is expelled from the Edenic Herland. Yet unlike the "funny" Brute in the *Pictorial Review* article, Terry remains proudly incorrigible, a Brutish, unrepentant primal rapist. Gilman depicts him sneering at the powerful women of Herland who had mastered him: "'Sexless, epicene, undeveloped neuters!' he went on bitterly. He sounded like Sir Almwroth Wright." (And, lest the reference be missed, Gilman twice compares Terry to Wright.)[140] The fictional Herland could expel the Brute, but Gilman was aware that she and her contemporaries could not dispatch the figure of the thrillingly masculine primal rapist so easily.

Gilman had argued that woman was the race, and man was the sex; woman was civilization, and man was the savage. But Wright and Sedgwick had taken the cultural ground from beneath her feet. Both men were delighted to be considered "the sex" and the savage; as they saw it, this proved men had the inherent primal strength and potency to compel women to comply with their demands. They insisted that civilization could only continue its advance if women were forced to return to the home—forced to renounce their claims to the vote, to civic rights, to the masculine rights and privileges of civilization. Thus, as Wright and Sedgwick paradoxically described it, civilization itself depended on men's capacity for masculine savagery. It was because civilized white men retained the primal masculine violence of the savage rapist that Sedgwick and Wright saw a future for civilization.

In the final analysis, then, Wright and Sedgwick argued that civilized men's inherent capacity for masculine savagery was the ultimate legitimation of man's power over women, the final proof that man, but not woman, had the strength to dominate civilization. With an increasing number of middle-class men eager to see themselves in this light, Gilman's strategy of denigrating white men as unmanly and oversexed lost its power, and her critique of masculine dominance became ever less persuasive. By the 1920s, Gilman's critique of masculinity could barely get a hearing, while the middle class' fascination with the sexually uncontrolled masculine primitive had given power to new cultural figures like Rudolph Valentino's nostril-flaring, Englishwoman-kidnapping, lustful Arab sheik.

Conclusion

From the beginning, Gilman's strategy for achieving woman's advancement had rested on the white supremacism of the civilization discourse. In order to fight the truly debilitating discourses of gender which had kept her mother poor and dependent, and which had forced her, as a young wife, to choose between marriage and productive work, or, as she saw it, between her sex and her race, Gilman had revised the way civilization positioned the categories of gender and race. In so doing, she made a powerful argument for woman's advancement, but one which addressed the advancement of only white, Anglo-Saxon women.

As a feminist theorist, Gilman was both brilliant and, from our perspective, deeply flawed. No woman of her time wrote with more insight about the very real barriers white women faced in their quest to participate productively in the world outside their homes. Few proposed more sweeping and innovative reforms to make that participation possible. Probably no feminist theorist of her day was more influential or convinced more American women to embrace the cause of women's advancement.

Gilman's rewriting of the civilization discourse was crucial to her success as a feminist theorist. Gilman fully understood both the ideological power and the material implications of the masculinist discourse of civilization. It legitimized excluding women from activities they were working hard to join and damaged women economically and psychically. She herself had suffered from it as a young woman, when she contracted the "neurasthenia" which she believed tortured her for the rest of her life. By rewriting civilization and making white women central to civilization's advancement, she believed she was removing a major obstacle to the advancement of both women and "the race." In other words, she understood that "civilization," as a discourse, had material results on women's lives, and, by revising the ideology, she hoped to ultimately revise the practices.

Yet on a very basic level, Gilman was merely proposing to replace one kind of exclusion with another. White women's inclusion in civilization, under her scheme, was predicated on the exclusion of nonwhite men and women. According to Gilman, the key to understanding the legitimacy of women's claim for sexual equality was to understand that Anglo-Saxon women were, first and foremost, members of a superior race, and therefore equally able to participate in an advanced civilization. Civilized women had far more in common with civilized men than with primitive women of "lower" races. Therefore, white women must be able to participate in all the "racial" activities so necessary to the millennial quest for human evolutionary advancement. Writing in the tradition of the racist woman suffragists who argued that educated, refined white women deserved the vote far more than nonwhite men, Gilman based her feminism less on a liberal inclusiveness than on an insistence that the wrong criteria were being applied in civilization's exclusivity. "Let us in, but keep them out" was her true message.

For about twenty years, this racist feminism served Gilman and her followers very well. As Zona Gale put it, Gilman's theories "lit to energy many thousand of the unaware, the indolent, the oblivious, and made of them socially conscious beings."[141] Yet, ironically, by 1920, this racial basis of Gilman's feminism had contributed materially to its loss of effectiveness. It wasn't that white people rejected Gilman's racism: racism itself remained as strong as ever. Yet white women were realizing that it got them nowhere to claim that they were as civilized as men, because middle-class white men were increasingly uninterested in constructing male power in terms of advanced civilization and racial refinement. Instead, white men were defining male power in terms of the primal masculinity they shared with men of more primitive races. Men like Wright and Sedgwick enjoyed imagining themselves in terms of the combativeness, savagery, and sexual potency of the figure of the primitive rapist.

In this context, Gilman's old arguments in favor of women's advancement lost their effectiveness. White feminist women would get nowhere by comparing their advanced, civilized qualities to men's despicable primitive beastliness when antifeminist men were proudly claiming the figure of the primitive rapist was the original antifeminist who would rape the feminists into submission if they did not voluntarily return to domesticity. The middle class' new interest in primitivism as a source of masculinity weakened

Gilman's most important claim: that Anglo-Saxon men ought to see Anglo-Saxon women as racially akin to them, and to see this racial similarity as far more important than sexual difference. By 1920, some middle-class white men would take precisely the opposite position, finding an imagined kinship with African American men of the Harlem Renaissance precisely because they believed they found in them a common, primitive, cross-race, sexualized masculinity.[142] Harlem became, for many middle-class New Yorkers, an intriguingly exotic place of sexually exciting nightclubs. Most white American men, of course, remained unwilling to claim kinship with African Americans in the 1920s; yet as primitive masculinity became increasingly compatible with civilized manliness, Gilman's claim that white women were as civilized as white men—equally superior to the lower races—became increasingly irrelevant to middle-class formulations of male dominance.

By 1920, Gilman was being forgotten. It is perhaps not coincidental that as her analyses fell rapidly out of favor after World War I, she became increasingly convinced of two points: the dangers of unleashed sexuality, and the extreme importance of racial difference. She saw the 1920s' celebration of sexuality as a masculinity more excessive than any she had ever imagined, a masculinity which misguided women were foolishly emulating. Equally bad, the old racial distinctions—the bedrock of her claim for women's advancement—were being entirely ignored; the entire nation was being swamped by an influx of "inferior" races, and no one cared. Both, to her mind, were evidence that the essential values of "civilization" were being betrayed.[143] And she was right: by 1920 the civilization discourse she had studied as a girl had indeed lost much of its power.

Gilman's attack on male dominance had depended on the argument that the shared racial bonds between civilized men and civilized women far outweighed primitive, animalistic, sexual difference. She was therefore both lost and defeated when, in the 1920s, white men began to believe that nature intended men to dominate women, and that the proof lay in the "primitive, animalistic" sexual aggressiveness they believed civilized men shared with black men and Arab sheiks. Gilman's story suggests once again how tightly turn-of-the-century American culture interwove issues of gender and race.

5

Theodore Roosevelt: Manhood, Nation,
and "Civilization"

In 1882, a newly elected young state assemblyman arrived in Albany. Theodore Roosevelt, assuming his first elective office, was brimming with self-
importance and ambition. He was only twenty-three—the youngest man in
the legislature—and he looked forward to a promising career of wielding
real political power. Yet Roosevelt was chagrined to discover that despite his
intelligence, competence, and real legislative successes, no one took him seriously. The more strenuously he labored to play "a man's part" in politics,
the more his opponents derided his manhood.[1]

Daily newspapers lampooned Roosevelt as the quintessence of effeminacy. They nicknamed him "weakling," "Jane-Dandy," "Punkin-Lily," and
"the exquisite Mr. Roosevelt." They ridiculed his high voice, tight pants, and
fancy clothing. Several began referring to him by the name of the well-
known homosexual Oscar Wilde, and one actually alleged (in a less-than-
veiled phallic allusion) that Roosevelt was "given to sucking the knob of an
ivory cane."[2] While TR might consider himself a manly man, it was becoming humiliatingly clear that others considered him effeminate.

Above all other things, Roosevelt desired power. An intuitive master of
public relations, he knew that his effeminate image could destroy any
chances for his political future. Nearly forty years before women got the vote,
electoral politics was part of a male-only subculture, fraught with symbols of
manhood.[3] Besides, Roosevelt, who considered himself a man's man, detested having his virility impugned. Although normally restrained, when he
discovered a Tammany legislator plotting to toss him in a blanket, TR
marched up to him and swore, "By God! if you try anything like that, I'll kick
you, I'll bite you, I'll kick you in the balls, I'll do anything to you—you'd
better leave me alone!"[4] Clearly, the effeminate "dude" image would have
to go.

And go it did. Roosevelt soon came to embody powerful American manhood. Within five years, he was running for mayor of New York as the

170

"Cowboy of the Dakotas." Instead of ridiculing him as "Oscar Wilde," newspapers were praising his virile zest for fighting and his "blizzard-seasoned constitution."[5] In 1898, after a brief but highly publicized stint as leader of a regiment of volunteers in the Spanish American War, he became known as Colonel Roosevelt, the manly advocate of a virile imperialism. Never again would Roosevelt's name be linked to effeminacy. Even today, historians invoke Roosevelt as the quintessential symbol of turn-of-the-century masculinity.[6]

Roosevelt's great success in masculinizing his image was due, in large part, to his masterful use of the discourse of civilization. As a mature politician, he would build his claim to political power on his claim to manhood. Skillfully, Roosevelt constructed a virile political persona for himself as a strong but civilized white man.

Yet Roosevelt's use of the discourse of civilization went beyond mere public relations: Roosevelt drew on "civilization" to help formulate his larger politics as an advocate of both nationalism and imperialism. As he saw it, the United States was engaged in a millennial drama of manly racial advancement, in which American men enacted their superior manhood by asserting imperialistic control over races of inferior manhood. To prove their virility, as a race and a nation, American men needed to take up the "strenuous life" and strive to advance civilization—through imperialistic warfare and racial violence if necessary.

Thus, TR framed his political mission in terms of race and manhood, nationalism and civilization. Like G. Stanley Hall and Charlotte Perkins Gilman, Roosevelt longed to lead evolution's chosen race toward a perfect millennial future. Yet Roosevelt harbored larger ambitions than either Hall or Gilman. Hall merely wanted to develop a pedagogy that would produce the "super-man." Gilman only wanted to revolutionize society by civilizing women. Roosevelt, on the other hand, yearned to be the virile leader of a manly race and to inspire his race to wage an international battle for racial supremacy. He hoped that, through this imperialistic evolutionary struggle, he could advance his race toward the most perfect possible civilization. This, for Roosevelt, was the ultimate power of manhood.[7]

Civilized Manliness and Violent Masculinity: Claiming the Power of a Man

From early boyhood, Roosevelt longed for the authority of a powerful man. Like the young G. Stanley Hall, young Roosevelt learned early that achieving real manhood required serious attention and strenuous effort. The boy Teedie (as Theodore was called as a child) learned that male power was composed of equal parts kindhearted manly chivalry and aggressive masculine violence.[8]

On the one hand, Roosevelt grew up committed to Victorian codes of bourgeois manliness. He identified this Victorian moral manliness with his adored father, "the best man I ever knew. He combined strength and courage with gentleness, tenderness and great unselfishness. . . . He made us understand that the same standard of clean living was demanded for the boys as for the girls; that what was wrong in a woman could not be right in a man."[9] His father's unselfish, self-restrained manliness expressed itself, in part, through an upper-class sense of noblesse oblige: the senior Roosevelt devoted himself extensively to philanthropic activity, especially on behalf of New York's poor street urchins.[10] Yet Roosevelt's father also taught his son that this unselfish, charitable manliness implied a certain authority over the lower orders. On a trip to Italy, for example, he showed eleven-year-old Teedie a game of tossing broken pieces of cake into the open mouths of a crowd of hungry beggars. Teedie recorded the fun in his diary: "I fed them like chickens with small pieces of cake and like chickens they ate it. Mr. Stevens kept guard with a whip with which he pretended to whip a small boy. . . . For a 'Coup de Grace' we threw a lot of them in a place and a writhing heap of human beings."[11] Throughout his life, TR would cherish this Victorian ideology of moral manliness—strength, altruism, self-restraint, and chastity—and identify it with both the manful strength of his father and his own authority as a member of the upper class.

At the same time young Teedie was learning the virtues of unselfish, moral Victorian manliness, he was also attracted to a more violent masculinity. Like other exponents of "natural man," Teedie associated this sort of masculinity with "nature." One morning in 1865, when Teedie was about seven, he suddenly came upon the body of a dead seal, laid out on a slab in a Broadway market. The little boy was enthralled, and later described discovering the seal as an epiphany—the adventure which started him on his career as a naturalist. To the delicate, sickly boy, the dead animal seemed a tangible link to the aggressive, masculine world of boys' adventure novels. "That seal filled me with every possible feeling of romance and adventure," he recalled. "I had already begun to read some of Mayne Reid's books and other boys' books of adventure, and I felt that this seal brought all these adventures in realistic fashion before me."[12]

Why should a young boy see a dead animal as a representation of "romance and adventure"? To understand why Teedie associated dead animals, "nature," and manhood, we can look at Mayne Reid's *The Boy Hunters; or Adventures in Search of a White Buffalo,* one of Teedie's favorite books.[13] Reid's three young heroes are "hunter-naturalists" who travel alone from Louisiana to Texas to kill and skin an albino buffalo. On the way, they have many thrilling adventures: they are attacked by cougars, shoot antelope and cimmaron, kill an attacking grizzly bear, and finally face down hostile Indians. *The Boy Hunters,* then, is a traditional western adventure, in which white men (or boys) prove their manhood by fighting and vanquishing Indians and wild beasts.

To show how the boy hunters become men, Reid draws on two larger subthemes. First, *The Boy Hunters* draws unmistakably on a wider tradition of Western stories in which, as Richard Slotkin has shown, white heroes achieve manhood by becoming "like" Indian warriors, while nonetheless remaining unmistakably white. Indeed, the very quest for a white buffalo mentioned in Reid's title typifes this tradition: the boys hunt a buffalo, the stereotypical quarry of Indians, yet they hunt a buffalo which is rare and superior because it is white. Similarly, at the novel's climax, the boy hunters are on the verge of being tortured and executed by Indians when, suddenly, the boys are revealed to possess the long-lost pipe of Tecumseh's brother, who was a friend of their father's. Recognizing this as a basis for kinship with the boys, the Indians are filled with "astonishment as well as admiration for [their] courage."[14] Again the manly white boy hunters are both like and superior to the Indians. The boys' simultaneous kinship and superiority to the Indians implicitly tie them to the American national myth of the frontier, in which manly Indian fighters like Daniel Boone and Davy Crockett forge an American nation.[15]

Yet if Indian frontier mythology was one subtheme of *The Boy Hunters*— and one element of the romance Teedie saw in the dead seal—the masculine "naturalness" of violence was an even stronger subtheme. Reid laces his adventures with natural history lessons stressing how predatory "nature" was. He dramatizes this predation in "The Chain of Destruction," a chapter in which the boy hunters observe a virtual feeding frenzy: A hummingbird hunting for insects is killed by a tarantula, which is in turn killed by a chameleon, and so on. When the hero Basil shoots and kills the last creature, a thieving eagle, Reid italicizes the moral: "This was the last link in the *chain of destruction!*"[16] In nature, the large animals hunt the smaller—and man is the fiercest, most powerful animal of all.

"Eat or be eaten" was the lesson Mayne Reid drew from nature, but it is not the only lesson one might draw from stories about animal life. "Nature" is a cultural construct, not a transparent fact to be reported. Reid's lesson about nature's violence enthralled the sheltered, sickly young Roosevelt, however. When he saw the body of the dead seal in the marketplace, he felt he had suddenly come face-to-face with a distant, romantic world of powerful and violent masculinity. He was fascinated. "As long as that seal remained there, I haunted the neighborhood of the market day after day." Emulating Lucien, the Boy Hunter who carried a notebook to annotate his observations, he returned to the market with a ruler and notebook, took a series of "utterly useless" measurements, and "at once began to write a natural history of my own, on the strength of that seal." He moved heaven and earth to acquire the dead seal's skull, with which he began a childish "Roosevelt Museum of Natural History" in his bedroom.[17] By playing at being a naturalist, young Teedie brought himself into imaginary contact with the aggressive, masculine nature he identified with the fictional Western frontier, where boys demonstrated their heroic masculinity by killing fierce animals and battling wild Indians.

Stories like Mayne Reid's "Chain of Destruction," depicting nature as red in tooth and claw, predisposed young Teedie to embrace Darwinism. By age ten the budding boy-naturalist had discovered Darwin's *Origin of Species,* and he soon became familiar with evolutionary theory.[18] *The Boy Hunters,* written seven years before Darwin published *Origin of Species,* was not in itself Darwinistic. While Reid's "chain of destruction" affirmed man as the apex of creation, it ascribed no cosmic meaning to man's superiority. But Darwinism provided a millennial purpose for Reid's chain of destruction—it was the engine which drove evolution. Like G. Stanley Hall and Charlotte Perkins Gilman, Roosevelt believed that bitter evolutionary conflict allowed the fittest species and races to survive, ultimately moving evolution forward toward its ultimate, civilized perfection.[19]

From his earliest youth, then, Roosevelt's understanding of nature was tinged by the genre of the Western adventure story. As TR saw it, nature was brutal and primitive—a proving ground of manly prowess—as epitomized by conflict with bloodthirsty, lurking Indians. The sickly seven-year-old boy measuring the seal in the Broadway market is the earliest glimpse we have of the strenuous adult man who would slaughter African lions and elephants in the name of science and construct himself as a virile cowboy on the Western frontier.

Eighteen years after encountering the seal, now a budding young politician, Roosevelt was accused of effeminacy, and once again he constructed a powerful male identity for himself in the terms of the Western adventure story. What better way to counter his Oscar Wilde image than to replace it with the image of the masculine Western hero? Although this was clearly a smart political move on TR's part, it was no cynical pose. Roosevelt had been enthralled by the masculine aggressiveness of Western fiction ever since he was a small boy reading *The Boy Hunters*. On his first trip to the Badlands in 1883, he was giddy with delight and behaved as much like a Mayne Reid hero as possible. He flung himself into battle with nature and hunted the largest and fiercest game he could find. As a child, he had been atttracted to natural history as a displacement of his desire to be a Western hero. Now, shooting buffalo and bullying obstreperous cowboys, he could style himself the real thing.[20]

Although most of his biographers date his transformation into a "Western man" from his retreat to South Dakota following the tragic death of his wife in 1884, Roosevelt had already bought his ranch and begun to transform himself into a Western rancher while Alice Lee was very much alive. On his very first trip to the Badlands in 1883, Roosevelt—although chronically short of cash—committed himself to spending forty thousand dollars to buy a South Dakota cattle ranch. Financially this was a foolhardy and risky investment, as Edmund Morris has pointed out; yet politically it was a brilliant step to transform his image from effeminate dude to masculine cowboy.[21]

Alice's death completely devasted TR, but it also freed him to construct himself as a cowboy far more completely than he had previously planned.[22] Even in his grief, and during his temporary withdrawal from politics, Roosevelt made certain the folks back East knew he was now a masculine cowboy. On his way to take up "permanent" residence on his Dakota ranch in 1884, he gave a "final" interview to the *New York Tribune*.

> It would electrify some of my friends who have accused me of representing the kid-glove element in politics if they could see me galloping over the plains, day in and day out, clad in a buckskin shirt and leather chaparajos, with a big sombrero on my head. For good healthy exercise I would strongly recommend some of our gilded youth go West and try a short course of riding bucking ponies, and assist at the branding of a lot of Texas steers.

Let no one think that TR remained a gilded youth or effeminate dude. He was now a denizen of (as he would later put it) "Cowboy Land."[23] Six months later, Roosevelt was back in New York writing *Hunting Trips of a Ranchman,* the first of three books detailing his thrilling adventures as a

Western hero.[24] TR intended *Hunting Trips* to establish his new identity as a heroic ranchman. He even included his new "ranchman" identity in the title. But lest the reader miss the point, TR included a full-length engraved portrait of himself as ranchman opposite the title page.[25] Sans eyeglasses (which would mark his body as imperfectly evolved), TR stands in a woodland setting, wearing a fringed buckskin suit. His face is grave, restrained, resolute—manly—and he grips a long rifle. Yet, although he bears the weapons and manly demeanor of civilized man, he wears the clothing of savages.[26] Like the Boy Hunters tracking the albino buffalo, he is at once like the Indians and superior to them. Like the Mayne Reid adventure, *Hunting Trips of a Ranchman* detailed TR's exciting adventures hunting animals, as a participant in the violent chain of destruction he had read about as a boy. Now he, too, like the Boy Hunters, was publicly measuring the violent power of his own masculinity against the aggressive predation of "nature."

TR's second Western book, *Ranch Life and the Hunting Trail*, published three years later, continued to portray him as a heroic and manly Western rancher, this time drawing more explicitly on the discourse of civilization. TR depicted ranchers like himself as pivotal characters in the evolutionary struggle between civilization and savagery—the struggle to establish the American nation. On the one hand, they embodied all the virtues of upright civilized manliness. A rancher "must not only be shrewd, thrifty, patient, and enterprising, but he must also possess qualities of personal bravery, hardihood, and self-reliance to a degree not demanded in the least by any mercantile occupation in a community long settled."[27] Yet the rancher's location on the frontier between civilization and savagery also allowed him to share the savage's primitive masculinity: "Civilization seems as remote as if we were living in an age long past. . . .Ranching is an occupation like those of vigorous, primitive pastoral peoples, having little in common with the humdrum, workaday business world of the nineteenth century; and the free ranchman in his manner of life shows more kinship to an Arab sheik than to a sleek city merchant or tradesman."[28] Like the traditional frontier hero, Roosevelt the ranchman possessed savages' "natural" strength and vigor; yet he also retained the superior manliness of the civilized white man. By telling a few stories about his run-ins with Indians, in which only his own manly coolness and facility with a rifle saved his scalp, Roosevelt further cemented his new identity as a modern Western hero.[29]

TR's efforts to transform his Jane-Dandy political image succeeded brilliantly. In 1886, when he ran for mayor of New York as the "Cowboy of the Dakotas," even the Democratic *New York Sun* lauded his zest for fighting and

Fig. 12. Theodore Roosevelt constructs himself as a virile Western ranchman in this frontispiece from *Hunting Trips of a Ranchman* (1885). Courtesy of Cathy Carver.

his "blizzard-seasoned constitution" instead of ridiculing him as "Oscar Wilde."[30] Throughout his political life TR would actively cultivate this political persona of masculine denizen of "Cowboy Land."[31]

Yet Roosevelt's ranchman identity was not a merely a case of cynical political packaging. It stemmed from Roosevelt's understanding of the higher significance of his political leadership. Despite his single-minded quest for political power, TR never believed he craved power for its own sake. As he saw it, his political ambitions ultimately served the purposes—not of his own selfish personal advancement—but of the millennial mission to advance his race and nation toward a more perfect civilization.

The Winning of the West: Race War Forges the Identity of the Manly American Race

At the same time that Roosevelt was engaged in constructing himself as a manly Western hero, he was also writing a history which explained the larger significance of his new frontiersman identity to the advancement of civilization. In *The Winning of the West,* an ambitious four-volume history of the late eighteenth-century American frontier, Roosevelt depicts the American West as a crucible in which the white American race was forged through masculine racial conflict. By applying Darwinistic principles to the Western tradition, Roosevelt constructed the frontier as a site of origins of the American race, whose manhood and national worth were proven by their ability to stamp out competing, savage races.[32]

Even in these scholarly historical tomes, Roosevelt invoked his own persona as a manly frontiersman to signify that he, himself, shared his race's virility, as well as its manly racial destiny.[33] At the very outset of *The Winning of the West,* TR makes his personal connection with the frontier explicit: "For a number of years I spent most of my time on the frontier, and lived and worked like any other frontiersman. . . . We guarded our herds of branded cattle and shaggy horses, hunted bear, bison, elk, and deer, established civil government, and put down evil-doers, white and red . . . exactly as did the pioneers."[34] This stretches the truth: Roosevelt never spent "most of his time" on the frontier. Even during the twenty-six months he considered himself a permanent resident of South Dakota, TR spent more than thirteen months in New York.[35] Yet, despite his limited time on the frontier, Roosevelt saw his own life-work in terms of the frontier history he was relating. Invoking his ranchman persona both explicitly and implicitly, Roosevelt used *The Winning of the West* to frame the larger significance of both his political career and his ambitions as a leader of the American nation.

Like Mayne Reid's *Boy Hunters* and other Western adventures, Roosevelt's *Winning of the West* told a story of virile violence and interracial conflict. Yet while the hero of the traditional Western adventure was a *man* whose race was implicitly white, the hero of Roosevelt's story was a *race* whose gender was implicitly male. The hero of *The Winning of the West* was the manly American race, which was born in violence on the Western frontier. Like many Victorian novelists, TR began his story by relating his hero's origins and parentage. Chapter 1, subtitled "Spread of the Modern English Race," describes the history of the English race, which TR saw as the American race's parent.[36] TR outlined the familiar Anglo-Saxonist history of the English race, as it began in the forests of Germany, overran prehistoric Europe, and finally established itself as Anglo-Saxon England.[37]

The Winning of the West then narrates, in much greater detail, a similar origin tale for the American race as it began in the forests of Kentucky, overran the American continent, and began to establish itself as the great United States. The settlement of the American West, according to Roosevelt, echoed the establishment of ancient England in that a race of primarily Germanic descent reconstituted itself in an extended act of racial conquest. As Roosevelt saw it, this act of manly conquest established the American race as a race apart—a race different from its English parent.[38]

> Americans belong to the English race only in the sense in which Englishmen belong to the German. . . . The modern Englishman is descended from a Low-Dutch stock, which, when it went to Britain, received into itself an enormous infusion of Celtic, a much smaller infusion of Norse and Danish, and also a certain infusion of Norman-French blood. When this new English stock came to America it mingled with and absorbed into itself immigrants from many European lands.[39]

TR made much of this point: The American race was not the same as the English race, since it had been reconstituted of new racial stock in the act of winning a new and virgin continent. Americans were literally of a different blood than the British. However, since most of the new, immigrant additions to English stock in America had come from the same superior Germanic and Celtic races that had long ago formed the British race (Germans, Scandinavians, Irish, and Dutch), the new American race retained all the superior racial traits of the older British race. In other words, the American race was a brand new race, but it shared both ancestry and "blood" with the English race. Long after he wrote *The Winning of the West*, Roosevelt continued to insist that Americans were a new and separate race.[40]

Yet although the manly American race was forged of various immigrant races, all of those contributing races were European. Black Americans played no part in TR's frontier history, nor did he consider them part of the American race. As he saw it, African Americans were racial inferiors whose presence in America could only damage the real (that is, white) American race. TR lambasted slave importers as "the worst foes, not only of humanity and civilization, but especially of the white race in America." Slave importation was not only "ethically aberrant," it was a biological crime because it encouraged non-eugenic interbreeding. Worse, the African race remained a problem in perpetuity. The inferior "negroes" could live peacefully with the superior whites for generations, unlike the Indians, who picked fights with the white man and thus could be killed off. In short, in constructing his racial hero, TR envisioned an American race that was exclusively white.[41]

The Winning of the West goes on to tell a story of racial origins in which the hero, the manly white American race, proves its manhood by winning a series of violent battles with inferior, savage Indians. Roosevelt depicts the violence of this frontier race war as the mechanism which forges the various groups of white European immigrants into one powerful, unified American race. Most of *The Winning of the West*'s four volumes recount this race-forming warfare in loving detail.

The logic behind TR's story of heroic racial formation revolves around "civilization's" three basic aspects: race, gender, and millennialism. The millennial evolutionary imperatives behind nature's quest to develop the most perfect men and women demanded that white Americans and Indians, thrown together on one continent, compete to establish which race had the strongest, most powerful men. Warfare between the white man and the Indian was thus, as TR repeatedly put it, "inevitable."[42] Only virile, masculine combat could establish whose men were superior and deserved to control the land and its resources. But the outcome was never in doubt. The new American race, able to advance civilization to ever greater heights, was "predestined" to prevail against the barbarous Indians.[43] "It is a sad and dreadful thing that there should of necessity be such throes of agony and yet they are the birth-pangs of a new and vigorous people," sighed Roosevelt.[44] Thus, in the violence of race war, the manly American race was born.

Manhood was the key to the American frontiersmen's victory in this race war, just as it had been the key to Roosevelt's own frontiersman identity. "The west would never have been settled save for the fierce courage and the eager desire to brave danger so characteristic of the stalwart backwoodsmen." Like the heroes of Western novels, these virile frontiersmen were bold, resourceful and self-reliant.[45] "The young men prided themselves on their bodily strength, and were always eager to contend against one another in athletic games, such as wrestling, racing, jumping and lifting flour barrels."[46] Moreover, the men and women of the American race clung tenaciously to "natural" sex roles: "The man was the armed protector and provider, the woman was the housewife and child-bearer."[47] As TR described the virile backwoodsmen, in another context, they were "every inch men," whose manhood was essential to their racial character. "There was little that was soft or outwardly attractive in their character; it was stern, rude, and hard, like the lives they led; but it was the character of those who were every inch men, and who were Americans through to the very heart's core."[48]

TR repeatedly contrasts the virile manliness of the Americans to the brutal unmanliness of the Indians.[49] Manhood was the essential characteristic of the American race, whereas Roosevelt's Indians "seemed to the white settlers devils and not men." These devilish nonmen "mercilessly destroyed all weaker communities, red or white" and "had no idea of showing justice or generosity towards their fellows who lacked their strength."[50] Manliness meant helping the weak; Indians attacked the weak. Therefore, Indians—like the Negro rapists in contemporary reports of lynching—were the opposite of manly. Indeed, Roosevelt repeatedly described Indians as brutal despoilers of women and children, invoking (like so many of his contemporaries) the ubiquitous cultural figure of the savage primitive rapist. According to Roosevelt, the white frontiersman

> was not taking part in a war against a civilized foe; he was fighting in a contest where women and children suffered the fate of the strong men. . . . His sweetheart or wife had been carried off, ravished, and was at the moment the slave and concubine of some dirty and brutal Indian warrior, . . . seared into his eyeballs, into his very brain, he bore ever with him, waking or sleeping, the sight of the skinned, mutilated, hideous body of the baby who had just grown old enough to recognize him and to crow and laugh when taken in his arms. Such incidents as these were not exceptional.[51]

Roosevelt described this savage unmanliness in pornographic detail, lumping together every Indian atrocity he had ever heard of—events occurring years apart, in different parts of the country—so that it appeared that Indians were typically rapists and baby killers.[52] (In contrast, modern historians have found that rape was practically unknown among most Indian tribes.)[53] Drawing on the discourse of civilization, TR constructed his Indians in the same terms which were currently depicting African Americans as unmanly, congenital rapists.

Yet civilized manliness was not the only thing that made the American race superior to the barbarous Indians. The American frontiersmen also proved their racial superiority by the potency of their violent masculinity—their ability to outsavage the savages. Although the primitive Indians were powerfully violent foes, Roosevelt depicted the white frontiersmen's violence as even more powerful: "Their red foes were strong and terrible, cunning in council, dreadful in battle, merciless beyond belief in victory. The men of the border did not overcome and dispossess cowards and weaklings; they marched forth to spoil the stout-hearted and to take for a prey the possessions of the men of might."[54] Again, the virile white man is both like the Indians and superior to them. The strength of the white Americans' violence proved them the most masculine of men and the most advanced of races.[55]

One might think that by regressing to brutal savagery, American men might be devolving toward a lower evolutionary stage, instead of advancing to a higher civilization. And Roosevelt conceded that, in the short run, this brutal race war was more likely to retrograde than to advance manliness and civilization. "A sad and evil feature of such warfare is that the whites, the representatives of civilization, speedily sink almost to the level of their barbarous foes, in point of hideous brutality."[56] Yet, as Roosevelt saw it, this regression to savagery was only temporary and proved the Americans' racial superiority. Since the Indian men fought at the brutal level of savagery, it was they who forced the white men into equal brutality in order to prevail in the struggle for survival. The superior race needed to match their red foes' masculine savagery in order to win the war and safeguard the future of civilization.[57] Having met the savages on their own primitive ground and having proven themselves the fitter race and the better men, the American men could claim their continent and reclaim their place as the most advanced of civilized races. This temporary reversion to the primitive in order to build a more powerful civilization thus echoes G. Stanley Hall's pedagogical vision of a primitive boyhood giving civilized men the masculine power to resist overcivilization and develop into the super-man.

For, brutal as it was, this bloody war between red and white men had a higher purpose: it served the sacred interests of civilization. Here, Roosevelt's own political mission comes into sharper focus, and the meaning of his own frontiersman persona takes on a cosmic tint. The American race had a sacred duty to advance civilization by wresting the continent from the Indians and installing a higher civilization. Indeed, the white man's race war against the Indians was really a holy crusade for human evolutionary advancement.

> The most ultimately righteous of all wars is a war with savages, though it is apt to be also the most terrible and inhuman. The rude, fierce settler who drives the savage from the land lays all civilized mankind under a debt to him. . . . It is of incalculable importance that America, Australia, and Siberia should pass out of the hands of

their red, black, and yellow aboriginal owners, and become the heritage of the dominant world races.[58]

This cosmic imperative rendered moot all lesser questions of morality. "Whether the whites won the land by treaty [or] by armed conquest . . . mattered comparatively little so long as the land was won. It was all-important that it should be won, for the benefit of civilization and in the interests of mankind."[59] Without such conquests, all human progress would cease and civilization itself would stop. "The world would have halted had it not been for the Teutonic conquests in alien lands; . . . the world would probably have gone forward very little, indeed would not have gone forward at all, had it not been for the displacement or submersion of savage and barbaric peoples as a consequence of the armed settlement in strange lands of the races who hold in their hands the fate of the years."[60] By killing the Indians, the virile American frontiersmen were unselfishly safeguarding the future advancement of all civilization.

Here, then, is the millennial importance of the race-making work of manly frontiersmen like Crockett, Boone, and, by implication, ranchman Roosevelt himself. By 1896, when Roosevelt published the fourth and final volume of *The Winning of the West*, he had embarked on his political career as an advocate of manly imperialism; and it might have appeared that his work as a scholarly historian was related only tangentially to his growing political prominence. Yet in *The Winning of the West*, Roosevelt had distilled the larger significance of both his political philosophy and his ambitions for the United States. As he saw it, history proved that manhood and race were integrally connected—almost identical—and the future of the American nation depended on both. History showed that, from the time the American race was born in violent racial conflict on the frontier, the American race had been superlatively manly. Indeed, superior manhood itself had allowed the American race to prevail against the Indians, win a continent, and build a mighty nation. Thus, America's nationhood itself was the product of both racial superiority and virile manhood.

But mere nationhood alone was not enough for Americans, according to Roosevelt, who (like Hall and Gilman) saw a cosmic importance in advancing evolution. Americans had a sacred duty to strive to develop the highest possible civilization. For Roosevelt, the mechanism of this human evolution came through a Darwinistic survival of the fittest. The American race must continue striving manfully to wrest the world's "waste spaces" from the inferior races who were currently "cumbering" them. And if all domestic territory had been wrested from the savages, then American men must turn their attention overseas. Indeed, as Roosevelt originally envisioned *The Winning of the West,* its story would have continued until the Alamo fell in 1836. By concluding with a different racial foe, Roosevelt's history would have signaled that in his own time the American race needed to summon its manhood to face a new opponent in its struggle for racial expansion: the "semicivilized" mestizo races of Latin America.[61] And who was more fit to lead American men in this fight than the modest, scholarly western ranchman who was so well versed in their racial history?

The Meaning of the Strenuous Life

Roosevelt never had the time to write the two final volumes of *The Winning of the West.* Instead, he took up the mantle of his heroic Indian fighters himself, urging American men to embrace a virile imperialism for the good of the race and the future of all civilization. Beginning in 1894, unhappy with President Cleveland's reluctance to annex Hawaii, Roosevelt began to exhort the American race to embrace a manly, strenuous imperialism, in the cause of higher civilization.[62] In Roosevelt's imperialistic pronouncements, as in *The Winning of the West,* issues of racial dominance were inextricably conflated with issues of manhood. Indeed, when Roosevelt originally coined the term "the strenuous life," in an 1899 speech, he was explicitly discussing only foreign relations: calling on the United States to build up its army and to take imperialistic control of Cuba, Puerto Rico, and the Philippines. Ostensibly, the speech never mentions gender at all. Yet the phrase "the strenuous life" soon began to connote a virile, hard-driving manhood, which might or might not involve foreign relations, at all.

How did the title of an essay calling for American imperialism become a catchphrase to describe vigorous masculinity? To answer this question, we need to understand the logic behind Roosevelt's philosophies about American nationalism and imperialism. For Roosevelt, the purpose of American expansionism and national greatness was always the millennial purpose behind human evolution—human racial advancement toward a higher civilization. And the race that could best achieve this perfected civilization was, by definition, the one with the most superior manhood.

The Dangers of Unmanly Overcivilized Racial Decadence

It was not coincidental that Roosevelt's advocacy of manly imperialism in the 1890s was contemporaneous with a widespread cultural concern about effeminacy, overcivilization, and racial decadence. As we have seen with Hall and Beard, throughout Europe and Anglo-America intellectuals were worried about the emasculating tendencies of excessive civilization. Roosevelt shared many of his contemporaries' fears about the future of American manly power; and this gave his imperialistic writings an air of especial urgency.[63]

Although Roosevelt never despaired about the future of American civilization, he believed racial decay was distinctly possible. He warned the nation that overcivilized effeminacy could threaten the race's fitness to engage in the sort of race wars he had described in *The Winning of the West*. He fretted over "a certain softness of fibre in civilized nations, which, if it were to prove progressive, might mean the development of a cultured and refined people quite unable to hold its own in those conflicts through which alone any great race can ultimately march to victory."[64] Publicly, Roosevelt professed faith that the American race retained the superior manhood which had allowed it to wrest the continent from the Indians. He denied "that the martial type necessarily decays as civilization progresses."[65] Yet in his private letters Roosevelt conceded that he believed American racial decadence was distinctly possible.[66]

Whereas Hall had seen decadence in terms of a physical or biological evolutionary backsliding, and Gilman had seen it in terms of the growth of excessive sex traits, Roosevelt understood decadence in terms of the racial conflict through which he believed civilizations rose and fell. As he had shown in *The Winning of the West*, TR believed that manly racial competition determined which race was superior and deserved to control the earth's resources. A race which grew decadent, then, was a race which had lost the masculine strength necessary to prevail in this Darwinistic racial struggle. Civilized advancement required much more than mere masculine strength, of course; it also required advanced manliness. Intelligence, altruism, and morality were essential traits, possessed by all civilized races and men. Yet, as important as these refined traits were, they were not enough, by themselves, to safeguard civilization's advance and prevent racial decadence. Without the "virile fighting virtues" which allowed a race to continue to expand into new territories, its more civilized racial traits would be useless. If American men lost their primal fighting virtues, a more manful race would strip them of their authority, land, and resources. This effeminate loss of racial primacy and virility was what Roosevelt meant by overcivilized racial decadence.

In order to help American men ward off this kind of racial decadence, Roosevelt wrote a series of articles exhorting American men to eschew overcivilized effeminacy. In 1893, for example, he suggested in *Harper's Weekly* that athletics might be one way to combat excess civilization and avoid losing Americans' frontier-bred manliness:

> In a perfectly peaceful and commercial civilization such as ours there is always a danger of laying too little stress upon the more virile virtues—upon the virtues which go to make up a race of statesmen and soldiers, of pioneers and explorers. . . . These are the very qualities which are fostered by vigorous, manly out-of-door sports, such as mountaineering, big-game hunting, riding, shooting, rowing, football and kindred games.[67]

Elsewhere he urged men to take up politics in order to cultivate "the rougher, manlier virtues. . . . A peaceful and commercial civilization is always in danger of suffering the loss of the virile fighting qualities without which no nation, however cultured, however refined, however thrifty and prosperous, can ever amount to anything."[68] Decadence could only be kept at bay if American men strove to retain the virile fighting qualities necessary for a race of soldiers and pioneers.

This concept of overcivilized decadence let Roosevelt construct American imperialism as a conservative way to retain the race's frontier-forged manhood, instead of what it really was—a belligerent grab for a radically new type of nationalistic power. As Roosevelt described it, asserting the white man's racial power abroad was necessary to avoid losing the masculine strength Americans had already established through race war on the frontier. Currently the American race was one of the world's most advanced civilized races. They controlled a rich and mighty continent because their superior manhood had allowed them to annihilate the Indians on the Western frontier. If they retained their manhood, they could continue to look forward to an ever higher civilization, as they worked ever harder for racial improvement and expansion. But if American men ever lost their virile zest for Darwinistic racial contests, their civilization would soon decay. If they ignored the ongoing racial imperative of constant expansion and instead grew effeminate and luxury-loving, a manlier race would inherit their mantle of the highest civilization.

By depicting imperialism as a prophylactic means of avoiding effeminacy and racial decadence, Roosevelt constructed it as part of the status quo and hid the fact that this sort of militaristic overseas involvement was actually a new departure in American foreign policy. American men must struggle to retain their racially innate masculine strength, which had originally been forged in battle with the savage Indians on the frontier; otherwise the race would backslide into overcivilized decadence. With no Indians left to fight at home, then, American men must press on and confront new races, abroad.

Imperialism: The Masterful Duty of the Manly Race

From 1894 until he became president in 1901, Roosevelt wrote and lectured widely on the importance of taking up what Rudyard Kipling, in 1899, would dub "the White Man's burden." Kipling coined this term in a poem written to exhort American men to conquer and rule the Philippines. "The white man," as we saw in the Wells chapter, simultaneously meant the white race, civilization itself, and white males as a group. In "The White Man's Burden," Kipling used the term in all these senses to urge white males to take up the racial burden of civilization's advancement. "Take up the White Man's burden," he wrote, capitalizing the essential term, and speaking to the manly civilized on behalf of civilization. "Send forth the best ye breed"—quality breeding was essential, because evolutionary development (breeding) was what gave "the White Man" the right and duty to conquer uncivilized races.

> Go bind your sons to exile
> To serve your captives' need;
> To wait in heavy harness,
> on fluttered folk and wild—
> Your new-caught, sullen peoples,
> Half-devil and half-child.[69]

Like Teedie throwing cake in the mouths of hungry beggars, manly men had the duty of taking unselfish care of those weaker than themselves—to "wait in heavy harness" and "serve their captives' need." And by calling the Filipinos "half-devil and half-child," Kipling underlined the essential fact that whatever these races were, they were not *men*.

Roosevelt called Kipling's poem "poor poetry but good sense from the expansionist standpoint."[70] Although Roosevelt did not use the term "the white man's burden" in his writings on imperialism, he drew on the same sorts of race and gender linkages which Kipling deployed in his poem. TR's speeches of this period frequently conflate manhood and racial power, and draw extended analogies between the individual American man and the virile American race.

For example, "National Duties," one of TR's most famous speeches, represents both American men and the American race as civilized entities with strong virile characters—in popular parlance, both were "the white man." Roosevelt begins by outlining this racial manhood, which he calls "the essential manliness of the American character."[71] Part of this manliness centered around individual and racial duties to the home. On the one hand, individual men must work to provide for the domestic needs of themselves and their families. On the other hand, the men of the race must work to provide for their collective racial home, their nation.[72] Men who shirked these manly homemaking duties were despicably unsexed; or, as TR put it, "the willfully idle man" was as bad as "the willfully barren woman."[73]

Yet laboring only for his own hearth and nation was not enough to satisfy a real man. Virile manhood also required the manly American nation to take up imperialistic labors outside its borders, just as manhood demanded individual men to labor outside the home: "Exactly as each man, while doing first his duty to his wife and the children within his home, must yet, if he hopes to amount to much, strive mightily in the world outside his home, so our nation, while first of all seeing to its own domestic well-being, must not shrink from playing its part among the great nations without."[74] It would be as unmanly for the American race to refuse its imperialist destiny as it would be for a cowardly man to spend all his time loafing at home with his wife. Imperialist control over primitive races thus becomes a matter of manhood—part of a male-only public sphere, which TR sets in contradistinction to the home.

After setting up imperialism as a manly duty for both man and race, Roosevelt outlines the imperialist's appropriate masculine behavior—or, should we say, his appropriate masculine appendage? Roosevelt immediately brings up the "big stick." It may be a cheap shot to stress the phallic implications of TR's imagery, yet Roosevelt himself explained the meaning of the "big stick" in terms of manhood and the proper way to assert the power of a man: "A good many of you are probably acquainted with the old proverb: 'Speak softly and carry a big stick—you will go far.' If a man continually blusters, if he lacks civility, a big stick will not save him from trouble; and neither will speaking softly avail, if back of the softness there does not lie strength, power."[75] Just as a manly man avoided bluster, relying instead on his self-evident masculine strength and power, so virile American men should build a powerful navy and army, so that when they took up the white man's burden in primitive lands, they would receive the respect due to a masterful, manly race.

This imperialistic manliness underlay the virile power of both man and race; yet it was not self-seeking. It was intended only for the advancement of civilization. Therefore, Roosevelt insisted, Americans never directed their virile expansionism against any civilized race. "No nation capable of self-government and of developing by its own efforts a sane and orderly civilization, no matter how small it may be, has anything to fear from us."[76] Only barbarous nations incapable of developing "a sane and orderly civilization" —for example, the Hawaiians and the Filipinos—required the correction of the manly American race.

Unfortunately, Roosevelt conceded, this unselfish civilizing duty might well become bloody and violent. Civilized men had a manly duty to "destroy and uplift" lesser, primitive men, for their own good and the good of civilization: "It is our duty toward the people living in barbarism to see that they are freed from their chains, and we can free them only by destroying barbarism itself. The missionary, the merchant, and the soldier may each have to play a part in this destruction and in the consequent uplifting of the people."[77] Yet this unselfish racial uplift would be worth the bloodshed, even for the destroyed barbarians themselves. Both Indians on the Great Plains and the Tagalogs in the Philippines—at least, those who still survived—would be far happier after the white man had conquered them, according to Roosevelt.[78]

Roosevelt closed his speech by reiterating his analogy between the manful race and the race's men. By conquering and civilizing primitive races, the American nation was simply girding up its racial loins to be "men" of the world, just as they had long been "men" at home in the United States: "We gird up our loins as a nation, with the stern purpose to play our part manfully in winning the ultimate triumph; and therefore . . . with unfaltering steps [we] tread the rough road of endeavor, smiting down the wrong and battling for the right, as Greatheart smote and battled in Bunyan's immortal story."[79] In its imperialist glory, the virile American race would embody a warlike manliness, smiting down and battling its unmanly foes in the primitive Philippines. Were American men to be frightened from this work, they would show themselves, as TR put it, "weaklings."[80]

Roosevelt always considered imperialism a question of both racial and individual manhood. Privately, he scorned anti-imperialists as "beings whose cult is non-virility."[81] Publicly, he derided men who refused to take

*anti-imperialism
equated w/ adultery*

*patriotism
equated to w/
monogamy*

up the white man's burden as decadent, effeminate, and enemies of civilization: "In the ages distant future patriotism, like the habit of monogamous
marriage, will become a needless and obsolete virtue; but just at present the
man who loves other countries as much as he does his own is quite as noxious a member of society as the man who loves other women as much as he
loves his wife."[82] Like the advocates of free love, anti-imperialists professed a
civilized high-mindedness, but their actions showed them as unmanly and
weak as adulterers.

An unmanly, anti-imperialist race was as despicable as an unmanly, anti-
imperialist man. As TR saw it, overly peaceful races were like unsexed deca-
dents who refused to breed, whereas expansive races left heirs, just as fathers
left sons. "Nations that expand and nations that do not expand may both
ultimately go down, but the one leaves heirs and a glorious memory, and the
other leaves neither."[83] As TR saw it, the only way to avoid effete, unmanly
decadence—on the part of either race or man—was to embrace virile imperialism.

In short, racial health and civilized advancement implied both manhood
and imperialism. An effeminate race was a decadent race; and a decadent
race was too weak to advance civilization. Only by embracing virile racial
expansionism could a civilization achieve its true manhood. This, as TR saw
it, was the ultimate meaning of imperialism.

The Rough Rider: The War Hero Models the Power of a Manly Race

Roosevelt was not content merely to make speeches about the need for violent, imperialistic manhood. He always needed to embody his philosophy.
The sickly boy had remade himself into an adventure-book hunter-
naturalist; the dude politician had remade himself into a heroic Western
rancher. The 1898 outbreak of the Spanish-American war—for which he
had agitated long and hard—let Roosevelt remake himself into Colonel Roosevelt, the fearless Rough Rider.

Reinventing himself as a charismatic war hero allowed Roosevelt to model
the manful imperialism about which he had been writing for four years. TR
became a walking advertisement for the imperialistic manhood he desired
for the American race. Indeed, from the moment of his enlistment until his
mustering out four months later, Roosevelt self-consciously publicized himself as a model of strenuous, imperialistic manhood. In late April 1898,
against all advice, Roosevelt resigned as assistant secretary of the navy and
enlisted to fight in the just-declared war on Spain. Aged thirty-nine, with an

important subcabinet post, a sick wife, and six young children, no one but Roosevelt himself imagined he ought to see active service. Roosevelt's decision to enlist was avidly followed by newspapers all over the country. Several editorialized against his enlistment, saying he would do more good for the war effort as assistant secretary of the navy. Roosevelt enlisted nonetheless and lost no opportunity to publicize his reasons to friendly newspapers. As he explained to the *New York Sun*, it would be unmanly—hypocritical—to allow other men to take his place on the front lines after he had agitated so strenuously for war. "I want to go because I wouldn't feel that I had been entirely true to my beliefs and convictions, and to the ideal I had set for myself if I didn't go."[84] Embracing the glare of publicity, TR demonstrated to all that when a member of the manly American race took up the white man's burden, he risked his life willingly and joyously, for the good of civilization.

Roosevelt, commissioned at the rank of lieutenant colonel, raised a volunteer cavalry regiment which he described as "peculiarly American."[85] It was designed to reflect Americans' masculine racial power as well as their civilized manly advancement. TR accepted only a fraction of the host of men who tried to enlist in his well-publicized regiment. Most of those he accepted were Westerners—rough cowboys and frontiersmen, the heirs and descendants of the masculine Indian fighters who had been forged into the American race on the Western frontier. But, to emphasize the American race's civilized superiority to the Spanish enemy, TR also enlisted several dozen young Ivy League college graduates, many of them athletes. These Harvard and Yale men, presumably the beneficiaries of the race's most advanced moral and intellectual evolution, represented the ever-advancing heights of civilization to which the manly American race could aspire. The regiment's combination of primitive Western masculinity and advanced civilized manliness dramatized the superior manhood of the American race. They would undoubtedly whip the pants off the inferior Latin Spaniards, and show Americans the glories of imperialistic manhood.

The press, fascinated by the undertaking, christened the regiment "Roosevelt's Rough Riders."[86] Roosevelt's heroic frontiersman identity thus came full circle, as he no doubt intended. As Richard Slotkin has pointed out, the term "Rough Riders" had long been used in adventure novels to describe Western horsemen. Thus, by nicknaming his regiment the "Rough Riders," the nation showed it understood the historical connections Roosevelt always drew between Indian wars in the American West and virile imperialism in Cuba and the Philippines.[87]

But lest anyone miss the connections he was trying to draw between continued manhood and racial expansion, Roosevelt made certain the press, and thus the public, remained fully informed about the Rough Riders' doings. He encouraged several journalists to attach themselves to the regiment throughout its sojourn in Cuba and even rounded up an interested motion-picture crew.[88] The public avidly followed the newspaper reports of the Rough Riders' masculine cowboy heroics, manly collegiate athleticism, and overall wartime heroics.

Roosevelt, himself, was the core of the Rough Riders' popularity—he embodied the whole manly, imperialistic enterprise. Like his Western recruits, Roosevelt was both a masculine cowboy-hero and (by reputation and association, although not in reality) an Indian fighter. But TR was also a civilized Harvard man, manfully sacrificing his life of ease and privilege to take up the white man's burden and do his duty by the downtrodden brown Cubans. His widely reported, dashing exploits, including the heroic charge up "San Juan" Hill, proved the American race's violent masculinity had lost none of its potency since the bygone days of the Western frontier. According to Edmund Morris, when Roosevelt returned from the war he was "the most famous man in America."[89]

After his mustering out, TR the politician continued to play the role of virile Rough Rider for all he was worth. In November, he was elected governor of New York, campaigning as a war hero and employing ex-Rough Riders to warm up the election crowds. By January 1899, his thrilling memoir, *The Rough Riders,* was appearing serially in *Scribner's Magazine.* And in 1900 his virile popularity convinced Republican party leaders that Roosevelt could counter Bryan's populism better than any other vice-presidential candidate. Roosevelt had constructed himself and the Rough Riders as the epitome of civilized, imperialistic manhood, a model for the American race to follow. His success in modeling that imperialistic manhood exceeded even his own expectations and ultimately paved the way for his presidency.

"The Strenuous Life"

On April 10, 1899, Colonel Roosevelt stood before the men of Chicago's elite, all-male, Hamilton Club and preached the doctrine of "The Strenuous Life." As governor of New York and a fabulously popular ex-Rough Rider, he knew the national press would be in attendance; and though he spoke *at* the Hamilton Club, he spoke *to* men across America. With the cooperation of the press and at the risk of his life, TR had made himself into a national hero— the embodiment of manly virtue, masculine violence, and white American racial supremacy—and the antithesis of overcivilized decadence. Now he urged the men of the American race to live the sort of life he had modeled for them: to be virile, vigorous, and manly, and to reject overcivilized decadence by supporting a strenuously imperialistic foreign policy. When contemporaries ultimately adopted his phrase "the strenuous life" as a synonym for the vigorous, vehement manhood Roosevelt modeled, they showed they correctly understood that his strenuous manhood was inextricably linked to his nationalism, imperialism, and racism.

Ostensibly, "The Strenuous Life" preached the virtues of military preparedness and imperialism, but contemporaries understood it as a speech about manhood. The practical import of the speech was to urge the nation to build up its army, to maintain its strong navy, and to take control of Puerto Rico, Cuba, and the Philippines. But underlying these immediate objectives lay the message that American manhood—both the manly race and individual white men—must retain the strength of their Indian-fighter ancestors, or another race would prove itself more manly and overtake America in the Darwinian struggle to be the world's most dominant race.

Roosevelt began by demanding manliness in both the American nation and American men. Slothful men who lacked the "desire and power" to strive in the world were despicable and unmanly. "We do not admire the man of timid peace. We admire the man who embodies victorious effort."[90] If America and its men were not man enough to fight, they would not only lose their place among "the great nations of the world," they would become a decadent and effeminate race. Roosevelt held up the Chinese, whom he despised as the most decadent and unmanly of races, as a cautionary lesson: If we "play the part of China, and be content to rot by inches in ignoble ease within our borders," we will "go down before other nations which have not lost the manly and adventurous qualities."[91] If American men lacked the manly fortitude to go bravely and willingly to a foreign war, the race would decay, preached TR, the virile war hero.

In stirring tones, the Rough Rider of San Juan Hill ridiculed the over-civilized anti-imperialists who had lost the "great fighting, masterful virtues." Lacking the masculine impulse toward racial aggression and unmoved by virile visions of empire, these men had been sapped of all manhood.

> The timid man, the lazy man, the man who distrusts his country, the over-civilized man, who has lost the great fighting, masterful virtues, the ignorant man, and the man of dull mind, whose soul is incapable of feeling the mighty lift that thrills stern men with em-

pires in their brains—all these, of course shrink from seeing the nation undertake its new duties; shrink from seeing us build a navy and an army adequate to our needs; shrink from seeing us do our share of the world's work. These are the men who fear the strenuous life. . . . They believe in that cloistered life which saps the hardy virtues in a nation, as it saps them in the individual.[92]

Like "cloistered" monkish celibates, these "over-civilized" men "shrink, shrink, shrink" from carrying the "big stick." Dishonorably, they refused to do their manly duty by the childish Filipinos. Had the United States followed these anti-imperialists' counsel and refused to undertake "one of the great tasks set modern civilization," Americans would have shown themselves not only unmanly but also racially inferior. "Some stronger, manlier power would have to step in and do the work, and we would have shown ourselves weaklings, unable to carry to successful completion the labors that great and high-spirited nations are eager to undertake." As TR saw it, the man, the race, and the nation were one in their need to possess virile, imperialist manhood.[93]

Then TR got down to brass tacks, dwelling at length on Congress' responsibility to build up the armed forces.[94] After again raising the specter of Chinese decadence, which American men faced if they refused to strengthen their army and navy, Roosevelt stressed America's duty to take up the white man's burden in Cuba, Puerto Rico, and the Philippines. If the American race was "too weak, too selfish, or too foolish" to take on that task, it would be completed by "some stronger and more manful race." He ridiculed anti-imperialists as cowards who "make a pretense of humanitarianism to hide and cover their timidity" and to "excuse themselves for their unwillingness to play the part of men."[95]

"The Strenuous Life" culminates with a Darwinian vision of strife between races for the "dominion of the world," which only the most manful race could win.

I preach to you then, my countrymen, that our country calls not for the life of ease but for the life of strenuous endeavor. . . . If we stand idly by . . . then the bolder and stronger peoples will pass us by, and will win for themselves the domination of the world. Let us therefore boldly face the life of strife, resolute to do our duty well and manfully.[96]

American men must embrace their manly mission to be the race which dominates the world. Struggle for racial supremacy was inevitable, but the most manful race—the American race—would triumph, if it made the attempt. Its masculine strength was proven by military victories over barbarous brown races. Its manly virtue was evident in its civilized superiority to the primitive childish races it uplifted. White American men must claim their place as the world's most perfect men, the fittest race for the evolutionary struggle toward a perfect civilization. This was the meaning of "The Strenuous Life."

We can now answer the question, "How did the title of an essay calling for American dominance over the brown races become a catchphrase to describe virile masculinity?" Roosevelt's desire for imperial dominance had been, from the first, intrinsically related to his views about male power. As he saw it, the manhood of the American race had been forged in the crucible of frontier race war; and to abandon the virile power of that violence would be to backslide toward effeminate racial mediocrity. Roosevelt wanted American men to be the ultimate in human evolution, the world's most powerful and civilized race. He believed that their victory over the Indians on the frontier proved that the American race possessed the racial superiority and masculine power to overcome any savage race; and he saw a glorious future for the race in the twentieth century, as it pressed on toward international dominance and the perfection of civilization. The only danger which Roosevelt saw menacing this millennial triumph of manly American civilization came from within. Only by surrendering to overcivilized decadence—by embracing unmanly racial sloth instead of virile imperialism—could American men fail. Thus, American men must work strenuously to uphold their civilization. They must refuse a life of ease, embrace their manly task, and take up the white man's burden. Only by living that "strenuous life" could American men prove themselves to be what Roosevelt had no doubt they were—the apex of civilization, evolution's most favored race, masterful men fit to command the barbarous races and the world's "waste spaces"—in short, the most virile and manly of men.

In later years, as Americans came to take international involvement for granted and as imperialism came to seem less controversial, the phrase "the strenuous life" underwent a subtle change of meaning. Always associated with Roosevelt, it came to connote the virile manhood which he modeled for the nation as imperialistic Western hero and Rough Rider—the peculiar combination of moral manliness and aggressive masculinity which he was able to synthesize so well. As Roosevelt's presidency wore on, Americans grew accustomed to taking up the white man's burden, not only in the Philippines, but also in Cuba, Panama, and the Dominican Republic. The "strenuous life" came to be associated with any virile, manly effort to accomplish

great work, whether imperialistic or not.[97] Yet on a basic level, "the strenuous life" retained TR's original associations with the evolutionary struggle
of the American race on behalf of civilization. "The strenuous life," as it came
to be used, meant the opposite of "overcivilized effeminacy." Or, as Roosevelt
summed it up himself in his *Autobiography,* the man who lives the strenuous
life regards his life "as a pawn to be promptly hazarded whenever the hazard
is warranted by the larger interests of the great game in which we are all engaged."[98] That great game, for Roosevelt, was always the millennial struggle
for Americans to perfect civilization by becoming the most manly, civilized,
and powerful race in the world.

"Civilization" in the White House: Race Policy and Race Suicide

In 1901, Theodore Roosevelt finally grasped the ultimate manhood which
he had sought for so long: to be the preeminent manly leader of the virile
American race. As president, TR believed his duty was to usher the manly
American nation ever closer to the racial preeminence and perfect civilization he had long predicted for it. Not surprisingly, then, considerations of
manhood, race, and "civilization" shaped many of Roosevelt's presidential
policies.

Internationally, as Frank Ninkovich has so eloquently shown, Roosevelt
relied on the ideology of civilization to frame his foreign policy. Ninkovich
refutes those historians who see TR as engaging in realpolitik or upholding
balances of power between the European nations, and argues that TR's concern was always to uphold the interests of "civilization." Or, as Secretary of
State Elihu Root summed up TR's diplomatic objectives, Roosevelt always
"viewed each international question against the background of those tendencies through which civilization develops and along which particular civilizations advance or decline." As we have already seen in his pre-presidential
speeches, TR believed that manhood required civilized nations to pacify and
rule savage and barbarous nations. The Roosevelt Corollary to the Monroe
Doctrine stemmed directly from this ideology of manly, civilized steward-
ship of the savage and barbarous races.[99]

As Roosevelt described it in his *Autobiography,* this diplomacy of "civilization" was essentially a diplomacy of manliness. "In foreign affairs, the principle from which we never deviated was to have the Nation behave toward
other nations precisely as a strong, honorable, and upright man behaves in
dealing with his fellow-men."[100] Like the manly man, the manly nation kept

its promises, fearlessly faced down strong, civilized nations, and was patient with weak, barbarous ones.[101] For example, Roosevelt wrote that the Monroe Doctrine was intended to apply, not to "civilized commonwealths" like Canada, Argentina, Brazil, or Chile (all with large white populations), but only to uncivilized "tropical states" which (like unmanly men) were too "impotent" to do their own duty or defend their own independence.[102] Yet always behind this upright moral manliness lay the virile masculine potency of the race's capacity to wield "the big stick."

President Roosevelt's belief in manly civilization shaped his domestic policies, too, especially regarding interracial relations. His actions toward both Japanese immigrants and African Americans were shaped by his long-standing assumption that when men of different and incompatible races lived together, they would battle until one race reigned supreme, just as they had on the American frontier.[103] Yet although TR believed that African American and Japanese men both presented a racial challenge to white American men, his policies toward the two races differed because, as he saw it, the two races had attained different degrees of civilization.

Roosevelt believed that "Negroes" were the most primitive of races—"a perfectly stupid race."[104] As he had written in *The Winning of the West,* he always believed that their very presence in the United States was a tragic but irreversible historical error.[105] Black Americans were somewhat less backward than "Negroes" anywhere else in the world because they had extensive contact with civilization in the United States. Yet even so, Roosevelt warned, it might take "many thousand years" before "the descendant of the Negro" in the United States evolved to become even "as intellectual as the [ancient] Athenian."[106]

The disparity in racial capacity between black and white threatened the nation with race war, since the "fundamental . . . fact of the conflict between race and race" at such different evolutionary points inevitably led men into racial violence.[107] TR deplored such racial violence as uncivilized and made headlines in 1903 and 1906 by denouncing lynching. (He also repeated uncritically the myth that African American men had catalyzed those lynchings by raping white women, thus reinforcing widespread belief in black men's lack of manliness.)[108] Yet, although he deplored lynching, Roosevelt assumed racial violence was all but inevitable when men of such dissimilar races lived together.[109]

Thus Roosevelt saw the "Negro Problem" as a question of male power. The men of the masterful white American race had an irresistible evolutionary imperative to assert control over any race of inferior men in their midst.

The Negro race was, unfortunately, permanently resident in the United States. Racial violence was thus a natural and inevitable part of manhood in a racially diverse society. Yet this posed another problem, because violence was itself barbarous and incompatible with a highly advanced civilization.

The only way to solve this dilemma, Roosevelt believed, was to focus explicitly on manhood. Because race difference was extreme and inescapable, the only solution was to pretend races did not exist, and invoke a democratic individualism which would allow each man (however racially unequal) to compete as a man. As he wrote to Albion Tourgée,

> I have not been able to think out any solution of the terrible problem offered by the presence of the negro on this continent, but of one thing I am sure, and that is that inasmuch as he is here and can neither be killed nor driven away, the only wise and honorable and Christian thing to do is to treat each black man and each white man strictly on his merits as a man, giving him no more and no less than he shows himself worthy to have.[110]

Racial strife was unavoidable; racial inequality a terrible and immutable fact. The only solution was to trust to manhood and natural selection, allowing each man to compete fairly, as a man facing other men, regardless of race. If any African American man proved himself as manly as white American men in fair competition, he should be given an equal chance.

In other words, where African Americans were concerned, Roosevelt substituted an individual contest between men—the democratic merit system—for a collective contest between men—race war. To carry out this substitution, Roosevelt made ostentatious efforts to appoint blacks to federal positions, though he always complained qualified black candidates were inordinately difficult to find. (Historians note, however, that these appointments dwindled markedly as time passed.)[111] But although Roosevelt championed the right of individual, superior black men to compete with white men, he was confident that the Negro race, as a whole, was so far inferior to the white American race that no real evolutionary challenge would ensue.[112]

He was less confident about the Japanese. He believed them "a great civilized power of a formidable type, and with motives and ways of thought which are not quite those of the powers of our race."[113] Because Japanese men were civilized, they were serious contenders for evolutionary supremacy and could pose a threat to white Americans' manly dominance. After all, they too had proven their masculinity through imperialistic race war, defeating the Russians in 1904, as the American frontiersmen had defeated the

Indians. Yet, however advanced, Japanese civilization was nonetheless both inferior to and incompatible with white American civilization.

Thus, it would be extremely dangerous to allow Japanese men to immigrate freely into the United States. On the one hand, the less civilized Japanese men were less manly and so willing to work for lower wages than American men. On the other hand, the Japanese were somewhat civilized and so were desirable and competent workers. Here was a particularly dangerous situation: If Japanese workingmen were allowed to settle in the United States, they could emasculate American men as breadwinners. Roosevelt thus believed "the California Legislature would have had an entire right to protest as emphatically as possible against the admission of Japanese laborers, for their very frugality, abstemiousness and clannishness make them formidable to our laboring class."[114] "Frugal" and "abstemious," the civilized but inferior Japanese men were willing to settle for a lower standard of living, and would force wages down, ruining American men's ability to provide for their families. Allowing Japanese men to immigrate and compete with white American men would thus be, as TR put it, "race suicide."[115]

In order to avoid this masculine racial competition, with its threat of race suicide, Roosevelt stood firm on proscribing all permanent Japanese immigrants, although temporary Japanese visitors—for example, students and tourists—would be acceptable.[116] The men of such totally different and unassimilable civilizations, living side by side, must inevitably compete in the daily struggle for economic survival and eventually battle for control of the American land and resources. "To permit the Japanese to come in large numbers into this country would be to cause a race problem and invite and insure a race contest."[117] It was therefore essential "to keep the white man in America . . . out of home contact with them."[118] America must remain a white man's country.[119]

TR's views on manhood and civilization thus shaped his presidential policies toward both African Americans and Japanese immigration, but in contrasting ways. Because TR believed African Americans, already resident in the United States in large numbers, were generally primitive and inferior, he was willing to make a virtue of necessity by allowing black men to compete with white American men on an equal basis. He believed that if natural selection took its course, African American men would be weeded out as unfit, and the manly white American race would remain supreme. Japanese men, however, were civilized, and thus formidable, manly competitors. To allow natural selection to work—to allow Japanese men to compete, as men, with white American men—would be dangerous to the white American race's supremacy. "Civilized" Japanese men, thus, should be excluded, while "primitive" African American men should be allowed to compete.[120]

Allowing Japanese immigration was not the only way the white American race could commit race suicide, however. Roosevelt was even more worried about a similarly suicidal racial tendency: native-born white Americans' falling birth rate. In his warnings about racial decadence, Roosevelt had always insisted that women's reluctance to breed was as dangerous to the race as men's reluctance to fight. Either way, a race would lose power and allow inferior races to surpass it in the Darwinistic quest for global supremacy.

Although historians today usually think of race suicide purely in terms of the birthrate controversy, the issue was tied to a host of broader fears about effeminacy, overcivilization, and racial decadence. The term "race suicide" was first coined in 1901 by sociologist Edward A. Ross. In his address "The Causes of Race Superiority," Ross raised all the fears of decadent manhood that had been so often evoked throughout the 1890s.[121] In terms reminiscent of the "neurasthenic paradox," Ross warned that the same manly virtues which had once allowed the "Superior Race" to evolve the highest civilization now threatened that race's very survival. He delineated the racial characteristics which had made white Americans superior to all other races —self-reliance, foresight, the ability to control their passions—in short, manliness. Yet, Ross argued, when faced with competition from less manly, racially inferior immigrants, these manly traits would prove the superior race's undoing. As it competed with these immigrants, the "very foresight and will power that mark the higher race dig a pit beneath its feet."[122] The superior race's manly self-denial gave it the drive to provide a rising standard of living for its children. But when manly white men competed for a livelihood with their racial inferiors, the inferior men, able to survive on less, would drive down wages; and the superior race's standard of living would decline. Unwilling to sire children they could not provide for, the superior American men would have fewer and fewer children. Thus manfully controlling their emotions, American men would "quietly and unmurmuringly eliminate" themselves.[123]

Race suicide thus expressed the ultimate racial nightmare—impotent, decadent manhood. In Ross' vision, the same manly traits which allowed a superior race to develop the most advanced civilization would leave it unable to compete with more primitive, less manly races. Civilized races' *manliness* thus threatened to destroy their *virility*. Again, we get the dynamic of the "neurasthenic paradox": Victorian manliness is both the hallmark of an advanced civilization and a threat to civilization's future. Manly sexual self-control was an excellent trait—proof of civilized advancement—but, taken too far, it would lead to the downfall of civilization and the ultimate unmanning of American manhood.

Roosevelt shared Ross' concern about the dangers of a falling birthrate.[124] TR had first voiced concern about the birthrate in 1894, about the same time he began to worry about national decadence and to agitate for a more vigorous imperialism. "Unquestionably, no community that is actually diminishing in numbers is in a healthy condition; and as the world is now, with huge waste places still to fill up, and with much of the competition between the races reducing itself to the warfare of the cradle, no race has any chance to win a great place unless it consists of good breeders as well as of good fighters," he warned.[125] In the midst of chronicling the manly American race's heroic conquest of savage Indians, the author of *The Winning of the West* fretted that "the warfare of the cradle" could undo the warfare of the frontier. There was no point in wresting the world's "waste spaces" from the primitive races if the frontiersmen's heirs simply refused to breed! Throughout the 1890s, in his published writings on the imperialistic duty of the manly race and in his private correspondence, TR raised the specter of race suicide.[126]

Roosevelt was not alone in his concerns. In the early 1890s, many commentators were wringing their hands about dwindling white birthrates, and pointing to the 1890 census to show that the native-born white birthrate had taken a sudden drop.[127] Yet although the birthrate was indeed dropping, as the alarmists claimed, this was nothing new. The birthrate had been dropping steadily ever since national statistics began to be kept in 1790; as early as 1843, Americans had been commenting on it.[128] What was new in 1890, however, was the growing debate about whether civilization was growing decadent and effeminate.

The race suicide controversy, then, was (like neurasthenia) one of many ways middle-class men addressed their fears about overcivilized effeminacy and racial decadence. Throughout the 1890s, elite American commentators bemoaned the falling birthrate, often blaming women's colleges or the new immigration.[129] Historians, following these sorts of articles, sometimes suggest increased immigration and new demands for women's rights explain these panicked fears.[130] Yet it would probably be more accurate to suggest that TR and his contemporaries saw both immigration and women's advancement, as well as the falling birthrate, as part of a wider threat to their race, manhood, and "civilization."

Roosevelt's personal dismay about the falling birthrate remained relatively private until 1903 when, as president, he allowed a letter expressing his fears about race suicide to be published. In October 1902 Roosevelt had written author Bessie Van Vorst, praising her *The Woman Who Toils,* an exposé of the hardships faced by women factory workers, then running serially in *Everybody's Magazine.* Van Vorst scarcely mentioned the birthrate, but she did suggest that factory girls liked the independence of wage work and thus were in no hurry to marry. This elicited a Rooseveltian tirade against race suicide. Possibly hoping to bolster sales, Van Vorst obtained TR's permission to reprint his letter as a preface to her book. Thus the nation became acquainted with Roosevelt's views, and the phrase "race suicide" came before the general public for the first time.[131]

"You touch upon what is fundamentally infinitely more important than any other question in this country—that is the question of race suicide, complete or partial," TR wrote. Denouncing the selfish wish to live for individual pleasure, TR called instead for "the strong racial qualities without which there can be no strong races"—courage, high-mindedness, unselfishness. The absence of these sorts of virtues showed a reprehensible inability to consider the good of the race and was a symptom of "decadence and corruption in the nation." A man or woman who, considering only his or her own individual convenience, deliberately avoided having children was "in effect a criminal against the race, and should be an object of contemptuous abhorrence by all healthy people." Men must be "ready and able to fight at need, and anxious to be fathers of families," just as women must "recognize that the greatest thing for any woman is to be a good wife and mother." Refusing to bear children was the same sort of racial crime as refusing to fight for racial advancement; for no matter how refined its civilization, a race which refused to fight or breed was doomed to racial extinction.[132] In short, Roosevelt, like Edward Ross, painted race suicide as a disease of excessive civilization—potentially the greatest danger facing the American race—yet, he insisted, the danger could be overcome. The masterful American race could regain its manly primacy through willful procreative effort.

Roosevelt's warning caught the attention of the American public and popularized "race suicide" as both a term and a problem.[133] Genteel magazines across the country carried letters and editorials commenting on the president's stand. *Popular Science Monthly,* for example, agreeing that "it is surely a serious problem when the more civilized races tend not to reproduce themselves," published sixteen letters and articles on race suicide between 1903 and 1905.[134]

Elite magazines' discussions mostly revolved around how to keep civilization manly and powerful. Many commentators accepted Roosevelt's argument and wrung their hands over civilization's future. Some complained that less civilized races outbred the native-born whites.[135] Others claimed a decadent love of luxury was sapping white Americans' will to sacrifice for their children. Some fretted that the white American race, like an overbred hybrid, had simply become sterile.[136] The anti-imperialist *Nation* agreed that a negative birthrate heralded national decadence, but it turned race suicide into an argument against TR's imperialism, suggesting that "a people who cannot bring to maturity an average of more than nineteen children to twenty parents ought not to think of having colonies and of civilizing inferior races."[137] Although feminists objected that TR's pronouncements limited women to earning their "right to a footing on earth by bearing children and in no other way," and questioned "the note of savagery that rings in [TR's] voice when he discusses war and 'race suicide,'" they had little impact on the national debate.[138]

Outside the genteel press, however, the race suicide debates developed unexpectedly into a new and respectable way to celebrate masculine sexuality. In April 1903, only two months after his letter was published, Roosevelt embarked on a Western speaking tour and was delighted to discover that the public now saw him as a patron saint of large families: "I found to my utter astonishment that my letter to those Van Vorst women about their excellent book had gone everywhere, and the population of each place invariably took the greatest pride in showing off the children."[139] Always the resourceful publicist, TR grabbed the chance to encourage the American race to breed. In St. Paul, Minnesota, Mayor R. A. Smith of Washington County presented TR with a picture of a local couple, their nine children, forty-eight grandchildren, and two great-grandchildren. "That is the stuff out of which we make good American citizens," TR enthused.[140] In South Dakota, Roosevelt hailed the large numbers of children who attended his appearances, repeatedly declaring "that he was glad to see that the stock was not dying out."[141] In Redlands, California, Roosevelt joked, "The sight of these children convinces me of the truth of a statement just made to me by Gov. Pardee, when he said that in California there is no danger of race suicide. You have done well in raising oranges, and I believe you have done better raising children."[142] Throughout TR's presidency, Americans deluged the White House with letters and photographs of their large families, receiving in reply presidential letters of congratulations.[143]

In these exchanges Roosevelt and his audience affirmed the potency of their civilization by affirming the sexual power of American manhood. By repeatedly invoking multitudes of rosy, white, native-born children, these cries of "No race suicide here!" joyfully reassured men that white American manhood was not growing decadent or overcivilized—just look what American paternity could produce! As these humorous protestations multiplied, they took on a ritual quality. At one typical interchange in 1905, Roosevelt was preparing to address the Society of Friendly Sons of St. Patrick at Delmonico's in New York when he was handed a telegram. During the course of the banquet one of the diners, Peter McDonnell, had become a grandfather, and his son Robert had cabled him the good news. TR jocularly announced that "as a sop to certain of my well-known prejudices," he had been shown the telegram, and he then read it aloud to the assembled Friendly Sons. "'Patrick just arrived. Tired after parade. Sends his regards to the President. . . . No race suicide in this family.'" According to the *New York Times,* "Pandemonium resulted. Men yelled and laughed and waved flags and behaved like boys on a lark." When the enthusiasm quieted down enough for TR to continue, he cried out, glass in hand, "And gentlemen, I want you to join with me in drinking the health of Patrick, Peter, Robert, and above all, of the best of the whole outfit, Mrs. McDonnell, the mother." More pandemonium ensued. The Friendly Sons howled their delight, ritually reaffirming their collective joy in healthy paternity, while "Mr. Roosevelt sat back in his chair and witnessed the proceedings with a broad, lasting smile."[144] As TR beamed down on the ecstatic gathering, the message was clear. Overcivilized effeminacy be damned—*they* were men.

This episode typifies these ritual calls of "No race suicide here!" Characteristically, only men took part in these interchanges. Not only was the Friendly Sons banquet all male, for example, but the telegram announcing "No race suicide in this family!" was written by the father to the grandfather, who passed it to the President. In the earlier examples, Mayor Smith and Governor Pardee, respectively, told TR there was "no race suicide" in their bailiwicks. These mutual affirmations that all present were palpably virile can be seen as ritualized claims by men to manhood.

When motherhood comes up in these protestations of "no race suicide here," the tone shifts to a more holy note, designating women as different, purer, and outside the conversation. Mrs. McDonnell, in TR's toast, is "the best of the outfit." No reason need be specified—the goodness of mothers was an unquestioned Victorian verity. But in the context of this public affirmation of male sexual potency, reverence for pure, passionless womanhood reaffirmed its *difference* from virile manhood. Furthermore, the tone of the "no race suicide here" exchanges was just ribald enough to implicitly exclude respectable women from taking part. The humorous, pleasurable allusions to male sexual potency, veiled and proper though they were, marked the discussion as masculine.

It is probably no coincidence that at the same time TR began speaking publicly about race suicide, his letters and writings began to evince a new tone of awestruck veneration of mothers' goodness. "The pangs of childbirth make all men the debtors of all women" became a new catchphrase in his letters and speeches. "The woman who has had a child . . . must have in her the touch of a saint," he avowed.[145] While Roosevelt had always subscribed to conventional Victorian views of womanhood, this vocal, humble reverence for motherhood was new. Perhaps he needed to reaffirm that good women were not sullied by contact with male sexuality but became, as mothers, far purer than any carnal man could ever understand. He may well have been ambivalent about unleashing so much new public affirmation of male sexuality. Roosevelt had long been prudish about any public expression of sexuality—he considered Chaucer "altogether needlessly filthy," for example.[146] Unlike some of his contemporaries (for example, Gilman's nemeses, William T. Sedgwick and Almroth Wright), Roosevelt never showed any interest in fortifying masculinity by praising the primal savage rapist. In his discussion of race suicide, Roosevelt came as close as he ever would to publicly praising male sexuality as an intrinsic aspect of powerful masculinity.

The race suicide discussion which Roosevelt catalyzed made it possible, for the first time since the eighteenth century, for respectable American men to publicly celebrate male sexuality. Throughout the nineteenth century, middle-class men had relegated the expression of male sexuality to a shadowy position in the private domain. Publicly, respectable men praised manly self-control and sexual restraint. But now—as the Sons of Saint Patrick's whoops and hollers showed—male sexuality could be lauded openly as a public service. And in the context of widespread cries of "overcivilized effeminacy" and men's interest in remaking manhood, this new acceptance of male sexuality took on added resonance. This widespread discussion of race suicide between 1903 and 1910 probably facilitated the development of modern ideologies of gender, in which sexual expressiveness became a hallmark of healthy manhood or womanhood.[147] Perhaps no public figure but Roosevelt, with his combination of manly civilized morality and violent frontiersman masculinity, could have raised male sexuality in a way at once so direct and so acceptable. Once again TR had succeeded in combining manliness (morality) and masculinity (sexuality). Not everyone could stomach the combination. Humorists, especially, had a field day ridiculing the incongruity of the dignified president making official pronouncements praising sex.[148] Yet, nonetheless, in the context of the race suicide danger, male sexuality could be seen in a new and eminently respectable light.

The key to reconciling male sexuality with the wider public good, in this way, was the imperative to achieve white racial supremacy. As popularly understood, Darwinism held that natural increase was a necessary component of the survival of the fittest. A race proved its evolutionary fitness by overrunning other races—by both outfighting and outbreeding them. Rising fecundity was thus a proof of racial superiority. Yet the census had shown that native-born, white Americans' birthrate was declining. White American men thus had the responsibility to marry and father multitudes of children in order to reverse this trend and keep the American race superior. It was this racial imperative, as understood through popularized Darwinism, that justified the new public celebration of male sexuality. G. Stanley Hall would soon describe the male orgasm as the "annunciation hour" of holy evolution, just as TR would continue to describe the siring of many healthy children as a public service. No longer was the power of middle-class manhood constructed primarily in terms of keeping masculine sexual passion under firm, willful control. In this light, male sexuality became a most important factor in maintaining race supremacy. Under the terms of the race suicide debates, expressive male sexuality was not an unmanly loss of self-restraint—it was a patriotic racial duty.

In defining "race suicide," Ross had posed a paradox—the same paradox that Beard had posed in his description of "neurasthenia." Civilized, self-restrained manliness was simultaneously the defining characteristic of white racial supremacy and its undoing. The same manly traits which had made white Americans the superior race now prevented them from maintaining their birthrate and led to overcivilized racial decadence. Roosevelt's particular way of understanding this relation of manhood to white racial supremacy provided a solution to Ross' paradox, just as Hall's ability to find primitive masculinity in civilized boyhood had provided a solution to Beard's. White Americans' civilized manliness and racial supremacy would be saved by rehabilitating primitive masculine sexuality. American men would remain as manly as ever, except now they would celebrate their sexual potency rather than merely restrain it. The "masculine"—in the guise of a vigorous sexuality—would come to the aid of the "manly" and safeguard the future of the American race. "No race suicide here!"

The Fantasy Incarnate: Into the Pleistocene

In 1908, having rashly promised not to run for a third term, Roosevelt was forced to consider what came after his presidency. Throughout his life, he had sought to embody the most superior manhood—to be the supreme leader and president of the manly American race. Now that this glorious achievement had come and gone, TR tried to resign himself to abdicating his manly racial leadership. Yet the millennial logic of civilization held that if a man didn't press forward with the quest to perfect his manhood, he would weaken and grow less manly. Could TR find anything to top the manly racial leadership of the presidency? Or had he himself, like an overcivilized race, evolved as far as he could, and did he now face devolution and decadence? If he could no longer be president, what must he do to embrace the "strenuous life"?

Although nothing could ever top the presidency, TR spent his first year after leaving office doing the next most virile thing he could imagine: traveling back in time to the period when primitive man first appeared on earth. That was the way Roosevelt characterized his eleven-month safari to Africa. From the moment Roosevelt first considered taking an African hunting trip, he saw his vacation as a visit to the primeval past: "I cannot say how absorbed I was in your account of that wonderful river voyage through a primeval world," TR wrote an acquaintance traveling in Africa, in 1904. "Think of the 20th Century suddenly going back into the world as it was when the men of the unpolished stone period hunted the mammoth and the woolly rhinoceros! My dear sir, when I get through this work, whether it is a year from now or five years from now, if I have the physical power and you still desire me, I shall most certainly accept for that trip into equatorial Africa."[149] By projecting pure primitivism onto Africa, Roosevelt constructed it as a place where Stone Age men battled large, fierce animals—where he could fully savor both the advancement of his own superior civilized manliness, and the violent power of his primitive masculinity.[150] This view was not unusual: even Victorian anthropologists saw Africa as a land arrested in the Stone Age.[151] Thus, TR was confident that in Africa he would travel to the moment of human origins and relive the primitive, masculine life of his most distant evolutionary forefathers.

In some ways, then, this trip reversed the logic of Roosevelt's political ambitions. From the time he began writing *The Winning of the West*, Roosevelt's prime objective had been to move his race forward, toward a perfect civilization. In this context, the trip to "Stone Age" Africa might seem a sudden reversal, as TR cast his vision backward toward savagery, to the time and place where human evolution first began. Yet, on another level, his African vacation was a perfect way to cap Roosevelt's political career. For, having led his manly race forward as far as he could, the virile president now could time-travel back to the moment of human origins, in order to gain a broader perspective on the evolutionary meaning of his manly racial leadership. This larger evolutionary significance of TR's safari was also suggested by the presence of his twenty-year-old son Kermit. TR's manful son, whose bravery and prowess Roosevelt repeatedly praised in his written account of the trip, affirmed TR's virile reproductive role in the American race's evolution toward the ultimate civilization.

Perhaps the most pleasurable aspect of TR's time-traveling vacation was the way it allowed him to concentrate on the power of his own masculinity. For, as Roosevelt and his contemporaries imagined the primitive past, it was above all characterized by the purest form of primal, violent masculinity— in contrast to the overcivilized present, threatened by decadent effeminacy. By traveling to the ancient past and sharing the bloodly pastimes of his primitive ancestors, TR hoped to reexperience their pure, essential masculinity. Where other men of his time fantasized about primal savage rapists, Roosevelt's fantasies of primal masculine violence were about, not sex, but fights to the death between superior and inferior species.

Officially, Roosevelt's safari was a scientific expedition to collect zoological specimens for the Smithsonian Institution, not a vacation to provide bloody diversion for an ex-president. Stung by earlier allegations that he was a "game butcher," Roosevelt took great pains to assure the public that his aims were purely scientific.[152] Yet pristine science and violent masculinity had always been linked for Roosevelt. At age fifty Roosevelt knew far more about biology than he did as a young boy measuring the dead seal in the marketplace. Yet he still saw nature in terms of "kill or be killed"; he saw wild animals as links in a violent chain of destruction. These Darwinistic views of animals were so important to Roosevelt that in 1907 he had embroiled himself in a most unpresidential public squabble with several popular nature writers. He condemned them for depicting animals in non-Darwinistic terms—for suggesting that weaker animals could prevail in contests with stronger, or that animals possessed advanced, human traits. "Certain of their wolves appear as gifted with all the philosophy, the self-restraint, and the keen intelligence of, say, Marcus Aurelius," he jeered.[153] Manliness in wolves? Absurd! If animals possessed the highest traits of civilized man, hunting would be the murder of brother creatures, instead of the pleasurable reenactment of the Darwinian law of survival of the fittest.

In short, Roosevelt believed his African hunting trip was a return to the primitive past, where he could relive his earliest ancestors' violent Darwinistic masculinity. This was not the first time TR had constructed his manhood in a violent place of "origins." As a young man, he had claimed his manhood on the Western frontier, which he saw as the place where the manly American race was originally forged in bloody conflict with the savage Indians. Now, at age fifty, he had gone even further back in time, to the place of origins—not of the American race—but of the human race itself. Once again, he could construct his manhood by reenacting the white man's evolutionary combat with the primitive, thereby experiencing true masculinity in its purest, most powerful form. Experiencing, as if for the first time, the primal power of his own superior masculinity, far from the enervating decadence of modern civilization—what could be more pleasurable for the leader of the manly race?

African Game Trails, Roosevelt's account of his hunting trip, explicitly situates his hunting adventures in the ancient world of his own Stone Age ancestors. Roosevelt even titled his first chapter "A Railroad through the Pleistocene." (The Pleistocene is the epoch, a million years ago, when humans first appeared on earth.) As Roosevelt described it, in modern Kenya life for both "wild man and wild beast, did not and does not differ materially from what it was in Europe in the late Pleistocene." TR insisted that this comparison was "not fanciful"—that African people and African animals "substantially reproduce the conditions of life in Europe as it was led by our ancestors ages before the dawn of anything that can be called civilization."[154]

These primitive conditions, as TR imagined them, were fraught with masculine violence. Nature, in Pleistocene Africa as in prehistoric Europe, was a primal hotbed of cruelty and interspecies violence, where primitive men battled teeming multitudes of huge and terrible wild beasts. Africa today, according to Roosevelt, still swarmed with fierce animals closely akin to the prehistoric monsters his own Stone Age ancestors once battled in Europe.

> The great beasts that now live in East Africa were in that by-gone age represented by close kinsfolk in Europe. . . . African man, absolutely naked, and armed as our early paleolithic ancestors were armed, lives among, and on, and in constant dread of, these beasts, just as was true of the [European] men to whom the cave lion was a nightmare of terror, and the mammoth and woolly rhinoceros possible but most formidable prey.[155]

In this primitive epoch "the white man" could measure the power of his civilized manhood against both men and beasts who were as savage and fierce as the ones his own caveman ancestors had encountered. TR expected his inter-actions with both wild men and wild beasts of the Pleistocene to prove that, although he was civilized, he shared his ancestors' masculine prowess.

Yet although TR saw African men and African beasts as equally primitive, he related to their evolutionary primitivism in different ways. Roosevelt measured his manhood against that of African *men* by comparing their "primitiveness" to his glorious, civilized manliness. As he saw it, African men were weak, backward, and childlike—barely men at all. (Again we encoun-ter the unmanly savage children of Hall's "racial pedagogy.") For example, he described his safari's porters as "strong, patient, good-humored savages, with something childlike about them that makes one really fond of them. Of course, like all savages and most children, they have their limitations. . . . They are subject to gusts of passion and they are now and then guilty of grave misdeeds and shortcomings; sometimes for no conceivable reason, at least from the white man's standpoint."[156] Charming but limited, these adult Afri-can men were like children. They had never evolved the civilized manliness which allowed the white man to restrain his gusts of passions. TR developed a great paternalistic fondness for these "children," and described their dances, songs, and chants—some composed in his honor—as charming ju-venile antics.[157] By constructing African men as primitive children, TR con-structed himself, in contrast, as a manly civilized paternalist, in much the same mold as G. Stanley Hall's manly racial pedagogue. When they took to calling him "Bwana Makuba," meaning "the chief or Great Master," Roosevelt was delighted, and proudly repeated the title several times in his book.[158] This daily adulation from the crowds of African porters—two hundred sixty were needed to carry the safari's gear—reinforced TR's view of himself as the manly white man, civilized and superior to the primitive childlike savages.[159]

To construct himself as the white man, emissary of civilization in the Afri-can jungle, Roosevelt required a few essentials; and sixty of the "childlike" porters were assigned to carry this equipment for Roosevelt's daily use.[160] Always a voracious reader, TR brought sixty pounds of books on safari, mostly the classics.[161] As he read Homer, Shakespeare, Milton, or Long-fellow under the African skies, he could ponder the glorious civilized accomplishments of his manly race at the same time he was visiting its Pleis-tocene past. Roosevelt also brought a portable bath tub, so that he could take daily hot baths, after which he would retire to drink his tea and eat his im-ported gingersnaps.[162] Books, bathtub, tea, and gingersnaps all provided concrete evidence that the Bwana Makuba upheld manly civilized values like cleanliness and the worth of enduring literature. He was thus superior to the savage porters who, TR presumed, lacked the ability to appreciate these finer things, and were fit only to lug them across East Africa.

Similarly, to commemorate his own position as the mighty former leader of a manly race, Roosevelt brought a large American flag, which flew at night over his capacious tent. TR noted that this flag "was a matter of much pride to the porters, and was always carried at the head or near the head of the march." This, TR implied, demonstrated the Africans' childlike reverence for both the American race and the American nation.[163] TR must have found it appropriate that the "childlike" Africans would revere the flag, symbol of the American nation: after all, TR's own brand of imperialistic nationalism was framed explicitly in terms of his race's manly duty to dominate and control childlike savages.

Yet although Roosevelt depicted Pleistocene African men as childlike and unthreatening, he depicted Pleistocene African animals as exceptionally strong and dangerous. This underlined his own masculine prowess in being able to kill them. Primitive man's violent and masculine life, as TR imagined it, had been filled with intense and unrestrained emotion, now lost to civilized man. In Africa, however, this passionate masculinity retained its primal purity.

> Watching the game, one was struck by the intensity and the evanescence of their emotions. Civilized man now usually passes his life under conditions which eliminate the intensity of terror felt by his ancestors when death by violence was their normal end. . . . It is only in nightmares that the average dweller in civilized countries now undergoes the hideous horror which was the regular and frequent portion of his ages-vanished forefathers.[164]

Hunting in the Pleistocene wild, Roosevelt believed, let him bravely face down the "hideous horror" of the eat-or-be-eaten struggle for survival which his Stone Age ancestors had faced. Here he could experience the pure, original emotions of primal masculinity. Like G. Stanley Hall, TR found in the violence of the primitive a safe way to relive the "hot life of feeling" which civilization had denoted "unmanly."

Roosevelt personally killed 269 mammals during his safari, including thirteen rhinos, eight elephants, seven hippos, seven giraffes, and nine lions. At the end of *African Game Trails,* he lists each kill, modestly insisting "we did not kill a tenth, nor a hundredth part of what we might have killed had we been willing."[165] In killing hundreds of animals and depicting this carnage as restrained behavior, Roosevelt was able to paint himself as simultaneously the ultimate in civilized manly restraint and in primitive masculine prowess. These kills, many of which he describes, allowed Roosevelt to imagine that he possessed the primal masculine virility of his primitive Stone Age ancestors, civilized man that he was.

Only once, in Roosevelt's account, did anything challenge Roosevelt's fantasy of himself as the masculine hunter and manly Bwana in the primal place of racial origins. In eastern Kenya, sixty Nandi warriors were brought in to show Roosevelt how they spear-hunted lion. At first, TR was enthralled: here was the pure, primordial masculinity he had journeyed to the Pleistocene to encounter. The Nandi, TR explained, were a savage, warlike tribe who, scarcely tamed, found civilized British rule "irksome." They were gloriously masculine—"splendid savages, stark naked, lithe as panthers, the muscles rippling under their smooth dark skins." Armed with only one spear each, the Nandi warriors flushed out a "magnificent" lion, "in his prime, teeth and claws perfect, with mighty thews, and savage heart."

Roosevelt waxed lyrical in his description of the ensuing Darwinistic struggle between two consummately primal creatures: the perfectly masculine Nandi, and the matchlessly feral lion. The lion's "life had been one unbroken career of rapine and violence; and now the maned master of the wilderness, the terror that stalked by night, the grim lord of slaughter, was to meet his doom at the hands of the only foes who dared molest him." The hunt itself was a "wild sight," as the Nandi gradually surrounded the lion until—as the lion charged—they speared and killed him. Then, raising their shields over their heads, the warriors chanted a victory song and marched around the dead lion. "This savage dance of triumph," TR wrote, "ended a scene of as fierce interest and excitement as I ever hope to see." What could inspire fiercer interest than a fight between Pleistocene man and a primitive monster, battling to see which was fitter to survive? Here was the essence of primal masculinity.[166]

Indeed, TR was so taken with this drama of primal masculinity that the next day he proposed to repeat it—with one small cast change. Now, Roosevelt wanted to kill the lion *himself,* and to employ the Nandi warriors as mere beaters. After all, he had journeyed to Africa to experience this primal masculine violence himself, not merely to watch savage Africans do it. By repeating the lion hunt, using yesterday's primal warriors as today's subservient beaters, TR could savor the peerless power of his violent masculinity.

Unfortunately for Roosevelt, however, the Nandi warriors refused to cooperate. Lion hunting meant manhood to the Nandi as much as to Roosevelt, it turned out—the more so now that the British colonizers had forbidden them to hunt lion without special permission.[167] Yet, much as they longed to hunt lions, the Nandi men absolutely refused to hunt for Roosevelt unless all agreed that only they be permitted to kill the lion. This permission to hunt in the white man's presence was highly unusual on safaris; generally Africans were permitted to kill only animals that were about to maul a white.[168] Roosevelt had agreed to these conditions for the first hunt, although he had found it a "sore temptation" to break his manly word to the Nandi and shoot the lion himself. But he had no interest in attending any more lion hunts unless he, himself, would be the mighty hunter. TR's terse, one-sentence summary of this incident suggests his frustration with the Nandi's absolute refusal to let him be the virile lion killer.[169] Despite cajolery, arguments, maybe even threats, the Nandi went home and TR continued his Pleistocene vacation without them.

With this brief but irritating exception, Roosevelt's African trip allowed him to fully live out his self-image as the ultimate in white manhood, the apex of evolution—which perhaps qualifies his trip as the ultimate in fantasy vacations. Time-traveling back to the Pleistocene allowed TR to position himself as wielding simultaneously the manly power of civilization and the masculine power of the primitive. On the one hand, he was a white man visiting the Stone Age, the manly Bwana Makuba, whose unquestioned civilized superiority allowed him to command the army of "childlike" native men who served him on safari. On the other hand, he was the Mighty Hunter, a man of the powerful American race, whose masculine force allowed him to pit his manhood against fierce, primitive wild animals proving that he had lost none of the virility of his primal ancestors. In both cases, he was reinforcing his identity as "the white man" by forging it anew in the crucible of the primitive, violent place of racial origins. The pleasure of the expedition, then, lay in the way it positioned TR as the ultimate in powerful, civilized manhood, by counterposing him to the African "primitive." And the cultural meaning TR drew from the expedition was based on the same discourse he had invoked in *The Winning of the West,* "The Strenuous Life," and his fulminations against race suicide. Always, TR linked the power of a race to its manhood, the power of manhood to race, and the power of both to "civilization."

Conclusion

Theodore Roosevelt is often invoked as turn-of-the-century America's prime example of a new and strenuous manhood. This chapter has attempted to show that one cannot understand Theodore Roosevelt's evocation of powerful manhood without understanding that, for Roosevelt, race and gender were inextricably intertwined with each other, and with imperialistic nationalism. In an era when traditional ideologies of manhood were being actively renegotiated, Roosevelt reinvigorated male authority by tying it to white racial supremacy and to a militaristic, racially based nationalism.

Theodore Roosevelt was not a representative American man. He was privileged and powerful, and some of his views were surely idiosyncratic. Yet, as we have seen, his impulse to remake male power by linking it to racial dominance using the discourse of civilization was not unusual. In diverse ways throughout the United States, men who felt the loss of older ideas of male authority—who feared that Victorian manliness was no longer enough to explain the source and workings of male power—turned to ideas of white supremacy. *Men's* power was growing murky. But *the white man's* power, the power of civilization, was crystal clear. And as race became interwoven with manhood through discourses of civilization, Americans' assumptions about manhood moved ever closer to what twentieth-century men would recognize as "masculinity."

From the early 1890s, Roosevelt worked diligently to show American men how this racially based male power worked, and to urge them to claim that power for themselves, both as individual men and as a nation. *The Winning of the West* invited American men to see themselves as a masculine race of Indian fighters. Roosevelt's 1890s advocacy of manly imperialism, in speeches like "The Strenuous Life" and "National Duties," promised American men they could achieve virile power if only they took up the white man's burden. As president, his fulminations against race suicide rehabilitated public celebrations of male sexuality, in the interest of keeping American manhood strong, potent, and able to outbreed the world's inferior races.

Americans fearful about the dwindling potency of Victorian manhood found Roosevelt's formulations of racially dominant manhood exhilarating. For many, Roosevelt himself came to embody the essence of powerful manhood.[170] In 1900, *New York World* columnist Rose Coghlan insisted approvingly (if improbably) that TR was as thrillingly masculine as a primal rapist: "a first-class lover," TR would "come at once to the question, and, if the lady repulsed him, bear her away despite herself, as some of his ancestors must have done in the pliocene age."[171] According to Mark Sullivan, TR was "the outstanding, incomparable symbol of virility in his time."[172]

As Roosevelt's formulations of manhood gained popular attention, they began to take on a life of their own, beyond TR's intentions. For example, where TR's own version of his African safari stressed both manliness and masculinity, popular accounts stressed a far more vulgar and salacious masculinity. A number of fictionalized versions of Roosevelt's safari hit the market before TR could get *African Game Trails* into print. In these unauthorized versions, enterprising journalists fed the public's appetite for stories of violent, sexualized masculinity. The subtitle of Marshall Everett's *Roosevelt's Thrilling Experiences in the Wilds of Africa Hunting Big Game* promised to describe Roosevelt's *Exciting Adventures . . . Mingling with the Savage People, Studying . . . Their Curious Marriage Ceremonies and Barbarous Treatment of Young Girls and Women.*[173] This titillating invocation of "barbarous" African sexual practices hinted at the masculine figure of the primal rapist, who remained implicit in any story of African masculinity, even though TR did not intend this. Unlike TR, Everett stressed masculine sexuality; he discretely but definitely peppered his book with photos and etchings of bare-breasted African women.[174] Everett's depictions of Roosevelt's violent exploits as a mighty hunter are more heroic than TR's; his unmanly African men, more cartoonish. For example, while Roosevelt described bagging his first hippo as an exercise in patience and marksmanship, in Everett's version, Roosevelt is charged by a maddened herd of hippos, kills *two* huge hippos in short order, and single-handedly clubs the rest of the herd off, as his comical "native" companions cower and shriek.[175] Roosevelt had seen Africa as a place of origins, where the white man could prove his superior manhood by reliving the primitive, masculine life of his most distant evolutionary forefathers. The popular press agreed, but their formulations used Roosevelt's distinguished persona to legitimize a more vulgar celebration of both the aggression and the sexuality they associated with primitive masculinity.

Over the next several decades, middle-class constructions of male power would become firmly based on the violence and sexuality of this journalistic version of primitive masculinity. Roosevelt had worked long and hard to revitalize American manhood by predicating it on white racial dominance. While TR would have detested these new middle-class ideologies of sexualized masculinity, his actions—and the actions of those he influenced—helped produce modern twentieth-century ideologies of powerful American manhood.

CONCLUSION
Tarzan and After

Race, gender and power—these were the defining attributes of the discourse of civilization. "Civilization" wove these attributes together by rooting them in a progressive, millennial tale of human history. On this level, "civilization" was a recognizable and coherent set of ideas and practices, shared by many, if not most, middle- and upper-class Americans at the turn of the century. Yet despite this ostensible coherence, the discourse of civilization had no intrinsic political meaning. In different hands, "civilization" could legitimate a variety of contradictory political positions. G. Stanley Hall, Theodore Roosevelt, and the male organizers of the 1893 Columbian Exposition used "civilization" to assert the power of white manhood. Charlotte Perkins Gilman and the Columbian Exposition's Board of Lady Managers used "civilization" to oppose male supremacy. Ida B. Wells and Jack Johnson used "civilization" to oppose white racism. All these Americans shared the belief that as civilization had evolved and advanced, both gender differences and racial differences had likewise evolved. Yet all drew different political conclusions from their belief in the historical connections between race, gender, and "civilization."

In the long run, though, the versions of "civilization" with the most influence were the ones that asserted white male supremacy. Charlotte Perkins Gilman had a loyal readership but her cultural influence never approached Theodore Roosevelt's. Ida B. Wells' 1894 antilynching campaign threw whites temporarily on the defensive, yet Wells never came near eradicating the myth of the Negro rapist. Moreover, as Victorianism lost its cultural power, defenders of white male power turned to masculinist versions of civilization in order to supplement old-fashioned ideologies of civilized "manliness" with newer sorts of primitive "masculinities." Increasingly, "the natural man," with his powerful "masculine" passions, was admired and celebrated by eminent men like G. Stanley Hall, Sir Almroth Wright, and William T.

Sedgwick. Yet Victorian ideologies of civilized, manly self-restraint never disappeared. Instead, men like Hall, Roosevelt, and Sedgwick invoked "civilization" to combine a variety of ostensibly contradictory ideologies of manhood. The logic of "civilization" gave coherence to these potentially confusing blends of manliness and masculinity, self-mastery and unrestrainable passion, refinement and savagery, by rooting them all in "civilization's" larger narrative of millennial advancement toward a higher race and perfect manhood.

By 1912, these ideas had permeated middle-class culture. That year, when the hullabaloo surrounding Roosevelt's safari had barely died down, a hack writer wrote a pulp-magazine adventure story set in a fictionalized Africa strongly reminiscent of TR's mythologized trip. In so doing, he invented a character who would become an enduring twentieth-century symbol of powerful masculinity. In *Tarzan of the Apes,* Edgar Rice Burroughs managed to combine many of the tropes we have already discussed. *Tarzan* suggests how ubiquitous the discourse of civilization, with its blend of race and gender, had become, and how useful it could be in remaking middle-class manhood.

Tarzan of the Apes

Edgar Rice Burroughs was, in many respects, a typical native-born, middle-class American man, with many reasons to be attracted to "civilization's" celebrations of powerful Anglo-Saxon manhood.[1] He was born in 1875 into a prosperous Chicago family whose forebears (his parents proudly noted) had fought in the American Revolution. His father was the vice president of a small company that manufactured storage batteries. At age thirteen, Ed had delighted in visiting the World's Columbian Exhibition, where his father's company was exhibiting an electric automobile. As an adult, however, Burroughs was unable to cash in on the White City's promise of civilized manly mastery. Like so many other middle-class sons of his generation, he was caught in a cycle of downward mobility. With business increasingly large scale and corporate, there were simply fewer opportunities for young men like him to get ahead. A career in the military proved unsatisfactory; he wangled discharge papers after ten months. When the Spanish-American War broke out, he tried to join Roosevelt's Rough Riders, but received a polite note of rejection signed by TR: the famous regiment was already over-enlisted. Other efforts to attain manly power and eminence proved equally unsuccessful. He took jobs as a railway policeman, as a construction timekeeper, as an office manager, as a salesman of books, of candy, of light bulbs. He started a series of small businesses that all failed utterly. Advancement eluded him.[2] He was, in short, precisely the sort of middle-class man who had most reason to crave potent new ways to remake ideologies of powerful manhood.

At age thirty-five, depressed about his inability to support his family, Burroughs began writing pulp fiction in his spare time, and finally achieved success. *Tarzan of the Apes* was one of the best-selling novels of the early twentieth century. After appearing in *All Story* magazine in 1912, it ran serially in at least eight major metropolitan newspapers.[3] In book form, it was published in 1914 and sold 750,000 copies by 1934.[4] It spawned twenty-seven sequels and forty-five movie versions.[5] *Tarzan's* phenomenal success can't be explained by its novelistic artistry. Its prose is wooden, its plot repetitive, its characters mostly one-dimensional. Rudyard Kipling suggested Burroughs wrote *Tarzan* simply "to find out how bad a book he could write and 'get away with.'"[6] The sole memorable feature of *Tarzan of the Apes* is the virile character of Tarzan—a powerfully appealing fantasy of perfect, invincible manhood. *Tarzan's* phenomenal success suggests it struck a deep chord with Americans interested in remaking manhood.[7]

Tarzan's plot can be quickly sketched. Lord John Greystoke, a young British officer on a diplomatic mission, and Lady Alice, his pregnant wife, are set ashore in Africa by mutineers. Within the year, they are dead; but an intelligent and motherly ape, Kala, adopts their infant son, names him "Tarzan," and rears him as an ape. Tarzan's apish education is supplemented by his investigations of the books and artifacts he finds at the beach cabin which (unbeknownst to him) belonged to his dead parents. Boy Tarzan becomes a fierce and mighty hunter. Although he is much smaller than the apes, he is more deadly because he has learned to use Lord John's hunting knife, supplemented with ropes which Tarzan makes out of vines. His great prowess allows him to become king of the apes. When Tarzan is twenty, five other humans are set ashore, also by mutineers. One is Jane Porter, with whom Tarzan falls in love, although he still thinks he is the son of an ape. Tarzan and Jane are separated, however, when Tarzan is called upon to save another white man, Lieutenant D'Arnot, from cannibals. (D'Arnot is from a French ship which arrives to rescue Jane's party.) Tarzan follows Jane to America, where the book concludes, after Tarzan discovers he is the heir to Lord Greystoke and thus not an ape.[8]

The most interesting thing about *Tarzan of the Apes*, in terms of the civilization discourse, is the way it manages to combine many themes we have already seen, including Pleistocene Africa, the figure of the savage little boy, the manliness of the lynch mob, and the figure of the primal rapist. Burroughs began writing *Tarzan of the Apes* in late 1911, about a year after Theodore Roosevelt returned from his highly publicized African safari. Burroughs' fictionalized Africa echoes hack journalists' sensationalized versions of TR's trip. He describes a savage and primal jungle, populated with man-eating cannibals and fierce tigers. Although Burroughs claimed he had researched the "flora and fauna of Africa and the customs of native tribes" in the Chicago Public Library, human meat was never a staple of the African diet, and tigers are indigenous only to Asia.[9] One *All Story* reader pointed out that it was not surprising that Burroughs placed tigers in Africa since "newspaper cartoonists blundered into the same pitfall at the time of Colonel Roosevelt's hunting trip."[10] Burroughs' Africa might not be realistic, but it was a recognizable version of a popular primitivist fantasy—the same masculine fantasy which led Roosevelt to Africa and made journalists invent fictionalized versions of TR's African exploits to satisfy popular curiosity.[11]

Like Roosevelt journeying through the Pleistocene, Burroughs constructed Africa as a place of origins, frozen at the moment the earliest human beings appeared on earth. For Roosevelt, these primal humans had been native African big-game hunters like the Nandi warriors. For Burroughs, however, the original primal humans were the apes who reared Tarzan. Burroughs gives his apes a spoken language, a monarchical government, and a religious ceremony called the "Dum-Dum" which required the ritual use of drums and dancing. Burroughs repeatedly describes the apes as the "progenitors of man" or "our fierce, hairy forebears."[12] The apes signify the primal origins of the civilizing process, the original archetypal savages. For example, the Dum-Dum represents the earliest of all human rituals: "From this primitive function has arisen, unquestionably, all the forms and ceremonials of modern church and state, for through all the countless ages, back beyond the uttermost ramparts of a dawning humanity our fierce, hairy forebears danced out the rites of the Dum-Dum."[13] In *Tarzan*'s sequel, the apes are called simply "the first men."[14] By placing Tarzan in this primal ape culture, Burroughs places him explicitly at the most primitive moment of human origins, when "natural man" appeared in his purest, most primal form. Thus Burroughs, like Roosevelt, constructed Africa as a place where "the white man" could prove his superior manhood by reliving the primitive, masculine life of his most distant evolutionary forefathers.

A childhood in this primal, masculine environment makes Tarzan an exemplar of perfect manhood, and Burroughs repeatedly describes him as such: "an embodiment of physical perfection and giant strength," a "forest god," "a perfect type of the strongly masculine."[15] He is the most resourceful, powerful, courageous man imaginable. Combining the ultimate in Anglo-Saxon manliness with the most primal masculinity, Tarzan is violent yet chivalrous; moral yet passionate. Above all, he has a superb body. If manhood is a historical process that constructs the male body as a metonym for power and identity, *Tarzan*'s cultural work was to proclaim that "the white man's" potential for power and mastery was as limitless as the masculine perfection of Tarzan's body.

Tarzan's perfect masculinity stems from two factors—his white racial supremacy, inherited from his civilized Anglo-Saxon parents, and his savage jungle childhood with the primitive apes. As Burroughs puts it, Tarzan was "only a little English boy. . . . In his veins, though, flowed the blood of the best of a race of mighty fighters, and back of this was the training of his short lifetime among the fierce brutes of the jungle."[16] Tarzan's civilized "blood," combined with his savage training, make him invincible. On the one hand, Tarzan's perfect manhood stems from his civilized racial inheritance. Throughout the book, Tarzan is defined by his race. Even the name "Tarzan," Burroughs informs us, means "white skin" in ape language.[17] Tarzan is not merely white, however; he is the ultimate in Anglo-Saxon racial advancement, the son of Lord and Lady Greystoke, whose old and noble bloodlines are especially superior. As Burroughs puts it, Tarzan is the "aristocratic scion of an old English house," and "the offspring of highly bred and intelligent parents."[18] He thus represents the cutting edge of civilized racial evolution and possesses the inborn intelligence and manly character of the most highly bred Anglo-Saxons. On this level, then, *Tarzan* constructs superior manhood as a racial attribute, inherited by men of civilized races even if they never meet their parents and are reared by savages.

Yet Tarzan's perfect masculinity also stems from his primitive, savage upbringing. After his human parents die, Tarzan is adopted by a female ape and reared as if he were an ape himself. This savage childhood gives him superhuman strength and abilities. By the age of ten, "he was fully as strong as the average man of thirty, and far more agile than the most practiced athlete ever becomes." As an adult, he easily carries burdens too heavy for ten men to lift and, armed only with a knife, effortlessly kills lions. Tarzan's senses, too, are extraordinarily keen, allowing him to smell smoke from a distant boat or to track long-gone prey through the jungle. According to Burroughs, these remarkable physical abilities stem from Tarzan's savage childhood in the jungle; they could never have developed in civilization. Because Tarzan was reared by apes, he attempted to perform apelike feats no civilized boy would have tried; and because he tried, he succeeded. "Man's survival does not hinge so greatly upon the perfection of his senses. His power to reason has relieved them of many of their duties, and so they have, to some extent, atrophied, as have the muscles which move the ears and scalp, merely from disuse."[19] Tarzan was, in short, simply using normal human senses that have atrophied in civilization, where men rely on reason instead of on their bodies.[20]

Thus, in *Tarzan of the Apes*, civilization has a paradoxical relationship to perfect manhood. On the one hand, only civilized races possess the most potent manliness; this is why Tarzan, the aristocratic Anglo-Saxon, always triumphs over beasts and savage black Africans. Yet civilization weakens the male body; this is why Tarzan's savage jungle upbringing gives him the physical strength and perfection no civilized Anglo-Saxon man could possess. Again we encounter the neurasthenic paradox which so bedeviled men like George Beard and G. Stanley Hall. If civilization denoted the most powerful, manliest manhood, yet, at the same time, civilization destroyed men's bodies, how could civilization—or manhood—survive? G. Stanley Hall found his answer in racial recapitulation, the racially mutable adolescent and the savage little boy. Burroughs' answer was fictional but similar to Hall's. Like Hall, Burroughs needed some way to combine the racial superiority of civilized white manliness with a powerful dose of primitive masculinity. And, like Hall, Burroughs suggested a civilized man could be powerful if, as a child, he repeated the primitive life of his savage ancestors.

The story of Tarzan's boyhood takes the logic of Hall's savage little boy to its ultimate extreme and revolves around the dynamic of racial recapitulation. By living fully the life of his most primal ancestors and only gradually ascending the ladder of evolution, Tarzan develops into a perfectly masculine Anglo-Saxon. As a child, Tarzan lives the life of an ape until, as an adolescent, he realizes his development has completely outstripped that of the apes.[21] At that point, Tarzan consciously decides to become a man. To mark his "evolution from the lower orders," as Burroughs puts it, Tarzan attires himself with jewelry and a loincloth, for "nothing seemed to him a more distinguishing badge of manhood than ornaments and clothing."[22] Logically enough, Tarzan begins his human incarnation with the characteristics of a primitive savage: in order to attain his loincloth, he kills a black man. Only later, after Tarzan meets Europeans, does he gradually become civilized. By the end of the book, he has evolved into "Monsieur Tarzan" who, immaculately dressed, drives a French automobile instead of swinging through the jungle.[23] Like Hall's savage little boy, Tarzan must live the life of an animal, and then of a savage, in order to become a man who is both masculine and civilized. And like Hall's recapitulating boy, Tarzan's savage boyhood allows him to become "the embodiment of physical perfection and giant strength"—the super-man.[24]

G. Stanley Hall liked *Tarzan of the Apes* so much he lectured on it in his college courses on human development.[25] Hall's discussion of racial recapitulation in *Adolescence* (1904) closely resembled Burroughs' description of Tarzan's boyhood. As Hall had put it, eight years before *Tarzan's* publication, "Indeed, the boy of ten or eleven is tolerably well adjusted to the environment of savage life in a warm country where he could readily live independently of his parents, discharging all the functions necessary to his personal life, but lacking only the reproductive function."[26] There is no evidence that Burroughs ever worked his way through the turgid prose of *Adolescence*. The similarity between Tarzan's savage boyhood and Hall's savage little boy suggests only that during these decades, a number of Americans, working in very different contexts, were interested in recapitulation and the relationship between boyhood savagery and adult masculinity.

Like Hall's savage boy, young Tarzan lives a life of primal violence. From earliest childhood, Tarzan fights and kills fierce jungle animals. At the age of ten, armed only with a knife, he overcomes a huge bull gorilla.[27] Later he kills the ape-king of his tribe, who had been threatening Tarzan's ape mother, and cries out "I am Tarzan . . . I am a great killer."[28] "Every child is a born criminal," Hall had written. "All children are murderers."[29] Tarzan's violence, like that of Hall's savage boy, was a necessary part of his primal upbringing.

Nor was young Tarzan a great killer of only animals. He was, in fact, a one-man lynch mob, a proud murderer of African men. Burroughs celebrates this racial violence as particularly manly by depicting it in terms reminiscent of the lynching-for-rape scenario. The first man Tarzan lynches is Kulonga, a savage African warrior from the village of Mbonga, who has outraged pure womanhood by murdering Tarzan's ape mother, Kala. At this point in the plot, Jane has not arrived, so Kala, as the "mother" of a white man, is the closest available equivalent to a pure white woman. Burroughs describes her as such: Kala, unlike most apes, has the "round, high forehead" of a racially advanced human being, and "a great capacity for mother love and mother sorrow."[30] She showers Tarzan with a pure, selfless devotion any human mother would be proud to emulate. In describing Tarzan's grief after she is killed, Burroughs explicitly makes Kala the surrogate of Tarzan's dead white mother, and thus the closest possible representative of pure white womanhood: "To Tarzan she had been kind, she had been beautiful. Upon her he had lavished, unknown to himself, all the reverence and respect and love that a normal English boy feels for his own mother. He had never known another, and so to Kala was given, though mutely, all that would have belonged to the fair and lovely Lady Alice had she lived."[31] It was thus "natural"—in terms of the figure of "the natural man," whose first impulse was to lynch the despoiler of pure womanhood—for Tarzan to lynch the man who killed her. Even the method Tarzan uses to lynch Kulonga was the typical method of a lynch mob. Lynch mobs usually hanged their victims; frequently, they were then shot.[32] Tarzan lynches Kulonga by stealthily lowering a rope noose round his head, and then jerking him, struggling, up into the treetops. Lacking a gun to complete the grisly Southern rite, Tarzan then "plunged his hunting knife into Kulonga's heart. Kala was avenged."[33] And Tarzan had become a lyncher.

Lynching becomes second nature to Tarzan, part of his perfect masculinity. Here again, Burroughs' story echoes the narratives of Northern journalists reporting on Southern lynching. Lyncher Tarzan is described as far manlier than his African victims. Burroughs lampoons the "comical" cowardice of Tarzan's victims, just as newspaper columnists ridiculed the unmanly cowardice of lynch victims like "Chicken George."[34] These African men lack a manly character, so they deserve their fate. They are evil and foolish, "more wicked than his own apes, and as savage and cruel as Sabor [the tiger] as well."[35] Worst of all, the Mbongans are unmanly cannibals, who gleefully torture their victims, then butcher them.[36] Like the lynch victims represented in the Northern press, Tarzan's victims—cowards, cannibals, and despoilers of pure womanhood—lack all manhood. Tarzan's lynchings thus prove him the superior man.

Tarzan's lynchings differ from journalists' representations of Southern lynchings in one crucial respect, however: Tarzan *enjoys* his lynchings. Like Theodore Roosevelt killing animals in the African Pleistocene, Tarzan unashamedly finds killing a sport fit for a real man. As Tarzan scouts the Mbonga village, Burroughs explains his interest:

> Few were his primitive pleasures, but the greatest of these was to hunt and kill. . . . That he joyed in killing, and that he killed with a joyous laugh upon his handsome lips betokened no innate cruelty. He killed for food most often, but, being a man, he sometimes killed

for pleasure, a thing which no other animal does; for it has remained for man alone among all the creatures to kill senselessly and
wantonly for the mere pleasure of inflicting suffering and death.[37]

"Man" alone killed for pleasure. Killing was thus not only a species trait, it
was also a sex trait. When Jane Porter, Burroughs' paragon of white womanhood, shoots and wounds an attacking lioness, she promptly faints: the thrill
of slaughter was implicitly masculine. (The decadent Mbonga women loved
to kill, too, but their blood lust demonstrated the absence of sex distinction
among savages.)

After killing Kulonga, Tarzan murders black men frequently, lynching
them by the standard method of hanging. He no longer needs the reason of
avenging pure womanhood to justify his lynchings, however. Now, his mo-
tive is mere larceny: he needs the warriors' arrows and clothing. (Ida B. Wells
had said, "It is only necessary for a white man to blacken his face when he
commits a crime, throw the suspicion on the first Negro he meets, follow
him up until he is lynched, and then enjoy his stolen goods."[38] Once Burroughs establishes Mbonga men as unmanly despoilers of Kala's pure womanhood, they become fair game for Tarzan's larcenous impulses.) Had Tarzan
hesitated at this slaughter, he would have been unmanly and sentimental.
"Tarzan of the Apes was no sentimentalist. He knew nothing of the brotherhood of man. All things outside his own tribe were his deadly enemies. . . .
To kill was the law of the wild world he knew."[39] The law of the jungle was to
kill or be killed. The only difference between killing humans for their arrows
and killing animals for their meat, as Burroughs described it, was that humans must not be eaten. Fortunately, as Tarzan prepares to consume the cannibal Kulonga, his unfailing "hereditary instinct" makes him nauseous.[40]
The impulse to kill black men, like the impulse to avoid cannibalism, was a
racially superior man's inherent masculine instinct.[41]

The impulse for homicidal violence, then, is a basic component of masculinity in *Tarzan of the Apes*. Hall and Roosevelt, too, had constructed aggressive violence as an essential component of primal masculinity; yet they
had needed to contain masculine violence. Hall had made the impulse to homicidal violence a natural masculine attribute—but only for small boys and
deplorable imperialists. Roosevelt had praised homicidal force against Indian or Filipino opponents of American imperialist expansionism—but he
always claimed the "barbarians" had attacked first. Burroughs made no such
halfhearted apologies. He celebrated the "natural man's" masculine impulse
for aggressive, homicidal violence as unashamedly as William Sedgwick and

Almroth Wright had celebrated the masculine capacity to rape unruly feminists into submission.

Respectable men had begun to admire the "masculine" passions that their fathers' generations had constructed "manliness" to restrain. Although they certainly never intended to condone actual rape or murder, their approving representations of masculine violence contributed to the cultural process of remaking manhood and helped create modern gender ideologies which depicted the capacity for rape and violence as an admirable and definitive part of a masculine identity. Tarzan's perfect masculinity stemmed, in part, from his capacity for masculine violence. It is no accident that when Tarzan introduces himself to Jane Porter and her white companions, he identifies himself (in big block letters) as "TARZAN, THE KILLER OF BEASTS AND MANY BLACK MEN."[42]

Once Tarzan is decently clad, he can meet a civilized woman: Tarzan first encounters Jane soon after he lynches the Mbongan warrior for his loincloth. Brigands have left the beautiful Jane Porter stranded, with four companions, on a nearby beach.

With civilized characters in the story, Burroughs can discuss the relationship between manhood and civilization more directly. Three of Jane's companions are civilized white men; they serve to demonstrate Tarzan's savage masculine superiority to more civilized men. Mr. William Cecil Clayton is Tarzan's first cousin. He shares Tarzan's superior racial bloodlines and represents what Tarzan would have become, had his childhood been spent in civilization instead of with the apes. Clayton is brave, honorable, manly, and intelligent—but in the jungle, he is helpless as a baby. Tarzan repeatedly saves Clayton from imminent death, demonstrating his superior, primal masculinity.[43]

The other white men are Professor Archimedes Q. Porter and Samuel T. Philander, Jane's father and his oldest friend. These two wizened old pedants represent the utter effeminacy of too much civilization. Tarzan discovers them engrossed in scholarly debate, so oblivious of their jungle surroundings they don't even notice they are being stalked by a lion.[44] When Philander sees their danger and tells Porter to flee, Porter accuses him of "a most flagrant breach of courtesy in interrupting my learned discourse to call attention to a mere quadruped of the genus *Felis*. . . . I am deeply pained, Mr. Philander, that you should have evinced such a paucity of manly courage in the presence of one of the lower orders."[45] Porter's ideology of civilized manliness is ludicrous and impotent. As he sees it, manly self-mastery requires him to restrain even his passions for self-preservation! Porter is so fixated on civilization that he stubbornly refuses to recognize he is in the primeval jungle.[46] After Tarzan rescues him from the lion, he tries to notify "the directors of the zoo" that their lion is loose.[47] If Africa represents a place where civilized men can test their manhood against the primal, masculine life of savages, its benefits are completely lost on the overcivilized Professor Porter.

Jane Porter and her servant Esmeralda make up the female portion of the party from civilization. Jane is a sweet, nineteen-year-old Southern virgin from Maryland. Esmeralda is Jane's foolish black mammy. The "comic" Esmeralda serves to set off the superiority of Jane's pure white womanhood, just as the Mbonga cannibals set off the superiority of Tarzan's virile white masculinity. Whereas Jane is slender, refined, and beautiful, Esmeralda weighs two hundred and eighty pounds and dresses in gaudy, garish colors.[48] Whereas Jane is calm and intelligent, Esmeralda screams hysterically, rolls her eyes, and faints at the slightest provocation. As the quintessence of pure white Southern womanhood, Jane Porter is a perfect mate for a one-man lynch mob like Tarzan. With a real Southern lady on the scene, we can be sure that an attempted rape will ensue, and that Tarzan will be able to reenact the lynching-for-rape scenario with a more traditional cast of characters than he had with Kala and Kulonga.

Tarzan immediately falls in love with Jane, not least because of her racial characteristics. He is "spellbound" by Jane's "snowy skin" and her "soft mass of golden hair."[49] He is equally drawn by her helplessness: "He knew that she was created to be protected, and that he was created to protect her."[50] In the context of *Tarzan* and "civilization," Jane's delicacy and need for protection are clearly racial characteristics. They contrast with the savagery and independence of the primitive Mbongan women, who raise their own food, attack their own enemies, and never receive protection from the Mbongan men. When Tarzan thinks of Jane, he calls her "the beautiful white girl."[51]

Before Tarzan can reveal himself to Jane and declare his love, however, he hears "an agonized scream." Jane has been abducted by the most primal "black beast" rapist of all: Terkoz, a renegade ape who was thrown out of Tarzan's ape tribe for excessive cruelty. Terkoz, a "horrible man-like beast," intends to eat Jane, but as he drags her throat toward his "awful fangs," the sight of "that fair skin" changes his mind: "This hairless white ape" would make a fine addition to his harem. Terkoz throws Jane across his shoulders and carries her deep into the "impenetrable jungle."[52] Tarzan races after them.

In the ensuing scene, Tarzan's masculine power is constructed by his relationship to the figure of the primal savage rapist. Yet this relationship is complex and contradictory. At first, as Tarzan pursues the ape through the jungle, he continues as the one-man lynch mob, intent on defending the honor of pure white womanhood by killing the primal savage rapist. Yet once Tarzan actually catches up with Terkoz and the still-unraped Jane, Burroughs abandons the lynching-for-rape scenario in favor of an even more primal scene.

Now Tarzan sheds his identity as the civilized, manly avenger, and becomes an impassioned, primitive "natural man." Tarzan squares off with Terkoz in a primal Darwinistic scene of sexual selection; and two males, each perfect of their species, battle for the possession of a desirable female. Gilman had insisted that female sexual choice was the basis of evolution, but in *Tarzan's* version, females have no choice: to the victor will go the spoils. Her "eyes wide with mingled horror, fascination, fear and admiration, [Jane] watched the primordial ape battle with the primeval man for possession of a woman—for her." As she watches the "great muscles" of Tarzan's back and shoulders "knotted beneath the tension of his efforts, and the huge biceps and forearms [holding] at bay those mighty tusks," Tarzan's irresistible primitive masculinity overpowers Jane's civilized sexual reticence, and transports her back across the ages to the primal Darwinistic past, where males battled to prove their fitness to mate with the female. The "veil of centuries of civilization and culture was swept from the blurred vision of the Baltimore girl. When the long knife drank deep a dozen times of Terkoz' heart's blood . . . it was a primeval woman who sprang forward with outstretched arms toward the primeval man who had fought for her and won her." When Tarzan kills Terkoz, all civilization is swept aside, and Jane flings herself into the arms of her primal suitor, to be "smothered" with his hot kisses.[53]

Yet Jane is not a primal savage—that is what makes her so delicate and desirable. "As suddenly as the veil [of centuries of civilization] had been withdrawn it dropped again," and Jane abruptly blushes and tries to fight Tarzan off. Now that Jane has awakened him sexually, however, Tarzan's identity shifts once more. Jane's "perfect lips had clung to his in burning kisses that had seared a deep brand into his soul—a brand which marked a new Tarzan." Although Jane's pure, refined womanhood allows her to draw the "veil of civilization," Tarzan remains a savage, defined by his unleashed passions. His perfect manhood is rooted in the primitive masculinity so fully developed by his ape-life in the jungle. He cannot deviate from the primeval course of the battle he started when he challenged Terkoz for the possession of Jane. Having killed Terkoz, won his woman, and held her in his arms, only one course of action is possible. "Tarzan of the Apes did just what his first ancestor would have done. He took his woman in his arms and carried her into the jungle."[54] Like his first ancestor, Tarzan has become the original savage rapist.

Now, the impulse to rape becomes as central to *Tarzan*'s construction of perfect primitive masculinity as the impulse to kill. Here, again, Burroughs is not unique. Sir Almroth Wright and William T. Sedgwick, likewise, had suggested that the power to rape was an essential aspect of masculine power— that if woman chose to abandon her delicate womanly refinement, man would be equally justified in unleashing "his more brutal appetites toward woman."[55] In the 1890s, Charlotte Perkins Gilman, confident that no white man would want to emulate the unmanly "Negro" in the lynching-for-rape-scenario, had equated antifeminists with the original primal rapist. Yet by the 1910s, in the hands of men like Sedgwick, Wright, and Burroughs, the figure of the savage rapist had begun to lose its negative connotations (at least, as applied to "civilized" whites). A virile man would probably not actually commit rape; but as *Tarzan of the Apes* constructed powerful manhood, a virile man sometimes *wanted* to commit rape.

Burroughs couldn't allow Tarzan to actually rape Jane. In 1912, that would have been too shocking for most Americans to accept. Thus, Tarzan's identity shifts once again, to that of a chivalrous Anglo-Saxon. In a chapter titled "Heredity," Tarzan, the heir to highly civilized Anglo-Saxon nobility, decides not to rape Jane. As Tarzan bears Jane deeper into the jungle, the healthful exercise of traveling through the treetops cools his lust, and allows his racial Anglo-Saxon heredity to take over. His first emotion is one of race pride: he "felt rather than reasoned" that he must act "as a man, and not as an ape." Reared by the savage apes, he doesn't know how a man acts, but, he reasons, Terkoz has shown him how an *ape* acts. Had Tarzan not intervened, Terkoz would have raped Jane. Tarzan compares his own intentions with those of Terkoz. "True, it was the order of the jungle for the male to take his mate by force; but could Tarzan be guided by the laws of the beasts? Was not Tarzan a Man?" Tarzan, who hasn't yet learned how to speak, wishes he could ask Jane how men behave, but then realizes that by resisting his advances, Jane has already told him: civilized men are not rapists.[56] Tarzan's inherited instinct for chivalry, the racial characteristic of civilized Anglo-Saxons, has stopped him from committing rape.

Continued contact with a pure white woman allows Tarzan to discover more fully his inherited Anglo-Saxon manliness. At first, this discovery is symbolic: Jane shows Tarzan how to open the locket he always wears, revealing inside the images of his noble parents, Lady Alice and Lord John. Unwittingly, Tarzan has been carrying them with him all along. Tarzan's buried genetic links to his parents, like their long-hidden photographs inside his locket, are now becoming manifest. By the day's end, Tarzan is a new, almost civilized man. "Contact with this girl for half a day had left a very different Tarzan from the one on whom the morning's sun had risen. Now, in every fiber of his being, instinct spoke louder than training. He had not in one swift transition become a polished gentleman from a savage ape-man, but at last the instincts of the former predominated."[57] Tarzan has discovered within his breast the chivalrous "instincts" he has inherited from Lord John Greystoke. To reassure nervous Jane of his pure intentions before they retire for the night, Tarzan gives her his hunting knife: she can kill him before he will violate her.[58] The civilized race traits of the manly Anglo-Saxon predominate, and the savage rapist is no more.

Yet although Tarzan stops being a savage rapist, he never becomes entirely civilized. The potential for murderous violence always remains an intrinsic part of his perfect masculinity. Even after Lieutenant D'Arnot has begun to teach him the ways of civilization, Tarzan's first impulse upon encountering a group of Africans working in the fields is to fit his bow with a poisoned arrow. ("'Maybe they are friends,' suggested D'Arnot. 'They are black,' was Tarzan's only reply.")[59] When he follows Jane back to America and finds her unhappily engaged to a cad named Canler, Tarzan suggests treating Canler as violently as he once treated the rapist ape Terkoz. "This is not an African jungle," Jane replies. "You are no longer a savage beast. You are a gentleman, and gentlemen do not kill in cold blood." "I am still a wild beast at heart," Tarzan replies in a low voice.[60] Unrestrained masculine *sexuality* might not yet be acceptable in a middle-class representation of perfect primal masculinity, but barely restrained masculine *violence* was becoming essential.

Yet *Tarzan*'s conclusion suggests Burroughs was ambivalent about restraining Tarzan's capacity to rape. Because the civilized Tarzan lacks the primal rapist's sexual aggressiveness, he loses Jane to his effeminate cousin Clayton. Tarzan, now settled in France with D'Arnot, has traveled to America eager to woo and win Jane. He arrives just in time to rescue her from imminent death in a Wisconsin forest fire. (Jane is visiting the North.) Again, Tarzan carries Jane through the treetops, telling her that he is "Your savage, primeval man come out of the jungle to claim his mate."[61] Later, he convinces Canler to release Jane from her promise to marry him. Now that Jane is free to marry, Tarzan proposes marriage like a civilized man. But Jane is not attracted to the civilized, urbane, Frenchified Tarzan, as she was to the jungle savage. "She realized the spell that had been upon her in the depths of that far-off jungle, but there was no spell of enchantment now in prosaic Wisconsin. Nor did the immaculate young Frenchman appeal to the primal woman in her, as had the stalwart forest god."[62] Lacking the primal rapist to sweep her off her feet, as Tarzan did in Africa, Jane has time for sober reflection and decides that it would be more "logical" to marry Clayton, who has social position, a title, education, and whose refined "love she knew to be of the sort a civilized woman should crave."[63] She decides that her passion for Tarzan was simply a momentary atavism, attributable to "a temporary mental reversion to type on her part—to the psychological appeal of the primeval man to the primeval woman in her nature. If he should never touch her again, she reasoned, she would never feel attracted toward him."[64] Of course Tarzan can no longer touch Jane without her permission, since he is no longer the primal rapist. Thus, the romance is doomed. Jane agrees to marry Clayton. Though she soon realizes her mistake, Jane is civilized and feels she must honor her engagement; and Tarzan must now defer to her judgment instead of carrying her off. In the book's final sentence Tarzan repudiates his human inheritance as Lord Greystoke and claims to be what he knows he is not—an ape. If the perfect man loses his woman to a man like Clayton, masculinity and civilization must be incompatible. Thus, *Tarzan*'s ending can be read as an indictment of civilization's effeminacy, an elegy for the doomed primal rapist in the civilized man.[65]

Tarzan's readers refused to accept this denouement, however. *All Story*'s readers were enthusiastic about the rest of Burroughs' book, but they wrote letter after letter complaining about the "punk ending" and demanding a sequel—evidently to make certain that Tarzan and Jane were finally reunited.[66] The readers recognized that under the terms of the discourse, the perfectly masculine primal man must not only be a flawless physical specimen like Tarzan but sexually irresistible, too. Moreover, they felt that Tarzan's perfect, ape-reared masculinity was incompatible with refined civilization, and they wanted Tarzan to abandon his identity as urbane Frenchman and return to the jungle. A month after *Tarzan* was published, Burroughs was preparing to write the sequel, in which Tarzan abandons civilization, returns to Africa, and gets Jane.[67]

Tarzan of the Apes suggests that "civilization" was, indeed, a coherent and recognizable discourse. In *Tarzan*, Burroughs combined four themes which, at first glance, would seem to be unrelated—themes which we have seen deployed by other people in other ways. Burroughs situates *Tarzan* in an imaginary Africa, reminiscent of Theodore Roosevelt's Pleistocene safari. He gives Tarzan a savage boyhood which echoed the pedagogical theories of

G. Stanley Hall. He contrasts Tarzan's perfect white manliness with the primal, unmanly savagery of both apes and Africans, just as the White City and the Midway had done at the Chicago World's Fair; this was the formulation which Wells had inverted in her British antilynching campaign. He used the figure of the primordial savage rapist to represent a natural and uncivilized manhood, just as Charlotte Perkins Gilman and William Sedgwick had done.

If *Tarzan of the Apes* echoes all these other attempts to make or remake manhood, however, it is not because Burroughs was trying to imitate Hall, Gilman, Wells, or Sedgwick. He probably never heard of any of them. The similarity of all these peoples' uses of "civilization," and of the tropes they employed to express the relationship between powerful manhood and race, suggest once again how powerful and ubiquitous was the larger discourse of civilization, and how pervasive it had become in the cultural project to remake manhood.

Sons of Tarzan: Twentieth-Century Implications

Although developments after 1917 are outside the scope of my study, scattered sources suggest that throughout the twentieth century, Americans have drawn upon the discourses of civilization and the primitive to remake and represent powerful manhood. As times have changed, however, so have their strategies. As Victorian formulations of manliness have gradually evaporated, "the natural man's" primitive masculinity has increasingly overshadowed "the white man's" civilized self-mastery.[68]

In 1921, for example, American audiences thrilled to the virile Arab savagery of Rudolph Valentino in *The Sheik*, a movie strongly reminiscent of *Tarzan of the Apes*. *The Sheik*'s hero, Ahmed Ben Hassan, is a white man who, like Tarzan, was reared by a "primitive" race, far from his parents' advanced civilization. In the best-selling novel by Edith Maude Hull, from which the movie was adopted, Ahmed's parents were titled European aristocrats, just as Tarzan's parents were. Like Tarzan, Ahmed's uncivilized rearing makes him so strong and masculine that he has become the absolute ruler of his adopted barbarous tribe.[69]

Unlike *Tarzan*, however, *The Sheik* constructs powerful manhood primarily in terms of the unrestrainable masculine sexuality of the primitive savage rapist. Lake Tarzan after his battle with Terkoz, Ahmed kidnaps his white beloved, Diana Mayo, over her vehement protests. Like Tarzan, Ahmed is attracted to this aristocratic British woman because of her racial attributes: "The pale hands and golden hair of a white woman" are Valentino's first sub-titled words upon meeting Diana. Unlike Tarzan, however, Ahmed is not ashamed of his desire to rape Diana. Ahmed's very attractiveness is predi-cated upon his unrestrained sexual passions which, unlike Tarzan, he never renounces. Passion is the keynote of Valentino's performance. He grins, scowls, and widens his eyes astonishingly, mugging to a degree extreme even for silent film. This represents the savage intensity of his desire for Diana. Because actual on-screen rape was still not acceptable to the American pub-lic, Valentino never actually violates Diana, although several times he nearly does so. Nonetheless, his character is clearly a barely restrained version of the savage rapist. When his French friend chastises him, "Does the past mean so little to you, that you now steal white women and make love to them like a savage," Ahmed responds simply, "When an Arab sees a woman that he wants, he takes her." Hull's novel was less euphemistic. By the end of the fourth chapter, Ahmed has raped the bruised and resisting Diana twice.[70] "Little fool," he says smilingly when she tries to fight. "Better me than my men."[71] Eventually, Hull's Diana succumbs to Ahmed's overwhelm-ing sexual attractiveness, and their nightly encounters become consensual. The movie's Diana, too, falls in love with her passionate, sexually predacious abductor.

Tarzan, the instinctively chivalrous Anglo-Saxon, had renounced his masculine impulse to rape, even though it meant losing the woman he loved. By 1921, however, the movie-going public was eager to see perfect primal manhood on the verge of rape, if not yet as an actual rapist. Women in the audience swooned with passion. Libraries reported a sudden rush of interest in books about Arabs and Arabia; the press reported that hundreds of girls were running away to the Sahara; and the word "sheik" meaning "a masterful man to whom women are irresistibly attracted" became a staple of the 1920s' romantic vocabulary. This visceral response made Valentino a star and sug-gests that ideologies of passionate primitive masculinity had become perva-sive in American culture.[72]

The figure of the primal savage rapist outlived the silent movie era. By the 1940s, Victorianism had long been abandoned as old fashioned, and "deca-dent effeminacy" no longer seemed an impending blight. Yet the old primal rapist was appearing once again—this time, as a humorous caveman who turned up regularly in midcentury cartoons and comic strips. In midcentury America, different issues faced those working to remake manhood. Now, cartoonists invoked a "natural" caveman to lampoon the complexity of modern sexual relations and to contrast them to an imaginary time in prehistory, when civilized niceties like courtship, consent, and women's demands on men had not been invented. This latter-day primal rapist usually wore animal skins draped over one shoulder, carried a huge club, and hunted primal woman as he would have hunted a primal mastodon. Upon finding his prospective mate, he dragged her back to his cave by her hair, while she smiled approvingly. These cavemen were all humorous, for by the 1940s the attractiveness and power of the masculine primitive had so permeated American culture that people took it for granted.

Although this caveman was unquestionably primal and unquestionably masculine, he was usually represented as white. Yet the turn-of-the-century's racial assumptions had only been submerged, not forgotten. If the caveman-rapist trope was elaborated upon, the equation "primitive equals nonwhite" could easily resurface. For example, in the 1949 movie musical, *On the Town,* Clair (Ann Miller), an anthropologist, falls madly in love with Ozzie (Jules Munshin), a sailor, because he looks precisely like the caveman she is studying, *Pithecanthropus Erectus.* She shows Ozzie a model of this *Pithecanthropus Erectus*: it has Munshin's facial features and, like the typical cartoon caveman, wears animal skins draped over its shoulder and carries a huge club. Clair explains why she is drawn to Ozzie: "Yes, you see there are all too few modern males who can measure up to the prehistoric." Clair is a sophisticate who has all the civilized graces; but her desire for a caveman is presented as simultaneously humorous and plausible, as she sings a song about her longings for "a prehistoric man," a "primitive mate" who wears bear skin and beats tom-toms. Actual miscegenation is out of the question; but Claire's fantasies have unmistakable racial overtones. The song-and-dance number dramatizing her desires is set in a museum exhibit of "primitive" African and Polynesian-looking artifacts. As Miller tap-dances, Ozzie and his companions, dressed in the museum's masks, grunt, beat tom-toms, and imitate prehistoric man, using the museum's African and Polynesian artifacts. At one point, Ozzie, carrying a large club, wearing a headdress of animal tusks and an animal-skin loincloth, drags Clair across the floor by her hair, while Clair smiles beatifically and clasps her hands to her chest in a "my hero" attitude. At the end of the sequence, Ozzie-the-prehistoric-rapist gives a Tarzanesque yell.[73]

For the most part, these cartoonish caveman-rapists have disappeared from American culture, but today middle-class men are once again looking to their fantasies about "the natural man" and his primitive past to remake manhood. Since the 1980s, members of a new middle-class "men's movement" have been banding together to perform their own versions of ancient Indian rites.[74] In this, as David Leverenz has pointed out, they are unknowingly imitating men of the late nineteeth century, who banded together into fraternal orders like the New Improved Order of Red Men to perform their own allegedly "Indian" rituals.[75] In the 1990s, tens of thousands of American men—mostly white professionals—have assembled to sit in sweat lodges or engage in drumming, mask-making, dancing, or ritual invocations of West African or Native American gods. They believe these savage—they would say "premodern"—rites will put them back in touch with a lost, primal masculinity.

Like Burroughs, Hall, and Roosevelt at the turn of the century, these new-age apostles of the natural man have turned to the primitive to invent new truths about male identity and male power. Members of this men's movement reject many aspects of the gender ideology they grew up with, especially the notion that men must be aloof and domineering; yet they are equally unhappy with the concept of androgyny, which they associate with feminism. Lacking any established blueprint for a new masculinity, they invent an imaginary past when men's innate, "natural" manhood could be expressed with less constraint. According to Douglas Gillette, men's movement leader and coauthor of the recent *King, Warrior, Magician, Lover: Rediscovering the Archetypes of the Mature Masculine,* the movement is "about reclaiming masculine pride and searching for the essence of masculinity."

> Men now are caught in a sphere of the feminine. We've been wandering in a twilight zone of gender confusion with a cultural ideal of androgyny. Not to romanticize the past, because I don't think there was ever a golden age, but the men's movement is about the recovery of the ritual process we've lost and about getting in touch with the mythic consciousness—with our deep selves—in a postmodern way.[76]

By performing sacred Sioux or Chippewa rituals, drumming, dancing, or chanting to "the Spirit of Deep Masculinity, the West African god they call Hepwa," men in this movement are trying to regain lost, premodern knowledges about the meaning of their own manhood.[77] Like middle-class men at the turn of the century, they look to the lost, prehistoric past to explain what has gone wrong with civilized manhood.

The best-known statement of the movement's philosophy, Robert Bly's *Iron John: A Book about Men,* provides a good overview of some of the ways this movement uses the primitive to remake manhood.[78] *Iron John,* which sold over a half-million copies and was on the *New York Times* best-seller lists for well over a year, is an extended exegesis of a traditional northern European folk tale.[79] According to Bly, folk tales do for humans what instinct does for birds—they are the reservoirs of our species' ancient, accumulated wisdom.[80] Bly speculates that the folk tale "Iron John" "could be ten or twenty thousand years old," and presents it as a "natural" source of primal, instinctive wisdom about how boys should be initiated into manhood in order to fully embrace their power as men.[81]

Bly's method of analyzing "Iron John" is remarkably similar to G. Stanley Hall's method of analyzing adolescence. Like Hall, Bly invokes exotic-sounding customs from a variety of "premodern" cultures to explain what "natural" masculinity was like before it became endangered by modern cultural developments. Bly's theoretical orientation differs from Hall's, in that Hall interpreted primitive man in terms of Darwinism and racial recapitulation, whereas Bly turns to Jungian psychology to explain the course and meaning of human development.[82] Both Bly and Hall, however, turn to cultures they see as primitive in order to discover—that is, invent—a lost, pure, primal masculinity with the capacity to reinvigorate a weakened contemporary manhood. Bly complains that men today are miserable because they have lost their vibrant masculine energy and become "soft men." Gentle, nurturing, and passive, these soft men know how to value their "feminine" side, but, like the effeminate turn-of-the-century neurasthenics who so worried Hall, they are missing "something *fierce*" (Bly's italics).[83] Like Hall, Bly proposes to regain this lost masculine "*fierceness*" by giving young men access to the primitive.

In this light, Bly interprets "Iron John" as an ancient legend full of instinctive, primitive wisdom about true masculinity. "Iron John" tells the story of a young prince who becomes a strong and powerful man with the help of a "Wild Man" from the forest. This Wild Man, named Iron John, represents the lost masculinity of the primitive past; Bly describes him as "a large primitive being with hair down to his feet," and an "ancient hairy man." Iron John has the rare ability to initiate young men into manhood, because he possesses what modern men have lost: the instinctive primal power of true manhood. Bly dubs this the "Wild Man energy" and defines it as "forceful action undertaken . . . with resolve." (A cynic might suggest that "Wild Man energy" is simply old-fashioned "macho" power shorn of its negative connotations, but Bly insists it is different because it is "less cruel.")[84]

Like the turn-of-the-century exponents of primitive masculinity, Bly constructs the Wild Man's manhood in terms of the primitive. Like Hall, Bly associates the Wild Man with the spontaneity of childhood. Like Roosevelt, Bly associates the Wild Man with wildness in nature and wild animals. Like Burroughs, Bly associates the Wild Man with a liberated male sexuality, although unlike Tarzan, Bly's Wild Man is not a rapist. Like all three, Bly associates the Wild Man with men of color: "The native American has much Wild Man in him."[85] Bly's Wild Man, in short, is a direct descendent of what turn-of-the-century men once called "the natural man"—a primal, unfettered man, unrestrained by civilization.

Yet although Bly suggests the primitive can revitalize manhood, he is no more willing to abandon civilization than Hall or Roosevelt were. Like them, Bly constructs powerful manhood as simultaneously primitive and civilized: "The Wild Man is not opposed to civilization; but he's not completely contained by it, either."[86] By following Iron John, Bly's seeker of powerful manhood can heal "the fundamental historical split in the psyche between primitive man and the civilized man."[87] Bly doesn't want men to actually *become* primitive Wild Men, any more than Hall or Roosevelt did. Like them, he simply wants to add "primitive" masculine virtues to "civilization's" positive attributes.

Bly believes that to get in touch with these lost, primitive masculine qualities, civilized young men need older mentors to guide them, possibly using ancient initiation rituals: "The Wild Man's job is to teach the young man how abundant, various, and many-sided his manhood is. The boy's body inherits physical abilities developed by long-dead ancestors, and his mind inherits spiritual and soul powers developed centuries ago."[88] Hall may have looked to the natural evolutionary processes of racial recapitulation, while Bly looks to the therapeutic processes of psychology, but the import is the same. Both men want to revitalize civilized manhood by reviving a lost, instinctive masculinity which boys inherit from their ancient ancestors; and both insist that the only way to recapture that submerged, ancestral masculinity is by embracing the primitive.

Bly claims he is profeminist, but he frequently blames women for making men "soft" and miserable. Sometimes he blames the feminist movement, who "in a justified fear of brutality have labored to breed fierceness out of men."[89] More frequently, however, he blames mothers for committing "psychic incest"—unconsciously turning their sons against their fathers, in order to keep the sons' love for themselves.[90] Bly frequently sounds like a new-age Philip Wylie, as he accuses 1990s mothers of what 1950s misogynists called "smother love." Because of their unconsciously incestuous mothers, many young men never learn to trust older men. As students, these young men will occupy college presidents' offices, and if they become teachers, they will "deconstruct" older writers instead of appreciating them.[91]

Bly praises the Sioux Indians for their custom of forbidding boys over the age of seven to look their mothers in the eyes, thereby avoiding this psychic incest. He warns that "Much sexual energy can be exchanged when the mother looks the son directly in the eyes and says, 'Here is your new T-shirt, all washed.'"[92] He even accuses mothers of trying to claim civilization for their own, in order to undermine the true power of manhood. "Some mothers send out messages that civilization and culture and feeling and relationships are things which the mother and the daughter, or the mother and the sensitive son, share in common, whereas the father stands for and embodies what is stiff, maybe brutal."[93] Yet after repeatedly blaming women for thwarting their sons' access to primal masculinity, Bly always—somewhat unconvincingly—claims it's not really women's fault. It's the fault of older men, who have neglected their duty to properly initiate boys into manhood. Mothers are inherently destructive, so men must construct a more powerful, primal manhood to offset the injurious power of this rampant femininity.

Bly and his movement have every right to engage in the ongoing historical process of making and remaking manhood. Gender is always being made and remade; and there is no reason to ask today's men to be less active in this process than their fathers and grandfathers were. Yet history suggests that the discourse of civilization, with its admiring reference to an unchanging masculine primitive, is a double-edged sword for those who, like Bly, claim to want racial and sexual equality. It is dangerous to construct gender out of race, and the Native American trappings of Bly's own movement show that even in the 1990s, "the primitive" still retains echoes of race.

The impulse to find a pure, lost, powerful masculinity in primitive prehistory possesses a long and dubious history. One hundred years ago, middle-class men eager to remake manhood invented a primal and unchanging manhood from the distant past. In their hands, this tactic simply remade racial and sexual oppression. Feminists like Charlotte Perkins Gilman tried to turn this discourse to their own purposes (much as some women are doing today)[94]; yet, in the long run, this tactic proved misguided, as Gilman discovered to her dismay. Today, men are finding a primal and holy masculinity in the primitive past once more. Once again, they are representing that past in terms of the manhood of nonwhite "premodern" men, especially Native Americans. Like Roosevelt and Hall, these men claim to admire women's advancement but show disturbing signs of antifeminism.

Men have frequently legitimated the ongoing oppression of one type of "other" by praising the unchanging, primal origins of a different type of "otherness." Turn-of-the-century men found something primal and holy in the evolutionary relationship between civilized white men and their ancient savage past, as represented by men of other races; and they used this "primitive masculinity" to legitimate their continuing power over women. Conversely, white Southerners found something primal and holy in the relationship between chivalrous white men and pure white women; and they used this holy "chivalry" to justify a savage reign of racial terror and lynch law, to legitimate their continuing power over African Americans.

Discourses of civilization and the primitive have proven a slippery slope for those who dream of a more just society. Frequently, those who have criticized the "civilized" present by invoking a lost "primitive" past have strongly supported white supremacy, male dominance, or both. Race and gender have been interwoven so tightly in discourses of the civilized and the primitive that they have been impossible to disentangle. Indeed, in 1890, the very attraction of civilization was its mix of whiteness and manhood. Throughout America's history, men and women eager to remake gender have been able to ignore—or to exploit, consciously or not—the ways that issues of race pervade discussions of gender.

This underlines the larger point of my study. My objective in analyzing the turn-of-the-century discourse of civilization has been to contribute to recent scholars' observations that race and gender cannot be studied as if they were two discrete categories. In the past, as in the present, these two categories of difference have worked in tandem, in ways that are no less real for sometimes not being apparent. This suggests two implications for contemporary America.

First, the history of manhood and "civilization" suggests that contemporary difficulties facing poor and working-class men of color in the United States may have a cultural basis, in addition to their widely recognized economic and social basis. Whiteness has long been an intrinsic component of middle-class ideologies of manhood. This may well complicate many men's ability to gain the status of "men" in our patriarchal society. In other words, for men, just as for women, gender can complicate and exacerbate the cultural forces leading to racism.

My major point is simpler, less tentative, and should by now be self-evident. This study suggests that neither sexism nor racism will be rooted out unless both sexism and racism are rooted out together. Male dominance and white supremacy have a strong historical connection. Here, surely, is a lesson that we all can learn from history.

NOTES

Chapter One

1. Al-Tony Gilmore, *Bad Nigger! The National Impact of Jack Johnson* (Port Washington, N.Y.: Kennikat Press, 1975), 41; Randy Roberts, *Papa Jack: Jack Johnson and the Era of White Hopes* (New York: Free Press, 1983), 99. Both books provide excellent broader discussions of Johnson's life and cultural importance.

2. Roberts, *Papa Jack,* 31.

3. Gilmore, *Bad Nigger!* 25–6; Elliott J. Gorn, *The Manly Art: Bare-Knuckle Prizefighting in America* (Ithaca, N.Y.: Cornell University Press, 1986), 218, 238–9.

4. Gilmore, *Bad Nigger!* 26.

5. Jack London, *Jack London Reports: War Correspondence, Sports Articles, and Miscellaneous Writings,* ed. King Hendricks and Irving Shepard (Garden City: Doubleday, 1970), 264.

6. Roberts, *Papa Jack,* 85–6.

7. "Is Prize-Fighting Knocked Out?" *Literary Digest* 41 (16 July 1910): 85.

8. "A Review of the World," *Current Literature* 48 (June 1910): 606.

9. "The Psychology of the Prize Fight," *Current Literature* 49 (July 1910): 57.

10. Roberts, *Papa Jack,* 114.

11. On the riots, see Gilmore, *Bad Nigger!* 59–73; "Is Prize-Fighting Knocked Out?" 85; Roberts, *Papa Jack,* 108–9.

12. *New York Herald,* 5 July 1910, quoted in Gilmore, *Bad Nigger!* 65–6.

13. "Is Prize-Fighting Knocked Out?" 85.

14. Gilmore, *Bad Nigger!* 75–93.

15. Gilmore, *Bad Nigger!* 14; Roberts, *Papa Jack,* 74–5.

16. See, e.g., "Reflections on a Suicide," *New York Times,* 14 September 1912, 12.

17. Roberts, *Papa Jack,* 146; "Mob Threatens Johnson," *New York Times,* 20 October 1912, 12.

18. Roberts, *Papa Jack,* 138–54; Gilmore, *Bad Nigger!* 95–116.

19. Roberts, *Papa Jack,* 158–219; Gilmore, *Bad Nigger!* 117–33.

20. Gilmore, *Bad Nigger!* 148.

21. Theodore Roosevelt, "The Recent Prizefight," *Outlook* 95 (16 July 1910): 550–1.

22. Gilmore, *Bad Nigger!* 81, 108.

23. Hazel V. Carby, *Reconstructing Womanhood: The Emergence of the Afro-American Woman Novelist* (New York: Oxford University Press, 1987), 18. A number of important recent theoretical articles have thoughtfully considered the relation between race and gender in history. They include Evelyn Brooks Higginbotham,

"African-American Women's History and the Metalanguage of Race," *Signs* 17 (December 1992): 251–74; Iris Berger, Elsa Barkely Brown, and Nancy A. Hewitt, "Symposium—Intersections and Collision Courses: Women, Blacks, and Workers Confront Gender, Race, and Class," *Feminist Studies* 18 (Summer 1992): 283–326; and Gerda Lerner, "Reconceptualizing Differences Among Women," *Journal of Women's History* 1 (Winter 1990): 106–22. Two fine articles utilizing these sorts of approaches are Laura F. Edwards, "Sexual Violence, Gender, Reconstruction, and the Extension of Patriarchy in Granville County, North Carolina," *North Carolina Historical Review* 68 (July 1991): 237–60; and Ruth Feldstein, "'I Wanted the Whole World To See': Race, Gender and Constructions of Motherhood in the Death of Emmett Till," in *Not June Cleaver: Women and Gender in Postwar America, 1945–1960,* ed. Joanne Meyerowitz, (Philadelphia: Temple University Press, 1994).

24. For a cross-cultural anthropological discussion, see David D. Gilmore, *Manhood in the Making: Cultural Concepts of Masculinity* (New Haven, Conn.: Yale University Press, 1990).

25. For two otherwise very useful examples, see Mark C. Carnes, *Secret Ritual and Manhood in Victorian America* (New Haven, Conn.: Yale University Press, 1989), and Jeffrey P. Hantover, "The Boy Scouts and the Validation of Masculinity," in *The American Man,* ed. Elizabeth H. Pleck and Joseph H. Pleck (Englewood Cliffs, N.J.: Prentice-Hall, 1980), 285–302.

26. Peter G. Filene, *Him/Her/Self: Sex Roles in Modern America* (Baltimore: Johns Hopkins University Press, 1986), 70.

27. Two examples of this approach are Michael C. Adams, *The Great Adventure: Male Desire and the Coming of World War I* (Bloomington: University of Indiana Press, 1990); and Filene, *Him/Her/Self.* For debates over whether or not there was a "masculinity crisis," see, for example, Filene, *Him/Her/Self,* 69–93; Michael S. Kimmel, "The Contemporary 'Crisis' of Masculinity in Historical Perspective," in *The Making of Masculinities,* ed. Harry Brod (Boston: Allen and Unwin, 1987), 121–54; Margaret Marsh, "Suburban Men and Masculine Domesticity," *American Quarterly* 40 (June 1988): 165–86, and Clyde Griffen, "Reconstructing Masculinity from the Evangelical Revival to the Waning of Progressivism: A Speculative Synthesis," in *Meanings for Manhood: Constructions of Masculinity in Victorian America,* ed. Mark C. Carnes and Clyde Griffen (Chicago: University of Chicago Press, 1990), 183–204.

28. Two fine examples of this approach are Donna Haraway, *Primate Visions: Gender, Race, and Nature in the World of Modern Science* (New York: Routledge, 1989), and Mary Poovey, *Uneven Developments: The Ideological Work of Gender in Mid-Victorian England* (Chicago: University of Chicago Press, 1988).

29. For a more complete discussion of this approach to gender, see Teresa de Lauretis, *Technologies of Gender: Essays on Theory, Film, and Fiction* (Bloomington: University of Indiana Press, 1987), 1–30. See also Judith Butler, *Gender Trouble: Feminism and the Subversion of Identity* (New York: Routledge, 1990); Michel Foucault, *The History of Sexuality,* vol. 1: *An Introduction* (New York: Vintage, 1978); Denise Riley, *Am I That Name? Feminism and the Category of "Women" in History* (New York: Macmillan, 1988); Joan Wallach Scott, *Gender and the Politics of History* (New York: Columbia University Press, 1988); and Joan W. Scott, "Experience," in *Feminists Theorize the Political,* ed. Judith Butler and Joan W. Scott (New York: Routledge, 1992), 22–40.

30. Gilmore, *Bad Nigger!* 14; Roberts, *Papa Jack,* 74.

31. Roberts, *Papa Jack,* 66–7, 160–1.

32. Roberts, *Papa Jack,* 124–6.

33. Jack Johnson, *Jack Johnson is a Dandy: An Autobiography* (New York: Chelsea House, 1969), 22; Roberts, *Papa Jack,* 185–214.

34. Roberts, *Papa Jack,* 54–67, 122.

35. For an excellent treatment of agency and gender, see Poovey, *Uneven Developments.*

36. See, for example, Joe L. Dubbert, "Progressivism and the Masculinity Crisis," in *The American Man,* 303–20; Filene, *Him/Her/Self,* 69–93; John Higham, "The Reorientation of American Culture in the 1890s," in *Writing American History: Essays on Modern Scholarship* (Bloomington: Indiana University Press, 1978), 73–102; Kimmel, "The Contemporary 'Crisis' of Masculinity," 121–54; and James R. McGovern, "David Graham Phillips and the Virility Impulse of the Progressives," *New England Quarterly* 39 (1966): 334-55.

37. Marsh, "Suburban Men and Masculine Domesticity," 165–86; Griffen, "Reconstructing Masculinity," 183–204.

38. Mary P. Ryan, *Cradle of the Middle Class: The Family in Oneida County, New York, 1790–1865* (Cambridge: Cambridge University Press, 1981); Leonore Davidoff and Catherine Hall, *Family Fortunes: Men and Women of the English Middle Class, 1780–1850* (Chicago: University of Chicago Press, 1987). Although *Family Fortunes* discusses English, and not American, middle-class formation, many of the authors' observations, especially about the importance of manliness in class formation, are applicable to the United States.

39. Stuart M. Blumin, *The Emergence of the Middle Class: Social Experience in the American City, 1760–1900* (Cambridge: Cambridge University Press, 1989), 138–91, 298–310; Paul E. Johnson, *A Shopkeeper's Millennium: Society and Revivals in Rochester, New York, 1815–1837* (New York: Hill and Wang, 1978).

40. Ryan, *Cradle of the Middle Class,* 83–151, 116–27; Davidoff and Hall, *Family Fortunes,* 71–192; Nancy F. Cott, *The Bonds of Womanhood: "Woman's Sphere" in New England, 1780–1835* (New Haven, Conn.: Yale University Press, 1977).

41. On character, see Warren I. Susman, "Personality and the Making of Twentieth-Century Culture," in Susman, *Culture as History* (New York: Pantheon, 1984), 273–7; David I. Macleod, *Building Character in the American Boy: The Boy Scouts, YMCA, and Their Forerunners, 1870–1920* (Madison: University of Wisconsin Press, 1983).

42. On "manliness" see Davidoff and Hall, *Family Fortunes,* 108–13; Filene, *Him/ Her/Self,* 70–1; Charles Rosenberg, "Sexuality, Class and Role in Nineteenth-Century America," *American Quarterly* 35 (May 1973): 131–53; *Manliness and Morality: Middle-Class Masculinity in Britain and America, 1800–1940,* ed. J.A. Mangan and James Walvin (New York: St. Martin's Press, 1987); and Norman Vance, *The Sinews of the Spirit: The Ideal of Christian Manliness in Victorian Literature and Religious Thought* (Cambridge: Cambridge University Press, 1985). For an excellent analysis of the final demise of Victorian ideologies of self-restrained manliness in the 1920s, see Christina Simmons, "Modern Sexuality and the Myth of Victorian Repression," in *Passion and Power: Sexuality in History,* ed. Kathy Peiss and Christina Simmons (Philadelphia: Temple University Press, 1989) 157–77.

43. Davidoff and Hall, *Family Fortunes,* 207–8; Ryan, *Cradle of the Middle Class,* 140-2.

44. Ryan, *Cradle of the Middle Class,* 165–85.

45. Filene, *Him/Her/Self,* 73; Richard Hofstadter, *The Age of Reform: From Bryan to FDR* (New York: Vintage, 1955), 218.

46. Blumin, *Emergence of the Middle Class,* 290–5; Filene, *Him/Her/Self,* 70–3.

47. Lewis A. Erenberg, *Steppin' Out: New York Nightlife and the Transformation of American Culture, 1890–1930* (Chicago: University of Chicago Press, 1981), 33–59; John F. Kasson, *Amusing the Million: Coney Island at the Turn of the Century* (New York: Hill and Wang, 1978).

48. Gail Bederman, "'The Woman Have Had Charge of the Church Work Long Enough': The Men and Religion Forward Movement of 1911–1912 and the Masculinization of Middle-Class Protestantism," *American Quarterly* 41 (September 1989): 435–40.

49. Paula Baker, "The Domestication of Politics: Women and American Political Society, 1780–1920," *American Historical Review* 89 (June 1984): 620–47, especially 628–30, and *The Moral Framework of Public Life: Gender, Politics, and the State in Rural New York, 1870–1930* (New York: Oxford University Press, 1991), 24–55.

50. On immigrants and nativism, see John Higham, *Strangers in the Land: Patterns of American Nativism, 1860–1925* (New York: Atheneum, 1971), and Thomas F. Gossett, *Race: The History of an Idea in America* (Dallas: Southern Methodist University Press, 1963), 287–309.

51. Strike statistics in Alan Trachtenberg, *The Incorporation of America: Culture and Politics in the Gilded Age* (New York: Hill and Wang, 1982), 80; work force statistics from Mary Beth Norton et al., *A People and a Nation: A History of the United States,* vol. 2: *Since 1865, 2d ed.* (Boston: Houghton Mifflin, 1986), A-20.

52. [Gaius Glenn Atkins], "The Right and Wrong of Feminism: A Sermon Preached at the Central Congregational Church, Providence, R.I.," (Providence, 1914), 15.

53. On the woman's movement, see Mari Jo Buhle, *Women and American Socialism, 1870–1920* (Urbana: University of Illinois Press, 1981), 49–103; Nancy F. Cott, *The Grounding of Modern Feminism* (New Haven, Conn: Yale University Press, 1987); Filene, *Him/Her/Self,* 3–68.

54. George M. Beard, *American Nervousness: Its Causes and Consequences* (New York: G. P. Putnam's Sons, 1881); F. G. Gosling, *Before Freud: Neurasthenia and the American Medical Community, 1870–1910* (Urbana: University of Illinois Press, 1987); John S. Haller, Jr. and Robin J. Haller, *The Physician and Sexuality in Victorian America* (Urbana: University of Illinois Press, 1974), 3–43; T. J. Jackson Lears, *No Place of Grace: Anti-Modernism and the Transformation of American Culture, 1880–1920* (New York: Pantheon, 1981), 49–57; E. Anthony Rotundo, *American Manhood: Transformations in Masculinity from the Revolution to the Modern Era* (New York: Basic, 1993), 185–93; Tom Lutz, *American Nervousness, 1903: An Anecdotal History* (Ithaca, N.Y.: Cornell University Press, 1991).

55. George Chauncey, Jr. "Christian Brotherhood or Sexual Perversion? Homosexual Identities and the Construction of Sexual Boundaries in the World War I Era," in *Hidden from History: Reclaiming the Gay and Lesbian Past,* ed. Martin Duber-

man, Martha Vicinus, and George Chauncey, Jr., (New York: Meridian, 1989), 313–5; John D'Emilo and Estelle Freedman, *Intimate Matters: A History of Sexuality in America* (New York: Harper and Row, 1988), 225–7.

56. Harvey Green, *Fit for America: Health, Fitness, Sport, and American Society* (Baltimore: Johns Hopkins University Press, 1986); Donald J. Mrozek, *Sport and American Mentality, 1880–1910* (Knoxville: University of Tennessee Press, 1983).

57. Green, *Fit for America*, 242.

58. Green, *Fit for America*, 213, 242–50.

59. Theodore Roosevelt, "Value of an Athletic Training," *Harper's Weekly* 37 (23 December 1893): 1236.

60. See Carnes, *Secret Ritual*.

61. Hantover, "The Boy Scouts," 285–302; and see Macleod, *Building Character in the American Boy.*

62. Green, *Fit for America*, 182–215.

63. Albert J. Beveridge, *The Young Man and the World* (New York: Appleton, 1905).

64. Michael S. Kimmel, "Men's Responses to Feminism at the Turn of the Century," *Gender and Society* 1 (September 1987): 261–83.

65. Victoria Bissell Brown, "The Fear of Feminization: Los Angeles High Schools in the Progressive Era," *Feminist Studies* 16 (Fall 1990): 493–518.

66. Henry James, *The Bostonians* (New York: Modern Library, 1965), 343, quoted in Kimmel, "Contemporary 'Crisis,'" 146.

67. Marsh, "Suburban Men," 165–86.

68. Bederman, "The Women Have Had Charge," 432–65.

69. Gorn, *Manly Art,* 129–45; Roy Rosenzweig, *Eight Hours for What We Will: Workers and Leisure in an Industrial City, 1870–1920* (Cambridge: Cambridge University Press, 1983), 57–64; Christine Stansell, *City of Women: Sex and Class in New York, 1789–1869* (New York: Knopf, 1986), 76–100; Sean Wilentz, *Chants Democratic: New York City and the Rise of the American Working Class, 1788–1850* (New York: Oxford University Press, 1984), 257–64.

70. Erenberg, *Steppin' Out,* 33–59.

71. Gorn, *Manly Art,* 194–206.

72. Higham, "Reorientation," 78–9.

73. Rotundo, *American Manhood,* 251.

74. Marsh, "Suburban Men," 181 n. 4, corroborates my observations.

75. *The Century Dictionary: An Encyclopedic Lexicon of the English Language* (New York: Century, 1890), s.vv. "masculine," "manly."

76. Vance, *Sinews of the Spirit,* 8–10; E. Anthony Rotundo, "Learning about Manhood: Gender Ideals and the Middle-Class Family in Nineteenth-century America," in *Manliness and Morality,* 37–40, 43–6.

77. *The Century Dictionary,* s.v. "masculine."

78. *Oxford English Dictionary,* s.v. "masculinity." The only usage it cites earlier than 1860 is from 1748 and explicitly says the word is French. The earliest use I have found of the noun "masculinity" is a passage from an 1854 novel, which describes a beautiful and sensuous woman as "a tribute to masculinity." Elizabeth Oakes Smith, *Bertha and Lily: Or The Parsonage of Beech Glen, a Romance* (N.Y.: Derby, 1854), 211.

Thanks to Lyde Sizer for this reference. The adjective "masculine," of course, was a much older word: the oldest definition cited in the *Oxford English Dictionary* is from Chaucer in 1374.

79. Chauncey Goodrich and Noah Porter, *An American Dictionary of the English Language by Noah Webster, LLD* (Springfield, Mass.: Merriam, 1890), 505. Two dictionaries which omit "masculinity" are James Stormonth, *A Dictionary of the English Language* (New York: Harper and Brothers, 1885), and *An American Dictionary of the English Language by Noah Webster* (Springfield, Mass.: Merriam, 1847).

80. Gorn, *Manly Art,* 179–206.

81. For fine examples of other possibilities, see Donna Haraway, "Teddy Bear Patriarchy: Taxidermy in the Garden of Eden, New York City, 1908–36," in *Primate Visions,* 26–58; Anson Rabinbach, *The Human Motor: Energy, Fatigue, and the Origins of Modernity* (Berkeley and Los Angeles: University of California Press, 1990); and Mark Seltzer, *Bodies and Machines* (New York: Routledge, 1992).

82. A few words need to be said about the way I am using the term "race." Like gender, race is a way to metonymically link bodies, identity, and power. Its connection to bodies, however, is perhaps more tenuous than that of gender. While men's and women's reproductive systems are not as dualistically opposite as our culture represents them, at least reproductive organs do exist. Race, however, is purely a cultural sign. (See essays in *"Race," Writing, and Difference,* ed. Henry Louis Gates, Jr. [Chicago: University of Chicago Press, 1986].) Most anthropologists deny that any pure racial differences or strains can even be identified. Thus, race, like gender, is a way to naturalize arrangements of power in order to depict them as unchangeable when, in fact, these arrangements of power are actually socially constructed and thus historically mutable. In short, this study's assumption is that race does not exist in nature but only as a cultural construct.

83. Rowland Berthoff, "Conventional Mentality: Free Blacks, Women, and Business Corporations as Unequal Persons, 1820–1870," *Journal of American History* 76 (December 1989): 753–84.

84. David R. Roediger, *The Wages of Whiteness: Race and the Making of the American Working Class* (New York: Verso, 1991).

85. James Oliver Horton, "Freedom's Yoke: Gender Conventions among Antebellum Free Blacks," *Feminist Studies* 12 (Spring 1986): 55; James Oliver Horton and Lois E. Horton, "Violence, Protest, and Identity: Black Manhood in Antebellum America," in *Free People of Color: Inside the African American Community,* ed. James Oliver Horton, (Washington: Smithsonian Institution Press, 1993), 80–96.

86. Frederick Douglass, *Narrative of the Life of Frederick Douglass An American Slave* (1845; New York: New American Library, 1968), 82.

87. David Walker, "David Walker's Appeal: 1828," in *Chronicles of Black Protest,* ed. Bradford Chambers (New York: New American Library, 1968), 56; emphasis in the original.

88. Jim Cullen, "'I's a Man Now:' Gender and African-American Men," in *Divided Houses: Gender and the Civil War,* ed. Catherine Clinton and Nina Silber (New York: Oxford University Press, 1992), 76–91.

89. On the early history of the *National Geographic,* see Philip J. Pauly, "The World and All That Is in It: The National Geographic Society, 1888–1918," *American*

Quarterly 31 (Fall 1979): 516–32, esp. 527–8. For insightful discussions of the concept of the primitive at the turn of the century, see Haraway, *Primate Visions*, 26–58, and Marianna Torgovnick, *Gone Primitive: Savage Intellect, Modern Lives* (Chicago: University of Chicago Press, 1990), 26–33.

90. Major P. H. G. Powell-Cotton, "A Journey through the Eastern Portion of the Congo State," *National Geographic Magazine* 19 (March 1908): 157. See also Phillips Verner Bradford and Harvey Blume, *Ota: The Pygmy in the Zoo* (New York: St. Martin's Press, 1992).

91. Quoted in Stuart Anderson, *Race and Rapprochement: Anglo-Saxonism and Anglo-American Relations, 1895–1904* (Rutherford, N.J.: Farleigh Dickinson University Press, 1981), 25.

92. Rotundo, "Learning about Manhood," 40–2. See also Rotundo, *American Manhood*, 227–32.

93. See Carnes, *Secret Ritual*.

94. Amy Kaplan, "Romancing the Empire: The Embodiment of American Masculinity in the Popular Historical Novel of the 1890s," *American Literary History* 3 (December 1990): 659–90.

95. "The Real Domestic Problem," *Atlantic Monthly* 103 (February 1909): 287; and see 286–8.

96. For other discussions of the meaning of "civilization" at the turn of the century, see David Axeen, "'Heroes of the Engine Room': American 'Civilization' and the War with Spain," *American Quarterly* 36 (Fall 1984): 481–502; Nancy F. Cott, "Two Beards: Coauthorship and the Concept of Civilization," *American Quarterly* 42 (June 1990): 274–300; Frank Ninkovich, "Theodore Roosevelt: Civilization as Ideology," *Diplomatic History* 10 (Summer 1986): 233–45. E. Anthony Rotundo also discusses the part of "civilization" in remaking manhood: yet he erroneously assumes that civilization was always coded feminine (*American Manhood*, 251–5).

97. Foucault, *The History of Sexuality*, vol. 1; Michel Foucault, *Power/Knowledge: Selected Interviews and Other Writings*, trans. Colin Gordon (New York: Pantheon, 1972). Some outstanding recent examples of histories using this sort of methodology are Robert C. Allen, *Horrible Prettiness: Burlesque and American Culture* (Chapel Hill: University of North Carolina Press, 1991); Haraway, *Primate Visions*; Thomas Laqueur, *Making Sex: Body and Gender from the Greeks to Freud* (Cambridge, Mass.: Harvard University Press, 1990); and Rabinbach, *The Human Motor.*

98. George W. Stocking, Jr., *Race, Culture, and Evolution,* (New York: Free Press, 1968), 112–32, esp. 114, 121–2. For an excellent and exhaustive analysis of the history and development of the discourse of civilization, see George W. Stocking, *Victorian Anthropology* (New York: Free Press, 1987). On ideas of civilization in an early American Indian–European context, see Roy Harvey Pearce, *Savagism and Civilization: A Study of the Indian and the American Mind* (Baltimore: Johns Hopkins University Press, 1965).

99. For a discussion of the eighteenth–century roots of this idea, see Rosemarie Zagarri, "Morals, Manners, and the Republican Mother," *American Quarterly* 44 (June 1992): 192–211, esp. 203–5.

100. Cynthia Eagle Russett, *Sexual Science: The Victorian Construction of Womanhood* (Cambridge, Mass.: Harvard University Press, 1989), 144–8.

101. Ernest Lee Tuveson, *Redeemer Nation: The Idea of America's Millennial Role* (Chicago: University of Chicago Press, 1968); James H. Moorehead, *American Apocalypse: Northern Protestants and National Issues, 1860–1869* (New Haven, Conn.: Yale University Press, 1978).

102. Darwinism's reception in the United States is discussed in Richard Hofstadter, *Social Darwinism in American Thought* (Boston: Beacon Press, 1955); Robert C. Bannister, *Social Darwinism: Science and Myth in Anglo-American Thought* (Philadelphia: Temple University Press, 1979); and Cynthia Eagle Russett, *Darwin in America: The Intellectual Response* (San Francisco: Freeman, 1976).

103. For a fine discussion of the Victorian view of the teleological implications of human history from a somewhat different angle, see Christina Crosby, *The Ends of History: Victorians and "The Woman Question"* (New York: Routledge, 1991).

104. W. E. B. Du Bois, "The Conservation of Races," in *Pamphlets and Leaflets by W. E. B. Du Bois*, ed. Herbert Aptheker (White Plains, N.Y.: Kraus Thompson, 1986), 2–4.

105. *The Century Dictionary*, s.v. "masculine." For similar discussions of Victorian ideologies of middle-class manhood as a moral ideal to be achieved, see Charles E. Rosenberg, "Sexuality, Class and Role in Nineteenth Century America," *American Quarterly* 35 (May 1973): 131–53; and Rotundo, "Learning about Manhood," 33–51.

106. Quoted in Russett, *Sexual Science,* 148. See also Russett, *Sexual Science,* 130–55; and Mrinalini Sinha, "Gender and Imperialism: Colonial Policy and the Ideology of Moral Imperialism in Late Nineteenth-Century Bengal," in *Changing Men: New Directions in Research on Men and Masculinity,* ed. Michael S. Kimmel (Newbury Park, Calif.: Sage, 1987), 218–9.

107. Russett, *Sexual Science,* 143–8.

108. "A Happy Marriage," *Literary Digest* 41 (9 July 1910): 78.

109. Stocking, *Victorian Anthropology,* 106.

110. Zagarri, "Morals, Manners, and the Republican Mother," 204.

111. John F. Kasson, *Rudeness and Civility: Manners in Nineteenth-Century Urban America* (New York: Hill and Wang, 1990); Lawrence W. Levine, *Highbrow/Lowbrow: The Emergence of Cultural Hierarchy in America* (Cambridge, Mass.: Harvard University Press, 1988).

112. Quoted in Virginia C. Meredith, "Woman's Part at the World's Fair," *Review of Reviews* 7 (May 1893): 417.

113. James Gilbert, *Perfect Cities: Chicago's Utopias of 1893* (Chicago: University of Chicago Press, 1991), 41–2.

114. Robert W. Rydell, *All the World's a Fair: Visions of Empire at American International Expositions, 1876–1916* (Chicago: University of Chicago Press, 1984), 38–71. My discussion of the racial aspect of the fair draws heavily upon Rydell's excellent analysis. On the cultural meaning of the Columbian Exposition, see also Gilbert, *Perfect Cities,* 75–130; Kasson, *Amusing the Million,* 17–28; and Trachtenberg, *The Incorporation of America,* 208–34.

115. *The Century Dictionary*, s.v. "manly."

116. "The World's Columbian Exposition—A View from the Ferris Wheel," *Scientific American* 69 (9 September 1893): 169.

117. *Chicago Daily Inter Ocean,* 26 April 1893, supplement; cited in Rydell, *All the World's a Fair,* 249, n. 19.

118. Jeanne Madeline Weimann, *The Fair Women* (Chicago: Academy Chicago, 1981), 31. For a good, brief overview of the Woman's Pavilion, see Anne Firor Scott, *Natural Allies: Women's Associations in American History* (Urbana: University of Illinois Press, 1991), 128–34.

119. Weimann, *Fair Women,* 36.

120. Ibid., 51–2.

121. Ibid., 52, 260.

122. Ibid., 232–4.

123. Ibid., 233–4; 260–1.

124. Quoted in ibid., 259.

125. Weimann, *Fair Women,* 152. While the map shows some smaller structures, these were service buildings, not buildings housing exhibits.

126. "Exhibits Which Prove That the Sex is Fast Overhauling Man," *New York Times,* 25 June 1893, quoted in Weimann, *Fair Women,* 427. For a similar assessment, somewhat more humorously patronizing, see M. A. Lane, "The Woman's Building, World's Fair," *Harper's Weekly* 36 (9 January 1892): 40.

127. Russett, *Sexual Science,* 54–77.

128. For lists of Midway attractions, see map in "Opening of the World's Columbian Exposition, Chicago, May 1, 1893," *Scientific American* 68 (6 May 1893): 274–5; "Notes from the World's Columbian Exposition Chicago 1893," *Scientific American* 68 (27 May 1893): 323.

129. Rydell, *All the World's a Fair,* 61–2.

130. Quoted in ibid., 65. Gilbert rightly points out that non-ethnic exhibits mixed among the exotics might have kept some fair-goers from seeing the Midway in terms of the progress of human racial evolution; but even he concedes that the organizers did plan the Midway as "a unitary exhibit of ethnic variation tied together by concepts of evolution and movement through stages of civilization" (Gilbert, *Perfect Cities,* 109). And as the *Chicago Tribune* quote suggests, many fair-goers did see the Midway in these terms.

131. "Sights at the Fair," *Century Magazine* 46 (5 September 1893): 653.

132. For contemporary commentary on this dynamic, see "The World's Columbian Exposition—A View from the Ferris Wheel," 169; and Frederic Remington, "A Gallop through the Midway," *Harper's Weekly* 37 (7 October 1893): 996.

133. "Wonderful Place for Fun," *New York Times,* 19 June 1893, 9. On the Dahomans' reputation as the most primitive savages at the fair, see Rydell, *All the World's a Fair,* 66.

134. Elliot M. Rudwick and August Meier, "Black Man in the 'White City': Negroes and the Columbian Exposition, 1893," *Phylon* 26 (Winter 1965): 354–5; Ann Massa, "Black Women in the 'White City,'" *Journal of American Studies* 8 (December 1974): 319–37; Weimann, *Fair Women,* 103–5, 110–23; and F. L. Barnett, "The Reason Why," in *The Reason Why the Colored American Is Not in the World's Columbian Exposition,* [ed. Ida B. Wells] (Chicago, 1893), 63–81.

135. Rudwick and Meier, "Black Man," 354.

136. Massa, "Black Women," 319–37.

137. Weimann, *Fair Women,* 269; photo on 122.

138. Rudwick and Meier, "Black Man," 357.

139. Quoted in Weimann, *Fair Women,* 393.

140. Quoted in Weimann, *Fair Women,* 404.

141. Wells and Douglass' letter is reprinted in "No 'Nigger Day,' No 'Nigger Pamphlet!'" *Indianapolis Freeman,* 25 March 1893, 4. Unfortunately Wells and Douglass were unable to raise funds to cover printing full translations into four languages. Only the introduction was translated, into French and German.

142. [Ida B. Wells], "Preface," in *The Reason Why the Colored American Is Not in the World's Columbian Exposition,* no page number.

143. Frederick Douglass, "Introduction," in ibid., 2.

144. Ibid., 3.

145. Idid., 10–11.

146. Ibid., 12. Although Wells and Douglass were both partisans of women's equality, they accepted "manly" as a synonym for "civilized." This was not because they themselves identified civilization with men, but because they understood that hegemonic discourses of civilization marginalized African Americans by denigrating their manhood. Therefore, their antiracist version of civilization strategically mobilized "manliness" in the interest of rewriting the relation between civilization and race.

147. Douglass, *The Reason Why,* 9. Lest this sound like Douglass lacks respect for Dahomans, note that American cartoonists leapt to draw unflattering depictions of impossibly thick-lipped Dahoman men, clad (like women) only in brief grass skirts, necklaces, bracelets, and earrings. See Rydell, *All the World's a Fair,* 53, 54, 70.

148. *Crusade for Justice: The Autobiography of Ida B. Wells,* ed. Alfreda M. Duster, (Chicago: University of Chicago Press, 1970), 117.

149. Arthur Ruhl, "The Fight in the Desert," *Collier's* 45 (23 July 1910): 13.

150. Quoted in Gilmore, *Bad Nigger!* 35.

151. Quoted in ibid.

152. Ruhl, "Fight in the Desert," 13.

153. Clippings in Scrapbook 50, Alexander Gumby Collection, Special Collections Division, Columbia University, New York, New York.

154. Jack London, *Jack London Reports,* 277–8.

Chapter Two

1. Ray Stannard Baker, "What is a Lynching? A Study of Mob Justice, South and North," *McClure's Magazine* 24 (February 1905): 429.

2. Ida B. Wells, *A Red Record,* reprinted in *On Lynchings* (1895; Salem, N.H.: Ayer, 1987), 98.

3. "British Anti-Lynchers," *New York Times,* 2 August 1894, 4.

4. "An Idyll of Alabama," *New York Times,* 30 December 1891, 4. See also "The Cartwright Avengers," *New York Times,* 19 July 1893, 4.

5. Paula Giddings, *When and Where I Enter: The Impact of Black Women on Race and Sex in America* (New York: Bantam, 1984), 27–29; Bettina Aptheker, *Woman's*

Legacy: Essays on Race, Sex, and Class in American History (Amherst: University of Massachusetts Press, 1982), 67–8; Angela Y. Davis, *Women, Race, and Class* (New York: Vintage, 1981), 191–2.

6. Joel Williamson, *The Crucible of Race: Black-White Relations in the American South Since Emancipation* (New York: Oxford University Press, 1984), 117, 183–4. Williamson says this proclivity to rape began to be discussed "in and after 1889." This doesn't mean that excessive male sexuality hadn't been associated with African American men before 1889. Winthrop Jordan asserts that as far back as the early modern period, Europeans had asserted that Africans were especially licentious; and that, in the eighteenth and nineteenth centuries, white Americans had argued that black men desired white women (Winthrop Jordan, *White over Black: American Attitudes toward the Negro, 1550–1812* [New York: Norton, 1977], 32–43, 151–62, 398–9). Other scholars, however, have pointed out that the notion that black male sexuality posed a threat to white women took force only after the Civil War. See especially Martha Hodes, "Wartime Dialogues on Illicit Sex: White Women and Black Men," in *Divided Houses: Gender and the Civil War,* ed. Catherine Clinton and Nina Silber (New York: Oxford University Press, 1992), 230–42, and Martha Hodes, "The Sexualization of Reconstruction Politics: White Women and Black Men in the South after the Civil War," *Journal of the History of Sexuality* 3 (1992): 402–17.

7. "Some Fresh Suggestions about the New Negro Crime," *Harper's Weekly* 48 (23 January 1904): 120–1; [T. Thomas Fortune], "The Rape Racket," *New York Freeman,* 20 August 1887, 2; Frederick Douglass, "Why Is the Negro Lynched?" in *The Life and Writings of Frederick Douglass,* ed. Philip S. Foner, 4 vols. (New York: International, 1955), 4:491–523.

8. For statistics, see James Elbert Cutler, *Lynch Law* (New York: Longmans, Green, 1905), 170; and Robert L. Zangrando, *The NAACP Crusade against Lynching, 1909–1950* (Philadelphia: Temple University Press, 1980), 6.

9. Edward L. Ayers, *Vengeance and Justice: Crime and Punishment in the Nineteenth-Century South* (New York: Oxford University Press, 1984), 236–55, esp. 250; Williamson, *Crucible of Race,* 111–39.

10. LeeAnn Whites, "Rebecca Latimer Felton and the Wife's Farm: The Class and Racial Politics of Gender Reform," *Georgia Historical Quarterly* 76 (Summer 1992): 368–72.

11. Nell Irvin Painter, "'Social Equality,' Miscegenation, Labor, and Power," in *The Evolution of Southern Culture,* ed. Numan V. Bartley (Athens, Ga.: University of Georgia Press, 1988), 47–67.

12. Jacquelyn Dowd Hall, "'The Mind That Burns in Each Body': Women, Rape, and Racial Violence," in *Powers of Desire: The Politics of Sexuality,* ed. Ann Snitow, Christine Stansell, and Sharon Thompson (New York: Monthly Review Press, 1983), 335. On Southern white men's projection of repressed sexuality onto black men, see also Jacquelyn Dowd Hall, *Revolt against Chivalry: Jessie Daniel Ames and the Women's Campaign against Lynching* (New York: Columbia University Press, 1979), 148; and Trudier Harris, *Exorcising Blackness: Historical and Literary Lynching and Burning Rituals* (Bloomington: University of Indiana Press, 1984), 1–28.

13. I will be discussing only Northern views of lynching in this chapter. Although at times Northerners' opinions of lynching, civilization, and manhood were echoed

by Southerners, Southern commentators frequently employed more extreme rhetoric than Northerners. Moreover, Southern ideologies of manhood were slightly different from Northern, due to differing emphasis on factors like "honor." Perhaps most important, few Northern men actually formed lynch mobs. I don't want to overstate the differences. Southerners, perhaps even more than Northerners, constructed male dominance by drawing on white supremacy through ideologies of civilized manliness. But since this study does not get into issues of specifically Southern views of manhood and race, I have decided to discuss only Northerners' views of lynching. On Southern ideas of "honor," see Ted Ownby, *Subduing Satan: Religion, Recreation, and Manhood in the Rural South, 1865–1920* (Chapel Hill: University of North Carolina Press, 1990). For a discussion of Southern manliness and honor during an earlier period, see also Bertram Wyatt Brown, *Southern Honor: Ethics and Behavior in the Old South* (New York: Oxford University Press, 1982).

14. "Mob Law in Arkansas," *New York Times*, 23 February 1892, 4.

15. Quoted in "The Burning of Negroes," *Public Opinion* 16 (October 5, 1893): 3.

16. John D'Emilio and Estelle B. Freedman, *Intimate Matters: A History of Sexuality in America* (New York: Harper and Row, 1988), 178–82.

17. D'Emilio and Freedman, *Intimate Matters*, 68–9; John S. Haller and Robin M. Haller, *The Physician and Sexuality in Victorian America* (Urbana: University of Illinois Press, 1974), 191–234; Cynthia Eagle Russett, *Sexual Science: The Victorian Construction of Womanhood* (Cambridge, Mass.: Harvard University Press, 1989), 112–6.

18. On character, see Warren I. Susman, "Personality and the Making of Twentieth-Century Culture," in Susman, *Culture as History* (New York: Pantheon, 1984), 273–7; David I. Macleod, *Building Character in the American Boy* (Madison: University of Wisconsin Press, 1983).

19. On "manliness" see Leonore Davidoff and Catherine Hall, *Family Fortunes: Men and Women of the English Middle Class, 1780–1850* (Chicago: University of Chicago Press, 1987), 108–13; Peter G. Filene, *Him/Her/Self: Sex Roles in Modern America* (Baltimore: Johns Hopkins University Press, 1986), 70–1; *Manliness and Morality: Middle-Class Masculinity in Britain and America, 1800–1940,* ed. J. A. Mangan and James Walvin (New York: St. Martin's Press, 1987); and Norman Vance, *The Sinews of the Spirit: The Ideal of Christian Manliness in Victorian Literature and Religious Thought* (Cambridge: Cambridge University Press, 1985).

20. Karen Lystra, *Searching the Heart: Women, Men, and Romantic Love in Nineteenth-Century America* (New York: Oxford University Press, 1989), 58–87, 113–20; Ellen K. Rothman, *Hands and Hearts: A History of Courtship in America* (Cambridge, Mass.: Harvard University Press, 1987), 187–8, 198–200, 230–2.

21. D'Emilio and Freedman, *Intimate Matters,* 178–82; E. Anthony Rotundo, *American Manhood: Transformations in Masculinity from the Revolution to the Modern Era* (New York: Basic, 1993), 119–28. On deviant young middle-class men's contradictory approach to sexual passion in an earlier time, see Patricia Cline Cohen, "Unregulated Youth: Masculinity and Murder in the 1830s City," *Radical History Review* 52 (Winter 1992): 33–52.

22. Michel Foucault, *The History of Sexuality,* vol. 1: *An Introduction* (New York: Vintage, 1978).

23. For a fine discussion of the myth of the African American man as rapist, see

Angela Y. Davis' influential "Rape, Racism, and the Myth of the Black Rapist," in *Women, Race, and Class,* 172–201.

24. As discussed in the first chapter, "manly" referred to the highest forms of manhood, while "masculine" referred merely to any characteristics, good or bad, which all men had. As *The Century Dictionary* put it, "Masculine . . . applies to men and their attributes." Unlike "manly," which referred to traits which civilized men had, "masculine" referred to traits which savage men and civilized men both possessed.

25. As the *Encyclopedia Britannica* put it in 1898, "No full-blood Negro has ever been distinguished as a man of science, a poet, or an artist, and the fundamental equality claimed for him by ignorant philanthropists is belied by the whole history of the race throughout the historic period." *Encyclopedia Britannica,* 9th ed., s.v. "Negro."

26. Quincy Ewing, "The Heart of the Race Problem," *Atlantic Monthly* 103 (March 1909): 389.

27. Charles Carrington, *Rudyard Kipling* (London: Macmillan, 1978), 334.

28. "The White Man's Problem," *Arena* 23 (January 1900): 1–30.

29. Edward C. Gordon, "Mob Violence: 'The National Crime,'" *Independent* 46 (1 November 1894): 1400–1. Only in writings by black authors did the words "the black man" frequently appear. Even there, however, asymmetrical references to "the white man" versus "the Negro" abounded.

30. "Negro Lynching," *Providence Journal,* 2 February 1893, 5.

31. "Negroes Lynched by a Mob," *New York Times,* 10 March 1892, 1.

32. "Mob Law in Arkansas," *New York Times,* 23 February 1892, 4.

33. Quoted in "The Disgrace of Georgia and Alabama," *Current Literature* 37 (October 1904): 294.

34. One African American commentator pointed this out: D. E. Tobias, "A Negro on the Position of the Negro in America," *Nineteenth Century* 46 (December 1899): 966–7. I found no other writers who noticed this very salient point.

35. "The Cartwright Avengers," *New York Times,* 19 July 1893, 4. See also B. O. Flower, "The Burning of Negroes in the South: A Protest and a Warning," *Arena* 7 (April 1893): 631–7.

36. Albion Tourgée was the one white journalist I found who consistently and unequivocally opposed lynching. He died in 1905. On the absence of concern about racism or lynching among Progressive muckrakers, see Maurine Beasley, "The Muckrakers and Lynching: A Case Study in Racism," *Journalism History* 9 (Autumn-Winter 1982): 86–91.

37. Baker, "What is a Lynching?" 301–2.

38. Ibid., 429.

39. The biographical information in this chapter is taken primarily from [Ida B. Wells-Barnett], *Crusade for Justice: The Autobiography of Ida B. Wells,* ed. Alfreda M. Duster (Chicago: University of Chicago Press, 1970). Additional biographical information on Wells may be found in Bettina Aptheker, "Woman Suffrage and the Crusade against Lynching, 1890–1920," in Aptheker, *Woman's Legacy: Essays on Race, Sex, and Class in American History,* (Amherst: University of Massachusetts Press, 1982), 53–76; Paula Giddings, "Ida Wells-Barnett 1862–1931," in *Portraits of Amer-*

ican Women from Settlement to the Present, ed. G. J. Barker-Benfield and Catherine Clinton (New York: St. Martin's Press, 1991), 366–85; Giddings, *When and Where I Enter,* 19–31, 89–93; Thomas C. Holt, "The Lonely Warrior: Ida B. Wells-Barnett and the Struggle for Black Leadership," in *Black Leaders of the Twentieth Century,* ed. John Hope Franklin and August Meier (Urbana: University of Illinois Press, 1982), 39–50; Mary Magdelene Boone Hutton, "The Rhetoric of Ida B. Wells: The Genesis of the Anti-Lynch Movement" (Ph.D. diss., Indiana University, 1975); Dorothy Sterling, *Black Foremothers: Three Lives* (New York: Feminist Press, 1988), 61–117; Mildred Thompson, "Ida B. Wells-Barnett: An Exploratory Study of an American Black Woman, 1893–1930" (Ph.D. diss., George Washington University, 1979), 20–125; David M. Tucker, "Miss Ida B. Wells and Memphis Lynching," *Phylon* 32 (Summer 1971): 112–22; Vron Ware, *Beyond the Pale: White Women, Racism, and History* (New York: Verso, 1992), 167–224. Hazel V. Carby deftly analyzes Wells' antilynching pamphlets in the context of the 1890s black women's movement in *Reconstructing Womanhood: The Emergence of the Afro-American Woman Novelist* (New York: Oxford University Press, 1987), 95–120, and in "'On the Threshold of Woman's Era': Lynching, Empire, and Sexuality in Black Feminist Theory," in *"Race," Writing, and Difference,* ed. Henry Louis Gates, Jr. (Chicago: Univeristy of Chicago Press, 1985), 301–16.

40. See, e.g., Iola [Ida B. Wells], "A Southern Woman's Earnest Plea for Organization," *New York Freeman,* 9 July 1887, 1; Iola, "Woman's Mission—A Beautiful Christmas Essay on the Duty of Woman in the World's Economy," *New York Freeman,* 26 December 1885, 2.

41. Wells-Barnett, *Crusade for Justice,* 19–45.

42. Ibid., 52. For a full account of the lynching, see Wells-Barnett, *Crusade for Justice,* 47–52; Giddings, *When and Where I Enter,* 17–18; and Tucker, "Miss Ida B. Wells and Memphis Lynching," 115–6.

43. Iola [Ida B. Wells], "Freedom of Political Action—A Woman's Magnificent Definition of the Political Situation," *New York Freeman,* 7 November 1885, 2.

44. Ida B. Wells, 11 April 1887, diary 1884–1887, Ida B. Wells Papers, Department of Special Collections, University of Chicago Library; also quoted in Sterling, *Black Foremothers,* 77.

45. "The Lynchers' Winces," *New York Age,* 19 September 1891.

46. In 1891, after attacking the inferior conditions of Memphis' black schools in her paper, Wells was fired from her job as a teacher and was frustrated to discover that most of African American Memphis, instead of supporting her, blamed her for sticking her neck out. Wells-Barnett, *Crusade for Justice,* 37.

47. Tucker, "Miss Ida B. Wells and Memphis Lynching," 116–7; Wells-Barnett, *Crusade for Justice,* 53–58.

48. Ida B. Wells, *Southern Horrors: Lynch Law in All Its Phases,* reprinted in *On Lynchings* (1892; Salem, N.H.: Ayer, 1987), 4.

49. Quoted in Wells, *Southern Horrors,* 5.

50. Wells-Barnett, *Crusade for Justice,* 401.

51. See, for example, Iola [Ida B. Wells], "Iola's Southern Field—Save the Pennies," *New York Age,* 19 November 1892, 2; Iola, "The Reign of Mob Law: Iola's Opin-

ion of Doings in the Southern Field," *New York Age,* 18 February 1893 (Typescript in Ida B. Wells Papers, University of Chicago); Wells, *Southern Horrors,* 22–3.

52. Wells-Barnett, *Crusade for Justice,* 86; see also 219.

53. Ibid., 21.

54. Iola [Ida B. Wells], "Woman's Mission," 2. See also Iola [Ida B. Wells], "The Model Woman," *New York Age,* 18 February 1888, 2.

55. Wells diary, 28 June, 8 July 1886, 13 July 1887, Ida B. Wells Papers. The other ambitious young woman was Mary Church, later Terrell.

56. Wells-Barnett, *Crusade for Justice,* 8, 10.

57. Iola [Ida B. Wells], "Our Women," *New York Freeman,* 1 January 1887, 2 (reprinted from the *Memphis Scimitar*). See also Iola, "The Model Woman," 2.

58. Ida B. Wells, "Lynch Law in All Its Phases," *Our Day* 11 (May 1893): 345. See also Iola, "Freedom of Political Action," 2.

59. On the centrality of middle-class gender conventions to the African American middle class, of which Wells was a part, see Kevin Gaines, *Uplifting the Race: Black Politics and Culture in the United States Since the Turn of the Century* (Chapel Hill: University of North Carolina Press, 1995); and Evelyn Brooks Higginbotham, *Righteous Discontent: The Women's Movement in the Black Baptist Church, 1880–1920* (Cambridge, Mass.: Harvard University Press, 1993), esp. 184–229. Although my analysis of Wells' antilynching campaign, following Gaines and Higginbotham, stresses Wells' ladylike manipulations of middle-class gender ideology, Wells' activism also had a far more feisty side, which I have had to scant here. For an excellent, contrasting analysis of Wells' writings which stresses the uppity, feminist nature of her reworkings of Victorian gender, in the context of the black and white women's movements, see Carby, *Reconstructing Womanhood,* 108–16. Christina Simmons analyses a similar renegotiation of racist Victorian gender ideology in "African Americans and Sexual Victorianism in the Social Hygiene Movement, 1910–1940," *Journal of the History of Sexuality* 4 (Summer 1993): 31–75.

60. Wells, *Southern Horrors,* Preface (no page number), and 5.

61. Wells, *Southern Horrors,* 8, and see 7–10; emphasis in original.

62. Ibid., 6.

63. Ibid., 11–2.

64. Ibid., 14

65. Carby, *Reconstructing Womanhood,* 6; Carby, "On the Threshold," 303–4.

66. Albion Tourgée, "A Bystander's Notes," *Chicago Daily Inter Ocean,* 24 September 1892, 4.

67. George C. Rowe, "How to Prevent Lynching," *Independent* 46 (1 February 1894): 131–2.

68. *The Reason Why the Colored American Is Not in the World's Columbian Exposition,* [ed. Ida B. Wells], (Chicago, 1892); for the plans to print translations, see "No 'Nigger Day,' No 'Nigger Pamphlet!'" *Indianapolis Freeman,* March 25, 1893, 4.

69. Wells-Barnett, *Crusade for Justice,* 77–78, 82, 85–86. Also see Wells' comments in "Idol of Her People," *Chicago Daily Inter Ocean,* 8 August 1894, 2.

70. Although Wells' speeches were covered extensively by the English press, they are mostly unobtainable in this country. Mary Magdelene Boone Hutton's disserta-

tion, "The Rhetoric of Ida B. Wells: The Genesis of the Anti-Lynch Movement" (Indiana University, 1975) uses British press reports extensively to document both tours. The excerpts Hutton cities are similar in tone to interviews Wells gave to American papers immediately after returning, and to Wells' book, *A Red Record,* published early in 1895. Thus, I am using these sources, in addition to a few available English sources, to reconstruct what Wells said.

71. "A Sermon on Ibsen—A Coloured Woman in the Pulpit," *Christian World* 38 (14 March 1894): 187; quoted in Hutton, "The Rhetoric of Ida B. Wells," 127.

72. Ida B. Wells, Letter, "Lynch Law in the United States," *Birmingham Daily Post* (England), [16 May 1893]. Undated xerox in Ida B. Wells Papers. The article is reprinted and dated in Wells-Barnett, *Crusade for Justice,* 101, but the editor did not transcribe it accurately.

73. Wells rarely mentioned the word "Anglo-Saxon" explicitly during the British agitation—most likely because she herself did not want to reinforce the discourse, understanding that it ultimately worked against racial equality. She occasionally used the term "Anglo-Saxon" before and after the British agitation, always ironically or derogatorily. See I. B. Wells, "Afro-Americans and Africa," *A.M.E. Church Review* 9 (January 1892): 40–41; Ida B. Wells-Barnett, "Mob Rule in New Orleans" (1900), in *On Lynchings,* 46. Yet, despite her dislike for Anglo-Saxonism, she clearly understood the discourse and knew how to use it to her advantage in the British campaign.

Just as middle-class Northern white men liked to see themselves as manlier than Southern white men, so genteel British men were delighted to preen themselves as more manly and civilized than American men. Middle- and upper-class Britons, of course, were themselves suffering from their own insecurities about the dwindling potency of Victorian "manliness," and were working to remake powerful manhood. Widespread interest in remaking the potency of British manliness probably made genteel Britons especially responsive to Wells' message that manly Britons must impart civilization to the unmanly Americans.

74. Quoted in "An Anti-Lynching Crusade in America Begun," *Literary Digest* 9 (11 August 1894), 421.

75. Ida B. Wells, quoted in the *London Daily Chronicle,* 28 April 1894, 3, in Hutton, "The Rhetoric of Ida B. Wells," 135.

76. Wells, *A Red Record,* 74–5.

77. Ida B. Wells, "Ida B. Wells Abroad—A Breakfast with Members of Parliament," *Chicago Daily Inter Ocean,* 25 June 1894, 10; also in Wells-Barnett, *Crusade for Justice,* 179.

78. Ida B. Wells, "Ida B. Wells Abroad—The Bishop of Manchester on American Lynching," *Chicago Daily Inter Ocean,* 23 April 1894, 10; "Against Lynching—Ida B. Wells and Her Recent Mission in England," *Chicago Daily Inter Ocean,* 4 August 1894, 1; Wells-Barnett, *Crusade for Justice,* 95, 139, 141. As a young woman Wells had studied elocution; see Wells diary, 23 March 1886, Ida B. Wells Papers.

79. On images of black women as inherently unwomanly, see Carby, *Reconstructing Womanhood,* 20–61; Giddings, *Where and When I Enter,* 85–94.

80. Ida B. Wells, "Ida B. Wells Abroad—Her Reply to Governor Northen and Others . . . The English Papers and People Resent the Attack on a Woman," *Chicago Daily Inter Ocean,* 7 July 1894, 18.

81. Quoted in Wells, *A Red Record,* 84.

82. Wells-Barnett, *Crusade for Justice,* 111–13; 202.

83. The main documents of this public debate can be found in Wells, *A Red Record,* 80–90; Wells-Barnett, *Crusade for Justice,* 201–11, and "Draw No Color Line— Position of the W.C.T.U. Stated by Miss Willard," *Chicago Daily Inter Ocean,* 17 November 1894, 5. See also Ware, *Beyond the Pale,* 198–212.

84. Ida B. Wells et al. "Symposium-Temperance," *A.M.E. Church Review* (7 April 1891): 379–80. Thanks to Kevin Gaines for this reference.

85. See Ruth Bordin, *Woman and Temperance: The Quest for Power and Liberty, 1873–1900* (Philadelphia: Temple University Press, 1981).

86. Willard's address was reprinted in "Draw No Color Line," *Chicago Daily Inter Ocean,* 17 November 1894, 5. Her speech condemns white men for having liaisons with black women (though she says this practice has largely stopped after slavery), as well as black men for raping white women (though she stresses that the average black man would never be a rapist). She seems not to notice that this asymmetrical argument implies black women are unchaste: i.e., white women are raped, whereas black freedwomen have voluntary liaisons.

87. Wells, *A Red Record,* 89. Of course, Willard also was loathe to alienate the white Southern women she had worked so hard to recruit into the W.C.T.U.; see Bordin, *Woman and Temperance,* 72–94.

88. Wells, *A Red Record,* 87–88.

89. See Wells, *A Red Record,* 80–90; Wells-Barnett, *Crusade for Justice,* 111–3, 201–10. See also Albion Tourgée, "A Bystander's Notes—Lynching as a Fad," *Chicago Daily Inter Ocean,* 24 November 1894, 12.

90. See, for example, Wells, *A Red Record,* 12–14. Many African Americans pressured Wells to stop speaking of white women's unchastity; see Wells-Barnett, *Crusade for Justice,* 220-1.

91. For more on the results of Wells' British agitation, see Ware, *Beyond the Pale,* 173–8, 182–90.

92. "The Bitter Cry of Black America—A New 'Uncle Tom's Cabin.'" *Westminister Gazette* 3 (10 May 1894): 2; quoted in Hutton, "The Rhetoric of Ida B. Wells," 146.

93. "Lynch Law in America," *Christian World* 38 (19 April 1894): 287; quoted in Hutton, "The Rhetoric of Ida B. Wells," 156.

94. Xerox marked "The Birmingham Daily Gazette, May 18th [1893]" in the Ida B. Wells Papers.

95. Ida B. Wells, "Ida B. Wells Abroad—A Breakfast with Members of Parliament," 10; Hutton, "The Rhetoric of Ida B. Wells," 156–9, 170–1; Wells-Barnett, *Crusade for Justice,* 176, 190–7; "English Feeling upon America's Lynchings," *Literary Digest* 9 (14 July 1894): 308; "That Irish Begging Letter," *New York Times,* 9 September 1894, 12; "The Sneer of a Good Natured Democrat," *Indianapolis Freeman,* 16 June 1894, 4.

96. Quoted in Ida B. Wells, "Ida B. Wells Abroad—Lectures in Bristol, England, on American Lynch Law," *Chicago Daily Inter Ocean,* 19 May 1894, 16. A version is also in Wells-Barnett, *Crusade for Justice,* 157–58, but the editor did not transcribe it precisely.

97. Wells-Barnett, *Crusade for Justice,* 215–7; Hutton, "The Rhetoric of Ida B. Wells," 68–9.

98. Quoted in "How Miss Wells' Crusade is Regarded in America," *Literary Digest* 6 (28 July 1894): 366.

99. Quoted in "The Anti-Lynching Crusade," *Literary Digest* 6 (8 September 1894): 544.

100. Edward C. Gordon, "Mob Violence: 'The National Crime,'" 1400.

101. Since the South was solidly Democratic, Northern Democratic newspapers were more likely to defend Southern practices and politicians, while Republican newspapers were more likely to attack them. See, for instance, "An Anti-Lynching Crusade in America Begun," 421–2; and Editorial, *New York Times,* 16 March 1894, 4.

102. Reprinted as "Lessons for Busybodies," *New York Times,* 15 October 1894, 9; "London Week of Excitement," *New York Times,* 7 October 1894, 1. See also "English Criticism of the English Anti-Lynching Committee," *Literary Digest* 9 (27 October 1894): 757; and "British Anti-Lynchers," *New York Times,* 2 August 1894, 4. In the London *Spectator,* a debate on lynching raged in the "Letters to the Editor" column, while the editors simultaneously condemned lynching and called on Britons to stop interfering in American internal affairs. See Editorial, *Spectator* 72 (16 June 1894): 810; W. McKay, Letter, "Lynching in Georgia: A Correction," *Spectator* 73 (28 July 1894): 111; S. Alfred Steinthal, Letter, "Lynching in America," *Spectator* 73 (4 August 1894): 142; Chas. S. Butler, Letter, "The Lynching of Negroes in America," *Spectator* 73 (25 August 1894): 240; ΒΑΡΒΑΡΟΣ, Letter, "Lynch Law in the United States," *Spectator* 73 (8 September 1894): 303; and "Lynching in America and English Interference," *Spectator* 73 (11 August 1894): 1669–70.

103. "An Anti-Lynching Crusade in America Begun," 421.

104. Although some historians have suggested that no delegations of British Anti-Lynching Committees ever came to the United States, contemporary press reports suggest that Sir John Gorst—and perhaps a small committee—came as a representative of the London Committee. See "Sir John Gorst's Report," *New York Times,* 10 September 1894, 8; "Governor Northen is Aroused," *New York Times,* 11 September 1894, 2; "Southern Governors on English Critics," *Literary Digest* 9 (22 September 1894): 601–2; and Peter Stanford, "Serious Complications—The Anti-Lynch Sentiment in England Being Cooled," *Indianapolis Freeman,* 1 December 1894, 1.

105. "Gov. Northen is Aroused," *New York Times,* 11 September 1894, 2; "Southern Governors on English Critics," *Literary Digest* 9 (22 September 1894): 601–2.

106. "A Bad Week for the Lynchers," *Independent* 46 (18 September 1894): 1187.

107. "Killing of the Six Tennessee Negroes," *New York Times,* 9 September 1894, 12.

108. Quoted in "The Latest Lynching Case," *Literary Digest* 9 (15 September 1894): 577; Wells, *Southern Horrors,* 5.

109. Tucker, "Miss Ida B. Wells and Memphis Lynching," 121–2.

110. "How Miss Wells' Crusade is Regarded in America," 366 (see footnote 98); "Helping Miss Wells' Crusade," *New York Times,* 11 December 1894, 6.

111. Quoted in "The Anti-Lynching Crusade," 545 (see footnote 99). For a selection of Northern newspaper editorials in favor of or against the antilynch agitation,

see, in addition, "An Anti-Lynching Crusade in America Begun," 421–2; and "Remedies for Lynch Law: A Case in Point," *Indianapolis Freeman*, 4 August 1894, 4.

112. Wells, *A Red Record*, title page, 72. For a similar opinion, see "His 'Opinion' No Good," *Indianapolis Freeman*, 29 September 1894, 4. See also "Remedies for Lynch Law—A Case in Point," *Indianapolis Freeman*, 4 August 1894, 4; and Thompson, "Ida B. Wells-Barnett: An Exploratory Study," 116–22.

113. Ayers, *Vengeance and Justice*, 237–55; Williamson, *Crucible of Race*, 117–8. Tucker, on the other hand, credits Wells' campaign with curtailing lynchings in Memphis; see Tucker, "Miss Ida B. Wells and Memphis Lynching," 121–2.

114. Cutler, *Lynch Law*, 229–30; Peter Stanford, "Serious Complications—The Anti-Lynch Sentiment in England Being Cooled," *Indianapolis Freeman*, 1 December 1894, 1.

115. See, for example, "Lynching," *New York Times*, 27 May 1895, 5; "Lynching in the South," *New York Times*, 14 January 1896, 4. Compare these to "The Cartwright Avengers," published in the *Times* in 1893.

116. "Public Sentiment against Lynching," *New York Times*, 8 December 1895, 32; Cutler, *Lynch Law*, 233–45.

117. "Lynch Law," *Saturday Review* 71 (30 May 1891): 643. For other invocations of "natural man," see also Jus et Justitia, Letter, "The Causes of Lynching," *New York Times*, 18 July 1892, 10; and "Lynch Law in Michigan," *Public Opinion* 15 (3 June 1893): 200 (*Detroit Free Press* editorial).

118. B. O. Flower, "The Rise of Anarchy in the United States," *Arena* 30 (September 1903): 309–10.

119. Dean Richmond Babbitt, "The Psychology of the Lynching Mob," *Arena* 32 (December 1904): 589; see 586–9.

120. William James, "A Strong Note of Warning Regarding the Lynching Epidemic (1903)," *Essays, Comments, and Reviews* (Cambridge, Mass.: Harvard University Press, 1987), 170–1. This article was reprinted as "How Can Lynching Be Stopped?" in *Literary Digest* 27 (8 August 1903): 156. For press reaction, see "How To Put Down Lynching," *Nation* 77 (30 July 1903): 86; "The One Remedy for Mobs," *World's Work* 6 (August 1903): 3829–30, and "Murder," *Outlook* 74 (8 August 1903): 877–80.

121. James, "A Strong Note of Warning," 172. See also "Judge Lynch as an Educator," *Nation* 57 (28 September 1893): 223.

122. Elliot J. Gorn, *The Manly Art: Bare-Knuckle Prizefighting in America* (Ithaca, N.Y.: Cornell University Press, 1986), 237–47.

123. On "nature" as a cultural construction, see, for example, Maurice Bloch and Jean H. Bloch, "Women and the Dialectics of Nature in Eighteenth-century French Thought" in *Nature, Culture and Gender*, ed. Carol P. MacCormack and Marilyn Strathern (New York: Cambridge University Press, 1980), 25–41; Donna Haraway, *Primate Visions: Gender, Race, and Nature in the World of Modern Science* (New York: Routledge, 1989); Ludmila Jordanova, "Natural Facts: An Historical Perspective on Science and Sexuality," in *Nature, Culture, and Gender*, ed. MacCormack and Strathern (New York: Cambridge University Press, 1980), 42–69; Marianna Torgovnick, *Gone Primitive: Savage Intellect, Modern Lives* (Chicago: University of Chicago Press, 1990).

124. See, for example, Ida B. Wells-Barnett, "Lynching and the Excuse for It," *Independent* 53 (16 May 1901): 1133–6; Ida Wells-Barnett, "Lynching Our National Crime," *Proceedings of the National Negro Congress, 1909* (New York: Arno, 1969), 174–9; and Ida B. Wells-Barnett, "Our Country's Lynching Record," *Survey* 29 (1 February 1913): 573–4.

125. Wells had been a founding member of the African American woman's club movement and had been active in the woman suffrage movement. See Wells-Barnett, *Crusade for Justice,* 120–3, 242–5, 269–74, 279–88, 345–7. According to Thompson, Wells was criticized for being a woman heading a man's organization, and she was somewhat defensive about it; Thompson, "Ida B. Wells-Barnett: An Exploratory Study," 187–88.

126. On Wells' activities with the Negro Fellowship League, see Wells-Barnett, *Crusade for Justice,* 300–7, 330–3, 353, 356–8, 409–14, and Thompson, "Ida B. Wells-Barnett: An Exploratory Study," 183–91.

127. Carby, *Reconstructing Womanhood,* 6, 20–61; Giddings, *When and Where I Enter,* 82–9.

Chapter Three

1. *Chicago Record,* 4 April 1899, 8.
2. "Dr. Hall's Ultra Views," *Chicago Evening Post,* 4 April 1899, 4.
3. "Corporal Punishments," *New York Education* 3 (November 1899): 163.
4. For a complete biography of Hall, see Dorothy Ross' excellent *G. Stanley Hall: The Psychologist as Prophet* (Chicago: University of Chicago Press, 1972). On native-born Protestant culture in New England and the northeast, see, for example, Nancy F. Cott, *The Bonds of Womanhood: "Woman's Sphere" in New England, 1780–1835* (New Haven, Conn.: Yale University Press, 1977) and Mary P. Ryan, *Cradle of the Middle Class: The Family in Oneida County, New York, 1790–1865* (Cambridge: Cambridge University Press, 1981).
5. As Warren Susman has pointed out, "character" was synonymous with "manhood." Warren I. Susman, *Culture as History* (New York: Pantheon, 1984), 273–4.
6. Granville B. Hall to G. Stanley Hall, 3 April 1852, G. Stanley Hall Papers, Clark University Library, box 1, folder 2.
7. Abigail Beale Hall to G. Stanley Hall, 13 September 1859, Hall Papers. See also Abigail Beale Hall to G. Stanley Hall, 31 December 1853, Hall Papers, box 1, folder 2.
8. Michel Foucault, *The History of Sexuality,* vol. 1: *An Introduction* (New York: Vintage, 1978).
9. G. Stanley Hall, *Life and Confessions of a Psychologist* (New York: Appleton, 1923), 76–7, 131–3. Did the young boy, so aware of his own genitals' "dirtiness," identify with the castrated piglets? The question is unanswerable, but in a school essay on "Hogs," nine-year-old Stanley enthusiastically described, not the castrated hogs he knew from the barnyard, but wild boars armed with powerful "long tusks with which they kill folks" ("Composition Book," 1853, Hall Papers, box 1, folder 2).
10. Hall, *Life and Confessions,* 131, 134.
11. G. Stanley Hall, *Adolescence: Its Psychology and Its Relations to Physiology, An-*

thropology, Sociology, Sex, Crime, Religion and Education, 2 vols. (New York: Appleton, 1904), 1:438–9. Although Hall never wrote explicitly about his own discovery of masturbation, in *Adolescence* he described the process in terms which almost certainly echo his own experiences. Hall had a tendency to extrapolate about general tendencies from his own experiences and to use autobiographical episodes, phrased in the third person, as evidence to support his psychological theories.

12. Hall, *Life and Confessions,* 132.

13. Hall, *Adolescence,* 1:457–8.

14. Hall, *Life and Confessions,* 132–3.

15. John S. Haller, Jr., and Robin Haller, *The Physician and Sexuality in Victorian America* (Urbana: University of Illinois Press, 1974), 195–207; Gail Pat Parsons, "Equal Treatment for All: American Medical Remedies for Male Sexual Problems 1850–1900," *Journal of the History of Medicine* 32 (January 1977): 61–4; Lesley A. Hall, *Hidden Anxieties: Male Sexuality, 1900–1950* (Cambridge: Polity, 1991), 14–32, 54–62.

16. Haller and Haller, *Physician and Sexuality,* 211–25; Parsons, "Equal Treatment for All," 64–8.

17. Cynthia Eagle Russett, *Sexual Science: The Victorian Construction of Womanhood* (Cambridge, Mass.: Harvard University Press, 1989), 104–29.

18. Quoted in Parsons, "Equal Treatment for All," 61–2.

19. Ross, *G. Stanley Hall,* 35–7.

20. Gail Bederman, "'The Women Have Had Charge of the Church Work Long Enough': The Men and Religion Forward Movement of 1911–1912 and the Masculinization of Middle-Class Protestantism," *American Quarterly* 41 (September 1989): 432–65; T. J. Jackson Lears, *No Place of Grace: Antimodernism and the Transformation of American Culture, 1880–1920* (New York: Pantheon, 1981).

21. For additional views of neurasthenia, see F. G. Gosling, *Before Freud: Neurasthenia and the American Medical Community, 1870–1910* (Urbana: University of Illinois Press, 1987); Haller and Haller, *Physician and Sexuality,* 3–43; Lears, *No Place of Grace,* 49–57; E. Anthony Rotundo, *American Manhood: Transformations in Masculinity from the Revolution to the Modern Era* (New York: Basic, 1993) 185–93; Russett, *Sexual Science,* 104–16; and Tom Lutz, *American Nervousness, 1903: An Anecdotal History* (Ithaca, N.Y.: Cornell University Press, 1991).

22. For dates, see Gosling, *Before Freud:* 13.

23. George M. Beard, *American Nervousness: Its Causes and Consequences* (New York: G. P. Putnam's Sons, 1881).

24. Hall, *Adolescence,* 1:290. On Beard himself, see Charles E. Rosenberg, "The Place of George M. Beard in Nineteenth-Century Psychiatry," *Bulletin of the History of Medicine* 36 (1962): 245–59 and "Obituary," *New York Times,* 24 January 1883, 5. On Beard's friendship with Hall, see Hall, *Life and Confessions,* 235, and Ross, *G. Stanley Hall,* 150–1.

25. Beard, *American Nervousness,* 3; emphasis in original.

26. On this view of the body as a machine limited by the first law of thermodynamics, see Russett, *Sexual Science,* 104–29. See also Beard's own explanation of neurasthenia in terms of the laws of physics in George M. Beard, *Sexual Neurasthenia: Its Hygiene, Causes, Symptoms, and Treatment, with a Chapter on Diet for the Nervous*

(New York: Treat, 1884), 57–64. Lutz, in *American Nervousness,* offers insight on the connection between neurasthenia's "bankruptcy" metaphor and class issues surrounding the middle class and capitalism.

27. Beard, *American Nervousness,* 11.

28. Ibid., 6–8.

29. Ibid., vi.

30. Ibid., 92.

31. Ibid., 26.

32. Because neurasthenia's implications varied for men and women, this chapter will focus only on neurasthenia and men. I will postpone the discussion of neurasthenia and women to the next chapter.

33. Beard, *American Nervousness,* vi.

34. Ibid., 56, 26.

35. Ibid., 17, 100–38.

36. Ibid., 121.

37. Ibid., 33–4.

38. Ibid., 153–4.

39. R. B. Kershner, Jr., "Degeneration: The Explanatory Nightmare," *Georgia Review* 40 (Summer 1986): 416–44.

40. Ross, *G. Stanley Hall,* provides an excellent account of Hall's quest for professional eminence.

41. Beard, *American Nervousness,* 135–6.

42. G. Stanley Hall, "New Departures in Education," *North American Review* 140 (February 1885): 144–5; G. Stanley Hall, "Overpressure in Schools," *Nation* 41 (22 October 1885): 338.

43. Hall, "Overpressure in Schools," 338.

44. G. Stanley Hall, "Phi Beta Kappa Oration," *Brunonian,* 17 June 1891, 109–16. Hall, a prodigious public speaker, evidently found these ideas so meaningful that he frequently repeated chunks of this speech during the early 1890s. See, for example, G. Stanley Hall, "Address Delivered at the Opening of Clark University," *Clark University, Worcester, Massachusetts: Opening Exercise, October 2, 1889* (printed by the university), 9–32; and G. Stanley Hall, "Hints on Self Education," *Youth's Companion* 65 (16 June 1892): 310.

45. Hall, "Phi Beta Kappa," 109.

46. Ibid., 110.

47. Ibid., 111.

48. Kershner, "Degeneration," 416–44.

49. G. Stanley Hall, "The Study of Children," in *Report of the Committee of Education for the Year 1892–93,* 367–8. Copy in G. Stanley Hall, Collected Works (unpublished), at Clark University Library.

50. Stephen Jay Gould, *Ontogeny and Phylogeny* (Cambridge, Mass.: Harvard University Press, 1977); Carl Degler, *In Search of Human Nature: The Decline and Revival of Darwinism in American Social Thought* (New York: Oxford University Press, 1991), 4–47. For an excellent discussion of the interactions between cultural developments and Darwin's own writings, including a discussion of recapitulation, see Gillian Beer, *Darwin's Plots: Evolutionary Narrative in Darwin* (London: Routledge and Kegan Paul, 1983), esp. 104–45.

51. Gould, *Ontogeny and Phylogeny,* 69–166; Russett, *Sexual Science,* 49–77, esp. 53–4.

52. Gould, *Ontogeny and Phylogeny,* 69–114; 135–55.

53. See, for example, G. Stanley Hall, "Child Study and Its Relation to Education," *Forum* 29 (August 1900): 694, 696; Hall, *Adolescence,* 1:v.

54. G. Stanley Hall and Arthur Allin, "The Psychology of Tickling, Laughing, and the Comic," *American Journal of Psychology* 9 (October 1897): 12–13.

55. Ibid., 20.

56. G. Stanley Hall, "Heirs of the Ages," *Proceedings N. J. Association for the Study of Children and Youth* (March 1899): 10.

57. For example, see also G. Stanley Hall, "A Study of Fears," *American Journal of Psychology* 8 (January 1897): 147–249.

58. G. Stanley Hall, "Student Customs," *Proceedings, American Antiquarian Society* 141 (October 1900): 84–5.

59. Hall, *Adolescence,* 1:x–xi; see also 1:45.

60. G. Stanley Hall, "Pedagogical Methods in Sunday School Work," *Christian Register* 74 (November 1895): 719–20.

61. Of course, Hall didn't need recapitulation to associate boyhood with savagery. Middle-class culture already associated boyhood with the primitive. See Rotundo, *American Manhood,* 30, 36. However, when Hall put these older ideas about boyhood savagery in the context of recapitulation and of civilization's movement toward the millennium, he was able to imbue them with a much larger—even cosmic—cultural significance. For the cultural context of the late-century interest in "bad boys," see Steven Mailloux, *Rhetorical Power* (Ithaca, N.Y.: Cornell University Press, 1989), 100–29.

62. G. Stanley Hall and Theodate L. Smith, "Showing Off and Bashfulness As Phases of Self-Consciousness," *Pedagogical Seminary* 10 (September 1903): 97. This whole passage reappears almost verbatim in Hall, *Adolescence,* 2:59–60.

63. Hall and Smith, "Showing Off," 97–8.

64. See chapter 1.

65. G. Stanley Hall, "Some Fundamental Principles of Sunday School and Bible Teaching," *Pedagogical Seminary* 8 (December 1901): 463. See also Hall, "Child Study and Its Relation to Education," 700.

66. On the wider cultural rejection of this feminized religion, see Bederman, "The Women Have Had Charge."

67. Hall saw this vaccination process as one whereby actual "rudimentary organs" were temporarily developed, allowing boys to repeat the savage emotions of their primitive ancestors. These primitive emotional organs needed to be actively used so that they could later atrophy and make way for more evolutionarily advanced powers to develop. Hall and Allin, "The Psychology of Tickling," 17.

68. Hall, *Adolescence,* 2:452.

69. Ibid., 2:398.

70. G. Stanley Hall, "Address at the Dedication of the Haston Free Public Library Building, N. Brookfield Mass. September 20, 1894," in *The Haston Free Public Library Building* (Brookfield, Mass.: Lawrence, 1894), 20.

71. G. Stanley Hall, "The Ideal School as Based on Child Study," *Forum* 32 (September 1901): 27–32.

72. G. Stanley Hall, "The Education of the Heart (Abstract)," *Kindergarten Magazine* 2 (May 1899): 592–4.

73. Ibid., 593.

74. Ibid.

75. G. Stanley Hall, "Corporal Punishments," *New York Education* 3 (November 1899): 163, 164.

76. Ibid., 164.

77. Ibid., 165.

78. Months later, stung by the ridicule in Chicago, Hall denied that he had ever made the extreme statements reported in this transcript; but at the same time, he refused to repudiate them. Instead, he hedged on his precise position and seemed to wish the whole thing had never happened. Based on careful reading of his other works at the time, I believe Hall did make these statements, but tried to take them back when the newspapers made a fuss. He didn't want to sound like a crank or be ridiculed by the press; but he believed in the savage little boy. See C. E. Franklin, "Dr. G. Stanley Hall on Training of Children," *New York Education* 3 (December 1899): 226.

79. G. Stanley Hall, "The Kindergarten," *School and Home Education* 18 (June 1899): 508. See also G. Stanley Hall, "Some Defects of the Kindergarten in America," *Forum* 28 (January 1900): 582–3.

80. "Boxing for Babies," *Chicago Record,* 4 April 1899, 7.

81. "Defends Small Boys," *Chicago Inter-Ocean,* 4 April 1899, 3.

82. See Mailloux, *Rhetorical Power,* 100–29.

83. "A Preacher of Pain and Pessimism," *Chicago Times Herald,* 5 April 1899, 6.

84. "Dr. Hall's Ultra Views," 4.

85. "Ban on Dr. Hall's Idea," *Chicago Tribune,* 6 April 1899, 7. See also "Frowns on Pugilism," *Chicago Record,* 6 April 1899, 6.

86. "Made Up of Sarcasm," *Chicago Times Herald,* 7 April 1899, 3.

87. "Seconds Dr. Hall's Opinion," *Chicago Record,* 10 April 1899, 8. See also "School of Psychology a Center Point of Interest," *Chicago Times-Herald,* 7 April 1899, 3, for Rev. Jenkin Lloyd Jones' approving comments.

88. Theodore Roosevelt to G. Stanley Hall, 29 November 1899, reprinted in Ross, *G. Stanley Hall,* 318; emphasis in original.

89. Hall, *Adolescence,* 1:452–3.

90. G. Stanley Hall, "The Moral and Religious Training of Children," *Princeton Review* 10 (January 1882): 43.

91. G. Stanley Hall, "Universities and the Training of Professors," *Forum* 17 (May 1894): 302–3.

92. Hall, *Adolescence,* 1:511–2, 2:568–612. On Clarke, see Russett, *Sexual Science,* 116–8.

93. Hall, *Adolescence,* 2:590–612.

94. Joseph F. Kett, *Rites of Passage: Adolescence in America 1790 to the Present* (New York: Basic, 1977), 62–85.

95. Hall, *Adolescence,* 2:292–3.

96. G. Stanley Hall, "Child Study: The Basis of Exact Education," *Forum* 17 (May 1894): 439. See also Hall, "Universities and the Training of Professors," 302.

97. For a more in-depth picture of Hall's revised, adulatory views of sex, circa 1904, see *Adolescence,* 2:281–362 and G. Stanley Hall and Theodate L. Smith, "Curiosity and Interest," *Pedagogical Seminary* 10 (September 1903): 338–42. For an insightful analysis of the broader middle-class move to reclaim male sexuality as a positive good, see also Christina Simmons, "Modern Sexuality and the Myth of Victorian Repression," in *Passion and Power: Sexuality in History,* ed. Kathy Peiss and Christina Simmons (Philadelphia: Temple University Press, 1989): 157–77.

98. Hall, *Adolescence,* 2:123.

99. Ibid., 2:292–3.

100. Hall, "Pedagogical Methods in Sunday School Work," 719–20. Hall's assumptions about what race was the closest to becoming the "super-man" are manifest in his reckoning from the time of William the Conqueror—a date of importance only to the history of Anglo-Saxons.

101. Hall, "Universities and the Training of Professors," 302.

102. G. Stanley Hall, "On the History of American College Text-Books and Teaching in Logic, Ethics, Psychology and Allied Subjects," *Proceedings of the American Antiquarian Society,* n.s. 9 (April 1894): 154–5.

103. Hall, "On the History of American College Text-Books," 155.

104. Hall, "Universities and the Training of Professors," 302.

105. G. Stanley Hall, "Remarks on Rhythm in Education," *Proceedings of the National Education Association* (1894): 85.

106. Hall, "Universities and the Training of Professors," 303.

107. Hall, "On the History of American College Text-Books," 155.

108. For a detailed discussion of principles of male variability and female conservatism, see Russett, *Sexual Science,* 92–100. For Hall's explicit statement of these principles, see, e.g., G. Stanley Hall, "Normal Schools, especially in Massachusetts," *Pedagogical Seminary* 9 (June 1902): 183–4.

109. Harry Campbell, *Differences in the Nervous Organisation of Man and Woman* (London: Lewis, 1891), 173; quoted in Russett, *Sexual Science,* 95.

110. Hall, *Adolescence,* 2:569–610.

111. G. Stanley Hall, "Modern Methods in the Study of the Soul," *Christian Register* 75 (February 1896): 133.

112. Hall and Allin, "Psychology of Tickling," 30.

113. Hall, "Heirs of the Ages," 13. For other examples, see also Hall, "Some Fundamental Principles of Sunday School," 464; and Hall, "Child Study and Its Relation to Education," 702.

114. G. Stanley Hall, "Results of Child Study Applied to Education," *Transactions of the Illinois Society for Child Study* 1 (1895): 13.

115. G. Stanley Hall, "Child Study in Summer Schools," *Regents' Bulletin* 28, University of the State of New York (July 1894): 336.

116. Gould, *Ontogeny and Phylogeny,* 167–206; Russett, *Sexual Science,* 155–80.

117. Ross, *G. Stanley Hall,* 325.

118. Hall, *Adolescence,* 1:viii; emphasis added.

119. Ibid., 1:50.

120. His letters suggest that he continued to hold his old recapitulation-based theories privately, however. For Hall's continuing, embittered, and embattled belief

in racial recapitulation, see G. Stanley Hall to William A. White, 11 December 1912, in Hall Papers, box 26, folder 9, and G. Stanley Hall to Robert M. Yerkes, 18 May 1915 in Hall Papers, box 26, folder 10.

121. See, for example, G. Stanley Hall, "Eugenics: Its Ideals and What It Is Going To Do," *Religious Education* 6 (June 1911): 152–9, and "Make Humanity Better by Controlling Unfit, Says President Hall," *Boston Sunday Post,* 29 October 1911.

122. Hall, *Adolescence,* 2:722.

123. Ibid., 1:vii–viii.

124. Ibid., 2:648–748. See also G. Stanley Hall, "The Relations between Lower and Higher Races," *Proceedings of the Massachusetts Historical Society,* 2d ser., 17 (January 1903): 4–13, much of which Hall incorporated into *Adolescence.*

125. Hall, *Adolescence,* 2:649.

126. Ibid.

127. Ibid., 2:659–60.

128. Ibid., 2:748.

129. Ibid., 2:714–9.

130. Memo of courses taken by Grace Lyman, written by G. Stanley Hall, in Hall Papers, box 25, folder 8.

131. Programs in Hall Papers, box 16.

132. See, for example, G. Stanley Hall, "The Undeveloped Races in Contact with Civilization," *Bulletin of the Washington University Association* 4 (1906): 145–50; G. Stanley Hall, "How Far Are the Principles of Education along Indigenous Lines Applicable to American Indians?" *Pedagogical Seminary* 15 (1908): 365–9; and G. Stanley Hall, "A Few Results of Recent Scientific Study of the Negro in America," *Proceedings, Massachusetts Historical Society,* 2d ser., 19 (1905): 95–107.

133. "Stanley Hall to Sec. Root," *Boston Transcript* (7 March 1906).

134. "Final Word is Not Yet," *Worcester Telegram,* (18 March 1906). For a collection of news clippings on Hall's activities with the Congo National Reform Association, see his Collected Works at Clark University.

135. Quoted in "Opens Field of Thought," *Worcester Telegram,* (21 January 1906).

136. Hall, *Adolescence,* 2:651; on woman the domesticator of feral man, see also 1:224–5 and 2:116–7, 299, 372–3, and 375.

137. Hall, *Adolescence,* 2:93.

138. Ibid., 2:93.

139. Stephen Jay Gould has noted strong connections between recapitulation theory and Freud's ideas, which may well have made them especially interesting to Hall. Freud was himself a recapitulationist, and his ideas of children's developmental stages were surely influenced by recapitulation. See Gould, *Ontogeny and Phylogeny,* 155–64; for Hall's interest in Freud, see Ross, *G. Stanley Hall,* 368–94; and Saul Rosenzweig, *Freud, Jung, and Hall the King Maker: The Historic Expedition to America (1909)* (Seattle: Hogrefe and Huber, 1992).

140. G. Stanley Hall, "How Rage, Anger and Hatred Help Us to Success," *Boston Sunday American,* 15 August 1915, Feature section, p. 4.

141. It's not clear whether two of the captions were quotes from Hall. I cannot find them in the accompanying newspaper article. They certainly sound like Hall,

however, and are probably in the complete address from which the newspaper article is excerpted, G. Stanley Hall, "Anger as a Primary Emotion and the Application of Freudian Mechanisms to Its Phenomena," *Journal of Abnormal Psychology* 10:81–87. The third quote is from this address.

Chapter Four

1. Charlotte Perkins Gilman, "Our Place Today," in *Charlotte Perkins Gilman: A Nonfiction Reader,* ed. Larry Ceplair (New York: Columbia University Press, 1991), 55. Emphasis in original.

2. See, for example, Eliza Burt Gamble, *The Evolution of Woman* (New York: Knickerbocker Press, 1893); Otis Tufton Mason, *Woman's Share in Primitive Culture* (New York: Appleton, 1894); Matilda Joslyn Gage, *Woman, Church and the State: and a Historical Account of the Status of Woman through the Christian Ages, with Reminiscences of the Matriarchate* (Chicago: Kerr, 1893); Anna Garlin Spencer, *Woman's Share in Social Culture* (New York: Mitchell Kennerley, 1912); Catherine Gasquoine Hartley, *The Age of Mother Power: The Position of Women in Primitive Society* (New York: Dodd, Mead, 1914); and Harriet B. Bradbury, *Civilisation and Womanhood* (Boston: Register, 1916). See also Nancy F. Cott, *A Woman Making History: Mary Ritter Beard through Her Letters* (New Haven, Conn.: Yale University Press, 1991), 25–7.

3. Nancy F. Cott, *The Grounding of Modern Feminism,* (New Haven, Conn.: Yale University Press, 1987), 40–1; Carl Degler, "Introduction to the Torchbook Edition," *Women and Economics,* by Charlotte Perkins Gilman (New York: Harper and Row, 1966), xiii.

4. Gary Scharnhorst, *Charlotte Perkins Gilman: A Bibliography* (Metuchen, N.J.: Scarecrow Press, 1985). I have relied heavily upon this excellent and comprehensive bibliography in researching this chapter. Scharnhorst has also written a sensitive monograph on Gilman's writings, *Charlotte Perkins Gilman* (Boston: Twayne, 1985).

5. Scharnhorst, *Bibliography,* 99–100.

6. Annie L. Muzzey, "The Hour and the Woman," review of *Women and Economics, Arena* 22 (August 1899): 443; Mary A. Hill, "Charlotte Perkins Gilman: A Feminist's Struggle with Womanhood," *Massachusetts Review* 21 (Fall 1980): 503.

7. Both quoted in Hill, "Charlotte Perkins Gilman: A Feminist's Struggle," 503.

8. Polly Wynn Allen, *Building Domestic Liberty: Charlotte Perkins Gilman's Architectural Feminism* (Amherst: University of Massachusetts Press, 1988), 50–3; *Charlotte Perkins Gilman: A Nonfiction Reader,* ed. Ceplair, 7; Mary A. Hill, *Charlotte Perkins Gilman: The Making of a Radical Feminist, 1866–1896* (Philadelphia: Temple University Press, 1980), 172–3; Hill, "Charlotte Perkins Gilman: A Feminist's Struggle," 517; Ann Lane, *To "Herland" and Beyond: The Life and Work of Charlotte Perkins Gilman* (New York: Meridian, 1990), 255–6, 294. One excellent exception is Susan S. Lanser, "Feminist Criticism, 'The Yellow Wallpaper,' and the Politics of Color in America," *Feminist Studies* 15 (Fall 1989): 415–41.

9. Charlotte Perkins Gilman, "A Suggestion on the Negro Problem," *American Journal of Sociology* 1 (July 1908): 78–85. See also Charlotte Perkins Gilman, "Immigration, Importation, and Our Fathers," *Forerunner* 5 (May 1914): 117–9; Charlotte

Perkins Gilman, "Let Sleeping Forefathers Lie," *Forerunner* 6 (October 1915): 261–3; and Charlotte Perkins Gilman, "Is America Too Hospitable?" *Forum* 70 (October 1923): 1983–9.

10. Gilman, "A Suggestion on the Negro Problem," 80–1.

11. On racism as endemic in the nineteenth-century white woman's movement, see Angela Y. Davis, *Women, Race and Class* (New York: Vintage, 1981), 30–86, 110–49; Ellen Carol DuBois, *Feminism and Suffrage: The Emergence of an Independent Women's Movement in America, 1848–1869* (Ithaca, N.Y.: Cornell University Press, 1978); Paula Giddings, *When and Where I Enter: The Impact of Black Women on Race and Sex in America* (New York: Bantam, 1984); Gerda Lerner, "Black and White Women in Interaction and Confrontation," in *The Majority Finds Its Past: Placing Women in History* (New York: Oxford University Press, 1979), 94–111; Louise Michele Newman, "Laying Claim to Difference: Racial Ideology of the U.S. Woman's Movement, 1870–1920" (Ph.D. diss, Brown University, 1992).

12. Of course, her name was not Gilman until 1900. As a child, she was known as "Charlotte Perkins." After her first marriage to Charles Walter Stetson, in 1884, she was called "Charlotte Perkins Stetson" until her second marriage to George Houghton Gilman, in 1900. In the interest of clarity, however, I will anachronistically call her by the name most people know her by today, "Gilman," for the discussion of her adult life, and call her "Charlotte" as a child.

13. The following biographical account draws deeply on Mary A. Hill's excellent biography, *Charlotte Perkins Gilman: The Making of a Radical Feminist, 1860–1896.*

14. Charlotte Perkins Gilman, *The Living of Charlotte Perkins Gilman: An Autobiography* (1935; Madison: University of Wisconsin Press, 1991), 8–9.

15. Mari Jo Buhle, *Women and American Socialism, 1870–1920* (Urbana: University of Illinois Press, 1981), 53–69.

16. Hill, *Charlotte Perkins Gilman*, 30–2.

17. Gilman, *Living*, 19, 27; Hill, *Charlotte Perkins Gilman*, 41–2. Although Hill suggests that Gilman's lack of education was nothing extraordinary, noting that four years of total schooling was the national average in 1870, it seems likely that had financial woes not intervened, Thomas and Charlotte would have had more schooling than they did. Mary Perkins herself had been "well educated" as a girl (Gilman, *Living*, 7); and Frederick Perkins—indeed, the whole Beecher clan—valued education highly. When Mary Perkins received a bequest from an aunt when Charlotte was about fourteen, she immediately spent it on good schools for the children, a fact that suggests that if more money had been available, Gilman would have received a more extensive primary education (Gilman, *Living*, 27).

18. Hill, *Charlotte Perkins Gilman*, 19; Gilman, *Living*, 37.

19. Gilman, *Living*, 36–7.

20. George W. Stocking, *Victorian Anthropology* (New York: Free Press, 1987), 150–64, 169–86.

21. G. Stanley Hall, *Adolescence: Its Psychology and Its Relations to Physiology, Anthropology, Sociology, Sex, Crime, Religion and Education*, 2 vols. (New York: Appleton, 1904), 2:213, 455, 727.

22. On *Popular Science Monthly*, see *Men's Ideas/Women's Realities: "Popular Science," 1870–1915*, ed. Louise Michele Newman, (New York: Pergamon Press, 1985).

23. Gilman, *Living,* 37.

24. Richard Hofstadter, *Social Darwinism in American Thought,* rev. ed. (Boston: Beacon Press, 1955), 28–30.

25. See, e.g., Kathryn Kish Sklar, *Catharine Beecher: A Study in American Domesticity* (Chicago: University of Chicago Press, 1973; New York: Norton, 1976); Nancy F. Cott, *The Bonds of Womanhood: "Woman's Sphere" in New England, 1780–1835* (New Haven, Conn.: Yale University Press, 1977), 126–59.

26. Gilman, *Living,* 39.

27. Ibid., 42.

28. Ibid., 39.

29. See Hill, *Charlotte Perkins Gilman* 44–120. Hill devotes three chapters to explicating the youthful struggles between what Gilman called her "two opposing natures" (74)—or, as Hill describes it, between the masculinity which she associated with her father's public achievement and the femininity which she associated with her mother's domesticity.

30. Quoted in Hill, *Charlotte Perkins Gilman,* 74. Emphasis in original.

31. Quoted in Hill, *Charlotte Perkins Gilman,* 94.

32. Gilman, *Living,* 83.

33. Quoted in Hill, *Charlotte Perkins Gilman,* 115.

34. Gilman's fictionalized version of her neurasthenic breakdown, *The Yellow Wallpaper,* is well known. The following discussion is drawn mostly from her autobiography and analyzes the way Gilman herself interpreted her breakdown in light of her subsequent feminist interpretations of "civilization."

35. Gilman, *Living,* 89.

36. Ibid., 91.

37. Ibid., 95. On Charlotte's fears of brain disease, see also the quote from her diary in Hill, *Charlotte Perkins Gilman,* 148.

38. F. G. Gosling, *Before Freud: Neurasthenia and the American Medical Community, 1870–1910* (Urbana: University of Illinois Press, 1987), 55.

39. George M. Beard, *American Nervousness: Its Causes and Consequences* (New York: G. P. Putnam's Sons, 1881), vi, 96, 137. The other four developments—which mostly applied to middle-class men in their business capacities—were steam power, the periodical press, the telegraph, and the sciences.

40. Hall, *Adolescence,* 1:511–2; 2:639.

41. Mitchell himself believed that higher education was fine for women with large reserves of nervous energies, but extremely dangerous for women with any nervous deficiencies—and this would have included the hysterically depressed Gilman. See S. Weir Mitchell, *Doctor and Patient,* (Philadelphia: Lippincott, 1888), 147–54.

42. Gilman, *Living,* 95.

43. On the rest cure, see Gosling, *Before Freud,* 109–16, and S. Weir Mitchell, *Fat and Blood: An Essay on the Treatment of Certain Forms of Neurasthenia and Hysteria,* 4th ed. (Philadelphia: Lippincott, 1883).

44. Gilman, *Living,* 96. See also Charlotte Perkins Gilman, "Why I Wrote 'The Yellow Wallpaper'?" in *The Charlotte Perkins Gilman Reader: "The Yellow Wallpaper" and Other Fiction,* ed. Ann J. Lane (New York: Pantheon, 1980), 19–20.

45. Gilman, "Why I Wrote 'The Yellow Wallpaper'?" 20.

46. Gilman, *Living,* 96.

47. In 1899, Gilman referred to recapitulation theory in a Minneapolis lecture: see "Things As They Are," *Minneapolis Sunday Times,* 19 November 1899, and "Things As They Are," *Minneapolis Journal,* 20 November 1899; copies of both in Charlotte Perkins Gilman Papers, Schlesinger Library, Radcliffe College. See also Charlotte Perkins Gilman, *Women and Social Service* (pamphlet) (Warren, Ohio: National American Woman Suffrage Association, 1907 ?). These references show up after her breakdown, but she read so widely before she got sick that she undoubtedly knew about recapitulation theory, which was a well-known part of Darwinism.

48. Gilman's fictionalized version of her neurasthenic breakdown, "The Yellow Wallpaper," is pervaded with primitivist racial imagery, as Susan Lanser has shown. It is surely no accident that Gilman describes the remote house in which the heroine is imprisoned as "a colonial mansion," or that the wallpaper of the locked nursery was yellow—the skin color of the "barbarous" residents of the locked Asian harems so anathematized by feminists. See Lanser, "Feminist Criticism," 427–34.

49. Charlotte Perkins Gilman, *The Home: Its Work and Influence* (New York: Charlton, 1903).

50. Charlotte Perkins Stetson [Gilman], *Women and Economics: A Study of the Economic Relation between Men and Women as a Factor in Social Evolution* (Boston: Small, Maynard, 1898), 155–6; Charlotte Perkins Gilman, "The 'Nervous Breakdown' of Women," *Forerunner* 7 (August 1916): 202–6.

51. Gilman, *Living,* 97.

52. Ibid., 104.

53. See Scharnhorst, *Bibliography.*

54. Gilman, "Our Place Today," 53–5 (emphasis in original).

55. Scharnhorst, *Bibliography,* 99–101; Degler, "Introduction," xiii.

56. Quoted in Hill, *Charlotte Perkins Gilman,* 331.

57. Gilman, *Women and Economics,* 2–3.

58. Ibid., 5.

59. Ibid., 46.

60. Ibid., 207; see also 59.

61. Ibid., 73, 24–5.

62. Hall, *Adolescence,* 2:568–9.

63. Ibid.

64. Gilman, *Women and Economics,* 31.

65. Ibid., 30.

66. Ibid., 31–9, 58–9.

67. Ibid., 35.

68. Ibid., 23–5, 72–5.

69. Ibid., iii–v, 58–75, 122–45.

70. Ibid., 60.

71. Ibid., iii.

72. Ibid., iv.

73. "Woman as a Factor in Civilization," [Newspaper report on Gilman's lecture of the same title], *New Orleans Daily Picayune,* 11 December 1904.

74. Gilman, *Women and Economics*, 60.

75. Charlotte Perkins Gilman, "Two 'Natural Protectors,'" *Women's Journal*, 29 October 1904, 346.

76. Gilman, *Living*, 39–40.

77. Gilman, *Women and Economics*, 61–5.

78. Ibid., 69–72.

79. Ibid., 72.

80. Ibid., 74.

81. Ibid., 127.

82. Ibid., 129; emphasis added.

83. Ibid., 134.

84. Ibid., 142.

85. Ibid., 146.

86. Ibid., 140.

87. Ibid., 146–7.

88. Gilman's speech paraphrased in "Woman as a Factor in Civilization"; see also "Women Half Civilized," *New Orleans Times Democrat*, 11 December 1904.

89. Charlotte Perkins Gilman, "A Suggestion on the Negro Problem," 78–85.

90. Gilman, *Women and Economics*, 339.

91. Ibid., 332, 339.

92. Quoted in Stocking, *Victorian Anthropology*, 202. By 1896, the complete absence of evidence to support these claims of frequent primitive rape made some anthropologists question them (Stocking, *Victorian Anthropology*, 202–4).

93. Lester F. Ward, "Our Better Halves," *Forum* 6 (November 1888): 266–75; Lester F. Ward, *Pure Sociology* (New York: Macmillan, 1903), 290–416, esp. 313–23.

94. Charlotte Perkins Gilman, "Comment and Review," *Forerunner* 1 (October 1910): 26.

95. Charlotte Perkins Gilman, "The Man-Made World, or Our Androcentric Culture (New York: Charlton, 1911), 24.

96. Charlotte Perkins Gilman, "Masculine, Feminine, and Human," *Woman's Journal*, 16 January 1904, 18; emphasis in the original.

97. Gilman, *The Home*, 290.

98. Gilman, "Masculine, Feminine, and Human," 18; emphasis in the original.

99. Gilman, *Man-Made World*, 15.

100. Ibid., 22.

101. Ibid., 28; see also, e.g., 29, 58.

102. Patrick Geddes and J. Arthur Thompson, *The Evolution of Sex* (London: Walter Scott, 1889). For Gilman's statement of her debt to *Evolution of Sex*, see Hill, *Charlotte Perkins Gilman*, 265–6; and Gilman, *Living*, 259. For an explicit use of Geddes and Thompson's theories in *Man-Made World*, see, e.g., 78–9.

103. Geddes and Thompson, *Evolution of Sex*, 267.

104. Jill Conway, "Stereotypes of Femininity in a Theory of Sexual Evolution," in *Suffer and Be Still: Women in the Victorian Age*, ed. Martha Vicinus (Bloomington: Indiana University Press, 1972), 140–54.

105. Gilman, *The Man-Made World*, 28–9.

106. Cynthia Eagle Russett, *Sexual Science: The Victorian Construction of Womanhood* (Cambridge, Mass.: Harvard University Press, 1989), 80. On sexual selection, see Russett, *Sexual Science*, 78–101.

107. Gilman, *Man-Made World*, 23–24.

108. Ibid., 255-6.

109. Ibid., 85–6.

110. Ibid., 90–3.

111. Ibid., 141–2.

112. Ibid., 137–41.

113. Ibid., 202.

114. Ibid., 234.

115. Ibid., 52.

116. Ibid., 29–34, 48–60.

117. Ibid., 30.

118. Ibid., 68–9. This was Gilman's essential position on the question of eugenics: return woman to the position of sexual selector, and all would be well for the race. See also Charlotte Perkins Gilman, "The Primal Power," *Forerunner* 4 (November 1913): 297; and Charlotte Perkins Gilman, "What May We Expect of Eugenics?" *Physical Culture* 31 (March 1914): 219–22. Gilman's view of human sexual selection was somewhat different from that of male scientists. Darwin and most biologists who believed in sexual selection believed that humans differed from all other animals, in that among humans it was natural for males to be the sexual selectors, while among animals, females were sexual selectors. As Cynthia Russett notes, this was an awkward position for them because, in other respects, these scientists assumed that what was "natural" for animals was also "natural" for humans (Russett, *Sexual Science*, 83–6).

119. Gilman, *Man-Made World*, 259.

120. [Charlotte Perkins Stetson], "The Review," *Impress* 2 (22 December 1894): 2.

121. [Charlotte Perkins Stetson], "Editorial Notes," *Impress* 1 (June 1894): 1.

122. Charlotte Perkins Gilman, "Two 'Natural Protectors,'" *Woman's Journal* 36 (29 April 1904): 65.

123. Sir Almroth Wright, "Suffrage Fallacies: Sir Almroth Wright on Militant Hysteria," *London Times*, 28 March 1912, 7–8; Sir Almroth E. Wright, *The Unexpurgated Case against Woman Suffrage* (London: Constable, 1913); "Feminism behind the Suffrage War," *New York Times*, 28 March 1912; Editorial, "Doctrine and Word Both Venerable," *New York Times*, 29 March 1912, 12; "Militant Women Break Higher Law," *New York Times*, 31 March 1912, sec. 3, p. 2; "Physician Who Killed the English Suffrage Bill," *New York Times*, 5 May 1912, sec. 3, p. 3; "A Famed Biologist's Warning of the Peril in Votes for Women," *Current Literature* 53 (July 1912): 59–62; "The 'Inferiority' of Women," *Literary Digest* 47 (8 November 1913) 865–6.

124. Wright, *Unexpurgated Case*, 19; emphasis in the original. For a brilliant explication of the larger cultural ramifications of this ideology of contract between man and woman, see Carole Pateman, *The Sexual Contract* (Stanford. Calif.: Stanford University Press, 1988). According to Pateman, liberal political theory presumes that before men replace a state of nature with a civil society by binding themselves to a

"social contract," they make a sexual contract. This sexual contract excludes women from the social contract. Instead, it binds women to provide services to man, in return for male protection. Although this view of the social contract is a new contribution to twentieth-century political theory, it would have come as no news to Wright or Sedgwick. Both presumed precisely such an agreement. If women abrogated the sexual contract, they warned, so would men. By breaking the sexual contract, women would by necessity break the social contract, which was predicated upon the sexual contract. Without a social contract, men would revert to a state of nature and become once again the natural man, the savage rapist.

125. Wright, *Unexpurgated Case,* 58; see also 32–5, 48–57, and Wright, "Militant Hysteria," reprinted in *Unexpurgated Case,* 81–4.

126. Charlotte Perkins Gilman, "The Brute in Man," *Forerunner* 4 (December 1913): 316–7.

127. George MacAdam, "Feminist Revolutionary Principle is Biological Bosh," *New York Times,* 18 January 1914, sec. 5, p. 2. This seems to have been Sedgwick's only major foray as an antifeminist activist. After this controversy, he seems to have devoted himself once again to his career in public health. According to the *Dictionary of American Biography,* he is remembered today as an early advocate of chlorinated water and pasteurized milk, and for his achievements in sewage disposal.

128. Ibid.

129. Ibid.

130. Editorial, "Feminism and the Facts," *New York Times,* 19 January 1914, 8.

131. Ida M. Metcalf, Letter, "The Rule of Brute Force," *New York Times,* 25 January 1914, sec. 3, p. 4. See also Helen Kendrick Johnson, "Two Suffrage Setbacks," *New York Times,* 21 January 1914, 8.

132. "Indignant Feminists Respond to Prof. Sedgwick," *New York Times,* 15 February 1914, sec. 5, p. 4; C. A. Woodward, "A Case For Feminism," *New York Times,* 22 January 1914; 10. See also "The 'Brute in Man' as as Argument against Feminism," *Current Opinion* 56 (May 1914): 370-1.

133. Charlotte Perkins Gilman, "The Biological Anti-Feminist," *Forerunner* 5 (March 1914): 64–7.

134. Ibid., 64.

135. Ibid., 66.

136. Ibid., 67; see also "Mrs. Gilman Calls Science to Witness," *New York Times,* 9 April 1914, 10.

137. Charlotte Perkins Gilman, "What the 'Threat of Man' Really Means," *Pictorial Review* 16 (June 1915): 2.

138. Charlotte Perkins Gilman, *Herland* (1915; New York: Pantheon, 1979).

139. Ibid., 142.

140. Ibid.; for another mention of Wright, see 130 (misspelling of "Almwroth" in original).

141. Zona Gale, "Forward," in Gilman, *Living,* xlv.

142. Nathan Irvin Huggins, *Harlem Renaissance* (New York: Oxford University Press, 1971), 84–136.

143. See, for example, Gilman, *Living,* 316–9, 323–4, 329–30; Charlotte Perkins Gilman, "Vanguard, Rearguard, and Mudguard," *Century* 104 (22 July

1922): 348–55; Charlotte Perkins Gilman, "Parasitism and Civilized Vice," in *Woman's Coming of Age: A Symposium,* Ed. Samuel D. Schmalhausen and V. F. Calverton (New York: Liveright, 1931), 110–26; Charlotte Perkins Gilman, "Is America Too Hospitable?" in *Charlotte Perkins Gilman: A Nonfiction Reader,* ed. Ceplair, 288–95; Charlotte Perkins Gilman, "Unity is Not Equality," *World Unity* 4 (August 1929): 418–20.

Chapter Five

1. This biographical discussion of Roosevelt's career as assemblyman draws primarily on Edmund Morris, *The Rise of Theodore Roosevelt* (New York: Ballantine, 1979), 159–202, 227–70.

2. Mark Sullivan, *Our Times: The United States 1900–1925* (New York: Charles Scribner's Sons, 1927), 2:226–9; Morris, *Rise,* 162; David McCullough, *Mornings on Horseback* (New York: Simon and Schuster, 1981), 256.

3. Paula Baker, "The Domestication of Politics: Women and American Political Society, 1780–1920," *American Historical Review* 89 (June 1984): 620–47, esp. 628–30; Paula Baker, *The Moral Framework of Public Life: Gender, Politics, and the State in Rural New York, 1870–1930* (New York: Oxford University Press, 1991), 24–55.

4. Morris, *Rise,* 166.

5. Ibid., 349–53.

6. See, e.g., Peter G. Filene, *Him/Her/Self: Sex Roles in Modern America* (Baltimore: Johns Hopkins University Press, 1986), 69–93, 71, 73; Joe L. Dubbert, *A Man's Place: Masculinity in Transition* (Englewood Cliffs, N.J.: Prentice-Hall, 1979) 131–3; and Harvey Green, *Fit for America: Health, Fitness, Sport and American Society* (Baltimore: Johns Hopkins University Press, 1986), 235–8.

7. For a fine discussion of many of the same themes from a slightly different angle, see Donna Haraway, "Teddy Bear Patriarchy: Taxidermy in the Garden of Eden, New York City, 1908–36," in *Primate Visions: Gender, Race, and Nature in the World of Modern Science* (New York: Routledge, 1989), 26–58.

8. On this sort of middle-class "boy culture," see E. Anthony Rotundo, *American Manhood: Transformations in Masculinity from the Revolution to the Modern Era* (New York: Basic, 1993), 31–55.

9. Theodore Roosevelt, *An Autobiography* (1913; New York, De Capo Press, 1985), 7.

10. Ibid., 10; McCullough, *Mornings,* 28–9.

11. *Theodore Roosevelt's Diaries of Boyhood and Youth* (New York: Charles Scribner's Sons, 1928), 122–3.

12. Roosevelt, *Autobiography,* 14; McCullough, *Mornings,* 115; and Morris, *Rise,* 46.

13. Captain Mayne Reid, *The Boy Hunters; or Adventures in Search of a White Buffalo* (Boston: Ticknor and Fields, 1852); Paul Russell Cutright, *Theodore Roosevelt: The Making of a Conservationist* (Urbana: University of Illinois Press, 1985), 5.

14. Reid, *Boy Hunters,* 363.

15. Richard Slotkin, *Regeneration through Violence: The Mythology of the American*

Frontier, 1600–1860 (Middletown, Conn: Wesleyan University Press, 1973); and Richard Slotkin, *The Fatal Environment: The Myth of the Frontier in the Age of Industrialization, 1800–1890* (New York: Atheneum, 1985).

16. Reid, *Boy Hunters,* 90–114, 120, emphasis in the original; see also McCullough, *Mornings,* 116.

17. Roosevelt, *Autobiography,* 15.

18. McCullough, *Mornings,* 116.

19. Darwin himself, of course, was far less eager to embrace violence as the engine of evolutionary progress than some of his "Darwinistic" followers.

20. On Roosevelt's first trip west, see Morris, *Rise,* 202–25. Tom Lutz's otherwise excellent *American Nervousness* suggests that Roosevelt was sent west "on the advice of his doctor for his asthmatic neurasthenia" (Tom Lutz, *American Nervousness, 1903: An Anecdotal History* [Ithaca, N.Y., Cornell University Press, 1991], 63; see also 79). This seems questionable. Roosevelt did suffer from asthma; but doctors believed asthma was a lung disorder, not a nervous disorder, and they did not associate it with neurasthenia. Moreover, I have found no evidence in Roosevelt's letters that he ever consider himself neurasthenic, nor that any of his physicians ever diagnosed him as neurasthenic. None of Roosevelt's biographers mention any diagnosis of neurasthenia. Thus, despite Roosevelt's real bouts with ill health, it seems unlikely that anyone ever linked his health problems with neurasthenia.

21. Morris, *Rise,* 222–3.

22. On Alice Lee's death, see Morris, *Rise,* 221–5, 284–5.

23. Interview, *New York Tribune* (28 July 1884), quoted in Morris, *Rise,* 281. For "Cowboy Land," see Theodore Roosevelt, "In Cowboy-Land," *Century* 46 (June 1893): 276–84; and Roosevelt, *Autobiography,* 94–131.

24. Morris, *Rise,* 297.

25. Theodore Roosevelt, *Hunting Trips of a Ranchman* (New York: G. P. Putnam's Sons, 1885), frontispiece.

26. In *The Winning of the West,* Roosevelt would describe this costume as "in great part borrowed from [the frontiersman's] Indian foes." See Theodore Roosevelt, *The Winning of the West,* 4 vols. (New York: G. P. Putnam's Sons, 1889–96), 1:114–5.

27. Roosevelt, *Ranch Life and the Hunting Trail* (New York: Winchester Press, 1969), 7.

28. Ibid., 6.

29. Ibid., 102–4.

30. Morris, *Rise,* 349–53.

31. See, for example, "The President Talks on the Philippines," *New York Times,* 8 April 1903, 3; "Mr. Roosevelt Sees a Cowboy Festival," *New York Times,* 26 April 1903, 1; and "President Calls for a Larger Navy," *New York Times,* 23 May 1903, 2.

32. For a discussion of the search for origins as a means to legitimize the present by inventing a lost, pure form of something, see Michel Foucault, "Nietzsche, Genealogy, History," in *Language, Counter-Memory, Practice: Selected Essays and Interviews,* ed. Donald F. Bouchard (Ithaca, N.Y. Cornell University Press, 1977), 139–64, esp. 139–45.

33. Roosevelt, *Winning,* 1:xiv. For other discussions of *The Winning of the West,* which properly define it as a story of racial origins, see Thomas G. Dyer, *Theodore*

Roosevelt and the Idea of Race (Baton Rouge: Louisiana State University Press, 1980), 54–67; Morris, *Rise,* 462–5; and especially Richard Slotkin, *Gunfighter Nation: The Myth of the Frontier in Twentieth Century America* (New York: Atheneum, 1992), 42–51, and Richard Slotkin, "Nostalgia and Progress: Theodore Roosevelt's Myth of the Frontier," *American Quarterly* 33 (Winter 1981): 608–37.

34. Roosevelt, *Winning,* 1:xiv.

35. See Morris, *Rise,* 270–342.

36. Roosevelt, *Winning,* 1:1.

37. Roosevelt is drawing on Anglo-Saxonist historiography here, but he never uses the term "Anglo-Saxon" because he believed it was historically imprecise and did not take into account the subsequent, positive race-mixing after the eleventh century (Roosevelt to Thomas St. John Gaffney, 10 May 1901, in *Letters of Theodore Roosevelt,* ed. Elting E. Morison et al., 8 vols. [Cambridge, Mass.: Harvard University Press, 1954], 3:76). Roosevelt preferred the term, "the English speaking races," because it seemed to him more precise, and because it allowed him to speak of races in the plural, showing that the Americans, Australians, South Africans, and British were multiple, related, but different races. On Anglo-Saxonism, see Stuart Anderson, *Race and Rapproachement: Anglo-Saxonism and Anglo-American Relations, 1895–1904* (Rutherford, N.J.: Farleigh Dickinson University Press, 1981), 11–73.

38. Roosevelt, *Winning,* 1:1–27.

39. Ibid., 1:20–1.

40. See, for example, Roosevelt to Finley Peter Dunne, 23 November 1904, in *Letters,* 4:1040–1; Roosevelt to Edward Grey, 18 December 1906, in *Letters,* 5:528–9. Some historians might ask whether Roosevelt means "nation" when he says Americans made up a new "race." Yet when discussing the origins of the "American race," *The Winning of the West* so blatantly referes to "racial" origins, "racial" traits and minglings of "blood" it is impossible not to understand that Roosevelt is referring explicitly to race. Roosevelt also insisted the European colonists had evolved into the manly American "race" well before they began to form the American nation; Roosevelt, *Winning,* 1:108–9. On the connections between concepts of "nation" and "race" during the period, see Dyer, *Roosevelt and the Idea of Race,* 28–30.

41. Roosevelt, *Winning,* 3:28–9; 1:8.

42. Ibid., 1:87; 3:40, 326.

43. Ibid., 3:1.

44. Ibid., 3:176.

45. Ibid., 1:124.

46. Ibid., 1:117.

47. Ibid., 1:113.

48. Theodore Roosevelt, *The Life of Thomas Hart Benton* (Boston: Houghton, Mifflin, 1887), 21. In a letter to Francis Parkman, Roosevelt described this chapter as containing "an idea of the outline I intend to fill up" in *Winning of the West.* Roosevelt to Francis Parkman, April 23, 1888, in *Letters,* 1:140.

49. Roosevelt, *Winning,* 1:106.

50. Ibid., 1:69.

51. Ibid., 1:94–5 and 1:95 n.

52. Slotkin, "Nostalgia and Progress," 623–34.

53. John D'Emilio and Estelle Freedman, *Intimate Matters: A History of Sexuality in America* (New York: Harper and Row, 1988), 8–9.

54. Roosevelt, *Winning*, 1:110.

55. Ibid., 1:192–3.

56. Ibid., 3:46.

57. Ibid., 2:230–1.

58. Ibid., 3:45–6.

59. Ibid., 3:44.

60. Ibid., 3:175–6.

61. Slotkin, *Gunfighter Nation*, 51.

62. Morris, *Rise*, 471. The earliest explicitly pro-imperialist article Roosevelt published that I can identify was a letter in the *Harvard Crimson* (2 January 1896), in *Letters*, 1:505. But his private letters show Roosevelt was identifying foreign policy as his dominant interest as early as 1894 (see Roosevelt to Henry Cabot Lodge, 27 October 1894, in *Letters* 1:408–9).

63. See, for example, Theodore Roosevelt, "The Monroe Doctrine" (1896), in *American Ideals and Other Essays, Social and Political* (New York: G. P. Putnam's Sons, 1897), 2:58–9. See also Theodore Roosevelt, "Phases of State Legislation," *Century Magazine* 39 (April 1885): 825, for hints of earlier concerns about decadence.

64. Theodore Roosevelt, "The Law of Civilization and Decay," *Forum* 22 (January 1897): 579.

65. Roosevelt, "Law of Civilization," 588–9.

66. For private expressions of Roosevelt's ambivalence on this matter—his deep fears that racial decadence was possible, combined with his faith that the American race was still strong and virile—see Roosevelt to Cecil Arthur Spring Rice, 11 August 1899, in *Letters*, 2:1051–3, and Roosevelt to Cecil Arthur Spring Rice, 16 March 1901, in *Letters*, 3:14–6. For other published expressions of his fears of decadence, see, e.g., Theodore Roosevelt, "Professionalism in Sports," *North American Review* 151 (August 1890): 191; and Theodore Roosevelt, "Manhood and Statehood," in *The Strenuous Life: Essays and Addresses* (1901: St. Clair Shores, Mich.: Scholarly Press, 1970), 254–7.

67. Theodore Roosevelt, "Value of an Athletic Training," *Harper's Weekly* 37 (23 December 1893): 1236.

68. Theodore Roosevelt, "The Manly Virtues and Practical Politics," *Forum* 17 (July 1894): 555.

69. Rudyard Kipling, "The White Man's Burden," in *The Five Nations: The Works of Rudyard Kipling*, 30 vols. (New York: Scribner's, 1903), 21:78.

70. Quoted in Willard Gatewood, *Black Americans and the White Man's Burden* (Urbana: University of Illinois Press, 1975), 183. See also 183–6 for a fine discussion of African Americans' scathing parodies and reactions to Kipling's poem.

71. Theodore Roosevelt, "National Duties," in *The Strenuous Life: Essays and Addresses* (1901; St. Clair Shores, Mich.: Scholarly Press, 1970), 280.

72. Ibid., 282.

73. Ibid., 281.

74. Ibid., 287.

75. Ibid., 288.

76. Ibid., 291.
77. Ibid., 293–4.
78. Ibid., 292–6.
79. Ibid., 296–7.
80. Ibid., 296.
81. Roosevelt to Henry Cabot Lodge, 19 January 1896, in *Letters,* 1:509.
82. Theodore Roosevelt, "The Monroe Doctrine," 2:51. For other instances where Roosevelt linked patriotism to monogamous marriage, and internationalists to unmanly adulterers or free-lovers, see Roosevelt to Osborne Howes, 5 May 1892, in *Letters,* 1:279, and Theodore Roosevelt, "What Americanism Means," *Forum* 17 (April 1894): 199.
83. Theodore Roosevelt, "Expansion and Peace," in *The Strenuous Life: Essays and Addresses* (1901: St. Clair Shores, Mich.: Scholarly Press, 1970), 37. See also Roosevelt, "National Duties," 285–6.
84. Roosevelt to Paul Dana [editor of the *New York Sun*], April 18, 1898, in *Letters,* 2:817.
85. Quoted in Morris, *Rise,* 673. Due to lack of transport space, the horses (except for those of Roosevelt and his superior officers) had to be left behind in Florida, so the cavalry became infantry. The image of Rough Riders on horseback remained, however—crucial for the regiment's cowboy image. Cowboys, after all, rode horses, and did not slog through the mud on foot.
86. Morris, *Rise,* 614. For the full story of the Rough Riders, see Morris, *Rise,* 615–61.
87. Slotkin, *Gunfighter Nation,* 79–87; see also 101–6.
88. Morris, *Rise,* 629.
89. Ibid., 665. Roosevelt's charge, of course, was really up Kettle Hill; see ibid., 650–6.
90. Theodore Roosevelt, "The Strenuous Life," in *The Strenuous Life: Essays and Addresses* (1901; St. Clair Shores, Mich.: Scholarly Press, 1970), 1–2.
91. Ibid., 6.
92. Ibid., 7.
93. Ibid., 9–10.
94. Ibid., 10–16.
95. Ibid., 17, 18.
96. Ibid., 20-1.
97. See, for example, "Mr. Roosevelt's Views on the Strenuous Life," *Ladies' Home Journal* 23 (May 1906): 17.
98. Roosevelt, *Autobiography,* 54. The quote is taken from the chapter entitled, "The Vigor of Life," which Roosevelt says is a synonym for "The Strenuous Life" (52).
99. Frank Ninkovich, "Theodore Roosevelt: Civilization as Ideology," *Diplomatic History* 10 (Summer 1986), 221–45; Elihu Root, "Roosevelt's Conduct of Foreign Affairs," in Theodore Roosevelt, *The Works of Theodore Roosevelt,* National Ed., 20 vols. (New York: Charles Scribner's Sons, 1926), 16:xiii; quoted in Ninkovich, "Civilization as Ideology," 223.
100. Roosevelt, *Autobiography,* 398–9.
101. Ibid., 516–7.

102. Ibid., 520–1.

103. Although Roosevelt was dubious about the southern and eastern European immigrants' ability to assimilate into the American race, political considerations prevented him from supporting immigration legislation as strong as he would have preferred. Still, he believed that within a few generations, the best specimens of these European races could be absorbed into the white American race—unlike the Japanese and African Americans, whom he believed would always remain unassimilable. On Roosevelt and European immigration, see John R. Jenswold, "Leaving the Door Ajar: Politics and Prejudices in the Making of the 1907 Immigration Law," *Mid-America* 67 (January 1985): 3–22, and Dyer, *Roosevelt and the Idea of Race*, 129–34.

104. Theodore Roosevelt, "National Life and Character" (1894) in *American Ideals and Other Essays, Social and Political* (New York: G. P. Putnam's Sons, 1897), 1:109. For a comprehensive discussion of Roosevelt's ideas about African Americans, see Dyer, *Roosevelt and the Idea of Race*, 89–122; and George Sinkler, *The Racial Attitudes of American Presidents* (Garden City, N.Y.: Doubleday, 1971), 341–73.

105. Roosevelt to Albion Winegar Tourgée, 8 November 1901, in *Letters* 3:190; Roosevelt, *Winning*, 3:28–9.

106. Theodore Roosevelt, "The Negro in America," (4 June, 1910) in *The Works of Theodore Roosevelt,* Memorial Ed., 24 vols. (New York: Charles Scribner's Sons, 1925), 14:194; Roosevelt, "National Life and Character," 110–1.

107. Roosevelt to Ray Stannard Baker, 3 June 1908, in *Letters,* 6:1047–8.

108. For Roosevelt's official condemnations of lynching, always tying the crime of lynching to the Negro rapist, see Theodore Roosevelt, "Address at Unveiling of Frederick Douglass Monument, at Rochester, June 10, 1899," in *Public Papers of Theodore Roosevelt, Governor, 1899[–1900]* (Albany: Brandow, 1900), 322–35; "President Denounces Mob Lawlessness," *New York Times,* 10 August 1903, 1; "Roosevelt for Reform of the Criminal Law," *New York Times,* 26 October 1905, 5; and Theodore Roosevelt, "Sixth Annual Message" (1906), in *Works,* Memorial Ed., 17:411–5.

109. Roosevelt to Charles Henry Pearson, 11 May 1894, in *Letters,* 1:376–7.

110. Roosevelt to Albion Winegar Tourgée, 8 November 1901, in *Letters,* 3:1901; see also Roosevelt to Lyman Abbot, 10 May 1908, in *Letters,* 6:1026.

111. Joel Williamson, *The Crucible of Race: Black-White Relations in the American South since Emancipation* (New York: Oxford University Press, 1984), 345–55.

112. Roosevelt to Charles Henry Pearson, 11 May 1894, in *Letters,* 1:376–7.

113. Roosevelt to Cecil Arthur Spring Rice, 16 June 1905, in *Letters,* 4:1233–4.

114. Roosevelt to George Kennan, 6 May 1905, in *Letters,* 4:1169.

115. Roosevelt to James Wilson, 3 February 1903, in *Letters,* 3:416.

116. Roosevelt to William Kent, 4 February 1909, in *Letters,* 6:1503. See also Theodore Roosevelt, "The Japanese Question," in *Works,* National Ed., 16:289; originally published in the *Outlook,* 8 May 1909.

117. Roosevelt to Philander Chase Knox, 8 February 1909, in *Letters,* 6:1511. See also Roosevelt, *Autobiography,* 392–3, 396.

118. Roosevelt to Arthur James Balfour, 5 March 1908, in *Letters,* 6:963.

119. For a fuller discussion of Roosevelt's views on the Japanese, see Sinkler, *Racial Attitudes,* 320–31, and Dyer, *Roosevelt and the Idea of Race,* 135–9.

120. Sinkler argues Roosevelt believed in a "great rule of righteousness": treat all

men according to their merits, and let all men compete on equal terms. The above discussion attempts to refute that type of argument by showing that Roosevelt believed in such competition only when he was certain that the white American race would prevail (Sinkler, *Racial Attitudes,* 317–8).

121. Edward A. Ross, "The Causes of Race Superiority," *Annals of the American Academy of Political and Social Science* 18 (July 1901): 67–89.

122. Ibid., 86.

123. Ibid., 88.

124. For a good catalog of Roosevelt's views on race suicide, see Dyer, *Roosevelt and the Idea of Race,* 143–67. See also Sinkler, *Racial Attitudes,* 337–40.

125. Roosevelt, "National Life and Character," 2:117.

126. Roosevelt, "Kidd's Social Evolution," *North American Review* 61 (July 1895): 97, 109; Roosevelt, "The Law of Civilization and Decay," 579, 586–7, 588–9; Roosevelt, "The Strenuous Life," 3–4. Roosevelt to Cecil Arthur Spring Rice, 5 August 1896, 29 May 1897, 13 August 1897, all in *Letters,* 1:554, 620–1, 647–9; and Roosevelt to Helen Kendrick Johnson, 10 January 1899, in *Letters,* 2:904–5.

127. John S. Billings, "The Diminishing Birth-Rate in the United States," *Forum* 15 (June 1893): 467–77; Francis A. Walker, "The Great Count of 1890," *Forum* 11 (June 1891): 406–18; Francis A. Walker, "Immigration and Degradation," *Forum* 11 (August 1891): 417–26.

128. Louise Michele Newman, ed., *Men's Ideas/Women's Realities: "Popular Science," 1870–1915* (New York: Pergamon Press, 1985), 107.

129. See, e.g., Grant Allen, "Plain Words on the Woman Question," in *Men's Ideas/Women's Realities,* ed. Newman, 125–31; originally published in *Popular Science Monthly* 36 (December 1889); and Walker, "Immigration and Degradation," 417–26. For overviews of the race suicide agitation, see Linda Gordon, *Woman's Body, Woman's Right: A Social History of Birth Control in America* (New York: Penguin, 1976), 136–58; and Newman, *Men's Ideas/Women's Realities,* 105–21.

130. See, e.g., Gordon, *Woman's Body,* 137–42, 148–57; Newman, *Men's Ideas/Women's Realities,* 107–12; John Higham, *Strangers in the Land: Patterns of American Nativism 1860–1925* (New York: Atheneum, 1971), 146–8.

131. Bessie and Marie Van Vorst, *The Woman Who Toils: Being the Experience of Two Ladies as Factory Girls* (New York: Doubleday, Page, 1903), 1–2; for the uncut letter, see Roosevelt to Bessie Van Vorst, 18 October 1902, in *Letters,* 3:355–6. This was the beginning of Roosevelt's public attack on race suicide, not his March 1905 speech to the National Congress of Mothers, as Linda Gordon has suggested in *Woman's Body,* 136–7, 142.

132. Roosevelt to Bessie Van Vorst, 18 October 1902, in *Letters,* 3:355.

133. It seems probable that Roosevelt's efforts can be credited with putting Ross' term "race suicide" into popular usage. Besides Ross' article coining the term, I have found no articles using the term "race suicide" published before February, 1903, when Roosevelt's letter was published; but the term was used extensively in the following months, and repeatedly described as a new term, associated with Roosevelt. See W. R. MacDermott, "The Suicide of the Race," *Westminister Review* 159 (June 1903): 695, and "Race Suicide," *Independent* 55 (21 May 1903): 1220.

134. "The Question of the Birth Rate," *Popular Science Monthly* 62 (April 1903): 567. For a complete list, see *Men's Ideas/Women's Realities*, ed. Newman, 121–2.

135. See, e.g., A. C. R., "Race Preservation," *New York Times*, 7 June 1903, 14. Actually, while the birthrate of African Americans was somewhat higher than that of white Americans, it was falling far more rapidly. See *Men's Ideas/Women's Realities*, ed. Newman, 120.

136. "Race Suicide," *Independent* 55 (May 21, 1903): 1220–1; "Topics of the Times: Presenting a Few of the Facts," *New York Times*, 1 May 1905, 8.

137. "The Question of the Birthrate," *Nation* 76 (11 June 1903): 469.

138. Reason vs. Instinct [pseud.], "No Fear of 'Race Suicide,'" *New York Times*, 4 March 1903, 8. See also Lydia Kingsmill Commander, "Has the Small Family Become an American Ideal?" *Independent* 56 (14 April 1904): 837–40.

139. Roosevelt to John Hay, 9 August 1903, in *Letters*, 3:549.

140. "No Race Suicide There," *New York Times*, 8 April 1903, 3.

141. "The President's Busy Day," *New York Times*, 7 April 1903, 2.

142. "President in California," *New York Times*, 8 May 1903, 3.

143. "Mr. Roosevelt's Views on Race Suicide," *Ladies' Home Journal* 23 (February 1906): 21; Roosevelt to Mr. and Mrs. R. T. Bower, 14 February 1903, in *Letters*, 3:425; "Roosevelt Thanks a Father," *New York Times*, 21 July 1904, 5.

144. Theodore Roosevelt, "Americans of Irish Origin," *Works*, National Ed., 16:39–40; "Roosevelt Praises the Hardy Irish," *New York Times*, 18 March 1905, 1.

145. Roosevelt to Hamlin Garland, 19 July 1903, in *Letters*, 3:520–1 is the earliest earliest example of the "birth pangs" phrase I could find. For other examples, see Theodore Roosevelt, "The American Woman as a Mother," *Ladies' Home Journal* 22 (July 1905):4; "Roosevelt Repeats Hymn to Methodists," *New York Times*, 17 May 1908, sec. 2, p. 8.

146. Roosevelt to Cecil Arthur Spring Rice, 3 May 1892, in *Letters*, 1:277. See also Roosevelt to Thomas Raynesford Lounsbury, 28 April 1892, in *Letters*, 1:275, and Roosevelt to Owen Wister, 27 April 1906, in *Letters*, 5:222.

147. For a wider discussion of this transformation, see Christina Simmons, "Modern Sexuality and the Myth of Victorian Repression," in *Passion and Power: Sexuality in History*, ed. Kathy Peiss and Christina Simmons (Philadelphia: Temple University Press, 1989), 157–77.

148. "Mr. Roosevelt's Views on Race Suicide," *Ladies' Home Journal* (23 February 1906): 21. See also, e.g., *The Foolish Almanack for the Year of 1906 and the Fifth since the Discovery of Race Suicide by President Roosevelt* (Boston: Luce, 1905) especially entries opposite March 15 and September 9; and William M. Gibson, *Theodore Roosevelt among the Humorists: W. D. Howells, Mark Twain, and Mr. Dooley* (Knoxville: University of Tennessee Press, 1980), 28, 57.

149. Roosevelt to Leigh S. J. Hunt, 11 February 1904, in *Letters*, 4:725. Hunt, a wealthy American who had made his money investing in Asia and Africa, ultimately financed Roosevelt's safari, along with Andrew Carnegie and Oscar Straus.

150. On the cultural meaning of "darkest Africa," see Patrick Brantlinger, "Victorians and Africans: The Genealogy of the Myth of the Dark Continent," in *"Race,"*

Writing, and Difference, ed. Henry Louis Gates, Jr. (Chicago: University of Chicago Press, 1986), 185–222.

151. See George Stocking, *Victorian Anthropology* (New York: Free Press, 1987), 185.

152. Theodore Roosevelt, "A Scientific Expedition," *Outlook* 91 (20 March 1909): 627–8, and Theodore Roosevelt, *African Game Trails: An Account of the African Wanderings of an American Hunter Naturalist* (New York: Charles Scribner's Sons, 1910), 3, 14–15. The safari, which included three Smithsonian naturalists, did furnish hundreds of animal skins for the Smithsonian. Donna Haraway has brilliantly analyzed how natural history museums of this period attempted to stem social decadence by exhibiting stuffed animals; and surely Roosevelt hoped the animals he had killed and sent to Washington would ultimately teach that sort of lesson. See Haraway, "Teddy Bear Patriarchy," 26–58.

153. Roosevelt, "Nature Faker," *Everybody's Magazine* 17 (September 1907): 429. See also Edward B. Clark, "Roosevelt on the Nature Fakirs," *Everybody's Magazine* 16 (June 1907): 770–7. For background on the Nature Faker controversy, see Ralph H. Lutts, *The Nature Fakers: Wildlife, Science and Sentiment* (Golden, Colo.: Fulcrum, 1990), and Matt Carmill, "Getting at the Heart of the Wild Things," *Natural History* (February 1991): 67.

154. Roosevelt, *African Game Trails,* 2.

155. Ibid. For other assertions that Africa was still as it was in the Pleistocene or Stone Age, see *African Game Trails,* 10–12, 18, 105, 378, and 418–9; Roosevelt to George Otto Trevelyan, 19 June 1908, in *Letters,* 6:1089; and Theodore Roosevelt, "Wild Man and Wild Beast in Africa," *National Geographic Magazine* 22 (January 1911): 19.

156. Roosevelt, *African Game Trails,* 94–5.

157. See, e.g., Roosevelt, *African Game Trails,* 258–60.

158. At least, that was what Roosevelt was told "Bwana Makuba" meant! Roosevelt, *African Game Trails,* 119, 260, 504, 506.

159. For the number of porters, see *Letters,* 7:13 n.

160. Ibid.

161. Roosevelt, *African Game Trails,* 29, 569–70.

162. Ibid., 349.

163. Ibid., 95; photo on 21.

164. Ibid., 239.

165. Ibid., 532–4.

166. Ibid., 406–10.

167. Ibid., 407.

168. Haraway, "Teddy Bear Patriarchy," 51.

169. Roosevelt, *African Game Trails,* 414.

170. Kathleen Dalton, "Why America Loved Theodore Roosevelt: Or Charisma Is in the Eyes of the Beholders," *Psychohistory Review* 8 (Winter 1979): 20–1.

171. "Rose Coghlan's Vivid Pen-Picture," *[New York?] World,* 22 June 1900, quoted in Morris, *Rise,* 728.

172. Sullivan, *Our Times,* 2:235.

173. Quoted in *Letters,* 7:85.

174. Marshall Everett [pseud. Henry Neil], *Roosevelt's Thrilling Experiences in the Wilds of Africa Hunting Big Game* (Chicago? 1910), 179–82; and see pictures of bare-breasted women on 44, facing 113, facing 144, 197, 199.

175. Everett, *Roosevelt's Thrilling Experiences,* 154–5. Compare to Roosevelt, *African Game Trails,* 142–6, 254–60.

Conclusion

1. For an exhaustive biography, see Irwin Porges, *Edgar Rice Burroughs: The Man Who Created Tarzan* (Provo, Utah: Brigham Young University Press, 1975), from which the following biographical discussion is drawn.

2. Ibid., 9–115.

3. Ibid., 156, 722.

4. Robert W. Fenton, *The Big Swingers* (Englewood Cliffs, N.J.: Prentice-Hall, 1967), 58.

5. Porges, *Edgar Rice Burroughs,* 796, 798–9; *Leonard Maltin's TV Movies and Video Guide,* ed. Leonard Maltin et al. (New York: Signet, 1988), 1051.

6. Quoted in Porges, *Edgar Rice Burroughs,* 132.

7. A number of fine articles have been written about the cultural meaning of *Tarzan of the Apes.* Indeed, *Tarzan's* importance to American culture is suggested by the variety of approaches scholars have taken in discussing it. Eric Cheyfitz has used *Tarzan* to investigate how difficult it has been for U.S. foreign policy to "translate" the meanings of other cultures into its own. ("*Tarzan of the Apes:* U.S. Foreign Policy in the Twentieth Century," *American Literary History* 1 [Summer 1989]: 339–66). David Leverenz has located Tarzan as one of a long series of American cultural heroes who represent the last gasp of an endangered overcivilized manhood in his excellent essay, "The Last Real Man in America: From Natty Bumppo to Batman," *American Literary History* 3 (Winter 1991): 751–81. Marianna Torgovnick's rich reading of *Tarzan of the Apes* in *Gone Primitive: Savage Intellects, Modern Lives* (Chicago: University of Chicago Press, 1990), 42–72, stresses its hidden subversiveness. She makes the excellent point that Burroughs' novel does not need to be interpreted as monolithically ethnocentric, racist, and sexist. On the one hand, the young Tarzan is willing—eager—to consider and learn from apes and other "natural" beings. Torgovnick reads this as an openness to cultural relativism which undermines Burroughs' overtly ethnocentric message. However, another reading is possible: in light of the turn-of-the-century popularity of recapitulation theory, one might also read Tarzan's openness to ape culture as Burroughs' depiction of Tarzan's recapitulation of more primitive evolutionary stages (see below). Similarly, Torgovnick suggests that the masculinist message of Tarzan's white male superiority is undermined by Tarzan's initial confusion about his identity, and the fact that this confusion is only mitigated by encounters with Africans and women. I agree that these sorts of encounters with "others" imply a variety of "anxieties" which could potentially undermine *Tarzan's* overt racist, sexist message. However, as I read it, these anxieties tend to heighten the reader's pleasurable anticipation of their resolution. Tarzan himself might appear insecure, but the narrative always promises that he will ultimately

prove his fabulous superiority as a noble white man. Thus, I read Tarzan's encounters with "others" as reinforcing, more than undermining, the book's white male supremacy—much like the traditional Western hero, whose manly superiority, as Richard Slotkin has pointed out, rests on his being simultaneously akin to and superior to savage "others."

8. Edgar Rice Burroughs, *Tarzan of the Apes* (1912; New York: Ballantine, 1983).

9. Burroughs, quoted in Porges, *Edgar Rice Burroughs,* 131.

10. Porges, *Edgar Rice Burroughs,* 136.

11. For the background of this view of Africa, see Patrick Brantlinger, "Victorians and Africans: The Genealogy of the Myth of the Dark Continent," in *"Race," Writing, and Difference,* ed. Henry Louis Gates, Jr. (Chicago: University of Chicago Press, 1986), 185–222.

12. Burroughs, *Tarzan of the Apes,* 28.

13. Ibid., 52.

14. Edgar Rice Burroughs, *Return of Tarzan* (1913; New York: Ballantine, 1941), 173.

15. Burroughs, *Tarzan of the Apes,* 112, 186, 162.

16. Ibid., 44.

17. Ibid., 34.

18. Ibid., 36, 210.

19. Ibid., 154.

20. Ibid., 154–5.

21. Ibid., 86.

22. Ibid., 96–7.

23. Ibid., 242, 244.

24. Ibid., 112.

25. G. Stanley Hall, *Life and Confessions of a Psychologist* (New York: Appleton, 1923), 363, 365.

26. G. Stanley Hall, *Adolescence: Its Psychology and Its Relations to Physiology, Anthropology, Sociology, Sex, Crime, Religion and Education,* 2 vols. (New York: Appleton, 1904), 1:44.

27. Burroughs, *Tarzan of the Apes,* 44–5.

28. Ibid., 56.

29. G. Stanley Hall, "Corporal Punishments," *New York Education* 3 (November 1899): 163.

30. Burroughs, *Tarzan of the Apes,* 28. Victorian anthropology held that primitive races had lower foreheads than more advanced, highly evolved races.

31. Ibid., 67.

32. Joel Williamson, *The Crucible of Race: Black-White Relations in the American South Since Emancipation* (New York: Oxford University Press, 1984), 188.

33. Burroughs, *Tarzan of the Apes,* 71.

34. Ibid., 96. For "Chicken George," see "Negro Lynching," *Providence Journal,* 2 February 1893, 5.

35. Ibid., 80. In the original version, Sabor was a tiger, but when *All Story* readers informed Burroughs that there were no tigers in Africa, Sabor became a lioness. See Porges, *Edgar Rice Burroughs,* 136–8.

36. Burroughs, *Tarzan of the Apes*, 81–2, 174–5.

37. Ibid., 73.

38. Quoted in "An Anti-Lynching Crusade in America Begun," *Literary Digest* 9 (11 August 1894): 421.

39. Burroughs, *Tarzan of the Apes*, 73.

40. Ibid., 72.

41. Ibid., 213.

42. Ibid., 103.

43. Ibid., 104–5, 110–3, 120–1.

44. Ibid., 127, 123–8.

45. Ibid., 124, 126.

46. Ibid., 125.

47. Ibid., 135.

48. Ibid., 155, 116, 102.

49. Ibid., 140.

50. Ibid., 134.

51. Ibid., 148.

52. Ibid., 153.

53. Ibid., 155–6.

54. Ibid., 156–7.

55. Sir Almroth Wright, "Suffrage Fallacies: Sir Almroth Wright on Militant Hysteria," *[London] Times*, 28 March 1912, 7–8; Sir Almroth E. Wright, *The Unexpurgated Case against Woman Suffrage* (London: Constable, 1913).

56. Burroughs, *Tarzan of the Apes*, 163.

57. Ibid., 168–9.

58. Ibid., 166–9.

59. Ibid., 213.

60. Ibid., 235.

61. Ibid., 233.

62. Ibid., 242.

63. Ibid.

64. Ibid., 242–3.

65. There is an alternative interpretation of the ending. Quite possibly Burroughs left the ending unsatisfyingly unresolved on purpose, in order to stimulate demand for a sequel. He was, after all, writing for money, not artistic satisfaction; and he had not been entirely successful in selling his fiction heretofore. The speed with which he began speaking of a sequel supports this theory. Burroughs' biographer rejects this interpretation, however, suggesting that Burroughs was not at all certain *Tarzan of the Apes* would be a success. Porges, *Edgar Rice Burroughs*, 123–8, 139.

66. Porges, *Edgar Rice Burroughs*, 139–40, 148–9.

67. Ibid., 148–9.

68. For a discussion of this sort of imagery deployed to construct manhood over the past two centuries, see Leverenz, "The Last Real Man in America," 753–81.

69. *The Sheik*, directed by George Melford, screenplay by Monte M. Katterjohn, Paramount, 1921; Edith M. Hull, *The Sheik: A Novel* (New York: Burt, 1921). Hull's novel was published first in Britain, in 1919. For a discussion of the popularity of

Hull's novel in the United States, see Irving Shulman, *Valentino* (London: Leslie Frewin, 1968), 158–60.

70. Hull, *The Sheik,* 59–61, 90.

71. Ibid., 90.

72. William K. Everson, *American Silent Film* (New York: Oxford University Press, 1978), 171; Robert Sklar, *Movie-Made America: A Cultural History of American Movies* (New York: Random House, 1975), 99; Shulman, *Valentino,* 166–7. Definition of "sheik" from *Webster's New World Dictionary of the American Language, College ed.* (New York: The World Publishing Company, 1953, 1962). For a more in-depth discussion of Valentino's racially and sexually ambiguous star persona, see Miriam Hansen, *Babel and Babylon: Spectatorship in American Silent Film* (Cambridge, Mass.: Harvard University Press, 1991), 245–94.

73. *On the Town,* directed by Gene Kelly and Stanley Donen, Metro-Goldwyn-Mayer 1949.

74. It should be noted that other, smaller men's movements exist today. Some are explicitly feminist; others are explicitly right wing. The following is not a critique of all men's movements, but specifically of the "Mytho-Poetic" men's movement whose chief spokesman is Robert Bly. See Jon Cohen, "Feminist Allies or Anti-Feminist Backlash: Analyzing (the) Men's Movement," *Nonviolent Activist* 9 (March 1992): 7–9; Susan Faludi, *Backlash: The Undeclared War against American Women* (New York: Doubleday, 1991), 304–12; *Women Respond to the Men's Movement: A Feminist Collection,* ed. Kay Leigh Hagan (San Francisco: Harper San Francisco, 1992).

75. Leverenz, "The Last Real Man in America," 754; see also E. Anthony Rotundo, *American Manhood: Transformations in Masculinity from the Revolution to the Modern Era* (New York: Basic, 1993), 287–9, and Mark C. Carnes, *Secret Ritual and Manhood in Victorian America* (New Haven, Conn.: Yale University Press, 1989).

76. Paul Galloway, "Cries that Bind: Men's Movement Drums up Support," *Chicago Tribune,* 21 June 1991, sec. 5, pp. 1, 5.

77. Jerry Adler et al., "Drums, Sweat and Tears," *Newsweek* (24 June 1991): 46, 52.

78. Robert Bly, *Iron John: A Book about Men* (Reading, Mass.: Addison Wesley, 1990).

79. *Women Respond,* ed. Hagan, xiii, has sales figures. According to Michiko Kakutani, *Iron John* was on the *New York Times* hardcover bestseller list for sixty-two weeks (Michiko Kakutani, "Beyond Iron John? How About Iron Jane," *New York Times,* 27 August 1993, sec. C, 1:3). *Iron John* was on the *New York Times* paperback bestseller list for at least fourteen weeks. (The paperback bestseller list of 31 May 1992 was the last listing I could find.)

80. Bly, *Iron John,* xi.

81. Ibid., 5.

82. The similarities between the Jungian Bly's ideas and Hall's are more than coincidental. Carl Jung, like Hall, strongly believed in racial recapitulation (Stephen Jay Gould, *Ontogeny and Phylogeny* [Cambridge, Mass.: Harvard University Press, 1977], 161–3). Some scholars have suggested that Jung's ideas were strongly influenced by Hall's; Hall's belief in a "Mansoul" and his ideas about a racial unconscious are strikingly similar to Jung's. See Emmet A. Hinkelman and Morris Adelman, "Appar-

ent Theoretical Parallels between G. Stanley Hall and Carl Jung," *Journal of the History of the Behavioral Sciences* 4 (1968): 254–7 and Dorothy Ross, G. *Stanley Hall: The Psychologist as Prophet* (Chicago: University of Chicago Press, 1972), 408–9.

83. Bly, *Iron John*, 2–4.

84. Ibid., 8.

85. Ibid., 223–4.

86. Ibid., 8.

87. Ibid., 13.

88. Ibid., 55.

89. Ibid., 46; see also 2 and 172.

90. Ibid., 182–90. See also Jill Johnston, "Why Iron John Is No Gift to Women," *New York Times Book Review* (23 February 1992): 1, 28–9, 31.

91. Bly, *Iron John*, 22, 184–7.

92. Ibid., 185.

93. Ibid., 24.

94. The prime example is Carissa Pinkola Estés' bestselling *Women Who Run with Wolves: Myths and Stories of the Wild Woman Archetype* (New York: Ballantine, 1992).

SELECTED BIBLIOGRAPHY

PRIMARY SOURCES

1. Archival Sources

Charlotte Perkins Gilman Collection. Arthur and Elizabeth Schlesinger Library on the History of Women in America, Radcliffe College, Cambridge, Massachusetts.

G. Stanley Hall Papers. Clark University Archives, Goddard Library, Clark University, Worcester, Massachusetts.

Ida B. Wells Papers, Department of Special Collections, University of Chicago Library, Chicago, Illinois.

2. Newspapers and Magazines

Arena	*National Geographic Magazine*
Atlantic Monthly	*New York Age*
Century Magazine	*New York Freeman*
Chicago Daily Inter Ocean	*New York Times*
Collier's	*North American Review*
Current Literature	*Outlook*
Everybody's Magazine	*Public Opinion*
Harper's Weekly	*Review of Reviews*
Independent	*Saturday Review*
Indianapolis Freeman	*Scientific American*
Literary Digest	*Survey*
McClure's Magazine	*Woman's Journal*
Nation	

3. Published Materials, Books, and Pamphlets

Beard, George M. *American Nervousness: Its Causes and Consequences.* New York: G. P. Putnam's Sons, 1881.

Bly, Robert. *Iron John: A Book about Men.* Reading, Mass.: Addison Wesley, 1990.

Burroughs, Edgar Rice. *Tarzan of the Apes.* 1912. New York: Ballantine, 1983.

Century Dictionary: An Encyclopedic Lexicon of the English Language. New York: Century Company, 1890.

Douglass, Frederick. "Why Is the Negro Lynched?" In *The Life and Writings of Frederick Douglass,* ed. Philip S. Foner, 4:491–523. New York: International Publishers, 1955.

Du Bois, W. E. B. "The Conservation of Races." In *Pamphlets and Leaflets by W. E. B. Du Bois,* ed. Herbert Aptheker, 2–8. White Plains, N.Y.: Kraus Thompson, 1986.

Everett, Marshall [Henry Neil]. *Roosevelt's Thrilling Experiences in the Wilds of Africa Hunting Big Game.* N. p., 1909.

Geddes, Patrick, and J. Arthur Thompson. *The Evolution of Sex.* London: Walter Scott, 1889.

Gilman, Charlotte Perkins. *Charlotte Perkins Gilman: A Nonfiction Reader.* Edited by Larry Ceplair. New York: Columbia University Press, 1991.

———. *The Charlotte Perkins Gilman Reader: "The Yellow Wallpaper" and Other Fiction.* Edited by Ann J. Lane. New York: Pantheon Books, 1980.

———. *The Forerunner.* Volumes 1–7, a magazine published from November 1909 to December 1916.

———. *Herland.* 1915. New York: Pantheon, 1979.

———. *The Home: Its Work and Influence.* New York: Charlton, 1903.

———. *The Living of Charlotte Perkins Gilman: An Autobiography.* 1935. Madison: University of Wisconsin Press, 1991.

———. *The Man-Made World or, Our Androcentric Culture.* New York: Charlton, 1911.

———. *Women and Economics: A Study of the Economic Relation between Men and Women as a Factor in Social Evolution.* Boston: Small, Maynard, 1898.

Hall, G. Stanley. *Adolescence: Its Psychology and Its Relations to Physiology, Anthropology, Sociology, Sex, Crime, Religion and Education.* 2 vols. New York: Appleton, 1904.

———. *Life and Confessions of a Psychologist.* New York: Appleton, 1923.

Hull, Edith M. *The Sheik: A Novel.* New York: Burt, 1921.

James, William. *Essays, Comments, and Reviews.* Cambridge, Mass.: Harvard University Press, 1987.

Johnson, Jack. *Jack Johnson Is a Dandy: An Autobiography.* New York: Chelsea House, 1969.

Kelly, Gene and Stanley Donen, codirectors. *On the Town.* Screenplay and lyrics by Adolph Green and Betty Comden; music by Leonard Bernstein with additional music by Roger Edens. Metro-Goldwyn-Mayer, 1949.

Melford, George, director. *The Sheik.* Screenplay by Monte M. Katterjohn; adapted from E. M. Hull, *The Sheik.* Paramount, 1921.

Reid, Mayne. *The Boy Hunters; or Adventures in Search of a White Buffalo.* 1852. Ridgewood, N.J.: Gregg Press, 1968.

Roosevelt, Theodore. *African Game Trails: An Account of the African Wanderings of an American Hunter Naturalist.* New York: Charles Scribner's Sons, 1910.

———. *American Ideals and Other Essays, Social and Political.* New York: G. P. Putnam's Sons, 1897.

———. *An Autobiography.* 1913. New York: Da Capo Press, 1985.

———. *Hunting Trips of a Ranchman.* New York: G. P. Putnam's Sons, 1885.

———. *The Letters of Theodore Roosevelt.* 8 vols. Edited by Elting E. Morison et al. Cambridge, Mass.: Harvard University Press, 1954.

———. *Ranch Life and the Hunting Trail.* New York: Winchester Press, 1969.

———. *The Strenuous Life: Essays and Addresses.* 1901. St. Clair Shores, Mich.: Scholarly Press, 1970.

———. *The Winning of the West.* 4 vols. New York: G. P. Putnam's Sons, 1889–96.

Ross, Edward A. "The Causes of Race Superiority," *Annals of the American Academy of Political and Social Science* 18 (July 1901): 67–89.

Ward, Lester F. "Our Better Halves." *Forum* 6 (November 1888): 266–75.

[Wells, Ida B., ed.] *The Reason Why the Colored American Is Not in the World's Columbian Exposition.* Chicago, 1892.

[Wells-Barnett, Ida B.] *Crusade for Justice: The Autobiography of Ida B. Wells.* Edited by Alfreda M. Duster. Chicago: University of Chicago Press, 1970.

Wells-Barnett, Ida B. *On Lynchings: "Southern Horrors," "A Red Record," "Mob Rule in New Orleans."* Salem, N.H.: Ayer, 1987.

Wright, Almroth E. *The Unexpurgated Case against Woman Suffrage.* London: Constable, 1913.

SECONDARY SOURCES

Anderson, Stuart. *Race and Rapprochement: Anglo-Saxonism and Anglo-American Relations, 1895–1904.* Rutherford, N.J.: Farleigh Dickinson University Press, 1981.

Baker, Paula. "The Domestication of Politics: Women and American Political Society, 1780–1920." *American Historical Review* 89 (June 1984): 620–47.

―――――. *The Moral Framework of Public Life: Gender, Politics, and the State in Rural New York, 1870–1930.* New York: Oxford University Press, 1991.

Bannister, Robert C. *Social Darwinism: Science and Myth in Anglo-American Thought.* Philadelphia: Temple University Press, 1979.

Bederman, Gail. "'Civilization,' the Decline of Middle-Class Manliness, and Ida B. Wells's Antilynching Campaign (1892–94)." *Radical History Review* 52 (Winter 1992): 5–30.

―――――. "'The Women Have Had Charge of the Church Work Long Enough': The Men and Religion Forward Movement of 1911–1912 and the Masculinization of Middle-Class Protestantism." *American Quarterly* 41 (September 1989): 432–65.

Beer, Gillian. *Darwin's Plots: Evolutionary Narrative in Darwin.* London: Routledge and Kegan Paul, 1983.

Berger, Iris, Elsa Barkely Brown, and Nancy A. Hewitt. "Symposium—Intersections and Collision Courses: Women, Blacks, and Workers Confront Gender, Race, and Class." *Feminist Studies* 18, (Summer 1992): 283–326.

Bloch, Maurice and Jean H. Bloch. "Women and the Dialectics of Nature in Eighteenth-Century French Thought." In *Nature, Culture and Gender,* ed. Carol P. MacCormack and Marilyn Strathern. New York: Cambridge University Press. 1980.

Buhle, Mari Jo. *Women and American Socialism, 1870–1920.* Urbana: University of Illinois Press, 1981.

Butler, Judith. *Gender Trouble: Feminism and the Subversion of Identity.* New York: Routledge, 1990.

Carby, Hazel V. "'On the Threshold of Woman's Era': Lynching, Empire, and Sexuality in Black Feminist Theory." In *"Race," Writing, and Difference,'* ed. Henry Louis Gates, Jr., Chicago: University of Chicago Press, 1985.

_____. *Reconstructing Womanhood: The Emergence of the Afro-American Woman Novelist.* New York: Oxford University Press, 1987.

Conway, Jill. "Stereotypes of Femininity in a Theory of Sexual Evolution." In *Suffer and Be Still: Women in the Victorian Age,* ed. Martha Vicinus. Bloomington: Indiana University Press, 1972.

Cott, Nancy F. *The Bonds of Womanhood: "Woman's Sphere" in New England, 1780–1835.* New Haven, Conn.: Yale University Press, 1977.

_____. *The Grounding of Modern Feminism.* New Haven, Conn.: Yale University Press, 1987.

_____. "Two Beards: Coauthorship and the Concept of Civilization," *American Quarterly* 42 (June 1990): 274–300.

Crosby, Christina. *The Ends of History: Victorians and "The Woman Question."* New York: Routledge, 1991.

Cullen, Jim. "'I's a Man Now': Gender and African-American Men in the Civil War." In *Divided Houses: Gender and the Civil War,* ed. Catherine Clinton and Nina Silber. New York: Oxford University Press, 1992.

Davidoff, Leonore, and Catherine Hall. *Family Fortunes: Men and Women of the English Middle Class, 1780–1850.* Chicago: University of Chicago Press, 1987.

Davis, Angela Y. *Women, Race, and Class.* New York: Vintage, 1981.

Degler, Carl. *In Search of Human Nature: The Decline and Revival of Darwinism in American Social Thought.* New York: Oxford University Press, 1991.

de Lauretis, Teresa. *Technologies of Gender: Essays on Theory, Film, and Fiction.* Bloomington: University of Indiana Press, 1987.

D'Emilio, John, and Estelle Freedman. *Intimate Matters: A History of Sexuality in America.* New York: Harper and Row, 1988.

Dyer, Thomas G. *Theodore Roosevelt and the Idea of Race.* Baton Rouge: Louisiana State University Press, 1980.

Edwards, Laura F. "Sexual Violence, Gender, Reconstruction, and the Extension of Patriarchy in Granville County, North Carolina." *North Carolina Historical Review* 68 (July 1991): 237–60.

Feldstein, Ruth. "'I Wanted the Whole World To See:' Race, Gender and Constructions of Motherhood in the Death of Emmett Till." In *Not June Cleaver: Women and Gender in Postwar America,* ed. Joanne Meyerowitz. Philadelphia: Temple University Press, 1994.

Filene, Peter G. *Him/Her/Self: Sex Roles in Modern America.* Baltimore: Johns Hopkins University Press, 1986.

Foucault, Michel. *The History of Sexuality.* Vol. 1: *An Introduction.* New York: Vintage, 1978.

Gaines, Kevin. *Uplifting the Race: Black Politics and Culture in the United States Since the Turn of the Century.* Chapel Hill: University of North Carolina Press, 1995.

Gates, Henry Louis Jr., ed. *"Race," Writing, and Difference.* Chicago: University of Chicago Press, 1986.

Giddings, Paula. *When and Where I Enter: The Impact of Black Women on Race and Sex in America.* New York: Bantam, 1984.

Gilmore, Al-Tony. *Bad Nigger! The National Impact of Jack Johnson.* Port Washington, N.Y.: Kennikat Press, 1975.

Gordon, Linda. *Woman's Body, Woman's Right: A Social History of Birth Control in America*. New York: Penguin, 1976.

Gorn, Elliott J. *The Manly Art: Bare-Knuckle Prizefighting in America*. Ithaca, N.Y.: Cornell University Press, 1986.

Gosling, F. G. *Before Freud: Neurasthenia and the American Medical Community, 1870–1910*. Urbana: University of Illinois Press, 1987.

Gossett, Thomas F. *Race: The History of an Idea in America*. Dallas: Southern Methodist University Press, 1963.

Gould, Stephen Jay. *Ontogeny and Phylogeny*. Cambridge, Mass.: Harvard University Press, 1977.

Gutiérrez, Ramón A. *When Jesus Came, the Corn Mothers Went Away: Marriage, Sexuality, and Power in New Mexico, 1500–1846*. Stanford: Stanford University Press, 1991.

Hall, Jacquelyn Dowd. "'The Mind That Burns in Each Body': Women, Rape, and Racial Violence." In *Powers of Desire: The Politics of Sexuality*, ed. Ann Snitow, Christine Stansell, and Sharon Thompson. New York: Monthly Review Press, 1983.

———. *Revolt against Chivalry: Jessie Daniel Ames and the Women's Campaign against Lynching*. New York: Columbia University Press, 1979.

Haller, John S., Jr., and Robin J. Haller. *The Physician and Sexuality in Victorian America*. Urbana: University of Illinois Press, 1974.

Haraway, Donna. *Primate Visions: Gender, Race, and Nature in the World of Modern Science*. New York: Routledge, 1989.

Higginbotham, Evelyn Brooks. "African-American Women's History and the Metalanguage of Race." *Signs* 17 (December 1992): 251–74.

———. *Righteous Discontent: The Women's Movement in the Black Baptist Church, 1880–1920*. Cambridge, Mass.: Harvard University Press, 1993.

Higham, John. "The Reorientation of American Culture in the 1890s." In *Writing American History: Essays on Modern Scholarship*. Bloomington: Indiana University Press, 1978.

Hill, Mary A. "Charlotte Perkins Gilman: A Feminist's Struggle with Womanhood." *Massachusetts Review* 21 (Fall 1980): 503–26.

———. *Charlotte Perkins Gilman: The Making of a Radical Feminist, 1866–96*. Philadelphia: Temple University Press, 1980.

Hodes, Martha. "Wartime Dialogues on Illicit Sex: White Women and Black Men." In *Divided Houses: Gender and the Civil War*, ed. Catherine Clinton and Nina Silber. New York: Oxford University Press, 1992.

Hofstadter, Richard. *Social Darwinism in American Thought*. Rev. ed. Boston: Beacon Press, 1955.

Hutton, Mary Magdelene Boone. "The Rhetoric of Ida B. Wells: The Genesis of the Anti-Lynch Movement." Ph.D. diss., Indiana University, 1975.

Jordanova, Ludmila. "Natural Facts: An Historical Perspective on Science and Sexuality." In *Nature, Culture, and Gender*, ed. Carol P. MacCormack and Marilyn Strathern. New York: Cambridge University Press, 1980.

Kaplan, Amy. "Romancing the Empire: The Embodiment of American Masculinity in the Popular Historical Novel of the 1890s." *American Literary History* 3 (December 1990): 659–90.

Kasson, John F. *Amusing the Million: Coney Island at the Turn of the Century.* New York: Hill and Wang, 1978.

Kershner, R. B., Jr. "Degeneration: The Explanatory Nightmare." *Georgia Review* 40 (Summer 1986):416–44.

Kimmel, Michael S. "Men's Responses to Feminism at the Turn of the Century." *Gender and Society* 1 (September 1987): 261–83.

Lane, Ann. *To "Herland" and Beyond: The Life and Work of Charlotte Perkins Gilman.* New York: Meridian, 1990.

Lanser, Susan S. "Feminist Criticism, 'The Yellow Wallpaper,' and the Politics of Color in America." *Feminist Studies* 15 (Fall 1989): 415–41.

Laqueur, Thomas. *Making Sex: Body and Gender from the Greeks to Freud.* Cambridge, Mass.: Harvard University Press, 1990.

Lears, T. J. Jackson. *No Place of Grace: Anti-modernism and the Transformation of American Culture, 1880–1920.* New York: Pantheon, 1981.

Lerner, Gerda. "Reconceptualizing Differences among Women." *Journal of Women's History* 1 (Winter 1990): 106–22.

Leverenz, David. "The Last Real Man in America.: From Natty Bumppo to Batman." *American Literary History* 3 (Winter 1991): 753–81.

———. *Manhood and the American Renaissance.* Ithaca, N.Y.: Cornell University Press, 1989.

Lutz, Tom. *American Nervousness, 1903: An Anecdotal History.* Ithaca, N.Y.: Cornell University Press, 1991.

Lystra, Karen. *Searching the Heart: Women, Men, and Romantic Love in Nineteenth-Century America.* New York: Oxford University Press, 1989.

Mangan, J. A., and James Walvin, eds. *Manliness and Morality: Middle-Class Masculinity in Britain and America, 1800–1940.* New York: St. Martin's Press, 1987.

Marsh, Margaret. "Suburban Men and Masculine Domesticity." *American Quarterly* 40 (June 1988): 165–86.

Massa, Ann. "Black Women in the 'White City.'" *Journal of American Studies* 8 (December 1974): 319–37.

McCullough, David. *Mornings on Horseback.* New York: Simon and Schuster, 1981.

Morris, Edmund. *The Rise of Theodore Roosevelt.* New York: Ballantine, 1979.

Newman, Louise Michele, ed. *Men's Ideas/Women's Realities: "Popular Science," 1870–1915.* New York: Pergamon Press, 1985.

Ninkovich, Frank. "Theodore Roosevelt: Civilization as Ideology." *Diplomatic History* 10 (Summer 1986): 221–45.

Ownby, Ted. *Subduing Satan: Religion, Recreation, and Manhood in the Rural South, 1865–1920.* Chapel Hill: University of North Carolina Press, 1990.

Painter, Nell Irvin, "'Social Equality,' Miscegenation, Labor, and Power." In *The Evolution of Southern Culture,* ed. Numan V. Bartley. Athens, Ga.: University of Georgia Press, 1988.

Pateman, Carole. *The Sexual Contract.* Stanford, Calif.: Stanford University Press, 1988.

Pearce, Roy Harvey. *Savagism and Civilization: A Study of the Indian and the American Mind.* 1953. Baltimore: Johns Hopkins University Press, 1965.

Poovey, Mary. *Uneven Developments: The Ideological Work of Gender in Mid-Victorian England.* Chicago: University of Chicago Press, 1988.

Porges, Irwin. *Edgar Rice Burroughs: The Man Who Created Tarzan.* Provo, Utah: Brigham Young University Press, 1975.

Riley, Denise. *Am I That Name? Feminism and the Category of "Women" in History.* New York: Macmillan, 1988.

Roberts, Randy. *Papa Jack: Jack Johnson and the Era of White Hopes.* New York: Free Press, 1983.

Roediger, David R. *The Wages of Whiteness: Race and the Making of the American Working Class.* New York: Verso, 1991.

Rosenberg, Charles. "Sexuality, Class and Role in Nineteenth-Century America." *American Quarterly* 35 (May 1973), 131–53.

Ross, Dorothy. *G. Stanley Hall: The Psychologist as Prophet.* Chicago: University of Chicago Press, 1972.

Rothman, Ellen K. *Hands and Hearts: A History of Courtship in America.* Cambridge, Mass.: Harvard University Press, 1987.

Rotundo, E. Anthony. *American Manhood: Transformations in Masculinity from the Revolution to the Modern Era.* New York: Basic, 1993.

———. "Learning about Manhood: Gender Ideals and the Middle-Class Family in Nineteenth-Century America." In *Manliness and morality: Middle-class masculinity in Britain and America, 1800–1940,* ed. J. A. Mangan and James Walvin. New York: St. Martin's Press, 1987.

Rudwick, Elliot M., and August Meier. "'Black Man in the 'White City': Negroes and the Columbian Exposition, 1893." *Phylon* 26 (Winter 1965): 354–61.

Russett, Cynthia Eagle. *Darwin in America: The Intellectual Response.* San Francisco: Freeman, 1976.

———. *Sexual Science: The Victorian Construction of Womanhood.* Cambridge, Mass.: Harvard University Press, 1989.

Ryan, Mary P. *Cradle of the Middle Class: The Family in Oneida County, New York, 1790–1865.* Cambridge: Cambridge University Press, 1981.

Rydell, Robert W. *All the World's a Fair: Visions of Empire at American International Expositions, 1876–1916.* Chicago: University of Chicago Press, 1984.

Scharnhorst, Gary. *Charlotte Perkins Gilman: A Bibliography.* Metuchen, N.J.: Scarecrow Press, 1985.

Scott, Joan W. "Experience." In *Feminists Theorize the Political,* ed. Judith Butler and Joan W. Scott. New York: Routledge, 1992.

———. *Gender and the Politics of History.* New York: Columbia University Press, 1988.

Simmons, Christina. "African Americans and Sexual Victorianism in the Social Hygiene Movement, 1910–40." *Journal of the History of Sexuality* 4 (Summer, 1993): 51–75.

———. "Modern Sexuality and the Myth of Victorian Repression." In *Passion and Power: Sexuality in History,* ed. Kathy Peiss and Christina Simmons. Philadelphia: Temple University Press, 1989.

Sinkler, George. *The Racial Attitudes of American Presidents.* Garden City, N.Y.: Doubleday, 1971.

Slotkin, Richard. "Nostalgia and Progress: Theodore Roosevelt's Myth of the Frontier." *American Quarterly* 33 (Winter 1981): 608–37.

Smith-Rosenberg, Caroll. "Captured Subjects/Savage Others: Violently Engendering the New American Subject." *Gender and History* 5 (Summer 1993): 177–95.

———. *Disorderly Conduct: Visions of Gender in Victorian America.* New York: Alfred A. Knopf, 1985.

Sterling, Dorothy. *Black Foremothers: Three Lives.* New York: Feminist Press, 1988.

Stocking, George W., Jr. *Race, Culture, and Evolution.* New York: Free Press, 1968.

———. *Victorian Anthropology.* New York: Free Press, 1987.

Susman, Warren I., *Culture as History.* New York: Pantheon, 1984.

Thompson, Mildred. "Ida B. Wells-Barnett: An Exploratory Study of an American Black Woman, 1893–1930." Ph. D. diss., George Washington University, 1979.

Torgovnick, Marianna. *Gone Primitive: Savage Intellect, Modern Lives.* Chicago: University of Chicago Press, 1990.

Trachtenberg, Alan. *The Incorporation of America: Culture and Politics in the Gilded Age.* New York: Hill and Wang, 1982.

Tucker, David M. "Miss Ida B. Wells and Memphis Lynching." *Phylon* 32 (Summer 1971): 112–22.

Ware, Vron. *Beyond the Pale: White Women, Racism, and History.* New York: Verso, 1992.

Weimann, Jeanne Madeline. *The Fair Women.* Chicago: Academy Chicago, 1981.

Whites, LeeAnn. "Rebecca Latimer Felton and the Wife's Farm: The Class and Racial Politics of Gender Reform." *Georgia Historical Quarterly* 76 (Summer 1992): 354–72.

Williamson, Joel. *The Crucible of Race: Black-White Relations in the American South Since Emancipation.* New York: Oxford University Press, 1984.

Zagarri, Rosemarie. "Morals, Manners, and the Republican Mother." *American Quarterly* 44 (June 1992): 192–211.

INDEX

Reason Why the Colored American Is Not in the World's Columbian Exposition, The (Douglass & Wells), 20, 38–40, 60, 250 nn. 146 and 147
recapitulation theory: in Gilman's thought, 131, 270 n. 47; and Hall's theories, 92–94, 95, 96, 99, 102, 104–6, 108, 109–10, 119–20, 222, 223, 263 nn. 61 and 67, 265–66 n. 120, 266 n. 139, 286 n. 82; in Jung's thought, 286 n. 82; and *Tarzan of the Apes* (Burroughs), 222, 223, 283 n. 7
Reid, Mayne, 172, 173–74, 175, 176
religion. *See* Bible; Christianity; evolutionary religion; Protestantism
Researches into the Early History of Mankind and the Development of Civilization (Tylor), 126
Roosevelt, Alice Lee, 175
Roosevelt, Kermit, 208
Roosevelt, Theodore: *African Game Trails,* 209, 211, 215; on African safari, 207–13, 215, 281 n. 149, 282 n. 152; *An Autobiography,* 196; career and impact summarized, 43, 44, 214–15; concepts of manliness/masculinity, 172–74, 184; discourse of civilization as used by, 171, 182–83, 185, 213, 217, 218; as example of manhood, 157, 174–77, 190, 192–93, 214–15; on football, 15; on gender, 180–81; and Hall, 100–101, 113; health problems, 275 n. 20; *Hunting Trips of a Ranchman,* 175–76, 177; immigration policy, 198–200, 201, 279 n. 103; imperialist foreign policy of, 184, 186–97, 214, 277 n. 62; on Jack Johnson, 4; on lynching, 197; and manliness, 172, 181, 182, 185, 188–90, 191–92, 193–97, 207, 210, 212; and masculine primitivism, 157, 176, 181–82, 185–86, 192, 207–9, 211–13, 214–15; masculinization of image of, 170–71, 174–77, 190, 275 n. 26; millennialism in thought of, 171, 177, 180, 183, 184,

196; "National Duties," 188, 214; press opinion of, 170–71, 176–77; on race and domestic policy, 197–206, 280 n. 120; on race and imperialist foreign policy, 184–96; on race and Western expansion, 171, 178–84, 195, 276 nn. 37 and 40; and race suicide concept, 199, 200–206, 280 nn. 131 and 133; *Ranch Life and the Hunting Trail,* 176; ranchman persona, 175–77, 178, 275 n. 26; on rape, 181, 205; and Rough Riders, 190–92, 218, 278 n. 85; "The Strenuous Life," 184, 192–96, 214; *The Winning of the West,* 178–84, 197, 214, 275 n. 26, 276 nn. 37, 40, 48
Root, Elihu, 196
Ross, Edward A., 200–201, 206, 280 n. 133
Rotundo, E. Anthony, 22, 247 n. 96
Rough Riders, 190–92, 218, 278 n. 85
Rough Riders, The (Roosevelt), 192
Rowe, George C., 60
Russell, Sir Edward, 68
Rydell, Robert, 31, 35

Sandow, Eugene, 15, 157
San Francisco Examiner, 41
Saturday Review, 71–72
savages and savagery: in discourse of civilization, 25, 28; Gilman on, 140; and Gilman's neurasthenia, 131–32, 270 n. 48; in Hall's theories, 77–79, 93–94, 95–101, 110–17, 119–20, 127, 225, 263 nn. 61 and 67, 264 n. 78 ; in modern men's movements, 235; in Roosevelt's thought, 176, 181–82, 189, 208, 210–12, 225 ; in *Tarzan of the Apes* (Burroughs), 220, 221–22, 223, 231–32. *See also* primal rapist; primitivism
Scribner's Magazine, 192
Sedgwick, William T., 159, 160–64, 166–67, 218, 229, 273 nn. 124 and 127
sex. *See* gender; manhood; womanhood